E-COMMERCE AND THE DIGITAL ECONOMY

Advances in Management Information Systems

Advisory Board

E-COMMERCE AND THE DIGITAL ECONOMY

MICHAEL J. SHAW
EDITOR

ADVANCES IN MANAGEMENT
INFORMATION SYSTEMS
VLADIMIR ZWASS SERIES EDITOR

M.E.Sharpe
Armonk, New York
London, England

References to the AMIS papers should be as follows:
Weitzel, T., Lamberti, H-J., and Beimborn, D. The standardization gap: An economic framework for network analysis. M.J. Shaw, ed., *E-Commerce and the Digital Economy. Advances in Management Information Systems*, Volume 4 (Armonk, NY: M.E. Sharpe, 2006), 54–73.

ISBN-13 978-0-7656-1150-5
ISBN-10 0-7656-1150-3
ISSN 1554-6152

Printed in the United States of America

The paper used in this publication meets the minimum requirements of
American National Standard for Information Sciences
Permanence of Paper for Printed Library Materials,
ANSI Z 39.48-1984.

BM (c) 10 9 8 7 6 5 4 3 2 1

ADVANCES IN IN MANAGEMENT INFORMATION SYSTEMS

AMIS Vol. 1: Richard Y. Wang, Elizabeth M. Pierce, Stuart E. Madnick, and Craig W. Fisher
Information Quality
ISBN-13 978-0-7656-1133-8
ISBN-10 0-7656-1133-3

AMIS Vol. 2: Sergio deCesare, Mark Lycett, Robert D. Macredie
Development of Component-Based Information System
ISBN-13 978-0-7656-1248-9
ISBN-10 0-7656-1248-8

AMIS Vol. 3: Jerry Fjermestad and Nicholas C. Romano, Jr.
Electronic Customer Relationship Management
ISBN-13 978-0-7656-1327-1
ISBN-10 0-7656-1248-1

AMIS Vol. 4: Michael J. Shaw
E-Commerce and the Digital Economy
ISBN-13 978-0-7656-1150-5
ISBN-10 0-7656-1150-3

Forthcoming volumes of this series can be found on the series homepage.
www.mesharpe.com/amis.htm

Editor-in-Chief
Vladimir Zwass
zwass@fdu.edu

CONTENTS

SERIES EDITOR'S INTRODUCTION

VLADIMIR ZWASS, EDITOR-IN-CHIEF

This is the first of several *AMIS* volumes devoted to the study of electronic commerce (e-commerce), a broad and encompassing way of conducting affairs with extensive reliance on networked information systems. As the volume shows full well, e-commerce transforms almost all aspects of our economic life, and not only that. The ongoing e-commerce-enabled and, in parts, e-commerce-driven transformation of the sectors of national and global economies has been termed the "digital economy" (Brynjolfsson and Kahin 2000). In this economy the structures, methods, and technologies of e-commerce emerge as a significant factor of business success or failure, of economic growth, and of social change.

In a well-accepted definition, e-commerce is the sharing of business information, maintaining of business relationships, and conducting of business transactions by means of telecommunication networks (Zwass 1996). This definition assigns priority to the long-term relationships with respect to the transactional, sell-buy, aspects. Indeed, the best transactions are the consummations of abiding, evolving, and strengthening relationships among economic actors. E-commerce not only facilitates these relationships; it changes the playing field and the forces active in it. Synonymous with e-business, e-commerce includes three principal segments: business-to-business (B2B), business-to-consumer (B2C, or e-tail), and the intraorganizational segment. It is the most visible component, e-tail, that has captured the popular imagination and is frequently confused with the entirety of e-commerce (as, for example, in the enthusiastic *Economist* article, "E-commerce Takes Off" [2004]). Yet, the lion's share of e-commerce, consistently over 90 percent of the volume, is actually taken up by B2B commerce—and that is without considering the difficult to account for, yet preeminent, intraorganizational e-commerce.

The momentum of e-commerce is inextricably intertwined with the emergence and the phenomenal rate of growth of the Internet-Web compound. However, looking *ex post,* e-commerce predates the emergence of the World Wide Web on the Internet telecommunication infrastructure. Thus, electronic data interchange (EDI) and electronic fund transfer (EFT) systems had been used for decades before the global network of networks, the Internet, was opened to commercial activity and the Web was devised as a distributed hypermedia database accessible over the Internet. However, the takeoff of e-commerce as we know it today can be dated to the early 1990s, when the Web was made ubiquitously accessible with browsers.

The scope of e-commerce can be seen in the so-called hierarchical framework, shown in Table 0.1 (Zwass 1996). E-commerce encompasses three meta-levels of activity and artifacts, ranging from the technological infrastructure to the products and the organizationally embedded structures. The infrastructure delivers the functionality of the World Wide Web over the Internet, and supports EDI and other forms of messaging over the Internet or over proprietary land-based and wireless networks. A variety of higher-level protocols, notably XML and the protocols facilitating the definition, discovery, and deployment of the publicly available software components known as Web services, make the infrastructure usable to the higher layers. The meta-level of services facilitates business transactions with messaging and with services enabling the matching, negotiation, exchange (and delivery in the case of digital goods), and settlement. The top meta-level enables coordination of economic activity through a marketplace or a hierarchy (that is, managerial means). This meta-level thus supports the two essential business governance modes, the markets and the lasting backbone supply chains, as well as their hybrids. A variety of electronic marketplaces is made available and the desired degree of collaboration is supported in the business webs of interorganizational supply chains.

A more detailed hierarchical framework (the "five Cs") classifies e-commerce activities into five domains: computation, connection, communication, collaboration, and commerce (Zwass 2003). This framework helps surface the e-commerce-enabled aspects of these activity domains, and details the attendant opportunities for entrepreneurial and intrapreneurial innovation. As with any deployment of information technology and of the business processes grounded in it, the economic benefits garnered by firms vary widely. Complementary assets, historical path dependence, and management skills are the general preconditions of economic payoff.

Several novel dynamics accompany the gradual transformation into a digital economy. Considering the entrepreneurial activity in the domain, "dynamics" is indeed the proper word. Only some of these developments can be mentioned here. In the B2B domain, these include reintermediation of electronic intermediaries (called also infomediaries) replacing the former intermediaries, sometimes leading to such ecosystems as those surrounding the online auctioneer eBay. Thus, instead of witnessing the predicted disappearance of intermediaries due to the potential for direct linkage between the suppliers and ultimate customers, we observe fragmentation of value-added services, sometimes called hypermediation (Carr 2000). The Internet-Web compound heightens collaboration between firms and their customers on innovations (Sawhney et al., 2003). Adaptable supply webs are replacing relatively stable supply chains. The role of firms that act as process specialists, for instance, in logistics or order processing, is heightened, leading to the possibility of global business-process outsourcing (in many cases through offshoring). Indeed, contemporary supply-chain management relies on the ubiquitous Internet-Web infrastructure. The success factors are: adaptability to market, product, and strategy shifts; agility to respond to short-term variations in demand or supply; and information-based alignment of incentives for the participant firms (Lee 2004). Several different aspects of flexibility require different approaches to supply-chain coordination (Gosain et al. 2004–5). A variety of online market structures have been studied and compared from various perspectives (for example, by Jap [2003] and Kambil and van Heck [1998]).

Notable e-commerce-based phenomena are transforming the B2C domain. Along with pure e-tail, they include synergistic multichannel marketing and sales. Trust-enhancement means, such as reputation systems, aim to compensate for the absence of the contact in the physical world (Dellarocas 2003). Ever higher levels of customization of products and of personalization of the Web pages are only some hedonic aspects of the Web shopping experience (Mathwick and Rigdon 2004). The communitarian aspects of the B2C domain, such as social network sites and loyalty-enhancing components of e-tail sites, are novel phenomena furnished by the forum of the Web. The growth potential of e-tail, with its attendant potential for channel restructuring and efficiencies, is vast, as Web sales make up at this time approximately 1.5 percent of the total retail volume in the United States and the European Union (UNCTAD 2003). The marketplace for digital goods and services has been entirely reshaped by the deployment of the Internet-Web compound, requiring deep understanding of the immutable rules of economics as applied to

Table 0.1

The Hierarchical Framework of Electronic Commerce

Meta-level	Level	Function	Examples
Products and structures	7	Electronic marketplaces and electronic hierarchies	Electronic exchanges, auctions, brokerages, dealerships, and direct search markets Interorganizational supply-chain management
	6	Products and systems	Remote consumer services (retailing, banking, stock brokerage) Infotainment-on-demand (fee-based content sites, educational offerings) Supplier-customer linkages Online marketing Electronic benefit systems Intranet- and extranet-based collaboration
Services	5	Enabling services	Electronic catalogs/directories, search engines, smart agents E-payment, including e-cash Digital authentication services Digital libraries, copyright-protection services Traffic auditing
	4	Secure messaging	EDI, e-mail, EFT
Infrastructure	3	Hypermedia/multimedia object management	World Wide Web with Java
	2	Public and private communication utilities	Internet and value-added networks (VANs)
	1	Wide-area telecommunications infrastructure	Land-based and wireless networks

Source: Zwass 1996, p. 6. Copyright ©1996 M.E. Sharpe, Inc. Reprinted with permission.

digital goods (Shapiro and Varian 1999). In the intraorganizational domain, Web-enabled enterprise systems, knowledge-management portals, and intranet-based workflow systems are notable technologies enabling new process designs and transformation of the firms.

E-commerce is still at the starting stage of its trajectory—and most of the predictions of the future are best left to the futurists. However, some of the transformations are already in process. Further far-reaching developments are expected from the exploitation of the potentialities of wireless computing in m-commerce. Notable among them are various location-dependent services, ubiquitous computing exploiting radio-frequency identification (RFID) and the 128-bit address of the IPv6 telecommunication protocol, and resource sharing in wireless grids (the latter is analyzed, for example, in McKnight et al. 2004). The ontology-based semantic Web services currently being implemented will offer an opportunity for further levels of effectiveness and efficiency in intra- and interorganizational integration. Combined, these developments will lead to massive communication among computers and other appliances to deliver the needed functionality automatically, limiting the need for human participation in more routine activities.

It has been stressed that e-commerce is a part of the economy at large, with several principal directions of embedding (Zwass 2002). The influence of e-commerce indeed derives from this embedding in the overall economy, rather than an autarkic development touted at its birth. As contrasted with purely virtual commerce, specific click-and-mortar approaches offer the potential for differentiation with value-added services, cost savings, market expansion, and higher trust levels (Steinfield et al. 2002).

Potentially bearing benefits, e-commerce does not offer them automatically. Creation of new value in a competitive marketplace is a difficult task; the capture of that value through a financial reward is far more difficult yet. Metrics need to be invented and validated to understand the processes of value creation and capture in the digital economy (Straub et al. 2002). A multiplicity of risks accompany e-commerce initiatives: the increasing reliance on the common infrastructure calls for heightened attention to the reliability, security, and quality of service of that infrastructure. A great variety of public policy issues call for resolution in the legal and regulatory domains, many of them in the international arena.

Indeed, digital divides persist internationally. This fact is reasonably well reflected by e-readiness, a measure of a country's readiness to take up opportunities of the digital economy, based on some 100 criteria. Applied to the world's sixty largest economies, the measure has yielded four tiers, with the spread of the overall score between 8.28 and 2.43 (The 2004 e-Readiness Rankings 2004). When combined with the Matthew effect of cumulating advantage, it is likely that the digital divides will persist, barring beneficial external developments. However, firm-level analysis of value creation in e-commerce reveals the differing dominant factors in value creation in the developed and developing countries (Zhu et al. 2004). By actively enhancing the relevant factors, the level of e-readiness can be raised.

The present volume offers a research perspective on many of the factors of e-commerce and digital economy. The coverage will be continued by the *AMIS* volumes to come.

REFERENCES

Brynjolfsson, E., and Kahin, B. Introduction. In *Understanding the Digital Economy,* E. Brynjolfsson and B. Kahin (eds.), Cambridge: MIT Press, 2000, pp. 1–10.

Carr, N.G. Hypermediation: commerce as clickstream. *Harvard Business Review,* 75, 1 (January–February 2000), 46–47.

Dellarocas, C. The digitization of word of mouth: Promise and challenges of online feedback mechanisms. *Management Science,* 49, 10 (October 2003), 1407–1424.

E-commerce takes off. Special Section, *Economist* (May 15–21, 2004), 1–20.

Gosain, S.; Malhotra, A.; and El Sawy, O. Coordinating for flexibility in e-business supply chains. *Journal of Management Information Systems*, 21, 3 (Winter 2004–5), 7–45.

Jap, S.D. An exploratory study of the introduction of online reverse auctions. *Journal of Marketing,* 67 (July 2003), 96–107.

Kambil, A., and van Heck, E. Reengineering the Dutch flower auctions: A framework for analyzing exchange organizations. *Information Systems Research,* 9, 1 (March 1998), 1–19.

Lee, H.L. The triple-A supply chain. *Harvard Business Review,* 82, 10 (October 2004), 102–112.

Mathwick, C., and Rigdon, S. Play, flow, and the online search experience. *Journal of Consumer Research,* 31 (September 2004), 324–332.

McKnight, L.W.; Howlson, J.; and Bradner, S. Wireless grids: Distributed resource sharing by mobile, nomadic, and fixed devices. *IEEE Internet Computing,* 8, 4 (August 2004), 24–31.

Sawhney, M.; Prandelli, E.; and Verona, G. The power of innomediation. *MIT Sloan Management Review* (Winter 2003), 77–82.

Shapiro, C., and Varian, H.R. *Information Rules: A Strategic Guide to the Network Economy.* Boston: Harvard Business School Press, 1999.

Steinfield, C.; Bouwman, H.; and Adelaar, T. The dynamics of click-and-mortar commerce: Opportunities and management strategies. *International Journal of Electronic Commerce,* 7, 1 (Fall 2002), 93–119.

Straub, D.W.; Hoffman, D.L.; Weber, B.W.; and Steinfield, C. Toward new metrics for net-enhanced organizations. *Information Systems Research,* 13, 3 (September 2002), 227–238.

The 2004 e-Readiness Rankings. *Economist* Intelligence Unit and IBM Institute for Business Value, April 30, 2004 (available at http://graphics.eiu.com/files/ad_pdfs/ERR2004.pdf. Accessed 11/10/04).

UNCTAD (United Nations Conference on Trade and Development). *E-commerce and Development Report 2003.* New York and Geneva: UNCTAD, 2003 (available at http://r0.unctad.org/ecommerce/docs/edr03_en/ecdr03.htm. Accessed 11/19/04).

Zhu, K.; Kraemer, K.L.; Xu, S.; and Dedrick, J. Information technology payoff in e-business environment: An international perspective on value creation of e-business in the financial services industry. *Journal of Management Information Systems*, 21, 1 (Summer 2004), 17–54.

Zwass, V. Electronic commerce: Structures and issues. *International Journal of Electronic Commerce,* 1, 1 (Fall 1996), 3–23.

———. The embedding stage of electronic commerce. In P.B. Lowry, J.O. Cherrington, and R. R. Watson (eds.), *The E-Business Handbook.* Boca Raton, FL: St. Lucie Press, 2002, pp. 33–43.

———. Electronic commerce and organizational innovation: Aspects and opportunities. *International Journal of Electronic Commerce,* 7, 3 (Spring 2003), 7–37.

ACKNOWLEDGMENTS

I would like to thank the authors of the chapters included in this volume for their efforts and valuable insights. I am grateful to Professor Vladimir Zwass for inviting me to edit this volume. The financial support from Abbott Lab, Caterpillar, and State Farm is gratefully acknowledged. Last, but not least, I would also like to thank Stella Shen, Michele Gribbins, Matt Nelson, Katherine Zhao, and Sharon Collins for their helpful comments and editorial assistance. The efforts of all these individuals and organizations contributed to making this volume better, very much like how the various partners in a value-web work together in the digital economy. I consider myself very fortunate to be able to work with such a distinguished group.

Michael J. Shaw
University of Illinois at Urbana-Champaign

E-COMMERCE AND THE DIGITAL ECONOMY

AN INTRODUCTION

MICHAEL J. SHAW

PROLOGUE

This volume provides a state-of-the-art survey of information systems research on *electronic commerce* (e-commerce). Its intended audience includes three groups—the research community, practitioners/professionals, and graduate business students—who would like to understand the current issues, state-of-the-art developments, and future directions facing the effort to advance e-commerce, especially from the information –systems (IS) and information –technology (IT) research standpoints.

IT continues to transform the way businesses are conducted. Yet the role of IT, its pace of growth, and the nature of the transformations have changed in the aftermath of the bursting of the Internet bubble. E-commerce as a business phenomenon has become, if anything, more mature. Although some of the excitement that surged along with the enthusiasm about the potential of the so-called new economy has dissipated, the key drivers of the new economy have remained intact. After some adjustments, slowly but surely, we have begun to see another stage of evolution take shape. It is therefore important for us to analyze the underlying transformations. While previously, e-commerce was primarily based on the Internet, we are entering an era where the digitization of things and activities around us—in homes, businesses, enterprises, marketplaces, and civil services—has become so encompassing that it touches on every aspect of the global economy. Hence we are witnessing a natural evolution into the *digital economy.*

The University of Illinois, where I work, celebrated the tenth anniversary of the release of Mosaic to the world as the first widely used Internet browser a while ago. The undergraduate students involved in creating Mosaic subsequently founded Netscape. Netscape as a company exists now only in the history books, but other companies, such as Amazon and eBay, have moved beyond being the icons of the new economy. Paying visits to their Web sites has become part of our regular life. Aside from changing consumers' behavior, an increasing number of companies whose core businesses are based on the Internet are generating respectable financial returns. Significantly, newcomers in the second and third generations, such as Google, are doing very well in continuing the evolution. The keyword is evolution.

By now it has become clear that e-commerce in the business context, for most companies, can be best seen as a *complement.* Likewise, to understand e-commerce, one needs to take a holistic view, because there are as many transformations occurring in consumer experiences as there are in the whole industrial value chains. Just as e-commerce has transformed industry structure by giving companies new ways to run their businesses, it has also empowered consumers by providing them with more choices, more information, and more ways to buy.

While the digital economy, when realized, can improve the welfare of many, the picture is not entirely rosy, and major barriers remain. The business logic that can tie IT capabilities with business value, enterprise adoption, and consumer acceptance is still fuzzy. Concerns over security, risks, and legal issues remain mostly unresolved. Considerable resistance in moving e-commerce and the digital economy forward still stems from the lack of trust, both in business-to-consumer (B2C) and business-to-business (B2B) relationships. There are gaps between technological capabilities and user acceptance of these capabilities. To reap the full benefit from this important development, which represents the confluence of technological and business innovations all at once, society as a whole, and the business community in particular, we need to take a holistic and comprehensive perspective in seeing the opportunities ahead, dealing with the challenges, and taking actions accordingly.

To that end, this volume attempts to lay down the framework for understanding (1) business transformations and trends, (2) emerging opportunities, and (3) barriers to overcome in the rapid developments spanning e-commerce and the digital economy. To standardize the terms, we refer to the transformed business practices as electronic business, or *e-business.* We view it as a new era in the evolution of IT management. It is our hope that this volume gives clarity to the vision behind this emerging era.

THE TECHNOLOGY ENABLER

An effective infrastructure is essential in order to coordinate various business units and processes into an e-business. The enterprise information system supports supply chain processes and process coordination within and between enterprises. In addition, the infrastructure also includes (1) a global information network for supporting various electronic services, such as brokerage and contracting, payment and banking, and transaction processing; (2) electronic access to external data; and (3) electronic connections to customers that support such activities as filling orders and customer service.

Using the Web as the infrastructure not only gives an enterprise a better means to coordinate with its supply chain partners, but, as important, it provides a new channel to reach out to customers. With the Web channel serving as the virtual storefront, there are opportunities for product marketing, customer relationship management, and product branding. In addition, a new kind of *consumer process* is emerging, one that combines information aggregation, navigation, and interactive exchanges.

The general trend behind various developments in advancing Web technologies is this: In an e-business, there will be increasing use of modularity and the component model to increase portability, interoperability, and plug-and-play functionalities. The underlying paradox is that the enterprise systems will be more *integrated* because of the greater use of *distributed* but modularized components. The ongoing developments in software modularity and especially Web services all converge on that trend.

With Web services, we will likely see more highly modularized companies, with each unit specialized in its core competency but always prepared to link up with business partners and their enterprise systems. The component concept can be applied at several different levels: (1) *the software and system level,* where software modules have been used as the building blocks to make the functional components portable and interoperable; (2) *the process and application level,* where business processes and applications, such as order fulfillment, customer services, and so forth, have been managed as separate modules, sometimes running at remote sites by applications service providers (ASPs); and (3) *the enterprise level,* where business units can be quickly assembled to form virtual enterprises that explore a window of market opportunities.

Although the concept of software modularity and the use of software components are not new, Web services promise to meet both of these goals. Knowing the underlying reasons for that is important in thinking about the roadmap for the digital economy. First, the core technology supporting Web services is based on commonly agreed upon Web standards that are open, modular, widely accepted, and uniform. As a result, the adoption and diffusion of these standards are potentially much easier than previous similar technologies. Second, there are strong links between Web services and applications, which make it possible to encourage grassroots-level developments. Third, Web services can be used to support enterprise processes, making it possible for companies to adopt an "on-demand" strategy for investing their IT infrastructure. Related to this trend is the accelerating pace in developing e-business standards both vertically within particular industries and horizontally across industries.

ORGANIZATIONAL TRANSFORMATIONS

A distinct feature of an e-business system is its capability to adapt and react, making the organization more agile. The trend for e-business organizations to shift gradually from hierarchical to networked organizations is in line with the general trend of the economy. With the increasing use of information systems in most organizations, organizations are moving toward flatter and more adaptive structures, sometimes referred to as market-oriented networked organizations (MNOs). Instead of the command and control innate to traditional, hierarchical organizations, MNOs require more coordination, and the coordination is done in a way similar to the way goods are allocated in the marketplace, through decentralized pricing and exchanges. A supply chain network is a type of MNO where the business units are assembled through market forces. On the other hand, a supply chain network may be a type of hierarchical organization if it is totally vertically integrated. E-commerce is moving e-businesses toward the MNO model. Successfully implementing e-business technology reduces transaction costs and, therefore, the boundaries between markets and internal organizations are shrinking in favor of market orientation. Because of this shifting of firms' boundaries, the organizational transformations are closely linked with the supply chain transformations described in the next section.

The Web can enhance various types of coordination. It has a special impact on the coordination mechanisms that require stronger partnerships. Web technology can help move interorganizational information systems to a more advanced phase, where technologies such as XML will become standard, so that the information being exchanged can incorporate semantic structures. The major impact of the Web on coordinating e-businesses, in terms of forcing change in business models, will be the sharing, not only of information, but also knowledge and decision processes. Eventually, they can lead to the sharing of business processes between partners in the form of e-processes.

PROCESS/SUPPLY CHAIN TRANSFORMATIONS

The Web infrastructure provides opportunities to redefine the fulfillment process. Increasingly, e-businesses will adopt network organizations of specialized units coordinated through electronic networks to replace the traditional hierarchical organization. Because of their agility, these network organizations can be configured and reconfigured rapidly. The Web also provides new ways to coordinate workflow, manage documents, and enhance group work.

In running an e-business, the Web-based supply chain model provides opportunities for several companies to work together and form a virtual enterprise. PC "makers" such as IBM or HP still have their brand-name labels, but they no longer actually make computers. Instead, they focus their efforts on marketing, quality assurance, product development, customer service, and building the whole "supply web." There are many examples following this trend of "supply webs." A variety of companies acting as contract manufacturers have emerged as highly efficient manufacturers and supply chain managers that operate factories around the world. The electronics giants whose names their products carry are just as quickly getting out of making things, concentrating instead on developing new products and persuading consumers to buy them. But the story of forming a supply web is more than outsourcing the manufacturing operations. *It is about the ability to form a global supply chain quickly while being able to link with the supply chain partners electronically.* Through the e-business infrastructure, companies in the whole supply chain (or, more accurately, the whole supply web) act as one virtual company. The customers cannot tell that many companies are involved in the supply web. To them, the products are made by one company bearing the brand name.

While the examples just described most concern manufacturing enterprises, the same transformations are occurring in the service industries as well (which has led to the national debate on the merits of outsourcing). These process and supply chain transformations are taking place because, with the Web providing the links for sharing information among channel partners and the component technology providing the interoperability to integrate business processes, companies will use more outsourcing in their business models. As a result, companies will concentrate on their specialized products or services, that is, their core competencies, while working closely with their suppliers for other components or services. Because of the potential to manage e-business organizations in these dynamic, innovative ways, the ability to manage these transformed processes has become an important core competency in running any e-business.

CHANNEL MANAGEMENT

For most e-businesses, the emerging Web channel for purchasing, distributing, and marketing has created enormous opportunities for reaching out to new markets and customers. While there are companies specializing in e-commerce and using the Web as the only channel, most companies still maintain traditional channels. How to manage the Web channel alongside the other channels has increasingly become an issue for any e-business. The prominent channel management strategies used in running e-businesses are summarized as follows:

1. Using the Web to enhance traditional channels. This is a commonly used cross-marketing model. Major TV networks, for instance, often use the Web to provide more detailed coverage than their traditional channels, thus enhancing their brands and their traditional channels.
2. Using traditional channels to promote the Web channel. All e-commerce companies use traditional media to promote their brands. Some traditional retailers put kiosks in their stores to provide Web access to assist any need for additional product search, or to allow customers to return goods purchased online to local stores.
3. Using the Web channel to explore new markets. Because of the specific demographics of Web users, some companies use the Web to reach out to segments of the market they do not normally reach. Furthermore, the Web enables an e-business to reach out to consumers around the world.
4. Adding new Web-exclusive product lines. For the same reason, some companies use the

Web to sell new products. This is especially effective when the business traditionally depends on powerful dealers/distributors and, therefore, selling the same products directly is not an immediate option. Also, major consumer goods companies have found the Web an effective channel to test market new product lines.

5. Integrating the Web and traditional channels. This is the "click and mortar" model, which is aiming at combining the best of traditional and Web channels. Pure dot-com companies need more traditional distribution channels to provide more efficient logistics and better customer services. Traditional channels need to add the Web channel to gain new capabilities for searching, navigation, and interactive, hyper-linked information retrievals.
6. Using the Web to cannibalize traditional channels. Sometimes the new Web channel takes over the major share of the business. When this is inevitable in a given industry, a company might as well cannibalize the resources and focus its effort on the Web channel—rather than being preempted by competitors' aggressive Web channels. This happens in industries where the Web will inevitably become the main channel.
7. Using the Web to build alliances between traditional and Internet companies. The alliances recently built between carmakers and pure e-commerce companies, for example, belong to this model, which stems from the desire to build synergy between the Web and traditional channels.

What these channel management issues imply is that the enterprise information systems for an e-business can no longer be just for integrating traditional enterprise functions in accounting, production, marketing, and so forth. There must be additional components to provide capabilities for *channel coordination.* As with any of the other channels used by enterprises to reach their customers, the Internet has its strengths and weaknesses. It is, therefore, a risky proposition when a business relies on the Internet as its sole channel. Increasingly, it has become important for any enterprise to master how to integrate multiple channels (bricks-and-mortar stores, mail catalogs, call centers, the Internet site, portal site, etc.) and to build as much synergy among them as possible. These channels can be complementary in providing customer service, returns of goods, cross-marketing, merchandising, and other activities involved in shopping and purchasing. The use of multiple channels presents two challenges for enterprise information systems. The first is to integrate fully the channel activities. The second is to support the logistics and back-end infrastructure so that the transactions coming through the various channels can be processed seamlessly.

It is not surprising that consumers have learned to adopt multichannel behaviors. Increasingly more people, when making a purchase of goods or services, are going to the Web to investigate the products first and then go to the physical shops to buy what they have already decided on. This is referred to as *cross-channel* shopping and the crossing points can happen in several points in the purchasing process, such as (1) the initial investigation and examination, (2) the order or purchase of the goods, (3) the submission of payment, and (4) the possible services and/or returns. Now a consumer can go to either the Web or the physical shop for each of the four steps. To manage these new consumer behaviors, it is key to provide effective links among the channels so as to ensure making the sale while maintaining good services.

B2B OPPORTUNITIES

The Web provides an e-business with multichannel opportunities to interact with the marketplace. On the other side of the value chain, there is an increasing need to shift supply chain activities to interact more with B2B intermediaries, markets, and exchanges.

What activities do enterprise systems need to incorporate to fulfill the demands of these functions? For B2B supply chains, there will be more and more *market-making* and *aggregation* activities even for the supply chains of main products and their components. As a result, the supply chain management function for an e-business needs to coordinate and integrate the transaction flows among channel partners on a more dynamic basis. There are five B2B e-business models across a supply chain. Starting from the upstream of the supply chain, they are: (1) *manufacturer direct,* such as Dell or Cisco; (2) *e-distributors,* such as W.W. Grainger; (3) *neutral exchange and auction sites,* such as Freemarkets.com; (4) *buyer-side catalog aggregators,* such as Ariba or Commerce One; and (5) *industrywide (vertical) marketplaces,* such as Transora and Covisint.

In supporting B2B procurement, for instance, the B2B model can be based on Web-based catalogs, supply/demand aggregation, markets, or exchanges. For Web-based catalog systems, there are two key considerations. First, the suppliers' product information will have to be interoperable, so that the customers can navigate between the product catalogs of different suppliers. Second, the catalog search and related activities must be integrated with the enterprise legacy systems, so that the front-end information search processes and the back-end support processes can be seamlessly integrated. For supply/demand aggregation, market, and exchange models, the key to successful e-business development is to integrate transactions across multiple sites.

A complete e-business framework must enforce integration with B2B transactions. Channel partners, supply chain processes, and customer relationship management needs are equally important for managing an e-business. The framework also includes the ability to coordinate and integrate with other e-businesses. Compared to traditional systems, the new generation of enterprise systems will be open, flexible, modular, and interoperable. As important, it will fully integrate with the Web channel for supporting B2C and B2B transactions.

The three major areas where B2B e-commerce models have made the most impact are: (1) the productivity gains made possible by transformations in e-procurement and supply chain processes; (2) the increasing opportunities to participate in electronic marketplaces to further improve the efficiency of both the supply- and buyer-sides; and (3) the resulting B2B infrastructure to help streamline the activities and transactions across the whole vertical supply chains. It is clear that B2B e-commerce will continue its path of transforming supply chain relations, industrial organizations, and interorganizational structures.

What is less clear is how to evaluate a given B2B e-commerce system for a specific enterprise environment. Unlike traditional engineering projects or investments in new equipment, B2B e-commerce usually involves not only infrastructure investments, but also transformed processes and varying enterprise organizational structures. How to assess the precise value of B2B e-commerce is still an unsolved problem, and a solution is much needed to make technology investment and implementation decisions. Some preliminary studies suggest that, for instance, for the effective implementation of B2B e-commerce, an enterprise must consider a number of process, organization, and supply chain attributes to determine the value of a B2B e-commerce project. It is therefore important to identify and understand these attributes and their relationships to the implementation strategies adopted. This valuation methodology can be extended to the assessment of general e-business projects, as explained in the following section.

VALUE PROPOSITIONS AND JUSTIFICATION

The contribution of IT to productivity gains has now been generally recognized, after a considerable period in which the IT productivity paradox was at the center of debate. With e-business systems now under the spotlight of major capital investments, there are similar issues raised regarding the value of e-business systems. Some of the questions asked are practical ones. When millions of dollars of investments are being poured into e-business system projects in most larger companies, it is natural for IT managers to face the challenges of quantifying the value of e-business investments.

There are several challenges involved in assessing the value of e-business technology to an enterprise:

1. E-business technology is transformational. The adoption of e-business technology often requires changing business processes, organizational structure, and even supply chain relationships. Because it is not an isolated component, e-business technology must be evaluated in the enterprise context.
2. E-business technology is dynamically evolving. New versions of enterprise e-business systems arrive constantly. Sometimes they only require incremental changes, but at other times they bring about destructive innovation.
3. E-business technology is implemented for strategic as well as for operational objectives. The intangible yet strategic benefits of e-business systems are usually the hardest to estimate precisely.

It is important to note that the value of any given e-business project depends on the alignment between the strategic intent of the firm in question and the processes that embody the IT. For a consumer service firm, the IT that enables comprehensive customer services is much more valuable than the same IT for, say, a jet engine company selling primarily to other manufacturers. Depending on the nature of the e-business systems, their value can be systematically assessed at several levels, including

1. The strategic level,
2. The process level, and
3. The IT level.

To elaborate, there are four major value areas at the strategic level: supply chains, customer service, operational areas, and innovation, each of which will be discussed below.

With respect to supply chains, the impact of interorganizational systems (IOS) has been positive in improving the efficiency of business processes and the overall performance of manufacturing organizations. Electronic processing and communication of interorganizational data improves the timeliness and accuracy of information, allowing firms to plan and manage such assets as inventory better. This type of impact is first and foremost on the operational level and results in faster transactions, cost reduction, higher productivity, and improved quality. On the B2B side, e-business systems such as IOS provide competitive advantages by increasing the bargaining power of the buying organization by bettering coordination among supply chain partners and by increasing the information available about the business processes and demands across the whole supply chain. Technologies such as EDI and XML have resulted in the greater integration of firms with their suppliers. Interorganizational technologies also lead to shifts between different forms of coordination. Choosing a specific IT-based coordination structure creates risks in the form of relationship-specific investments, shifts in bargaining power, and the need for trust and commitment to an ongoing relationship. Web-based B2B e-commerce systems are radically different from other IT-based systems, and, therefore, it is questionable if the valuation methods and criteria developed previously are still valid. Moreover, the impact of the Web is increasingly difficult to isolate because of the transformation of processes and organizational structures.

On the customer side, e-business systems generally are aimed at helping improve the whole cycle of customer relations, that is, the acquisition, enhancement, and retention of customers. Activities involved in these different phases include direct marketing, sales force management, customer services, call-center coordination, and personalization. The value of acquiring new customers can be quantified by balancing acquisition costs and the lifetime value of customers. Enhancing customer service and the retention of existing customers are strategic factors that can be measured by the additional revenues generated by the services and the opportunity costs of losing customers due to poor service. The very nature of e-business technologies gives enterprises unprecedented capabilities to focus on the customers, enhancing all activities concerning customer acquisition, retention, and services. The value of these benefits is readily quantifiable. The more difficult measurements are such intangibles as brand image, reputation, and goodwill. Moreover, the key to customer facing is also about better integration of IS on the customer end and those managing supply chains and other business processes. While e-business technologies greatly enhance relations with customers, the back-end support is critical. That is the hidden side of valuation of e-business initiatives on the B2C front.

For the operational benefits, value is not uniform across processes and business units; therefore, a variety of strategies are needed. The type of business units, products, and suppliers and the characteristics of the enterprise have been shown to be important predictors of the level of improvement. Understanding the value of technologies and how they benefit different users, as well as business units, is critical in increasing the adoption of such systems.

In terms of innovation, many e-business systems are implemented as experiments for potential future competitive and strategic positions. In a similar vein, e-business initiatives can help enhance organizational learning because of their focus on enterprise integration, customer facing, and supply chain coordination. Managers view them as the initial steps toward greater future investments, depending on how future strategic positions and the technology should evolve. The underlying value of this type of e-business system is analogous to that of investing in financial *options*. This concept becomes especially important when considering the vast uncertainties involved in the future developments of e-business technologies.

By following this *strategy-process-IT* valuation framework, a firm can better quantify the benefits of e-business investments. This framework provides a more balanced analysis on the value of e-business projects and helps identify the intangible benefits better. Different companies may have different weights assigned to the four strategic components, leading to varying priorities assigned to process management and IT projects.

UBIQUITOUS COMMERCE

A significant development is taking shape in the effort to push the boundaries of e-commerce further. With the advent of wireless, mobile technology and devices that can be taken almost anywhere and to most business environments, we will see a new paradigm for business information management. That is, the information processing power will become more person- and location-oriented, as opposed to the current paradigm that is machine-oriented based on desk-top computing architecture. Because of the ubiquitous nature of the "points of execution," when this paradigm is implemented in e-commerce, we call it *ubiquitous commerce*, or u-commerce. The devices used to execute u-commerce include handheld mobile devices (personal digital assistants

(PDA), two-way pagers, cellular phones, net phones, and in-vehicle devices), laptops, desktops, workstations, and audio/video appliances. These devices are networked together to form a strong and integrated back-end and a highly mobile front-end infrastructure.

U-commerce builds on the Web information infrastructure to add three important capabilities to make Internet access ubiquitous—mobility, an interface to address access needs of the general population, and powerful distributed computing. Further, the architecture is envisioned to consist of a device-independent ubiquitous commerce platform that is integrated with the enterprise information, supply chain network, and electronic market infrastructures. U-commerce infrastructure consists of a core device-independent middleware platform, which is integrated with three major categories of information infrastructure—organization, supply chain, and market. This middleware is built on the Web infrastructure with the added capability of being accessed by consumers through a variety of wired and wireless devices. As these various devices have very different displays and processing and communication capabilities, the commerce platform should not only be flexible enough to add new devices, but also be secure and reliable. It is critical for their e-commerce applications to be integrated with these enterprise systems.

The arrival of radio frequency identification (RFID) tags, which can be attached to most merchandise to provide real-time product and pricing information, will create even more opportunities for u-Commerce. There will be increased visibility across the value chains, thus bringing about much more adaptive pricing and market-making options for companies. The additional data and information that come from these ubiquitous chips will put even more pressure on the enterprise IT infrastructure for providing sufficient bandwidth capacities and processing capabilities. The real-time data transmitted among RFID and enterprise servers require new standards to be established in the industries affected, so that a more uniform architecture can be deployed by the companies using this technology for new enterprise applications.

OPEN AND DYNAMIC ENTERPRISES

Compared to vertically integrated corporations, modern enterprises form and use supply chain networks to work with other companies to meet market demands. Because of the current rapid pace of new product introductions and product updates, an enterprise needs to be able to form a global supply chain quickly with its selected partners to explore emerging market opportunities. Ideally, there should be an interoperable "supply chain platform," where the enterprises can plug in to be connected with their suppliers or distributors. This interoperability not only needs the support of a global information infrastructure, which is greatly assisted by the Internet, but also the availability of sharable business processes for such supply chain activities as procurement and order fulfillment.

The benefits of *interoperable supply chains with standardized business processes* are driving companies who are competitors to adopt the same supply chains, platforms, and processes. Such supply chains make it attractive to collaborate to explore the increased bargaining power with the suppliers of their industry. Recent examples of such industrywide efforts are abundant, especially in the auto and the computer industries. In the former, the major manufacturers formed an industrywide e-marketplace called Covisint. In the latter, a consortium called the RosettaNet established supply chain collaboration and developed process standards. An interesting research question is how to enforce collaboration from fierce rivals in an industry to ensure fair allocation of benefits among the companies for their efforts.

The use of plug-and-play e-processes greatly increases a company's ability to work with its business partners, even if they use different enterprise systems. It means:

- More flexible business relationships with more partners linked by sharable e-processes;
- Lower set-up costs when working with new supply chain partners, and thus easier-to-explore, new business opportunities with greater bargaining power;
- Greater visibility and information-sharing across the supply chain, making the supply chain more efficient with less inventory;
- Greater integration in executing main supply chain processes, such as order fulfillment, thus reducing cycle times; and
- Improved operational efficiency enjoyed by all supply chain participants.

Effectively setting e-business and IT standards can help provide the necessary infrastructure for achieving these plug-and-play capabilities. The idea of developing interoperable supply chains has the potential to fundamentally transform the structure of many industries. This trend will continue, and it will force companies to adjust their practices accordingly.

OVERVIEW OF THE ORGANIZATION OF THIS VOLUME

To address these and related issues, this volume contains a collection of research papers by leading thinkers in the field, who collectively paint a canvas of the key developments, research projects, and findings in e-commerce and the digital economy. There are sharply focused close-up views and broad strokes of impressionist visions. Both types of research are important and in combination they help this volume cover the vast transformations still underway. The volume consists of four major clusters of chapters, which are described below.

IT Standards and the Transformation of Industry Structure

Companies are unbundling their enterprises into modular business processes in order to focus on their core competencies while outsourcing the noncore businesses. Furthermore, the standardized global information infrastructure enables the same companies to open up the borders of the enterprise in order to share processes and information with their partners in global supply chains. *Process sharing and standardization* are keys to the seamless plug-and-play infrastructure provided by the underlying supply chains. The open systems paradigm helps provide component interoperability and commonly recognized standards, which are important to establish connectivity and full integration. (Companies that used traditional enterprise resource planning systems have painfully found that hierarchical systems, while they also achieve connectivity and integration, are too rigid, restricting, and closed).

Web technology overcomes problems of system incompatibility by encapsulating enterprise systems as object components made accessible by standardizing components of the systems. This standards-setting effort includes the standardization of interoperable hardware, compatible interfaces, communications protocols, data formats, and, increasingly, business processes. This improves e-business management by (1) reducing production costs through lower procurement and distribution costs, (2) better utilizing resources through enterprise specialization, and (3) providing greater integration of supply chain activities. Large companies (e.g., Intel, Dell) have learned that their competitive advantages are determined to an increasingly great extent by their supply chain partners. Because these same suppliers are supplying to other companies, the best way to make supply chains more efficient is to let the whole industry (e.g., semiconductor, PC) adopt the same standards for IT, data, and supply chain processes. To avoid conflicting interests among competitors, standards development organizations (SDOs) play a central role for this type of vertical standards setting and development. RosettaNet is a prominent example of such a standards development organization.

The four chapters included in this section address and highlight the importance of e-business standards, standardization in B2B collaboration, the business impacts, and the standardization gap.

Emphasis on Consumers and Customization

E-business systems integrate enterprise applications from customer relationship management to supply chain management. They also help integrate business processes across the supply chain to facilitate such supply chain processes as order fulfillment and product development. The common infrastructure is interoperable and the processes sharable. This integration of processes and enterprise systems enables companies to interact with their customer on one hand, while remaining fully aware of the current status of supply chain information on the other. The abilities to achieve greater integration and customization have enabled innovative companies, such as IKEA, to get customers involved in an expanded part of the value-adding chain. The Web provides opportunities to accelerate that trend. As a result of customer facing, companies will be better able to customize their product offering and at the same time manage the demands of the market. This increasing emphasis on demand management in a proactive fashion in order to better balance supplies and demands requires more effective integration of customer relationship management and supply chain management.

There are four chapters included in this section that address the issues of focusing on customers, human factors, bundling of electronic content, and online auctions, respectively.

Management of IT Infrastructure

The enterprise IT infrastructure has been extended beyond simple networking to include mobile infrastructure. The new business infrastructure will have two components: one, a powerful backbone system with an interoperable platform running the major applications and business processes; the other, a highly portable, networked, and mobile front end that acts as a collection of nerve cells and tentacles for data collection, information sensing, and front-end processing. In addition to providing connectivity, the information infrastructure also provides interoperability on the enterprise and supply chain levels. To keep the infrastructure flexible and adaptive and to minimize pouring investments on fixed assets, companies will move to the on-demand model for supporting enterprise IT infrastructure, relying more on sharable IT services rather than building all of the infrastructure capacities in house.

Four chapters are included that point out important trends in, respectively, applying P2P technologies to B2B applications, topographical leveraging of sharable services, global mobile commerce, and the business model for mobile commerce typefied by NTT DoCoMo's i-Mode.

Trust, Security, and Legal Issues

By the very nature of the Web, e-business systems are based on the principle of open systems with a market orientation. Any e-business system must be ready to interact with consumers and be connected with a partner's system and to share the common processes. The market orientation of e-business systems provides additional B2B and B2C opportunities and choices. The main inhibitors remain the concerns over the lack of trust from consumers in B2C relations and also from business partners in B2B relations. In order to continue to make positive impacts and avoid the negative consequences looming on the horizon, the digital economy must resolve the unsettled issues with respect to the intrusions on privacy, the lack of trust of online transactions, the ongoing disputes over intellectual properties, and the risks of fraud in e-commerce. Greater research efforts in these areas are critically important for e-commerce and the digital economy to reach their full potential.

Three chapters cover this important area, addressing issues concerning trust in online consumer exchange, trust issues in the public key infrastructure (PKI) market, and private law on the Internet.

Because of the multidisciplinary nature of e-commerce and the digital economy, the chapters included utilize a wide range of research methods from various reference disciplines. We summarize the research methods used by each chapter in the following list.

Chapter	Research Methods
(1)	Industrywide surveys, economic value analysis, case studies
(2)	Supply chain analysis, operations modeling, case studies
(3)	Accounting data analysis and financial evaluation
(4)	Economic analysis, network effect theory and simulation
(5)	Questionnaire-based survey, Delphi study, focus-group interviews
(6)	Human factors, usability, human–computer interaction (HCI) theory
(7)	Consumer behavior, pricing theory, choice-based conjoint analysis
(8)	Information economics, auction theory
(9)	Business modeling, IT evaluation
(10)	Performance evaluation of information systems, industry analysis
(11)	Industrywide survey, business value analysis, user acceptance analysis
(12)	Case studies, economic value analysis, strategic management
(13)	Behavior theory, psychology, sociology
(14)	Economic theory, lemons principle, information security
(15)	Law and economics, Internet policy analysis, case studies

IT has been the driving force behind the developments that are the focus of this volume and to a certain extent this volume is about putting IT in the business context most effectively. The omnipresent electronic links and movements toward digitization in the economy essentially have added a new dimension to most, if not all, business decisions, processes, and strategies. The full impact of IT is yet to come and we are near the inflection points for new IT developments, such as personal mobile technology, Web services, and the integration of home and workplace IT, before the next wave of innovation. While the recent argument from some pundits that IT does not matter anymore is laughable, we in the business research community do need to do a better job of defining how IT still matters. That is the goal of this volume.

PART I

INFORMATION TECHNOLOGY STANDARDS AND THE TRANSFORMATIONS OF INDUSTRY STRUCTURE

CHAPTER 1

MEASURING THE BUSINESS BENEFITS OF WEB-BASED INTERORGANIZATIONAL SYSTEMS

A CO-ADOPTION MODEL FOR STANDARDS DEVELOPMENT

MATTHEW L. NELSON, MICHAEL J. SHAW, AND MARY SCHOONMAKER

Abstract: *One of the important sources of competitive advantages of information technology (IT) comes from the practice of interorganizational systems (IOS), which have taken on even more important roles because of the advent of Internet technologies, such as XML and Web services, for facilitating business-to-business transactions. This study evaluates the impacts made by the ongoing adoption of Web-based IOS standards. By first developing a co-adoption model for standards development, we are able to evaluate factors that include compatibility, relative advantage, environmental variables, and such control variables as seller versus buyer, technology conversion type, and location in supply chain. An empirical study covering twelve implementations of the target technology and standards is conducted with the RosettaNet consortium. A comparative analysis of the field study results based on the theoretical model is conducted. The intent of this comparison is to measure the business consequences of implementing Web-based IOS, examine key relationships, and assess potential influential factors leading toward adoption and diffusion in an industrial group setting. Recommendations for future research and managerial implications are also provided.*

Keywords: *Information Technology (IT) Standards Diffusion, Interorganizational Systems (IOS), Standards Development Organization (SDO), Supply Chain Interoperability*

INTRODUCTION AND BACKGROUND

This chapter examines one of the emerging trends in the digital economy regarding the open enterprise model and standards setting. The focus is on the assessment of business value and adoption strategy. We started out by merely seeking to identify supply chains interested in the use of consistent interorganizational systems (IOS) standards. What we found, however, were supply chains faced with extraordinarily competitive pressures and sharply rising manufacturing costs and the fact that industrial group survival was hanging in the balance—a situation that many industrial groups are now confronting. In coping with the competitive pressures, the group of firms we studied positioned themselves on the cusp of transformation enabled by intense industrywide collaboration and IOS standardization. This group collectively funded and launched industrywide standardization initiatives with elements that include a nonprofit standards development organization (SDO), called RosettaNet, to coordinate and oversee the development and deployment of vendor-neutral, platform-independent IOS standards that are modularized around cross-company business processes. The novelty of their approach has legitimately earmarked the industrial group as one of the first of its kind using an open enterprise model that other industrial groups now seek to replicate. The key research question is: Do the standards-setting adoption practices and e-process initiatives used by the supply chains in this industrial group generate value?

In the broader context, the development of IOS standards has reached a fevered pitch across many industrial groups. The Chemical Industry Data Exchange (CIDX), for example, is a nonprofit industry-based SDO for the chemical industry. CIDX has assembled seventy-five member firms and developed fifty-two sets of IOS standards since the year 2000, including a host of pending standards at various stages in the development cycle. HR-XML, a nonprofit industry-based SDO, was launched in 1999 and has assembled over 150 member firms and developed twenty-seven sets of human–resource related IOS standards, with many more in the development queue. Similarly, RosettaNet, a nonprofit SDO serving the semiconductor, electronic component, and information technology (IT) industries has assembled over 500 member firms since its launch in 1998 and developed fifty-three sets of IOS standards, with fifty-two in the development queue. New SDOs are emerging on a regular basis and other industrial groups are opting to redirect efforts of existing SDOs toward utilization of modern-day IOS standards-related innovations (e.g., Accord, Open-GIS).

This activity has caught the attention of researchers and practitioners alike. Dubbed the "next great frontier for reducing costs, enhancing quality, and speeding operations" (Jones 2000; Hammer, 2001), the use of consistent and compatible IOS standards in an industrial group setting solidifies business-to-business (B2B) connections and streamlines cross-company business processes. The key technological advancements spawning this activity are a grouping of related innovations that include eXtensible Markup Language (XML), Simple Object Access Protocols (SOAP), Web Services Description Language (WSDL), Universal Description Discovery and Integration (UDDI), and other application programming interfaces (APIs) (Hagel and Brown, 2001). Integrating cross-company business process standards with these innovations provides the opportunity for creating electronic business documents, common field attributes, consistent data tags, and compatible communication protocols (Berners-Lee 2001, 2003). With an industry-based SDO acting as the lead coordinator, these IOS standards are structured around shared cross-company business processes and jointly agreed to and developed by members of the extended industrial group. We refer to these integrated innovations as Web-based IOS, or XML-based IOS (to highlight the underlying technology).

The existence of this phenomenon, however, is raising a host of new challenges with respect to the adoption and deployment of Web-based IOS (Koch 2003). Some firms with a large electronic data interchange (EDI) installed base are reluctant to quickly deploy Web-based IOS due to their concerns that this will entail costly reengineering of back-end legacy systems and their associated business processes. Other firms that serve multiple industrial groups are delaying deployment of new IOS standards since they are uncertain as to which set of standards will take hold on a cross-industry (horizontal) basis. Still others (including some entire industrial groups) are postponing deployment projects to reap lessons learned and best practices from early adopter firms (and industries). In fact, in a review of fifteen different industry-based SDOs by the authors, the adoption issue was discovered to be among the top three priorities in all SDOs reviewed. Thus, the questions driving this line of research include: What are the business consequences of implementing Web-based IOS in a supply chain (industrial group) setting? What are the significant factors influencing the adoption and diffusion of Web-based IOS in organizations? Do these consequences or influencing factors change depending on the role played by an organization within the supply chain?

The work reported in this paper represents part of an ongoing inquiry by the authors to examine the factors influencing the adoption and diffusion of IOS standards. An earlier paper (Nelson et al. 2002) introduced and defined a theoretical model depicting potential antecedent conditions as well as consequences of diffusion measures. This provided insight into the technology under study and the use of interoperability standards and shed some light on the mutual operational and economic benefits provided to firms on each side of the IOS. The scope of that paper's empirical analysis was limited to a single implementation instance of an XML-based IOS between a manufacturer and distributor (Nelson et al. 2002). This paper builds on these findings and expands the empirical analysis to twelve implementations (organized into four cases) of the target technology across eight firms from a single industrial group. This structure enables a closer examination of the role and consequences of industrywide collaboration, an industry-based SDO, and the IOS standardization process.

The paper is structured as follows. First, based on a review of prior innovation diffusion and IOS literature, a theoretical framework is proposed to examine potential influential factors leading toward adoption and diffusion. Second, a field study utilizing RosettaNet's IOS standards is presented, examining twelve instances of the target technology. Third, the empirical results are compared to the theoretical model and the findings stated. Managerial implications are summarized and recommendations for future research are discussed throughout.

CO-ADOPTION MODEL OF WEB-BASED IOS STANDARDS

Based on a review of IOS and innovation diffusion literature the following factors are under consideration for influencing the adoption and diffusion of the target technology. The measurement variables can be classified into four constructs: *compatibility, relative advantage, environmental,* and *control variables* (see Figure 1.1). The dependent variables are in the bottom center of Figure 1.1 and include *adoption* and three measures of diffusion (*volume, diversity,* and *breadth*). All measurement and dependent variables are defined below. This paper's intent is to measure the business consequences of implementing Web-based IOS, examine key relationships, and assess potential influential factors leading toward adoption and diffusion in an industrial group setting. This research builds on the theoretical model and findings from earlier work in this line of inquiry by the authors (Nelson et al. 2002).

Compatibility

Compatibility examines the extent to which the innovation is consistent with existing tasks and needs and prior experiences and business processes of the adopters (Agarwal and Prasad 1999; Cho and Kim 2001; Cooper and Zmud 1990). Cooper and Zmud (1990) provide a framework for assessing compatibility of a new technology by evaluating assumption gaps between the characteristics of the new technology versus the task characteristic needs of the organization. This framework proves to be useful in this study for two reasons. First, the scope includes three different cross-company business processes: (1) *purchase order (PO) generation, change, and cancel,* (2) *shipments from made-to-stock items* (i.e., ship from stock and debit), and (3) *notification of advance shipments.* Thus, similar technological innovations are applied to different business processes that necessitate different task characteristics. Second, the alternative technical solutions include XML-based IOS, Web-based POs, electronic data interchange (EDI), and manual-based

Figure 1.1 **Co-Adoption Model of Web-based IOS Standards**

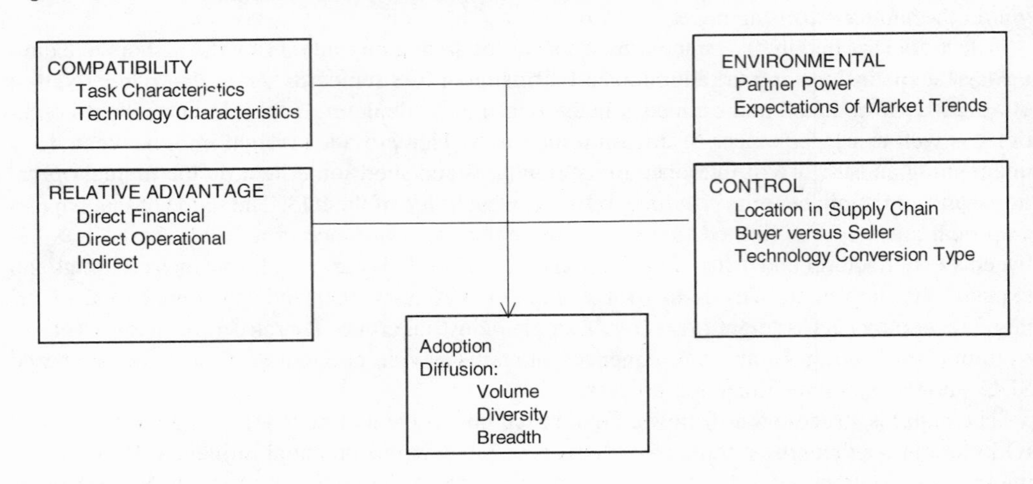

process solutions. This will provide a useful framework for evaluating the alternative technical solutions to the share business process types. Firms were asked to rate each solution's ability to meet underlying cross-company business process needs on a Likert Scale from 1 (Strongly Disagree with Compatibility) to 5 (Strongly Agree with Compatibility).

Relative Advantage

Relative advantage is the extent to which a potential adopting organization views the innovation as offering *direct* and *indirect* financial and operational benefits over previous ways of performing the same tasks (Agarwal and Prasad 1997). The financial indicators include Return on Investment (ROI, transaction cost savings, investment, and payback. The operational performance indicators include throughput (processing capability per unit of time) and cycle time. Thus, firms were required to calculate transaction costs prior to and after implementation of the target technology. The direct cost components include technical standards negotiation time (between the two participants), hardware, software, and implementation-related expenses. The initial up-front investments associated with implementing the new technology were isolated in order to calculate the ROI and payback financial indicators. The direct operational impact of the new technology was based on its impact on cycle time and throughput.

Environmental

Two environmental factors under consideration include *partner power* and *expectations of market trends. Partner power* is measured as the percentage of sales (or purchases) that a business partner is dependent on from their customer (or supplier). This use of the power variable is consistent with the industry under study, availability of substitute suppliers, low manufacturing capacity utilization rates, and relatively low switching costs. This is consistent with Hart and Saunder's notion of supplier dependence in dyadic relationships (Hart and Saunders 1998) and similar to

Iacovou's findings regarding external pressure in EDI adoption (Iacovou et al. 1995). *Expectations of market trends* is an infrequently used variable in study of innovation diffusion (Cho and Kim 2001, Fichman 1992). For the present study, the definition for this variable is consistent with Cho's: "Expectation for market trend is the degree of expectation that the target technology will be pervasively adopted in the industry in the future" (Cho and Kim 2001). Industry-based SDOs are funded, to a large extent, from contributions by member and partner organizations. Thus, partner organizations have a "vested" interest in developing and setting the most appropriate standards to be utilized within their industry.

Control Variables

Three control variables are used in this study and they include *buyers versus sellers, location in supply chain,* and *technology conversion type.* Each respondent firm will either be a *buyer* or *seller* organization with respect to the underlying cross-company business process. Similarly, each firm fulfills a role in the supply chain with respect to the underlying cross-company business process. For a given firm it may be as a distributor, an original equipment manufacturer (OEM), or an outsourcing partner. Since this study examines both pre- and post-implementation of the innovations, *technology conversion type* refers to the firms' former (pre-implementation) technical solution utilized to conduct the cross-company business process. The prior technology types vary from manual-based to semi-automated, EDI, or Web-based IOS solutions.

Innovation Measures

The innovation measures (dependent variables) measure the extent of Web-based IOS adoption and diffusion. Adoption is defined as "a decision is reached to invest resources necessary to accommodate the implementation effort" (Cooper and Zmud 1990). Fichman defines internal diffusion as "the extent of use of an innovation across people, projects, tasks, or organizational units" (Fichman, 2001,p. 454). Since our study examines diffusion both internally and externally to an organization, Fichman's definition will be extended to the extent of use of an innovation across people, projects, tasks, organizational units, or external trading partners. Three additional diffusion dimensions are used: *volume, diversity,* and *breadth* (Massetti and Zmud 1996). *Volume* refers to the ratio of business documents transmitted via the technology innovation channel, over the total number of business documents exchanged (regardless of the technology). *Diversity* refers to the count (or total instances) of the target technology that the organization has implemented. *Breadth* refers to the count of different trading partners with whom the respondent has co-adopted the target technology. The use of these definitions is consistent with other EDI studies (Hart and Saunders 1998; Massetti and Zmud 1996). For analysis and discussion purposes, diversity and breadth are measured at the organizational level (as opposed to an individual business process level). Similarly, adoption is measured at the SDO level (as opposed to a specific type of Web-based IOS). That is, adoption indicates that a firm has reached a decision to participate in an industry-based SDO that develops Web-based IOS standards.

RESEARCH FRAMEWORK

A field study was conducted to compare the theoretical model to a real work environment. The study was organized into four cases (see Figure 1.2) and was conducted during a twelve-month span in 2001 and 2002. Each case represents a shared business process called PIPä, or partner

Figure 1.2 **Case Study Research Framework**

		Shared Business Process				
Prior Technology	**Role in Supply Chain W.R.T. Business Process**	**Sell Side**	**Shared Business Process Description**	**Buy Side**	**Role in Supply Chain W.R.T. Business Process**	**Prior Technology**
Case #1 Semi-automated (Fax/E-mail)	Manufacturer	Company A-1	⟷ *Ship from Stock & Debit*	Company B-1	Distributor	Semi-automated (Fax/E-mail)
Case #2 EDI	Outsourcing Partner	Company C-2	⟷ *PO Generate, Change, & Cancel*	Company D-2	Manufacturer	EDI
Case #3 Proprietary IOS	Outsourcing Partner	Company E-3	⟷ *PO Generate*	Company F-3	Manufacturer	Semi-automated
Case #4 Semi-automated (Flat File)	Outsourcing Partner	Company G-4	⟷ *Notify of Advance Shipment*	Company H-4	Manufacturer	Semi-automated (Flat File)

interface process, between two separate companies "paired" on each end of the IOS, with the exception of Case #2, which includes three *closely related* shared business processes grouped into a single case. Thus, the scope of the field study includes six instances of Web-based IOS (for a total of twelve different installations) between eight respondent firms. The participating firms are members of the same industrial group where a nonprofit SDO exists and is responsible for coordinating the IOS standards development process on behalf of the industrial group. Most measures required firms to provide pre- and post-implementation data. Confidentiality of data and field study results was a concern of all respondent firms. Thus, firm names, precise location in supply chain, and other information have intentionally been excluded. Field study participants were selected based on three criteria: (1) both organizations in the dyadic relationship were willing to participate, (2) both organizations agreed to implement the Web-based IOS, and (3) both organizations would provide a lead point of contact to participate in the study. Interviews and data collection surveys were administered with all respondent firms.

Case Descriptions

Case #1 is between Company A-1, a manufacturer/seller to Company B-1, a distributor/buyer. Case #1's shared business process is ship from stock and debit, which enables the distributor to make unscheduled shipments of goods directly from their own inventory and request a debit authorization from the manufacturer. Both companies in Case #1 had previously completed this cross-company business process utilizing a semi-automated solution (e.g., faxes and e-mails). Case #2 is between Company C-2, an outsourcing manufacturer/seller to Company D-2, an original equipment manufacturer (OEM)/buyer. Case #2's shared business process is a grouping of three closely related cross-company business processes for purchase order (PO) generate, change, and cancel. Both companies in Case #2 had previously completed these cross-company business processes utilizing EDI. Case #3 is between Company E-3, an outsourcing manufacturer/seller to Company F-3, OEM/buyer. Case #3's shared business process is purchase order (PO) generate. Company F-3 had formerly generated the POs on a semi-automated basis, while Company E-3 conducted the shared business process on a manual basis. Case #4 is between Company G-4, an outsourcing manufacturer/seller to Company H-4, an OEM/buyer. Case #4's shared business process pertains to communicating advanced shipment notification and information between the seller and buyer. Both companies in Case #4 had previously completed this cross-company business process utilizing a semi-automated solution (e.g., flat file data exchanges via e-mail and FTP). For all cases, the participating SDO was the RosettaNet consortium.

SDO Background

Founded in 1998, RosettaNet is a nonprofit consortium focused on developing XML-based IOS standards for the high-technology industry, including computer and consumer electronics, electronic components, logistics, semiconductor manufacturing, and telecommunications segments. To fully address the business needs of supply chain companies across the trading network, RosettaNet maintains an ongoing symbiotic relationship with the solution provider community. Like RosettaNet, many of these newly formed XML standard-setting bodies have not limited their standards to consistent field attributes and definitions, but rather they have the standards repertoire to include business dictionaries, networking protocols, and technical dictionaries organized around shared business processes between partner organizations. RosettaNet has developed standards for more than seventy-five of these shared business processes, or PIPs™, ranging from

Request Engineering Change to *Cancel a Purchase Order* to *Notify of Authorization to Build.* The content of each is complete with messaging service standards, business dictionaries, technical dictionaries, and business process choreography. These XML-based shared business process standards form point-to-point connections via the Internet that enable execution of the relevant business processes within and between different organizations on a global basis. They are, in effect, modularized Web-based IOS.

RESULTS AND DISCUSSION

A comparison was made between the field study results and the co-adoption model of Web-based IOS. The intent of this comparison was to measure the business consequences of implementing Web-based IOS, examine key relationships, and assess potential influential factors leading toward adoption and diffusion in an industrial group setting. This section is structured around the three research questions driving this inquiry:

1. What are the business consequences of implementing Web-based IOS in a supply chain (industrial group) setting?
2. What are the significant factors influencing the adoption and diffusion of Web-based IOS in organizations?
3. Do these consequences or influencing factors change depending on the role played by an organization within the supply chain?

Business Consequences of Implementing Web-Based IOS

The consequences of implementing Web-based IOS solutions are categorized into four areas; direct financial impact, direct operation impact, technology compatibility, and indirect impact. Firms were requested to assess most measures on both a pre- and post-implementation basis.

Field study results indicate substantial direct financial and operational benefits are enabled from implementing the Web-based IOS solutions. The direct financial benefits resulted in transaction cost savings ranging from 16 percent to 87 percent for cases 1 through 3, with more moderate savings experienced in case 4. The direct operational benefits resulted in throughput improvements ranging from no change to nineteen-fold improvements and cycle-time reductions ranging from slight to 99 percent. Two key drivers have emerged that influence the degree of benefits afforded to organizations: (1) underlying cross-company business process type and (2) the technology conversion type. See Table 1.1 for summarized findings associated with the direct financial and operational measures.

Field study results indicate that Web-based IOS solutions are more compatible with meeting underlying cross-company business process task needs than EDI and semi-automated solutions. Five task needs were found to be common among all shared business process types and include (in order from most to least important): data accuracy and integrity, timeliness, effective communications, collaboration levels, and transaction volumes. Web-based IOS and EDI solutions earned more than twice the compatibility rating of semi-automated solutions. This finding is not surprising, since semi-automated solutions include informal process steps, with a hybrid of e-mails, faxes, and phone calls. From a Web-based IOS versus EDI perspective, the Web-based IOS solution earned greater compatibility levels in four of the five common task needs (in order of largest to smallest): collaboration levels, data accuracy and integrity, effective communications, and timeliness. We observed that firms generally treat Web-based IOS and EDI solutions to have the

Table 1.1

Direct Financial and Operational Impact

Firm	Web-based IOS solution	Buy/sell side	Direct financial impact: Trans cost savings	Direct financial impact: ROI (Y1)	Direct financial impact: Payback (years)	Direct operational impact: Thru-put capability	Direct operational impact: Cycle time
Case #1							
A-1	SHIP FROM STOCK AND DEBIT	Sell side	–87%	High	1.9	650% increase	91% reduction
B-1		Buy side	–40%	High	1.8	67% increase	40% reduction
Case #2							
C-2	PO GENERATE, CHANGE, CANCEL	Sell side	–32%	Moderate	10.4	PO CREATE (no change), PO CHANGE (tested at 19x increase)	PO CREATE (no change), PO CHANGE (tested at 85% decrease)
D-2		Buy side	–16%	Moderate	14.8	PO CREATE (tested at 2x increase), PO CHANGE (tested at 2x increase)	PO CREATE (98% decrease), PO CHANGE (98% decrease)
Case #3							
E-3	PO GENERATE	Sell side	–37%	Moderate	4.2	100% increase	99% reduction
F-3		Buy side	–32%	Moderate	8.6	Tested at 2x increase	99% reduction
Case #4							
G-4	NOTIFY OF ADVANCE SHIPMENT	Sell side	Slight	Slight	Slight	Slight	Slight
H-4		Buy side	Slight	Slight	Slight	Moderate	Moderate

Table 1.2

Compatibility Rating of Technical Solutions versus Business Process Task Needs

	Compatibility rating of business process task needs vs. technical solution											
	Ship from stock and debit			Request PO			Change PO and cancel PO			Overall SDO		
Business process task needs	Semi-auto	Web-based IOS	EDI	Semi auto	Web-based IOS	EDI	Semi-auto	Web-based IOS	EDI	Rank	Web-based IOS vs. semi-auto	Web-based IOS vs. EDI
Improved data accuracy and integrity	2.0	5.0	3.0	2.0	5.0	4.0	1.5	5.0	4.0	1	3.1	1.1
Enhanced timeliness	2.0	5.0	4.0	2.5	4.8	4.0	2.0	4.5	4.0	2	2.4	0.7
Effective communication	2.0	5.0	4.0	2.8	5.0	4.3	3.0	5.0	4.0	3	2.3	0.9
Collaboration levels with S.C. Partners	2.0	5.0	3.0	2.0	4.5	3.3	2.0	5.0	3.0	4	2.7	1.6
Ability to manage transaction volumes	3.0	4.0	5.0	2.5	4.8	4.5	2.5	4.5	4.5	5	2.0	0.0

*Ratings based on a 5-point Likert scale of 1—Strong Disagree with Compatibility to 5—Strongly Agree with Compatibility.

Table 1.3

Indirect Benefits of Web-based IOS

- Improved resource allocation time
- Product cost savings (advantages)
- Reduced negotiation time of technical standards
- Compliance with supplier or customer mandates
- Improved employee morale
- Increased accuracy
- Improved response times
- Enables and improves the "blanket" PO process
- Nightly batch vs. real-time processing

same compatibility rating with respect to the ability to handle large transaction volumes.

The field study also uncovered a number of indirect benefits that are enabled through implementing Web-based IOS solutions. The most common indirect benefits include reduced negotiation time of technical standards and improved resource allocation time, while the most important indirect benefits include compliance with business partner mandates and product cost advantages. There are substantial time savings associated with having an independent (nonprofit) supply-chain focused organization dedicated to establishing consistent standards for Web-based IOS solutions. The mere existence of an SDO provides benefits that are over and above the direct financial and operational benefits enabled by the technology. Examples include enabling and facilitating a *real* blanket PO process, designing (and encouraging) modularity in IOS architecture, reduced tensions between business partners regarding noncore issues, government tax breaks for enabling interconnectivity between organizations, reduced internal IT development expenditures, and others. See Table 1.3 for a list of indirect benefits enabled by Web-based IOS.

Supply Chain Logistical Influences on Consequence Measures

The field study included an equal number of buyer and seller respondent firms. From a partner power perspective, buyer firms have the power advantage in all four cases. In three cases, this power advantage is due to the organizations' relative position in the supply chain. That is, these three cases involve buyer firms that are OEMs and seller firms that are outsourcing partners. The final case's power advantage is due to the significantly larger firm size of the buyer (distributor) compared with that of the seller (manufacturer). Despite these power advantages, seller firms unanimously indicated they were not coerced into adopting the innovation. Seller organizations, in fact, earned greater direct financial benefits from implementing Web-based IOS solutions than buyer firms at nearly a 2:1 ratio. The direct operational and indirect benefits were relatively balanced between buyer and seller organizations. Finally, firms with semi-automated solutions (as their pre-implementation technological solution) were generally found to have greater direct financial and operational performance improvements than firms with other technology conversion types.

Diffusion Levels and Determinants

Table 1.4 includes current and projected diffusion levels of Web-based IOS solutions during the twelve and twenty-four months following the survey date. Field study results indicate substantial growth projected in all three diffusion measures: volume, diversity, and breadth. With the exception of respondent F-3, volume growth projections range from 100 percent to 800 percent over the next twelve to twenty-four months. During the next twenty-four months, firms are forecasting to triple the number of implementations (diversity) to 857 and more than double the number of trading partners (breadth) to 347. From a sell side versus buy side comparison, buyers are projecting greater diffusion in diversity and breadth over the next twelve and twenty-four months than sellers. From a volume perspective, sellers are forecasting slightly greater growth over the next twelve months, but buyers are expecting significantly greater growth over the next twenty-four months. These results are consistent with buyer power dominance and the probable need for sellers to catch-up with technology.

Collectively, several emerging patterns in the field study shed light on influential factors toward achieving greater Web-based IOS diffusion levels. First, buyer firms (manufacturers and distributors) in this industry are setting the technological trends with the sellers (outsourcing partners) following suit. Although coercive adoption techniques are absent, partner power and expectations of market trends are influencing this industrial group with a positive relation to greater diffusion. Second, firms are differentiating the adoption decision versus the diffusion decision. A firm's adoption decision is increasingly more related to their decision to participate or not participate in their industrial group's SDO. A firm's diffusion decision, on the other hand, is increasingly related to the specific type of Web-based IOS under consideration. Thus, environmental factors (partner power and expectations of market trends) and indirect benefits have jointly resulted in the respondent's adoption decision to participate in the industry-based SDOs. The relative advantages of the technology (including direct financial and operational benefits) are key constructs that will sustain interest in Web-based IOS solutions and likely lead toward greater levels of diffusion.

CONCLUSIONS

This paper develops a conceptual Web-based IOS adoption and diffusion model and then empirically evaluates the model in a field study involving four case studies within the RosettaNet consortium. Field study findings indicate substantial improvements in all direct financial and operational measures (ROI, transaction cost, payback, cycle time, and throughput), with transaction cost savings ranging from 16 percent to 87 percent. The study also revealed Web-based IOS solutions earned twice the compatibility rating than semi-automated solutions and greater compatibility levels in four of the five common task needs as compared to EDI solutions.

The most common indirect benefits included reduced negotiation time of technical standards, improved resource allocation time, enhanced compliance with business partner mandates, and product cost advantages. Additional indirect benefits that are over and above direct transaction cost savings were derived as a result of the mere existence of an industry-based standards development consortium. Environmental factors and indirect benefits jointly resulted in firms' decisions to participate in an industry-based standards development consortium. The relative advantage of the innovations (transaction cost savings, ROI, operational improvements) are the key constructs in sustaining interest in the target technology and likely leading toward greater levels of diffusion.

Regarding supply chain location influences, buyer firms possessed the partner power advantage primarily due to their OEM status and firm size. Seller firms earned the greatest direct financial and operational benefits from Web-based implementations, while buyer firms were projecting greater diffusion levels.

With respect to adoption and diffusion determinants, a framework is emerging regarding the role of an SDO toward achieving greater adoption and diffusion levels of Web-based IOS solutions through their respective supply chains and industrial groups. Environmental factors and

Table 1.4

Projected Diffusion Levels of Web-based IOS

ORG	Buy/sell side	Current volume Ratio	Growth rate projections: Volume (%) Next 12 months	Volume (%) Next 24 months	Diversity (%) Next 12 months	Diversity (%) Next 24 months	Breadth (%) Next 12 months	Breadth (%) Next 24 months
Case #1								
A-1	Sell side	Low	200	400	1,200	1,900	300	700
B-1	Buy side	Low	250	450	29	100	50	200
Case #2								
C-2	Sell side	Med	400	800	100	200	300	500
D-2	Buy side	Low	149	398	165	429	114	329
Case #3								
E-3	Sell side	Med	150	250	67	150	40	100
F-3	Buy side	Low	0	0	167	233	67	133
Case #4								
G-4	Sell side	Low	80	100	100	200	25	88
H-4	Buy side	Low	100	300	165	429	114	329
Totals	Sell side	Low	144	244	147	274	81	181
	Buy side	Low	139	367	137	360	96	289
	Total		140	348	138	351	94	271

indirect benefits jointly resulted in firms' decisions to adopt (or participate) in an SDO. However, the relative advantage measurement variables (transaction cost savings, ROI, operational improvements) are keys to sustaining interest in Web-based IOS that will likely leading toward greater levels of diffusion.

REFERENCES

Agarwal, R., and Prasad, J. The role of innovation characteristics and perceived voluntariness in the acceptance of information technologies. *Decision Sciences* 28, 3 (1997), 557–582.

———. Are individual differences germane to the acceptance of new information technologies? *Decision Sciences* 30, 2 (1999), 361–391.

Berners-Lee, T. Business model for the semantic Web: Enterprise application integration and other stories: Why, when XML gives us interoperability, do we need the semantic Web? W3C, 2001 (available at www.w3.org/DesignIssues/Business).

———. Web services: Program integration across application and organization boundaries. W3C, 2003 (available at www.w3.org/DesignIssues/WebServices.html).

Cho, I., and Kim, Y. Critical factors for assimilation of object-oriented programming languages. *Journal of Management Information Systems* 18, 3 (2001), 125–156.

Cooper, R., and Zmud, R. Information technology implementation research: A technological diffusion approach. *Management Science* 36, 2 (1990), 123–139.

Fichman, R. G. Information technology diffusion: A review of empirical research. In *Thirteenth International Conference on Information Systems.* Dallas, TX: Association for Computing Machinery, 1992, pp. 195–206.

Hagel III, J., and Brown, J.S. Your next IT strategy. *Harvard Business Review* 79, 9 (2001), 106–113.

Hammer, M. The superefficient company. *Harvard Business Review* 79, 8 (2001), 82–91.

Hart, P., and Saunders, C. Emerging electronic partnerships: Antecedents and dimensions of EDI use from the supplier's perspective. *Journal of Management Information Systems* 14, 4, (1998), 87–111.

Iacovou, C.; Benbasat, I.; and Dexter, A. EDI and small organizations: Adoption and impact of technology. *MIS Quarterly* (December 1995), 465–485.

Flynn, Peter, ed. The XML FAQ Special Interest Group, v.2.1, 2002 (available at www.ucc.ie/xml/#index).

Jones, J. Ballmer: It's the tags, stupid. *InfoWorld,* April 28 (2000). Available at www.infoworld.com/articles/ic/xml/00/04/18/000418icfosekey.html

Koch, C. "The battle for Web services." *CIO Magazine* 17, 1 (2003), 54–64.

Massetti, B., and Zmud, R. Measuring the extent of EDI usage in complex organizations: Strategies and illustrative examples. *MIS Quarterly* 20, 3 (1996), 331–345.

Nelson, M.; Shaw, M.; Shen, S.; Schoonmaker, M.; Qualls, W.; and Wang, R. 2002. "Co-adoption of XML-based interorganizational systems: A case of adopting RosettaNet standards." In Michael J. Shaw (ed.), *e-Business Management.* Berlin, Heidelberg: Springer-Verlag, 2002, 417–437.

CHAPTER 2

IMPACT OF STANDARDIZATION ON BUSINESS-TO-BUSINESS COLLABORATION

BARCHI PELEG AND HAU L. LEE

Abstract: *Over the past few years, a growing number of organizations have shifted the focus of their supply chain management practices from internal operations to cross-enterprise collaboration. Through advanced information sharing and knowledge exchange practices, companies are able to build products that better meet customer expectations and deliver them to the marketplace at the right time and place, while simultaneously improving the efficiency of their internal operations. Such collaborative activities require numerous process steps involving business-to-business (B2B) information technology (IT) applications. Having standards for these underlying B2B applications can have tremendous value, since standardization enables such initiatives to be repeated with the same partner, or with a more extensive set of partners, more easily, faster, and in a less costly manner. While the value of B2B collaboration, especially when based on standards, is no doubt significant, the efforts required for such implementation processes are usually quite costly, involving investment in IT infrastructure as well as in human resources. Resources are required to potentially re-engineer the business processes, train the employees, and select and install the required IT infrastructure. This paper discusses the costs and benefits of cross-enterprise collaboration, as well as the added value of standardization. We present a case study of one company that went through a large-scale collaboration effort with one of their major customers in a joint effort to streamline the company's planning and replenishment processes. We describe the benefits realized by both business partners, as well as the challenges they faced and the efforts needed to make this project successful.*

Keywords: *Business Process Reengineering, Business-to-Business (B2B) Collaboration, Case Study, Cost and Benefit Evaluation, Standardization, Standards*

INTRODUCTION

Today's competitive environment drives a growing number of companies to the realization that success cannot rely solely on improving the efficiency of their internal operations. Rather, to gain new levels of competitiveness they must extend their focus beyond their own four walls, and collaborate with their business partners across the extended value chain. Taking advantage of e-business solutions within application areas such as customer relationship management (CRM), supply chain management (SCM), supplier relationship management (SRM), and enterprise resource planning (ERP) can be of great value and help companies to better prepare for and respond to changing customer demands. Consider the example of TaylorMade, which became part of Adidas-Salomon in 1998. The company had continued losing revenue because of its difficulty in gauging customer demand and in optimizing its supply chain and supplier relationship. Implementing new SCM, SRM, and CRM solutions provided the company with a more accurate picture of actual inventory and demand patterns. This information was used to improve collaboration with the company's suppliers—many of them located in Asia—through sharing and extending demand-planning processes. As a result, significant savings were realized in transportation costs, and the customer service level was dramatically improved. The reduction of supply chain inefficiencies allowed TaylorMade-Adidas to double its sales in three years and double its inventory turns from 2001 to 2002 (Barlas 2002).

Tight coordination among business partners when carrying out such processes as product development, material procurement, logistics, and order fulfillment, enabled by a higher level of information sharing, can bring value to all parties across the extended enterprise. The value of information sharing has been explored extensively in the literature. Some of the relevant research articles include Gavirneni et al. (1999), which shows the cost reduction that a supplier can realize when retail customer information, in the form of inventory replenishment policy and ongoing actual inventory level, is shared. Lee et al. (2000) show that demand information sharing can provide significant inventory reduction and cost savings to the supplier when demands are highly correlated over time. Aviv (2001) studies the value of collaborative forecasting, where the supply chain members jointly maintain and update a single forecasting process in the system. An extensive numerical study showed that such practices provide significant benefits to the supply chain, leading to an average of 19.43 percent cost reduction. Lee and Whang (2000) summarize the types of information most commonly shared, and discuss how and why they were shared.

However, to gain the most from such initiatives and remain agile, flexible, and efficient, business partners have to exchange a significant amount of information across the extended supply chain. In the past, business partners used slow, manual, and error-prone collaboration tools such as phone, fax, and e-mail, which significantly limited the extent, scope, frequency, and timeliness of such information exchange, and consequently, the value of the integration efforts. Furthermore, such communication methods were not scalable in instances where high volumes of data had to be transferred on a regular basis. Consequently, the benefits that could be realized based on such forms of collaboration were usually limited. Early attempts to automate information exchange between business partners revolved primarily around electronic data interchange (EDI) systems, which focus on the exchange of information between trading partners based on common document formats. While EDI systems no doubt represent a significant improvement over manual methods, they suffer from several major drawbacks. First, the cost and complexity of the required software can be quite high, as are the ongoing, transaction-based costs of using EDI. Another limitation of EDI is its rigid structure, which makes it most suitable for routine data transfer, while not suitable for the exchange of complex documents (such as design drawings or product bills of materials). Many companies also find EDI inflexible to fit their business processes, especially when the rapidly changing environment these companies are operating in forces them to frequently update the content and structure of the information to be transferred. Finally, EDI is documentcentric, while an increasing number of companies are looking for a solution based on a process-oriented approach. Over time, the advent of the Internet provided the basis for an alternative to EDI, and gave business partners the ability to more quickly and easily exchange business documents. Such business-to-business (B2B) solutions undoubtedly provided much value to their users, but the lack of agreement on the underlying structure and dialogues of e-business processes significantly complicated related implementation projects and dramatically lowered the realized benefits. In addition, even when successful, such implementation projects could not be easily duplicated to processes with other business partners. In light of this, the use of standards can bring great value to business partners by making such collaborative efforts easily repeatable and reliable, thus significantly lowering the level of investment required for subsequent implementation projects.

This paper introduces a framework to analyze the value of B2B collaborative solutions, and to gain a better understanding of the added value of standardization. In addition, we present a case study of one company that went through a large-scale project with one of their trading partners in a joint effort to streamline the company's planning and replenishment operations. The project involved the implementation of advanced collaborative forecasting and inventory management processes based on RosettaNet standards, and was perceived by both parties as very successful. The remainder of the paper is structured as follows: in section 2 we provide a framework for assessing the costs and the benefits of cross-enterprise collaboration based on the use of B2B applications, in section 3 we discuss the added value as well as the associated costs of standardization, in section 4 we describe a case study that demonstrates the benefits as well as the challenges associated with such implementation projects, and in section 5 we provide a conclusion.

VALUE OF CROSS-ENTERPRISE COLLABORATION

Improved collaboration across the entire supply chain can have a positive impact on a variety of business processes, resulting in cost reduction and enhanced profitability. Peleg (1999) describes the impact of cross-enterprise collaboration in the early days of B2B applications. The benefits can be categorized as follows.

- *Product design:* Integrating suppliers into a new product design process can significantly reduce the length of the design cycle, increase the quality of the new product, allow for faster production ramp-up, and reduce the manufacturing costs. Furthermore, collecting early customer feedback to make new products that better match customer preferences could lead to higher market share and increased profitability. For example, the broad collaborative initiative General Motors took to improve its development cycle, which included linking with key suppliers throughout the vehicle development process, resulted in dramatic improvements—a 70-percent reduction in product development cycle time and more than $1 billion in savings (Gutmann 2003).
- *Forecast:* Sharing forecast information as well as other supportive data between two business partners, such as a retailer and a manufacturer, can help both of them to build a more accurate forecast, based on all information available to both parties. By being closer to the end customers, the retailer may have a better view of external forces that might impact expected consumption. In addition, the retailer may share with the manufacturer any planned sales promotions that are likely to impact consumption patterns. The manufacturer, on the other hand, has deeper knowledge of the product characteristics, and how external events such as weather can impact product sales. The manufacturer also possesses aggregate demand information from all other retailers that can be helpful in detecting trends or other change patterns. With better forecasting, the limited resources available to the manufacturer may be better allocated to allow them to be more responsive to customer needs, while at the same time increasing capacity utilization and reducing inventory levels and related holding costs. Consider, for example, the first Collaborative Planning, Forecasting, and Replenishment (CPFR) pilot, which was conducted in 1996 by Wal-Mart and Warner-Lambert and

involved Listerine products. In the pilot, the two companies exchanged forecasts as well as supportive data, such as past sales trends, promotion plans, and estimated impacts to events such as weather. The data were often exchanged in an iterative fashion via the Internet to allow the two companies to converge on a single forecast in case their original forecasts differed. The pilot was very successful, resulting in increased Listerine sales and higher fill rates, accompanied by a reduction of inventory investment (Aviv 2001).

- *Production:* Manufacturers continue to look for ways to squeeze efficiency out of their production facilities. Linkage to their supply chain partners gives production personnel guidance and direction to reduce errors, increase production rates, and minimize idle resources. With timely information available to them, manufacturers can dynamically schedule the right plants to make the right products and transfer customer order information to the plants. When production takes place in a make-to-stock environment, improved forecast accuracy allows production managers to prepare better plans that make the best use of the limited available resources. Further improvements may be realized by obtaining, on a regular basis, updated inventory status from both customers and suppliers, which can assist in better anticipation of future demand and parts availability. Overall, the manufacturer can improve demand fulfillment reliabilities, reduce total inventory levels, and improve capacity utilization. A strong indication of the demand for collaborative manufacturing is the increased demand for collaborative production management (CPM) systems, which has totaled more than $1.2 billion in 2000 and is expected to more than double to $2.5 billion by the end of 2005 (Gorbach 2001).
- *Procurement:* Sharing with suppliers sales and inventory information, demand forecast, and procurement and production schedules significantly improves the suppliers' ability to efficiently plan their operations and better meet future demand. At the same time, the manufacturer is more likely to receive the required material on time, reducing expensive expediting costs. Furthermore, updated inventory information and production plans received from suppliers allow the manufacturer to adjust production plans based on a more realistic picture of part availability. Knowledge of expected material availability also assists the manufacturer in quoting more feasible due dates to customer orders, thus improving customer service.
- *Logistics:* Over time, the scope of logistics outsourcing has expanded from transportation and warehousing to other value-added activities, such as order management (e.g., call center management, tracking and reporting), pick and pack (e.g., custom product sorting and packaging, custom packing for individual orders), inventory management, and other planning activities. Tight collaboration with logistics service providers can result in faster, accurate, and cost-effective logistics operations. Customer orders are more likely to be fulfilled on time, and at a lower cost.
- *Lateral Collaboration:* Information sharing among distribution centers or retailers provides the locations with the opportunity to redistribute inventories through lateral transshipments. That way, locations with excess goods can transfer some of their inventory to those locations that face shortages, resulting in mutual gains.
- *Performance Management:* Having visibility of performance measures across companies enables companies to detect problems in the so-called interface activities, i.e., operations that cut across multiple companies and may not be visible in a single company's internal performance measurement system. Such visibility enables companies to collaborate on identifying improvement areas promptly. The Mopar Division of Daimler-Chrysler improved the automobile service parts replenishments from suppliers to Mopar and to automobile dealers via such e-collaboration means (see Rajwat 2001).

The growing trend in recent years to outsource operations considered noncore to a company has intensified the need for extensive collaboration. With only a small portion of the operations conducted internally, the visibility and control a company may have over these operations becomes significantly limited. Frequent and accurate information flows between the outsourcing company and its business partners may help it to gain back most of the lost visibility.

In the last few years the use of e-commerce between organizations has become increasingly popular and has contributed largely to tighter relationships among supply chain partners. Companies who adopt B2B applications for conducting any of the business processes mentioned earlier are likely to improve the cooperation with their trading partners in the following ways:

- *Faster information exchange:* Substituting manual data-exchange processes with automated mechanisms substantially shortens the time involved with such activities, bringing the most updated information to the decision makers much faster.
- *Elimination of manual processes:* The use of B2B applications for data exchange eliminates many of the manual operations required previously, freeing up employees for more value-added tasks.
- *Improved accuracy:* "To err is human." The elimination of manual processes reduces the chance for errors, improving the quality of the available information and allowing the business partners to base their decisions on more accurate information.
- *Increased frequency:* The considerable reduction in time required for exchanging information between business partners provides them with the opportunity to increase the frequency of such transactions. Thus, decisions can be based on more updated information.

By obtaining and intelligently using more timely and accurate future demand information, companies are likely to improve their production planning, material purchasing, and inventory management, resulting in higher capacity utilization, lower inventory levels, reduced obsolescence costs, and higher order fulfillment rates. Through collaborative design processes, companies can significantly shorten the design cycle and introduce new products that better match customer tastes, thus giving them the opportunity to gain higher market share and increase their profitability. Efficient logistics networks can further improve the responsiveness to customer preferences, significantly improving customer satisfaction and loyalty. Overall, engaging in advanced collaborative initiatives may result in higher sales levels and increased profitability, combined with much more efficient internal operations.

The benefits of such applications, however, do not come without a cost. Developing a cross-organizational information system is expensive, time-consuming, and risky (Lee and Whang 1999). In addition to the initial investment required for purchasing the necessary hardware and software, substantial resources are required during the implementation process for revising the internal business processes, adjusting the information systems to best fit the specific requirements of the organization, implementing the new work procedures, and training all employees to assure smooth transition to the new systems. In addition, much time and effort must be invested to work jointly with each business partner to specify the type of information to be shared, the format of data to be transferred, the frequency of data exchange, as well as other aspects of the new B2B processes. The time required to complete an implementation project with a single business partner can range from several months to one or two years, sometimes even more. These types of investments can dramatically lower the net benefits of such implementation projects, especially in the short run. Moreover, unless the implemented systems are based on some standard exchange protocols and dialogues, implementation with each business partner is likely to require the same level of effort and resources to be invested.

THE ADDED VALUE OF STANDARDIZATION

In light of the implementation challenges, the use of standards is very appealing. With standardization, instead of establishing distinctly separate processes for information exchange with different trading partners, companies may use the available standard software, processes, and guidelines for automatic system-to-system exchange of information. That way, the time and effort required for each implementation process can be dramatically reduced, making those projects easily repeatable. Since each industry has unique requirements, many of the portals and standards developed so far are industry specific. Some examples include the RosettaNet consortium, which focuses on developing standards for information technology (IT), electronic component, semiconductor manufacturing, and telecommunications companies; the AIAG (Automotive Industry Action Group) association, which addresses the special concerns of companies in the automotive industry; and WWRE (WorldWide Retail Exchange), which was initiated for the purpose of enabling retailers and suppliers in the food, general merchandise, textile/home, and drugstore sectors to simplify and automate their supply chain processes. The AIA (Aerospace Industries Association of America) has also been developing a major initiative to develop data standards that will enable the exchange of information throughout the defense and aerospace supply chain.

Developing e-commerce among organizations on the foundation of established standards has the following additional benefits:

- *Scalable B2B model:* While the initial learning curve might be steep, the lessons learnt from implementing e-commerce applications based on standards with the first business partner can be applied to other business partners, and at a much faster pace and lower costs than if the implementation process is not based on any standards. That is, the initial implementation process can be successfully and relatively more easily duplicated with additional partners, leveraging the initial expenses across multiple accounts.
- *Higher rate of implementation across trading partners:* Due to the relative ease of implementation and the lower expected investments compared to implementation of Web-based applications that do not deploy any standards, more business partners would be willing to go through such an implementation process. Thus, total benefits to the company over the whole planning horizon are expected to increase.
- *Improved efficiency of internal operations:* With more business partners connected via B2B applications, the internal operations may be improved even further. For example, purchasing operations may become more efficient by providing buyers with means to automatically contact a larger number of potential suppliers for a price quote for a purchasing order, and to more efficiently compare all the bids received. That way, overall procurement costs are likely to decline.

While in the long run the use of standards is clearly of value, going through the first implementation project might actually require more resources when it is based on standards. Companies that have gone through such implementation projects report that much time and effort was invested initially in selecting the standards that best fit their needs, and in adjusting their business processes accordingly. This is true especially when an industrywide and acceptable standard has not yet been put in place. One risk of betting on one set of processes as the standard too early is that alternative standards may emerge later, rendering all the initial investments obsolete.

CASE STUDY: STMICROELECTRONICS E-CHAIN OPTIMIZATION PROJECT

In this section we illustrate the benefits as well as costs and risks associated with using standards in B2B implementation projects based on the experience of STMicroelectronics (ST), a leading European-based semiconductor manufacturer. More details of this case can be found in Peleg (2003).

Company Background

STMicroelectronics NV, headquartered in Geneva, Switzerland, was born in 1987 through the merger of two money-losing state-owned companies, SGS Microelettronica of Italy and Thomson Semiconducteurs of France. Despite its inauspicious beginning, the company has emerged to become the number one Europe-based and the world's number three chipmaker in sales in 2001 (after Intel and Toshiba), with reported sales of $6.36 billion. In December 2001, ST was named "Best French Company of the Decade" by French business magazine *L'Expansion* in its annual ranking of 1,000 companies, based on such criteria as sales growth, workforce growth, and current income.

ST is built on a solid multiple-application product portfolio. Over the years, the company has shown some of the best long-term management strategies and skills in the semiconductor industry, which helped it to remain relatively successful in hard times. A major part of that strategy has been balance—the company capitalizes on the diversity of its product lines, target markets, and customer base. Rather than depending on one geographical region, the company's sales are spread across Europe, Asia, North America, Japan, and several emerging markets. Moreover, ST has a wide array of product lines. The company specializes in memory chips, discrete components, and many types of analog and mixed-signal integrated circuits (ICs) used in communications technology, consumer electronics, computers, and industrial and automotive processes. ST's customer base includes more than 1,500 customers from diverse sectors of the industry.

One of the parameters that contributed to ST's success was its deep expertise in analog technology. The proliferation of cellular telephones, wireless computers, and consumer electronics products like DVD players created a resurgence of demand for analog devices in the 1990s, which ST was well positioned to exploit and few other companies could address. Just as Intel drove the microprocessor revolution in the 1980s by combining most of the digital devices needed for computation on a single chip, ST saw an opportunity to combine analog functions, such as sound, graphics, and power management, together with digital circuitry, such as logic and memory on a single chip, creating "system-on-chip" (SOC) devices.

ST's success also demonstrates the value of having a constellation of strategic alliances with market leaders in multiple businesses, building upon knowledge acquired from partners all over the globe, and disseminating that knowledge internally so that it can be used effectively throughout its own organization. The roots of this strategy go back to the first ten years following the foundation of the company, when ST focused on IC manufacturing while relying on strategic alliances and partnerships to complete the full vertical model. Through this experience, ST learned how to benefit from collaborative business models a long time before other semiconductor manufacturers, which had initially been fully vertical, started following the same model.

ST Supply Chain Structure

Figure 2.1 shows ST's supply chain, which is typical for the semiconductor industry. ST invests heavily in innovation to maintain its leadership in system-oriented technologies and global

Figure 2.1 **The ST Sypply Chain**

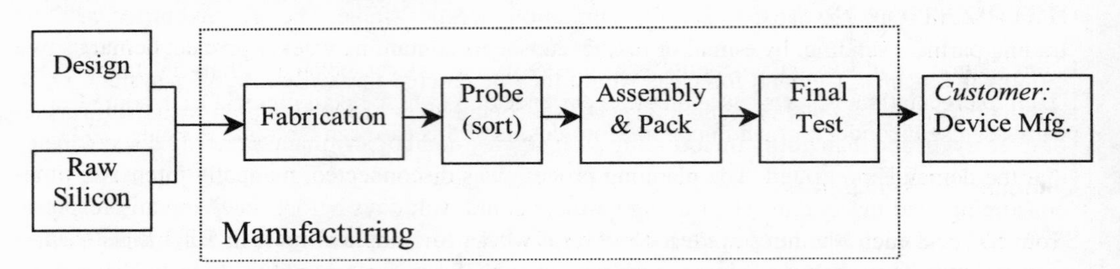

manufacturing infrastructure. It has sixteen advanced research and development (R&D) centers and thirty-nine design and application centers in Europe, the United States, and Asia.

The manufacturing process can be divided into four major steps. The front-end operations include wafer fabrication, in which devices are made on raw semiconductor wafers, and probing, in which each individual IC die on the wafer is tested to verify proper operation. The back-end operations include the assembly and pack of each individual IC die in a protective package. In addition, before shipping the packed ICs to the customers, each of them is tested again to ensure outgoing quality.

While many of the major chipmakers, including Lucent Technologies, Motorola Corp., and TI, are outsourcing a large portion of their operations to focus on core competencies, ST does not outsource much. Only about 10 percent of production is sent to foundries as a buffer during periods of high demand. The company makes the rest of its chips in-house, in seventeen main production sites that are spread across Europe, the United States, and Asia.

The major suppliers with whom ST works are those who provide the raw silicon and other raw material required for the manufacturing process. In addition, ST works closely with equipment vendors, who supply the tools required for the fabrication process.

ST has a diversified customer base among manufacturers in consumer electronics, telecommunications, computer peripherals, automobiles, and smart card/security devices. It is also a primary supplier to companies in the fast-growing electronics manufacturing services sector. For all its strong positioning in analog technology, ST quickly recognized that it cannot exploit its advantage in the SOC market through traditional arm's-length relationships with its customers. Therefore, ST has developed over the years global market-sensing capabilities and strategic partnerships with its customers, which are crucial sources of competitive advantage and have helped the company to bolster its performance through recent tough times in the industry. From 1998 to 2002, revenues from ST's global strategic alliances grew at a compound average growth rate of 14.9 percent, and reached 47 percent of its $6.32B in revenues in 2002.

ST Before Collaborative Forecasting and Inventory Management

A proper supply chain management strategy has always been essential for ST to manage its broad range of products and processes, as well as its strategic partnerships. Manufacturing at ST involves numerous technologies and customer specific expectations, and requires the highest level of flexibility. In 1991, ST started searching for a supply chain planner solution. By 1999, ST implemented an integrated planning and execution system, synchronizing thirty manufacturing sites, fifty sales offices, and thirty product divisions worldwide in a unique model. With time the company realized that internal synchronization was not sufficient, and that huge potential benefits might be realized if its internal supply chain model could interact with those of its partners.

At that time, ST and its trading partners were using manual processes to match trading partner demand with available capacity at ST's fabrication facilities (fabs). The process started with the trading partners sending, by e-mail or fax, spreadsheets containing weekly product demands two months in advance. Demand forecasts would then be entered manually into ST's system. Once trading partners' data were inputted, ST would reconcile their production plan with the information received, and then notify their trading partners by e-mail of any manufacturing discrepancies that the demands presented. The planning process was disconnected, manually intensive, time-consuming, and inaccurate. The trading partners could wait days before receiving any response from ST, and each planning cycle took several weeks to complete, making ST and its trading partners very inflexible and unresponsive to changes in market demands. Due to the lack of visibility to end-to-end supply chain data, the forecast information was distorted multiple times as it passed downstream between multiple partners. In addition, the isolated planning and lack of integration resulted in inefficiencies in capacity utilization, inventory management, product-mix decisions, and asset (capacity) investments. The high inventory levels and low capacity utilization reduced ST's return-on-net-assets (RONA), which is an important indicator of the company's profitability. ST figured that its RONA could be substantially improved if, rather than building up inventories, more funding was invested in profit-generating assets, such as additional capacity. Furthermore, ST predicted that, due to increased competition and higher customer expectations, the need for better service levels and improved coordination with its trading partners would increase, especially in the capacity requirement arena, thus putting even more pressure on ST to move away from the manual-intensive processes.

Due to the eight weeks of wafer fabrication time, ST had to plan its production two months in advance, making the system rigid and inflexible to changing demands. Still, trading partners frequently changed their orders within the two-months "booked" time period, forcing ST to keep a high level of inventory on hand at all times to ensure a high level of order fulfillment. High levels of inventory were also kept to mitigate the impacts of demand variability. Executives at ST attributed the build-up of inventory to the lack of communication between original equipment manufacturers (OEMs), contractors, and ST. ST needed a way to collect data faster and more efficiently, and to improve visibility to end-to-end supply chain data and performance. It was clear that real-time demand signals that are received automatically rather than through manual data entry would help reduce planning and order lead time, thus improving forecast accuracy and inventory management, which were essential for cost-efficient processes. Cross-enterprise supply chain visibility, reduction of the bullwhip effect (the distortion of demand data across the supply chain; see Lee, Padmanabhan, and Whang 1997), business process standardization, and re-engineering could dramatically affect savings and growth.

ST wished to provide a better service level (as measured by response time) and a higher rate of capacity utilization with enhanced information flows between ST and its trading partners. Their vision for a best-in-class supply chain management captured the four main processes needed for adequate demand satisfaction:

- *Planning:* An integrated planning environment that provides visibility, simulation, and optimization of the global ST/trading partner supply chain, including demand, supply, inventory, capacity, and product cost.
- *Sourcing:* Utilization of a worldwide automated system driven by the master production plan (MPS) that allows for the shortest lead time, maximum product flexibility, and real-time supplier performance evaluation, with centralized order management and optimum inventory management.

- *Making:* Worldwide visibility of production status, including a metric dashboard enabling rapid problem solving to optimize the manufacturing process.
- *Delivering:* An automated supplier managed inventory replenishment process, with worldwide visibility that optimizes product manufacturing and delivery performance.

The Need for Standards

With the advances in information technologies, ST had employed EDI with their trading partners. While EDI was sufficient to provide connectivity and data syntax, it did not contain semantic or process standards. In addition, EDI did not efficiently address real-time, B2B information exchange and application integration, which were critical for many new marketplace initiatives.

The dispersed geographical locations of ST's customer base added the challenge of how a global company could act locally and address the special needs of each of its markets. ST realized that it had to find and adopt a new, Internet-based standard that would specify how the data from different sources would be integrated to provide meaningful information, which in turn could be translated into powerful supply chain management knowledge and decisions. Building on the standards, which would allow ST to efficiently manage its global operations, the company could then personalize and replicate the processes in each region to best address the needs of the local customer base. This strategy was supported by market research that predicted that, through 2005, companies that adopt such standards for collaborative commerce would save 30 percent in integration cost down the road (Peterson and Thompson 2001).

RosettaNet Standards

While no single industry standard has achieved widespread, cross-industry adoption, by 1996 eXtensible Markup Language (XML)-based standards began to take hold, and have since emerged as the most promising set of standards due to their extensibility and Web-centricity. By the end of 1999, interest in the XML family of standards was commonplace, and some of the standard initiatives began gaining support and validation by industry consortia. In contrast to traditional standards rivalry, many XML-based standards have been developed to be compatible with one another.

In response to the growing need for industrywide e-business process standards, the RosettaNet consortium, a self-funded nonprofit organization, was formed in 1998 by forty leading IT organizations. Among the most unique factors contributing to RosettaNet's success was the stellar membership roster. To date, the consortium is composed of close to 500 of the industry's leading IT, electronic components, semiconductor manufacturing, solution provider, and telecommunications companies. Most of these members are involved in the development of RosettaNet standards, which support information exchange about products, services, marketing, manufacturing, sales leads, orders, and inventory. The standards are based on three elements: dictionaries, implementation framework, and Partner Interface Processes® (PIPs®). The technical and business dictionaries define the structure and contents of XML documents that are exchanged with the PIPs. They provide a common platform for conducting business within the supply chain, eliminate overlapping efforts by individual companies, and reduce confusion in the procurement process due to each company's uniquely defined terminology. The RosettaNet implementation framework (RNIF) provides exchange protocols for quick and efficient implementation of RosettaNet standards. The RNIF specifies information exchange between trading partner servers using XML, covering the transport, routing, and packaging of all PIP messages and business signals. The PIPs define business process dialogues among trading partners. In other words,

RosettaNet dictionaries provide the words, the RNIF acts as the grammar and the PIPs form the dialogue for the information exchanged by servers over the Internet as part of the whole electronic business exchange. RosettaNet's strategy is to develop plug-and-play interoperability between partners. With this said, the consortium has gained significant traction with high-tech manufacturers, largely because this is an industry that is committed and well aware of the needs for such communication standards. RosettaNet standards fill the gap in e-business exchange, strengthening trading relationships, improving operational efficiency, and providing new business opportunities. Analysts and visionaries view RosettaNet as an enabler of a new model that uses a common hub approach to accessing and sharing business information like inventory, pricing, and services (see Figure 2.2). From standard contractual commitments to franchised distribution sales and on through excess inventory sales, the vision consists of quick, accurate, low-cost, and increasingly secure ways to conduct semiconductor business.

The E-Chain Optimization Project

Sound supply chain management was imperative for ST's global business. With millions of units shipped by ST every hour, a total supply chain solution was essential. With design plants, manufacturing facilities, and distributors all over the world, communication of real-time information could have resulted in tremendous savings for the company. Connectivity with customers was also a critical factor, and so in 1998 ST began its pursuit of identifying the most efficient standards for B2B processes that would keep all parties linked. While the Internet was providing communication and worldwide infrastructure standards, it lacked those standards aimed at business applications. RosettaNet was identified as an initiative that fuelled B2B interaction by providing common dictionaries and PIPs that were central to ST's e-business projects, and so in October of 1999 ST formally embraced RosettaNet standards as a common information exchange to make its supply chain more efficient.

In June 2000, ST and one of its strategic trading partners decided to conduct the e-Chain Optimization (eChO) project, in which a new system based on RosettaNet standards would be implemented to enable collaborative planning with weekly collaborative forecasting and daily dynamic replenishments. The purpose of the eChO project was to create a scaleable, extensible, B2B-based collaborative planning and procurement solution, resulting in ST and its trading partners having the right inventory in the right place and at the right time, while obtaining lower costs. To achieve that, ST aimed to reduce the number of changes distorting the forecast while keeping flexibility, to improve forecast accuracy, to create an automated and collaborative planning process between ST and its trading partners, and to improve the payment mechanism. The new solutions were to be based on a vendor-managed inventory (VMI) model, which changed the vendor-customer relationship between ST and its trading partner from the traditional order-based system to a supplier managed/owned inventory system where ST ships products in response to the trading partner's anticipated consumption to maintain the on-site inventory. Also, ST's shipments were to be on consignment; that is, the inventory would reside at the site of the trading partner, but would remain on ST's books until it was used by the trading partner's production facilities. This resulted in a dramatic transformation of a superficial collaborative forecasting process to one that involves deep collaboration. The key objectives of the eChO project were to implement a robust collaborative forecasting and dynamic replenishment-planning tool through an automatic two-way exchange between ST and its trading partner that aimed to synchronize supply and demand. Such processes were expected to enable more accurate long-term capacity planning through constant updating of demand and consumption information. Collaborative

Figure 2.2 **The New Semiconductor Model**

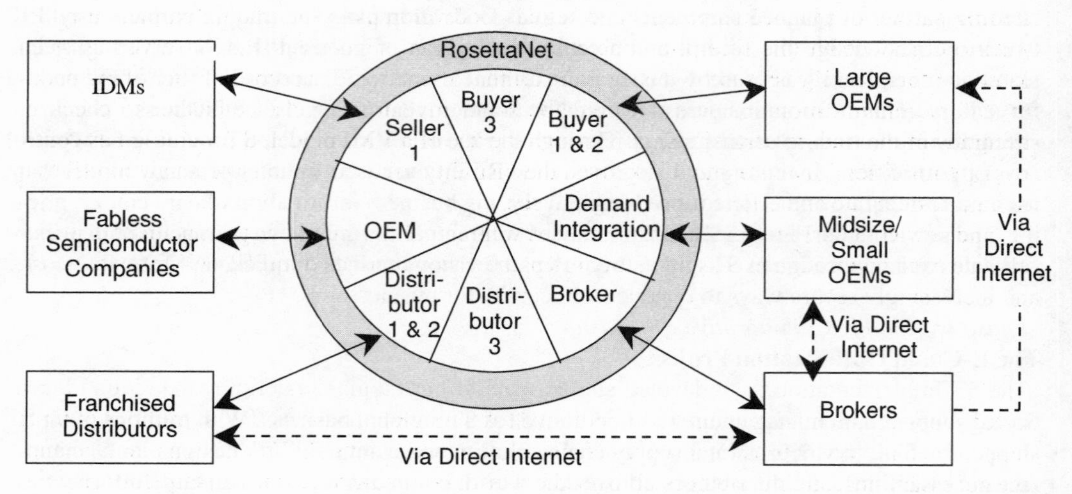

forecasting was complemented with the dynamic replenishment planning to provide a higher service level to the trading partner through the provision of a collaborative replenishment view. During this process, several metrics were monitored, including actual versus planned consumption control and ST plants/VMI stock levels. Customer demand was controlled by netting of ST plants, VMI stock, and goods in transit stocks. Shipment requests were automatically generated when inventory fell below a particular level. Demand and shipment requests were further fortified by a critical situation monitoring and alerts generation system.

The data exchange was enabled by several of RosettaNet's order management and inventory management PIPs, which support electronic processes for collaborative forecasting, inventory allocation and reporting, and shipping:

- *PIP 4A4, Notify of Planning Release Forecast:* ST and its trading partner used this PIP to exchange demand forecasts.
- *PIP 4B2, Notify of Shipment Receipt:* The trading partner used this PIP to report to ST the receipt of shipments.
- *PIP 4C1, Distribute Inventory Report:* ST and its trading partner used this PIP to exchange daily inventory reports, in which they specified the current inventory levels on-site and in transit.
- *PIP 3B2, Notify of Advance Shipment:* ST used this PIP to send advance shipment notification to its trading partner.
- *PIP 3B3, Distribute Shipment Status:* ST used this PIP to report shipment status while shipments were being transported to its trading partner.

PIP 4A4, together with private ST XML alert messages, supported the collaborative forecasting process and was used for the exchange of trading partner consolidated forecasts, consumption plans, minimum and maximum levels, as well as ST replenishment plans and capacity levels.

PIPs 3B2, 3B3, 4B2, and 4C1 handled the automatic replenishment planning and VMI model jointly developed by ST and its trading partner. ST used PIPs 3B2 and 3B3 for notifying the trading partner of planned shipments and actual goods in transit. The trading partners used PIP 4B2 to acknowledge the receipt and actual consumption of goods. PIP 4C1 served as a data integrity check and was used by the trading partner to send to ST a record of their daily ending inventory. This information was not used to update inventory levels, but rather to check the accuracy of the trading partner's data. Through the use of a VMI model, ST increased its control over its customers' inventory and improved the visibility to its customers' demand, contributing to a more accurate and efficient product delivery.

The new collaborative forecasting processes were implemented in two phases. In both phases, all data exchange between ST and its trading partner was conducted in PIP 4A4 format.

Phase 1: Monthly Collaborative Forecasting

The ST implementation team devoted approximately four months to defining the required technology, standards, infrastructure, and additional planning applications. By November 2000 ST had defined all the PIPs it wanted to use, as well as the relevant B2B applications. In December the necessary infrastructure was established, and testing was conducted in January 2001. By February 2001, ST started using this new system to exchange forecasts with its trading partner on a monthly basis.

The monthly planning cycle started when ST transmitted its capacity models to the trading partner. The trading partner's twelve-month master production plan (MPS) was generated automatically every thirty days. The MPS aggregated the trading partner's twelve-week factory plans for the various locations (four total in Europe, United States, and Asia) by converting them from daily into monthly buckets. It then added the marketing projection factor beyond twelve weeks to one year. The first iteration MPS was checked by the trading partner against the ST capacity model. Collaboration between the trading partner's corporate department and its sites occurred, and the MPS was updated several times until it fell within the ST capacity model. When the final MPS was ready, the trading partner sites' daily factory plans were reset to equal their input to the MPS.

Phase 2: Daily Collaborative Forecasting

To gain strategic benefits from eChO, ST and its trading partner decided to use the system for daily collaborative forecasting. Everything from information exchange to optimization calculations was automated. Consequently, the entire daily collaborative forecasting process took only four to five hours.

Each day, before 13:00 GMT, daily trading partner factory consumption plans (from the ST-owned consignment buffer on their site), which go out one year in daily buckets, are consolidated and sent in one transmission to ST. Daily receipts, daily inventory, and pulls from the inventory are also sent to ST's B2B server. As long as the trading partner provides an XML file in the proper PIP format, the trading partner and ST's B2B servers do not have to be the same. Each feed is converted by ST to STXML (an internal XML format) and is fed to the distribution requirements planning (DRP) module. The DRP module factors the above information as well as the ST goods in transit, the ST fab outs plan, and a sophisticated min/max module, which uses a dynamic and statistically grounded model with algorithms to optimize inventory balances based on consumption plans and historical data on deviations from plans. As soon as the actual consumption and consumption plan feeds have been received, min/max runs to calculate recommended time-phased target inventory levels by customer VMI site. The output of the DRP module is a shipment plan, called the replenishment plan, which is transmitted to the trading partners the same day.

The target inventory recommendation from min/max is sent to Leap,[1] an Internet-based replenishment distribution and planning application, for use in the net demand and shipment proposal calculations. Leap provides the following feeds to the trading partner:

- *Replenishment plan:* sent on to the customer as a forecast notification.
- *Alerts:* sent as proprietary XML.
- *Forecasted future inventory levels:* for both ST and Customer VMI locations.
- *Forecasted fab outs:* combined with the forecast notification.

When a pull from inventory occurs, the trading partner activates a self-billing invoice process and payment is issued to ST without any invoice from ST. Various reports are available on the portal on the dashboard to get a global view of all the above parameters and plans.

Implementation of VMI Model

PIPs 3B2, 3B3, 4B2, and 4C1 were implemented to handle the automatic replenishment planning and VMI model developed at ST. By managing the inventory located at the customer's site, ST is capable of increasing its control over its inventory and improving the visibility of its customer's demand. ST uses PIP 3B2 for notifying the trading partner of planned shipments, and PIP 3B3 for notifying the trading partner of actual goods in transit. The trading partner uses PIP 4B2 to acknowledge the receipt and actual consumption of goods. The information is sent to ST's replenishment planning application, to a logistics visibility system, to an enterprise data warehouse, and then on to ST's order entry/logistics system. These messages trigger goods in transit to move to its final destination as well as automatically update demand forecasts. These are the only means by which ST knows when a product has reached its destination. There are no delays using this acknowledgment process—messages are checked each day and the DRP is updated automatically.

PIP 4C1 serves as a data integrity check. The trading partner uses it to send to ST a record of daily ending inventory by part number. From ST's B2B transaction server, the data is sent to its logistics visibility system and enterprise data warehouse. PIP 4C1 reconciles the ending inventories at the VMI and at ST. This information is not used to update inventory levels, but rather to check the accuracy of the trading partner's data by comparing it with the information available at the ST inventory tracking system.

With the daily information received from the trading partner regarding its actual ending inventories, ST could more effectively forecast future demand and inventory needs. The data was used by ST's system, which checked the figures in real time against variables such as ST's capacity at eighteen worldwide factories and current materials supply. ST would return its projected supply to its trading partner with real-time precision and the trading partner could match its demand as needed.

Benefits of the eChO Project

While previously a significant investment was made in internal EDI systems both at ST and its customer sites, with time ST realized the primary limitation of EDI as being highly specific to a particular customer's requirements. In contrast, the RosettaNet standards defined a common platform for the business processes and served as a convenient vehicle for B2B messaging between ST and its trading partner. Even though the discovery process for the first implementation project took a total of three years, ST expected to be able to apply the key findings and duplicate the RosettaNet-enabled business processes to other trading partners at a much faster pace. Thus, and since the RosettaNet standards were likely to gain broad industry adoption in the future, ST expected to reap the benefits of compatibility with a large number of trading partners in the future.

Automating the forecasting and inventory management processes dramatically improved ST's process efficiency. Overall, 80 percent of manual transactions have been eliminated. The elimination of manual processes combined with the increased accuracy resulted in an estimated 50 percent reduction in contract costs. In addition, both ST and the trading partner projected automation to reduce the required number of planning man-hours by several full-time equivalents (FTEs).

Another benefit of the eChO project was that it provided ST the ability to develop with its trading partner a sophisticated VMI model, which resulted in a significant reduction in inventory levels. Prior to eChO, trading partners had to hold four to six weeks' worth of buffer inventory to ensure high fill rates. Once the eChO project took place and the two companies adopted a VMI model, ST's trading partner started sharing its forecast updates on a daily basis. At the same time, the higher level of automation and improved efficiency completely eliminated the two-week forecast generation period. Consequently, forecast accuracy was significantly improved, allowing ST to make more informed decisions regarding the inventory levels required for satisfying future demand. Rather than always holding a fixed level of buffer inventory, the trading partner now left it for ST to decide how much inventory to hold based on an agreed upon service level percentage.

One of the reasons for the required four to six weeks of buffer inventory was the high variability in market demand during the eight weeks of product lead-time. With a higher level of automation, and with the implementation of the DRP module, ST was able to cut out totally the four weeks of planning cycle time and thereby reduce the total planning and manufacturing cycle time by 50 percent, from eight to four weeks. Consequently, demand uncertainty decreased as well, which meant that ST only needed to carry two weeks' worth of inventory to satisfy the service level agreed upon with the trading partners. In fact, ST estimated that it has avoided a safety stock increase of more than 50,000 wafers, which had a significant inventory savings. Overall, with eChO, inventory levels have dropped dramatically for both ST and its trading partner, allowing ST to increase its inventory turns by 40 percent. That had a significant impact on ST's bottom line, due to the high unit cost.

At the same time, the increased visibility throughout the supply chain and the move to daily forecasting allowed ST to be more flexible and to respond faster to changes in the market and in customer demand. ST could conduct operations in real time and replan and reprioritize its manufacturing on a daily basis. With this newfound agility, ST was able to change its production schedule instantaneously, without having to rely on inventory. It has been estimated that ST has become ten times more responsive due to improved inventory management. Moreover, the increased visibility to supply chain operations made it easier to identify processes that are less than optimal and to collaboratively work to mitigate them, resulting in improved supply chain efficiency and reduced system costs.

With improved forecast accuracy and the VMI model, ST could also better utilize its capacity. Under the old system, trading partners used to contract capacity from ST according to their forecasted twelve-month demand. If demand was lower than expected, a part of ST's capacity would be left idle. ST could not use the excess capacity to fulfill other customers' demand and the trading partner would incur increased costs. Following the eChO project, ST was better positioned to allocate capacity according to more accurate forecasts. This freed up its fab capacity and allowed the company to serve more customers and increase its capacity utilization by 30 percent. This also helped the company to postpone capacity expansion and save on the related costs.

In addition to the savings and improved efficiencies, the eChO project helped foster greater customer loyalty between ST and its trading partner. By making it easier to do business with ST, the trading partner found it more desirable to continue doing business with ST, a factor that could potentially contribute to an increase in market share. In addition, the trading partner viewed ST's dynamic replenishment system as a logical extension of its own and considered ST part of its internal supply chain processes. In essence, ST could capitalize on rush orders, and thus provide an identifiable value-added service to the customer.

Challenges and Costs Associated with the eChO Project

While the eChO project undoubtedly brought much value to ST and its trading partner, the benefits were not realized without a cost. Initial expenses in IT infrastructure were substantial, even though some of the existing mid-tier and back-end systems and servers could continue to be used. They included investment in hardware, software, and a network, including one-time upfront license and ISP initiation fees. Ongoing operational costs were required for maintaining the technology infrastructure, including hardware, software, and network-related operational costs for providing updates, support, and maintenance, as well as monthly ISP network bandwidth costs.

Moreover, the implementation of the new IT infrastructure required significant human resources, coming from both external (contracted) and internal resources. These were required both for revising the business processes and providing the relevant training to all employees, and for selecting and installing the required IT infrastructure. These costs were in the same order of magnitude as the investments made in hardware and software license costs. In addition, while it was expected that in the long run the higher degree of automation would lower the company's labor and personnel costs, especially as ST expanded the implementation to more trading partners, in practice the eChO project led to an increase in the required man-hours for planning activities at ST. The main reason for that was that with the move from monthly to daily collaborative forecasting ST had to handle a considerable increase in the amount of data.

In addition, both ST and its trading partner, as any other company that wishes to become a member of RosettaNet and deploy its standards, were required to pay ongoing consortium fees. Adopting the RosettaNet standards posed some additional challenges. At the time, these standards were new and the use of XML was still in its nascent stage in the industry. A lot of time was spent trying to decide which RosettaNet PIPs to use. Moreover, since many of the PIPs were not well developed at the time, ST had to work closely with RosettaNet to better define them. Implementing the RosettaNet standards was also quite complicated and required substantial resources. In addition, ST had to spend a lot of time in revamping its entire ERP system. Despite all these hurdles, ST believed that after getting over the initial steep learning curve, it would be able to implement new PIPs with new trading partners much more easily and faster, in implementation projects that would take within six to ten months.

One of the biggest challenges ST was facing during the implementation process was changing the company's culture and mentality to handle the time reduction in all processes. With nearly instant responses, whole organizations had to mobilize at a far quicker pace and be able to supply any requested information much faster. Overcoming these barriers required time, effort, and commitment from both ST and its trading partner. In addition, ST had to consider how to set up a correct security infrastructure to protect the highly sensitive information that was being exchanged. ST made a strategic decision to reside its B2B server outside of the company rather than within its firewall. While this was necessary to allow it to receive messages from its external trading partner, it made the sensitive information being exchanged potentially accessible to the public. Steps had to be taken to overcome this problem and ensure security.

Key Success Factors

Looking back, ST could identify several key factors that contributed mostly to the success of the eChO project. The first was the clear e-business vision developed by ST and its trading partner. The company realized that to compete in the new semiconductor manufacturing landscape, their competitive advantage had to be built on speed and agility. To achieve the required short lead times and high degree of flexibility, ST articulated clear goals for each step in its plan to delivery process re-engineering. Having clear end goals in a SCM re-engineering project of this magnitude is immensely important, due to potential misunderstandings and conflict of interests that could arise among the parties involved. Armed with this unambiguous vision of the re-engineering objectives (together with a strong steering committee and finely honed communication channels), both the trading partner and ST managed to focus on the task at hand, which ultimately minimized redundant efforts and conflicting strategies.

Another key success factor was the willingness of ST and its trading partner to go through a three-year discovery, education, and implementation effort and to spend all the necessary resources to make the project successful. The time and other resources were used for building B2B infrastructure at the trading partner level; resolving various data integrity, security, and legal issues; and determining the best way to package the data extracted from the trading partner's ERP systems so that it was most beneficial to inventory forecasting efforts. As a matter of fact, cost breakdowns indicate that the implementation of RosettaNet PIPs made up only one-third of the costs, while the other two-thirds were attributed to alignment of the ERP systems and internal process re-engineering costs.

Since the participation and cooperation of ST's trading partner was crucial to the success of the eChO project, ST identified a partner that needed the solution as much, if not more, as ST needed it. This ensured that the trading partner was willing to engage in complex process re-engineering and to allocate heavy resources to the project. In addition, a strong, cross-functional steering committee was formed to drive the program with the correct collaborative management focus.

CONCLUSION

Cross-enterprise collaboration, especially when based on B2B solutions that provide the business partners with means to exchange a large amount of information in a fast and efficient way, can be of much value to all business partners. The benefits include customer expectations met with higher reliability and faster deliveries to the market, resulting in lower operating costs, higher sales levels, and overall improved profitability. Standards can help to increase or accelerate such benefits in the long run. With standardization, duplicating the collaboration efforts with multiple business partners becomes much easier and faster to implement and requires a significantly lower level of resources. Furthermore, it is much easier to entice business partners to participate, due to the relative ease of implementation and the lower investments required. Nevertheless, it is important for the company that initiates and leads such efforts to verify that all partners who engage in these initiatives gain some benefits by going through the process. Alternatively, proper incentives should be provided to the business partners to make it beneficial for them to adopt the new business practices.

Our case study of STMicroelectronics illustrated some of the benefits and challenges of a large-scale collaborative initiative with a major trading partner. While the implementation process took three years to complete and required significant investments in IT infrastructure and human resources, the realized benefits were quite impressive. Through a higher degree of automation, 80 percent of manual transactions were eliminated. This, combined with improved collaborative planning practices, allowed ST and their trading partner to reduce total planning and manufacturing cycle time by 50 percent. By capturing its partner demand signals faster and sooner, ST and its trading partner were able to dramatically reduce demand and supply variability, resulting in a 40 percent reduction in protective inventory. At the same time, the improved forecast accuracy and VMI model allowed ST to improve capacity utilization by 30 percent. The project contributed to increased visibility throughout the supply chain and allowed both companies to increase their market share for the specific products market.

In summary, while the investment made by ST and its trading partner during the eChO project for building the required processes, tools, and B2B infrastructure was substantial, both partners were able to realize significant benefits through decreased inventory levels and improved efficiency of internal operations. Furthermore, ST achieved the intangible benefit of increased customer intimacy. The efforts contributed to new levels of transparency and cooperation in operating a strategic partnership for mutual benefits. The next step ST will have to take to maximize the return on its investment is the expansion of the new processes to additional trading partners. With the tremendous infrastructure and knowledge base already in place and the scalable B2B model well defined, each new implementation would likely require much smaller investments while yielding similar or more benefits, thus significantly increasing ST's return on investment. Still, ST will have to select the appropriate candidates for future implementation projects—trading partners with relatively high scales of operations that are expected to realize sufficient gains from such projects to be willing to allocate the necessary resources to re-engineer their supply chain practices, deploy communications infrastructure, and in general manage the move to the new model. But the potential is great, and RosettaNet has become the cornerstone of ST's supply chain collaboration strategy.

NOTE

1. Saltare Leap—a suite of adaptive supply chain management applications specifically designed to intelligently address real-time inventory management and capacity allocation throughout the supply chain—is a trademark of Saltare, Inc. Vizional Technologies, Inc. announced on October 15, 2002, its acquisition of Saltare, Inc.

REFERENCES

Aviv, Y. The effect of collaborative forecasting on supply chain performance. *Management Science* 47, 10 (2001), 1326–1343.

Barlas, D. TaylorMade-Adidas golf. *Line56 Magazine,* October 25 (2002) (available at www.line56.com/articles/default.asp?ArticleID=4129&KeyWords=TaylorMade%2Dadidas++AND+Golf).

Gavirneni, S.; Kapuscinski, R.; and Tayur, S. Value of information in capacitated supply chains. *Management Science* 45, 1 (1999), 16–24.

Gorbach, G. Demand for CPM will more than double. *Manufacturing Systems* 19, 7 (2001), 26.

Gutmann, K. How GM is accelerating vehicle development. *Supply Chain Management Review* 7, 3 (2003), 34–39.

Lee, H.L.; Padmanabhan, V.; and Whang, S. The bullwhip effect in supply chains. *Sloan Management Review* 38, 3 (1997), 93–102.

Lee, H.L.; So, K.C.; and Tang, C.S. The value of information sharing in a two-level supply chain. *Management Science* 46, 5 (2000), 626–643.

Lee, H.L., and Whang, S. Sharing information to boost the bottom line. *Stanford GSB Research Reports,* 1999 (available at www-gsb.stanford.edu/research/reports/1999/whang_lee.html).

———. Information sharing in a supply chain. *International Journal of Technology Management* 20, 3/4 (2000), 373–387.

Peleg, B. Adaptec Inc., cross-enterprise integration. Stanford Global Supply Chain Management Forum Case, SGSCMF-002–1999, Stanford University, 1999, pp. 1–15.

———. STMicroelectronics e-chain optimization project. Stanford Global Supply Chain Management Forum Case, SGSCMF-001–2003, Stanford University, 2003.

Peterson, K., and Thompson, J. Standards: Important to rapid supply chain collaboration. *Gartner Research Note,* Technology, 03, October 2001.

Rajwat, P. See Commerce: Enhancing supply chain velocity at DaimlerChrysler. Stanford Global Supply Chain Management Forum Case, SGSCMF-001–2001, Stanford University, 2001.

CHAPTER 3

THE IMPACT OF B2B ELECTRONIC COMMERCE TECHNOLOGY, PROCESSES, AND ORGANIZATION CHANGES

A CASE STUDY IN THE PERSONAL COMPUTER INDUSTRY

DANIEL E. O'LEARY

Abstract: *We analyze the impact of changes in technology, processes, and organization on financial measures including* days in inventory, days in accounts receivable, *and* days in accounts payable, *through a case study that focuses on four firms in the personal computer (PC) industry (Compaq, Dell, Gateway, and Micron). The number of days that financial resources are locked up with product as part of the cash conversion cycle were measured and the impact of a portfolio of innovations, such as build-to-order production and merge-in-transit were investigated on disclosed and computed versions of those financial measures. This chapter describes the links between changes in systems and financial statement analysis and provides a rationale for different sets of changes in classic financial measures and a basis for benchmarking differences. Three of the four firms analyzed were actually able to generate negative days in the conversion cycle, meaning that others were literally accommodating the liquidity needs of those firms. Only Compaq had a conversion cycle with positive length. In addition, we analyze the relationship between disclosed measures and computed measures. We find that only firms with a negative conversion cycle disclose it, and that the absolute values of disclosed negative conversion cycles generally are longer than computed conversion cycles. This could result from differences in computational approaches, or use of different data. Finally, we compare the firms in the sample to see which measures changed the most and which gave corresponding competitive advantage. We find that Dell, Gateway, and Micron have substantial conversion cycle advantages over Compaq, providing them with a competitive advantage.*

Keywords: *Benchmarking, Business-to-Business (B2B) E-Commerce, Case Study, Financial Measures, Innovation, Personal Computer (PC) Industry*

INTRODUCTION

Best practices embedded in business-to-business (B2B) e-commerce have led to major changes in technology, processes, and organization structure that impact inventory, accounts receivable, and accounts payable. The purpose of this paper is to investigate some of those changes and trace their financial impact on firms in the personal computer (PC) industry.

A wide range of new technologies, including the Internet; changes in processes, such as buy direct, build-to-order, and merge-in-transit; and changes in organization structure, such as centralization of accounts payable and decentralization of accounts receivable, have led to major changes in financial positions. The fact that these changes have impacted financial positions has been disclosed in financial statements and discussed in news releases. However, there has been limited assessment as to the overall impact of the portfolio of changes. As a result, this paper summarizes many of those changes and analyzes the impact of those changes on measures disclosed as important by firms in the PC industry in their financial statements. These measures include *days in inventory, days in accounts receivable, days in accounts payable,* and their sum, *days of cash conversion cycle*. In particular, we find substantial changes in those four measures across the time period 1996–2002 and that processes deriving from e-business have led to major changes in financial benchmarks. Further, the extent to which technology, process, and organizational changes influence those ratios has become apparent, pushing financial statement analysis to consider their impacts.

The methodology used in this paper is a case study and small sample analysis. As a result, this study is a prototype analysis of the impact of processes and technology on an innovative subset of firms and lays out a methodology and set of findings that could be used in a larger sample study.

This chapter proceeds as follows. Section 1 provides a brief summary of the paper. Section 2 describes some of the financial changes at Dell Computer that provided motivation for the study. Section 3 summarizes some of the best practices in technology, processes, and organization structure changes. Section 4 analyzes their impact on accounts payable, accounts receivable, and inventory. Section 5 discusses the methodology. Section 6 discusses findings. Section 7 compares the disclosures of days in inventory, days in accounts receivable, and days in accounts payable to computed measures. Section 8 compares the findings across the firms to see where competitive advantage has been garnered. Section 9 briefly summarizes the paper and its contributions.

A CASE STUDY: DELL COMPUTER

Dell Computer has found it desirable to disclose information about days in inventory, accounts receivable, and accounts payable in their Form 10–Ks since the mid 1990s. Their disclosures over the time period 1994 to 2002 are summarized in Table 3.1.

An examination of Table 3.1 illustrates some major changes in Dell Computer's financial results over the time horizon from 1994 to 2002. In particular, between 1994 and 1997 Dell's financial ratio number of days in

- accounts receivable went from 50 to 37,
- inventory went from 33 to 13,
- accounts payable went from 42 to 54, and
- the conversion cycle of accounts receivable to accounts payable went from 41 to –4.

Although increased efficiencies continue past 2000, the changes are more incremental than revolutionary. For example, days in accounts receivable was reduced by about 9 percent per year over the time frame 1994 to 1997, but about 3 percent over the time frame 1997 to 2001. Similarly, days in inventory was reduced by over 20 percent per year over the time frame 1994 to 1997, but roughly 15 percent over the time period 1997 to 2001, with most of the reduction in that last period accruing to 1998. Further, days in accounts payable increased roughly 10 percent per

Table 3.1

Disclosed Turnover Measures

10-K	1994	1995	1996	1997	1998	1999	2000	2001	2002
Compaq									
Inventory turns	5.2	5.5	8.3	12.6	13.4	14.8	14.4	24	33
Equivalent days in inventory	70.2	66.4	44.0	29.0	27.2	24.7	25.3	15.2	11.1
Days in AP				40.0	54.0	58.0	52.0	53.0	54.0
Dell									
Days in AR	50	47	42	37	36	36	34	32	29
Days in inventory	33	32	31	13	7	6	6	5	4
Days in AP	42	44 (49)	33	54	51	54	58	58	69
Cash conversion cycle[1]					–8	–12	–18	–21	–36
Gateway									
Days in AR				26	23	22	23	20	17
Days in inventory				21	21	40	8	15	12
Days in AP				29	27	36	40	36	34
Cash conversion cycle[2]							–9	–1	–5

Notes:
AR = Accounts Receivable
AP = Accounts Payable
[1]Cash Conversion Cycle initiated in 1999.
[2]Cash conversion first disclosed in 2000.

year between 1994 and 1997, but less than 2 percent per year between 1997 and 2001. As a result, this paper examines the time period 1994 to 2000.

Many of those changes resulted from basic changes in the way that Dell did business. According to disclosures in the 10-K, those innovations derived from the way that production was done, to the logistics underlying distribution to doing business over the Internet. For example, in Dell's 1995 form 10-K, they note

> The Company employs a build-to-order manufacturing process that enables the Company to achieve rapid inventory turnover and reduced inventory levels ... operations benefited in 1995 from improvements in manufacturing logistics and ... from improved inventory management.

Further, although not acknowledged by Dell or other companies in the PC industry, once they had these processes and systems in place, it is likely that they would get better and better at using them. As a result, we would expect incremental yearly improvement beyond the big changes in measures due to new systems and processes.

What other innovations drove those changes in such a short time? Did the rest of the PC industry take advantage of those same changes?

SELECTED BEST PRACTICES IN ELECTRONIC COMMERCE: TECHNOLOGY, PROCESSES, AND ORGANIZATION

There are a number of best practices that have emerged in the PC industry, including build-to-order, selling direct, merge-in-transit, accounts payable management, accounts receivable management, using a reduced number of distributors, XML, and e-procurement. This paper focuses on those that can manifest themselves as reductions in the number of days of inventory, accounts payable, or accounts receivable, measures chosen for voluntary disclosure by the PC industry.

Selling Direct

Perhaps the key innovation used in the PC industry is that of selling direct, over the phone or over the Internet. As noted by Dell in their 1995 Form 10-K:

> Dell can price its products aggressively because it avoids typical dealer mark-ups and high inventory costs of physical stores. Second, it can offer a broader line of products because it is not constrained by physical retail shelf space. Third, the Company can accelerate time-to-market on new product introductions, which reduces obsolescence risk because it does not need to support an extensive pipeline of dealer inventory. Fourth, direct customer contact provides valuable information that is used to shape future product offerings and post-sale service and support. Fifth, the Company continually adds to its database of information about its customers, enabling it to market future product offerings more cost-effectively. Finally, by providing its end users with a full range of services, the Company believes it has a greater opportunity to develop customer loyalty than those who market through retail stores. The Company attempts to expand its direct marketing distribution channel through ongoing revision and improvement of its marketing and sales compensation programs to more effectively reach its customers and achieve improved market penetration, by improving its support systems, by pursuing additional distribution opportunities and by entering new markets.

The direct sales model continues to be important to Dell, as noted in their 2002 10-K:

> The direct model seeks to deliver a superior customer experience through direct, comprehensive customer relationships, cooperative research and development with technology partners, use of the Internet, computer systems custom-built to customer specifications, and service and support programs tailored to specific customer needs.

Further, the direct sales model is not only important to Dell. Other firms in the PC industry, for example, Compaq (Goh 1999), have found the direct sales approach important. Still other firms have tried to develop different models of the direct sales approach. For example, in the fourth quarter of 1997, Gateway introduced the concept of stores with no inventory. In particular, their Gateway country stores were designed to allow customers to evaluate the entire line of products, without carrying inventory. Customers could place an order at the store or contact Gateway directly. Having stores without inventory allows Gateway to engage a channel without influencing inventory.

Replacing the traditional distribution model of keeping inventory at stores with a direct-buy model could potentially decrease both raw material inventory and finished goods inventory. Finished goods inventory would be lower in a direct buying environment, since product would not need to be assembled until purchased. In addition, goods would be dispersed through a single point, rather than through multiple distribution chains, further pushing down finished goods inventory.

Build-to-Order (and Just-in-Time)

Dell was one of the first firms to build computers to order. As noted in Dell's 1995 10-K:

> The Company employs a build-to-order manufacturing process that enables the Company to achieve rapid inventory turnover and reduced inventory levels, which reduces the Company's exposure to the risk of declining inventory values. This flexible manufacturing process also allows the Company to rapidly incorporate new technologies and components into its product offerings.

A focus on simply build-to-order would be expected to decrease work-in-process inventory and finished goods inventory. However, build-to-order in the PC industry has evolved to include a just-in-time inventory approach. For example, Dell's model is based on just-in-time supply of raw materials. In addition, the complexity of the build-to-order process led to a need to consolidate their purchases, resulting in a smaller number of suppliers (Deck 2000). In addition, a smaller number of suppliers can result in a smaller administration cost.

Merge-in-Transit

O'Leary (2000) changes the classic process associated with shipping outsourced goods. In a classic outsourcing arrangement, firm 1 sells goods to the ultimate customer (firm 3), and an outsource firm (firm 2) actually makes the goods. Under the typical arrangement, firm 2 makes the goods and ships the goods to firm 1, which inventories the goods for some time period before they ship the goods to firm 3. However, there has emerged a new, more efficient approach, *merge-in-transit*. With merge-in-transit, firm 1 does not take possession of the goods. Instead, firm 2 ships the goods directly to firm 3. This results in less inventory for firm 1. So that firm 3 sees a single product and seller, the shipper (e.g., UPS or FedEx) merges the goods into a single shipment. Accordingly, merged-in-transit has been defined as follows: "This service collects shipments from multiple origin points and consolidates them, in transit, into a single delivery to the customer" (Dawe, 1997).

Merge-in-transit is either an issue of merging and forwarding, or synchronization. In the first case, as noted by Celestino (1999), generally a third-party logistics company receives the goods from multiple origins and assembles them at a single point near a customer, typically called a "merge point." In the second case, multiple shipments of goods may be shipped from multiple vendors, so that they all arrive at the customer at the same time.

With merge-in-transit, firms generally cut down the amount of particular types of inventory being stored in company warehouses, in some cases to zero. For example, Micron does not store monitors or printers in their own warehouses. Instead, the limited inventory that they do store is kept in FedEx warehouses (Cooke 1998), and it is generally kept there for a very short time. As an example, monitors might be outsourced, but PCs would be built in house. If a customer orders a PC with a monitor, then the PC company ships the PC, at virtually the same time as the outsourced monitor maker, so that the two are merged-in-transit and arrive at the customer at the same time. Merge-in-transit would result in fewer days in inventory since inventory would be held by the supplier until needed.

Accounts Receivable Management

Reportedly, PC industry firms have made changes in the organization of accounts receivable. According to Myers (2000), Dell's CFO, Jim Schneider, reorganized accounts receivable starting with his arrival in 1997. Schneider delegated responsibility for accounts receivable to individual business units. The theory was that those closest to the customer would handle the collection of receivables best. Furthemore, lockboxes closest to the customer could be used to get cash the quickest (Mellon 2002). Using lockboxes would result in fewer days in accounts receivable and higher working capital.

Accounts Payable Management

In Compaq's 1998 10-K, they noted:

> Accounts payable increased to $2.8 billion from $2.1 billion and days payable outstanding increased to 54 days from 40 days at December 31, 1997 and 1996, respectively, due to improved accounts payable management.

How does a firm "improve" accounts payable management? According to Myers (2000), for Dell, improved days in accounts payable meant centralizing accounts payable into three units worldwide. As seen in the above statement, "improved" also seems to mean increasing days in accounts payable.

Reduced Number of Distributors

For product distributed through traditional channels, for example, retail stores, best practices have included a reduction of the number of distributors (see Doyle 1999). The fewer the number of distributors, the less the inventory in the distribution pipelines. In addition, in order to fully exploit supply chain capabilities there needs to be an appropriate technical infrastructure. As noted by Compaq's chief operating officer, "It's easier to integrate systems with one, two or three large customers than it is to offer the same level of service to hundreds of customers" (Doyle 1999).

As announced on May 10, 1999, Compaq reduced the number of its distributors from thirty-nine to four. Only those four alliance partners were able to purchase built-to-order products directly from Compaq. As noted by Frank Doyle, now former CEO, "If you want speed you have to keep it simple." However, resellers were still able to purchase nonstandard, configure-to-order SKUs directly from Compaq or the four alliance partners. According to Doyle (1999), reduction of the number of suppliers could have ultimately reduced the amount of inventory at Compaq by a factor of two. However, with this announcement, it was clear that Compaq was pursuing traditional distribution, rather than direct distribution of its products. As a result, as noted by Ted Enloe of Compaq's CEO office, "Despite what you read about the direct approach, clearly, we remain committed to the channel." Unfortunately, it was difficult to trace the impact of this change because of Compaq's purchase of Digital and the corresponding need to integrate the two into a single firm, as well as the subsequent merger with Hewlett-Packard.

Software

Another source of improvement in operations is software. For example, reportedly Dell implemented credit and collections software in 1995 designed to facilitate an improved measure of days in accounts receivable (Slash DSO, 1999). As reported in Schmidt (1999), Micron in 1998 implemented software designed to facilitate collections. As part of the implementation of the collection software, Micron downloaded data from their enterprise resource planning system on a daily basis into a data warehouse, from which the data for the collection software was extracted. Compaq implemented SAP's financial application that is part of its enterprise resource planning system (Konicki and Maselli, 2001).

XML

Apparently, Dell was one of the first large commercial sites to employ XML (Neel 1999). In 1999, their site was updated to provide a customized view. Using XML allowed them to deliver an electronic version of the entire product database into the customer's purchasing system. As a result, the XML-backed site provides the ability to speed accounts receivable by facilitating correct order information and providing digital, rather than paper-based, information. Furthermore, XML could allow them to integrate with their customer e-procurement systems. Unfortunately, the impact of this innovation took place generally beyond the 1994 to 2000 time frame of our study.

E-Procurement

E-procurement is typically the electronic acquisition of nonproduction-oriented supplies and equipment, such as computers. Companies have set up procurement systems so that their employees can bypass purchasing departments and order goods directly from the manufacturer. Oftentimes, such links are over the Internet.

Not only does e-procurement make acquisition of computers and peripherals easier for customers, but it influences costs at the PC vendors. Orders come in electronically as direct orders and can be scheduled and accommodated using a build-to-order strategy. As a result, days in inventory can be affected by the percentage of orders that come in through e-procurement systems. Further, days in accounts receivable could be affected by such systems, since direct orders can be easily and quickly billed, or payment can be collected at the time of the order.

For example, as discussed by Goh (1999), another important approach was to begin integrating with the e-procurement systems of their major customers. In particular, Compaq was concerned with trying to make it easy for their customers to use the Internet to do business with them. Unfortunately, the impact of this innovation took place generally beyond the 1994 to 2000 time frame of our study.

Technology Convergence in the PC Industry

There is substantial evidence that technology used in one PC industry firm is rapidly emulated in other PC industry firms. For example, although in the early to mid 1990s Dell talked about build-to-order, shortly afterward Micron disclosed in their 10-Ks that they were using "assemble-to-order," the same concept.

Dell's use of merge-in-transit was discussed in the news in January 1998 (Order Assembly Centers 1998); Micron's use was discussed in May 1998. Use of merge-in-transit was also influenced by the particular transit company (e.g., UPS, DHL, or FedEx). If a transit company had developed the approach for one vendor, then others could use it. For example, on May 24, 1999, DHL announced that they would be opening their largest U.S. service center in Silicon Valley, at Sunnyvale California (*Electronic Buyer's News*, May 24, 1999), in order to meet the needs of the high-technology industries in the valley. They announced that the service center would provide merge-in-transit capabilities.

Similarly, virtually all of the PC industry firms sell direct. Some companies still sell in stores, and so their financial results reflect the multiple distribution chains.

IMPACT ON INVENTORY, ACCOUNTS RECEIVABLE, AND ACCOUNTS PAYABLE

What is the impact of these innovations on inventory, accounts receivable, and accounts payable?

Days in Inventory Decrease

Why should we expect these innovations to lead to a decrease in days in inventory? If a firm does build to order, then generally there should be a decrease in their work-in-process inventory and finished goods inventory.

In addition, if they engage in merge-in-transit, then some of their sales are goods that are fully outsourced, for example, monitors for Dell. Rather than having those monitors in their inventory and then ship them to their customers, the monitors are only in inventory for a short period of time, potentially just long enough for recognition of the sale. When the monitors are delivered, they are inventory for the PC manufacturer for a short moment, after which they become the property of the customer.

The same infrastructure that allows the PC manufacturers to merge-in-transit (e.g., electronic data interchange [EDI]) can also be used to facilitate decreases in raw material. Using EDI, inventory can be controlled to arrive just-in-time (JIT), further cutting down inventory. Each of these innovations can be rapidly diffused.

Days in Accounts Receivable Decrease

Why should we expect these innovations to decrease days in accounts receivable? First, a direct marketing approach, whether over the Internet or over the phone, should decrease accounts receivable, since for many orders cash is received up front, for example, from credit card purchases from individuals. Second, because the product is not yet built or assembled, the company has in effect received a cash advance on the product and any inventory required to build or assemble it. Third, if a portion of the order is merge-in-transit, then the PC firm will often receive payment for goods that it will not have to pay for until they are delivered to the customer, days later. Fourth, the same infrastructure that facilitates merge-in-transit also facilitates more rapid billing. EDI-based bills can be issued, speeding the billing process. Fifth, rather than having a centralized point to receive payments, at least one firm, Dell, pushed the accounts receivable task out to the business units, resulting in five lockbox locations in the United States (Myers 2000). Each of these technologies could be diffused to other similar firms.

Days in Accounts Payable Increase

Increases in days in accounts payable could be caused by a number of factors. One of the most important factors is being able to control internally when the bills are paid. Typically, this control is realized when a computer-based system is implemented to facilitate the billing.

Further, accounts payable can be centralized. In the case of Dell, starting in 1997 accounts payable was centralized to one location in the United States, one in Asia, and one in Europe (Myers 2000). A central location allows for tighter control. A central location also facilitates an increase in days in accounts payable since fewer locations are likely to mean longer transit time.

In addition, days in accounts payable can be increased with increased market power. Apparently, PC companies like Dell can persuade suppliers to take less than favorable terms for payment (see McGhie 2002). Further, market power is facilitated by aggregation of orders with fewer vendors, increasing volume with those vendors.

Merge-in-transit could also facilitate an increase in days of accounts payable. Merge-in-transit can employ multiple triggers for when payment is due.

SAMPLE AND DATA

The sample consists of four firms from the (Intel-based) PC industry for which PC-specific inventory, accounts payable, and accounts receivable information could be gathered: Compaq, Dell, Gateway, and Micron. During the period of analysis (1994 to 2000) these four firms were virtually entirely in the business of making and selling personal computers. IBM and Hewlett-Packard (HP) were not included because their results were compounded with other products.

The data were generated from the firms' 10-K forms for the years 1994 to 2000. In addition, an extensive review of the practitioner literature was made in order to gain knowledge about best practices used at particular PC industry firms.

Disclosed measures of days of inventory, accounts receivable, and accounts payable were captured from 10-K forms and are summarized in Table 3.1. Similarly, based on information disclosed in the 10-Ks, the same ratios were computed and are summarized in Table 3.2. The computations in this paper were based on the approaches discussed in the appendix, based on classic financial statement analysis.

I used computed ratios so that the different firms could be compared using a common measure. Disclosed ratios are not necessarily done using common approaches.

Table 3.2

Financial Statement Ratios

Company 10-K	1994	1995	1996	1997	1998	1999	2000
Compaq: computed ratios A (before Digital)							
Days in Inventory (CGS and average inventory)	45.0	58.8	42.0	29.0	31.2		
Days in AR	76.8	68.8	67.8	42.9	70.0		
Days in inventory (CGS)	89.9	60.9	31.1	32.1	29.1		
Days in AP	40.7	39.6	52.8	59.6	54.7		
Cash conversion cycle	126.1	90.0	46.1	15.5	44.5		
Days in production materials	57.4	29.5	15.5	15.7	17.1		
Days in WIP and FG	32.6	31.4	15.5	16.4	25.4		
Compaq: computed ratios B (with Digital)							
Days in inventory (CGS and average inventory)					30.5	29.0	27.5
Days in AR				43.7	93.3	76.5	68.7
Days in inventory (CGS)				32.7	34.2	29.0	28.6
Days in AP				61.1	75.5	67.0	58.9
Cash conversion cycle				15.4	52.1	38.5	38.3
Days in production materials				16.0	13.8	12.2	11.1
Days in WIP and FG				16.7	20.4	16.8	17.5
Dell: computed ratios							
Days in Inventory (and average inventory)	31.7	34.2	31.2	20.4	9.2	6.5	6.0
Days in AR	52.2	56.5	50.0	42.5	44.0	41.9	37.7
Days in inventory (CGS)	32.9	39.1	37.0	15.0	8.9	7.0	7.1
Days in AP	42.8	60.3	40.6	62.8	62.9	62.3	64.4
Cash conversion cycle	42.3	35.2	46.5	–5.3	–10.0	–13.4	–19.6
Days in production materials	29.3	34.9	33.7	13.4	7.2	6.0	6.1
Days in WIP and FG	3.6	4.1	3.4	1.7	1.7	1.0	1.0

(Continued)

Table 3.2 *(Continued)*

Company 10-K	1994	1995	1996	1997	1998	1999	2000
Gateway: computed ratios							
Days in Inventory (CGS and average inventory)			22.4	18.4	12.9	7.3	12.3
Days in AR		44.7	32.6	29.6	27.3	26.3	20.7
Days in inventory (CGS)		26.7	24.8	17.4	10.4	7.8	15.2
Days in AP		28.5	37.2	34.8	45.1	36.6	38.0
Cash conversion cycle		42.9	20.1	12.3	–7.4	–2.5	–2.0
Days in production materials		26.3	24.0	15.1	9.6	7.5	12.2
Days in FG		0.4	0.7	2.4	0.8	0.3	3.0
Micron: computed ratios							
Days in AP (purchases)	80.8	79.3	60.0	68.7	51.9	68.8	103.5
Days in Inventory (CGS and average inventory)		22.6	16.8	17.3	15.4	6.1	5.6
Days in AR	44.9	47.0	36.5	41.7	27.0	38.8	54.7
Days in inventory (CGS)	34.8	41.4	20.5	26.1	7.5	5.5	9.1
Days in AP	81.9	80.4	60.9	70.3	53.3	70.7	107.6
Cash conversion cycle	–2.3	8.0	–3.9	–2.5	–18.8	–26.5	–43.7
Days in production materials	31.5	38.0	17.3	21.0	5.0	4.5	6.7
Days in WIP and FG	3.9	3.4	3.1	5.1	2.5	0.9	2.4

Notes: AP = Accounts Payable; AR = Accounts Receivable; CGS = Cost of Goods Sold; WIP = Work in Process; FG = Finished Goods

BEST PRACTICE DISCLOSURES ABOUT PC COMPANIES

PC companies have implemented many of the best practices. This section summarizes available information about when those best practices were implemented.

Compaq

In 1997, Compaq indicated in their 10-K that they were " . . . in the process of building the capacity to build products to order (BTO) and configure products to order (CTO)." Others confirmed this, such as Court (1998). Disclosed days in inventory went from forty-four days in 1996 to twenty-nine days in 1997.

Compaq has worked to reengineer its processes while still maintaining traditional channels. Ultimately, this seems to limit their ability to control any of the measures to the extent of companies like Dell or Micron.

Unlike Dell and Gateway, Compaq did not disclose days in accounts receivable. As a result, there was no easy way to compute the disclosed cash conversion cycle.

Dell

According to company 10-Ks, build-to-order was initiated at least by 1994 and 1995. As a result, it is unlikely that we would see any major change over that time in days in inventory due to that innovation during 1994 to 2000. Similarly, the same direct model was maintained so that inventory and accounts receivable would not likely be further affected, except on a marginal basis. As seen in Table 3.2, in 1997 Dell disclosed a reduction of days in inventory from thirty-one to thirteen days. According to Dawe (1997), merge-in-transit was integrated into Dell's operations in 1997, the year of the major decrease.

In Table 3.1, it can be seen that Dell disclosed a major increase in days in accounts payable from 1996 to 1997. After that, days in accounts payable was relatively stable until 2002. It was in 1997 that Dell hired a new CFO who initiated a program of centralizing accounts payable, with an apparent impact of a twenty-one-day increase, as disclosed.

Disclosed days in accounts receivable decreased from fifty in 1994 to forty-two in 1996. During 1995, Dell implemented new software that allowed them to decrease the measure, according to the Institute of Management and Administration (Slash DSO 1999). Similarly, disclosed days in accounts receivable decreased from forty-two in 1996 to thirty-seven in 1997, the largest decrease over that time period. That time period corresponds to the shift of management of accounts receivable to local business units (see Mellon 2002, Myers 2000). As a result, disclosures seem somewhat consistent with major identifiable changes in processes and technology.

Gateway

In 1996, Gateway announced that their carrier was UPS (UPS Awarded Contract 1996). Since they have the same carrier as Micron, it is likely that innovations made available by UPS for one customer would be readily available for another. As a result, we would expect a similar timing for the use of merge-in-transit for Gateway and Micron. Micron implemented merge-in-transit in 1998 (Order Assembly Centers 1998). Computed days in inventory from 1997 to 1998 went from seventeen to ten.

Micron

Micron disclosed in their 10-K that they employed the approach of "assembled-to-order" (ATO) starting in 1996 and continuing through 1998. There was no such disclosure in 1995. From 1995 to 1996 their days in inventory went from 41.4 to 20.5.

Unlike Dell, who used UPS, Micron's carrier has been FedEx, which apparently implemented a merge-in-transit strategy in 1998 (Order Assembly Centers 1998), resulting in decreased inventory. Going from 1997 to 1998, Micron's days in inventory decreased from 26.1 to 7.5, based on ending inventory computations.

In 1998 Micron implemented data collection software, resulting in a reported 15 percent decrease in days in accounts receivable (Schmidt 1999).

There was no specific trend in days in accounts payable, although Micron appears to have implemented enterprise resource planning software.

COMPARISON BETWEEN DISCLOSED AND COMPUTED RATIOS

The purpose of this section is to discuss the relationship between disclosed ratios and computed ratios. Three of the four firms disclosed information about the ratios at some point in time. These disclosed ratios are summarized in Table 3.1. A comparison with the computed measures in Table 3.2 illustrates that either different numbers or different computational approaches were used.

The disclosed ratio quantities oftentimes differ from the computed ratio quantities. This difference could occur for a number of reasons. The two sets of computations may involve different data. For example, company computations could involve more detailed or differently timed data. Further, company computations may or may not be averaged data. Computations also could be different. Although the approach used to develop Table 3.2 was based on classic financial statement approaches, firms are not constrained to use those same approaches.

Compaq

Disclosed days in accounts payable were consistently less than computed days, by 21.1, 21.5, 9. and 6.9 days, respectively, from 1997 to 2000. Compaq did not disclose days in accounts receivable. Compaq's days in accounts receivable would be larger than other firms because of their dependence on a traditional sales model, rather than the Internet. Because it was larger, this may have influenced them not to disclose the information. Disclosed days in inventory was less than or equal to computed days in inventory for 1997 to 2000, but greater than computed days for 1994 to 1996 for average inventory, and 1995 to 1996 for ending inventory.

Dell

Disclosed days in accounts payable were consistently less than the computed quantity, by 0.8, 16.3, 7.6, 8.8, 11.9, 8.3 and 6.4, respectively, over the years from 1994 to 2000. Similarly, disclosed days in accounts receivable were consistently below computed days in accounts receivable (2.2, 9.5, 8, 5.5, 8, 5.9, and 3.7 for 1994 to 2000). Days in inventory, whether computed using a year-end inventory approach or average inventory, except for the first year, was the same or more than disclosed days in inventory.

Gateway

Disclosed days in accounts receivable and computed days in accounts receivable were very similar, with differences of 3.6, 4.3, 4.3, and –2.3 days occurring for 1997 to 2000, respectively, for computed minus disclosed. For inventory, where computed is based on cost of goods sold and average inventory, disclosed exceeded computed by –2.6, 8.1, 32.7 and 4.3 days. There was no consistent relationship between disclosed and computed inventory, using either average or year-end inventory.

Conclusions

For each of the disclosures there was a lack of a match:

- Disclosed days in accounts payable were consistently less than computed days in accounts payable, with substantial differences in some cases.
- Disclosed days in accounts receivable were consistently lower than computed days for Dell and Gateway.
- Disclosed days in inventory generally were less than computed days for both Dell and Compaq, but not Gateway, which did not have a consistent relationship.

There are a number of potential reasons for this lack of consistency. Perhaps firms did not want partners to know how long they were taking to pay accounts payables or how fast they were turning accounts receivable. Alternatively, different computational approaches could have been used or firms may have used disaggregated numbers (e.g., purchases) that were not available in public disclosures. Still another alternative is that firms manage discretionary disclosures so that they appear to have a particular direction over time.

COMPARISON BETWEEN FIRMS

Using the four measures of the conversion cycle, days in inventory, days in accounts receivable, days in accounts payable, and days in conversion cycle, for both disclosed and computed quantities, we can compare the four firms.

Days in Inventory

Disclosed

Of the three firms that made disclosures, each disclosed days in inventory. Each of the firms showed substantial improvement, with Compaq improving the most, from 70.2 days to 11.1 days. Gateway made only gradual improvement when compared to the other two firms. By 2000 Dell and Gateway had roughly one-third the number of days in inventory of Compaq, putting Compaq at a substantial competitive disadvantage in working capital.

Computed

Each of the firms improved substantially in the area of days in inventory, with Compaq showing the greatest improvement. However, by 2000, Dell, Gateway, and Micron each were substantially lower than Compaq. Compaq was at a substantial disadvantage.

Days in Production Materials and WIP and Finished Goods

Each of the four firms made separate disclosures of production materials and work in process (WIP) and finished goods. Computed days in those inventory categories are summarized in table 3.2. Differences in business models are apparent, particularly in the days in WIP and finished goods. While Dell, Gateway, and Micron had reduced their measure down to less than three days, Compaq never went below sixteen days during the entire time period of concern.

Similarly, although all four firms made substantial reductions in days in production materials, Gateway and Compaq had larger measures and thus were at a competitive disadvantage.

Days in Accounts Receivable

Disclosed

Each of the two firms that disclosed days in accounts receivable showed substantial improvement in this measure, with Gateway decreasing from twenty-six to seventeen and Dell decreasing from fifty to twenty-nine. This is the one measure that Gateway performed better on than Dell.

Computed

Dell and Gateway each showed substantial improvement in days in accounts receivable. However, there was no stable improvement with either Compaq or Micron. This suggests that the changes to accounts receivable processes were not made uniformly across the industry. Compaq and Micron were at a substantial disadvantage.

Days in Accounts Payable

Disclosed

Disclosed days in accounts payable increased substantially for Dell over the period 1996 to 2002. Compaq's increased from 1997 to 1998, but was then stable until 2002. Gateway's increased from 1998 to 1999, but then was stable to 2002, actually decreasing over the time period 2000 to 2002. It appears that the primary innovation diffusion occurred with Dell in 1996, Compaq in 1997, and Gateway in 1998.

Computed

Micron had the largest number of days in accounts payable, with 107 in 2000, providing them with substantial working capital. From 1995 to 1996, Compaq's days in accounts payable increased substantially, as seen in table 3.2 in the first panel, but then was relatively stable. Gateway was stable from 1995 through 2000, with the lowest days in accounts payable of all four firms.

Cash Conversion Cycle

Disclosed

Dell was the first to disclose the overall cash conversion cycle time, initiating that disclosure in 1998, when it was negative, although it had become negative in 1997. Gateway also disclosed their conversion cycle time in 2000. Compaq did not disclose days in accounts receivable, thus making conversion cycle disclosure impossible. Micron made no disclosures.

Computed

Dell, Compaq, and Gateway each improved substantially over the time period in the lengths of their cash conversion cycles, suggesting that the changes in processes and technology were very effective. Compaq made the greatest improvement in the computed cash conversion cycle, dropping from 126.1 to 38.3 days; however, their cycle time in 2000 was still substantially above that of the other firms and the only one of the four that was not negative, putting them at a considerable disadvantage in terms of working capital.

Analysis

The business processes that Compaq used, which were reflected in their conversion cycle, put them at a considerable disadvantage, particularly with respect to Dell and Micron. Gateway was competitive in each of the measures with Dell and Micron, except for days in accounts payable. This could be because some firms consider a large measure of accounts payable days as a sign of poor management; however, it could also be indicative of different degrees of market power.

SUMMARY

This paper has analyzed the impact of innovations that have occurred with the implementation of electronic commerce capabilities. In particular, we examined a portfolio of approaches to changes in technology, processes, and organization that would directly impact measures of days in inventory, accounts receivable, and accounts payable in the PC industry. For each of four firms, we identified different events and corresponding changes in the three measures. We then matched major events with major changes at the firms, tracing out the impact of the events on the firms' financial performances.

In addition, computed and disclosed measures were compared to see if there were any relationships over the time period 1994 to 2000. Disclosed measures of days in inventory, accounts receivable, and accounts payable were compared to computed measures, based on financial statement analysis. Disclosed measures were typically lower than computed measures. The issue of the relationship between disclosed and computed measures seems to require additional future research. However, it appears that there is management of such disclosures over time.

Finally, the firms were compared to each other across the four conversion cycle measures. It was found that Compaq was at a considerable disadvantage in terms of their ability to use emerging processes to speed their conversion cycle whereas Dell and Micron had a significant advantage in terms of increased current assets.

APPENDIX 3.1. FINANCIAL STATEMENT RATIOS

This appendix provides a brief summary of the financial ratios used as part of this analysis. These ratios and this discussion are based on Bernstein (1974).

One of the primary choices that is made in financial ratio computation is whether average or ending balances for balance sheet accounts should be used. In order to maintain consistency, and because some of the firms in the PC business have grown very rapidly, ending balances were used.

1. Days in Accounts Receivable (Collection Period)
= Ending Accounts Receivable / (Yearly Sales / 365 Days)

Days in accounts receivable reflects the nature of the supply chain and the extent to which customers are paying on time. If the distribution chain is "deeper" rather than shallower, the number of days can be larger. A distribution chain is deeper when there are multiple levels. In such settings, there can be a cycle effect of one party's collection depending on another. If there is a shallow distribution chain, for example, direct to the buyer, then collection is also more direct. In addition, this ratio will be lower if the firm is doing a good job of monitoring and ensuring that customers pay in a timely manner. (Bernstein, 1974, pp. 386–387)

2. Days in Inventory
= Ending Total Inventory / (Yearly Cost of Goods Sold / 365 Days)

Similarly, ratios for raw material, work in process, and finished goods could also be developed. In addition, rather than ending total inventory, average inventory could have been used. Both methods were used in the computation of this ratio, with "Avg. Inv." used to indicate average inventory was used.

The days in inventory provides a gauge as to how fast inventory can be converted into cash. Generally, in high-technology businesses like the PC industry, because of rapid obsolescence, it is generally desirable to drive down the number of days in inventory. Further, a lower number of days in inventory requires lower working capital. As noted in the main body of the paper, a range of business processes, including build-to-order, can influence days in inventory. (Bernstein, 1974, pp. 391–393)

3. Days in Accounts Payable
= Ending Accounts Payable / ([Yearly Cost of Goods Sold – Depreciation]/365 Days)

Alternatively, purchases could have been used if the information had been available. Unfortunately, purchase information was not generally available.

In 1997, Compaq noted in its 10-K, ". . . days payable outstanding increased . . . due to improved accounts payable management." Firms that have forty to sixty days in accounts payable are often said to be "effectively managing" the payables process. The higher the number of days, the lower the working capital requirements. At some point though, if days in accounts payable gets too large, then the company may find its creditors getting concerned. (Bernstein, 1974, pp. 395–396)

4. Days in the Cycle

Adding ratios 1 and 2 and subtracting 3 generates the number of days in the trade cycle. The higher the days in the trade cycle, the higher the working capital requirements. The computation of the days in the cycle led to the use of ending balances for accounts payable, accounts receivable, and inventory, rather than average balances. In the PC industry, some firms are able to generate negative days in the cycle. This is an unusual state of affairs. (Bernstein, 1974, p. 399)

REFERENCES

Bernstein, L. *Financial Statement Analysis*. New York: Irwin, 1974.
Celestino, M. Choosing a third-party logistics provider. *World Trade,* 12, 7 (1999), 54–56.

Cooke, J. Custom-built with speed. *Logistics Management and Distribution Report*, 37, 1 (January 1, 1998), 54–57.

Court, R. Dell's magic formula. May 27, 1998 (available at http://wired-vig.wired.com/news/print/0,1294,12564,00.html).

Dawe, R. Move it fast, eliminate steps. *Transportation and Distribution*, September 38, 9 (1997), 67–74.

Deck, S. Fine line. *CIO*, February 1, (2000), 88.

Doyle, T. Compaq retools distribution—streamlines distributors through four alliance partners. *VAR Business*, May 10 (1999) (available at www.varbusiness.com/showArticle.jhtml?articleID=18803288).

Electronic Buyers News. May 24, 1999. "DHL Opens Service Center in Silicon Valley."

Goh, E. Compaq e-business: A case study. Compaq Computer, unpublished presentation (1999).

Konicki, S., and Maselli, J. Apps made easy? March 12, 2001 (available at www.informationweek.com/828/entapps.htm).

McGhie, M. Cash-flow management. 2002 (available at www.digitaloutput.net).

Mellon receives Dell award. April 2, 2002 (available at www.mellon.com/cashmanagement/newsletter/updateataglance/up0072.html).

Myers, R. Cash crop: The working capital survey. *CFO*, August 1 (2000) (available at www.cfo.com/article.cfm/3015968?f=advancesearch).

Neel, D. Dell and Compaq fight it out online. *Infoworld,* 21, 46 (1999), 1, 40.

O'Leary, D. Supply chain processes and relationships for electronic commerce. In M. Shaw (ed.), *Handbook of Electronic Commerce.* Springer-Verlag, New York, 2000.

Order assembly centers. *Modern Materials Handling*, Mid May (1998) (available at www.mmh.com/article/CA110887.html).

Resources for current asset categories, South-Western Publishing (available at www.swlearning.com/accounting/students/ca_ar_resol.htm).

Schmidt, D. Eight pitfalls of collection automation. May 1999 (available at www.Bfmag.com).

UPS awarded Gateway 2000 distribution contract. Press release, United Parcel Service (June 10, 1996).

CHAPTER 4

THE STANDARDIZATION GAP

AN ECONOMIC FRAMEWORK FOR NETWORK ANALYSIS

TIM WEITZEL, HERMANN-JOSEF LAMBERTI, AND DANIEL BEIMBORN

Abstract: *Standardization is a key issue in information systems research and a theoretical as well as practical challenge for electronic commerce and the digital economy. Inherent in standards, the commonality property deriving from the need for compatibility implies coordination problems that are characteristic of information systems. From a theoretical perspective, the existence of network effects renders efficient neoclassical solutions improbable. As a consequence, corporate information management is increasingly occupied with coordinating standardization decisions as a basis for information and communication infrastructures.*

In this work, a standardization framework based on an analysis of network effect theory and computer-based simulations is developed and applied to corporate standardization problems. A fundamental finding is the existence of a standardization gap quantifying the magnitude of the standardization problem. A practical application of the framework empirically shows the size of a concrete standardization gap and how strategies can be developed internalizing this unrealized efficiency potential.

Keywords: *Agent-Based Computational Economics, Network, Network Effect, Standard, Standardization*

INTRODUCTION

"An economic theory of norms and standards (. . .) is still lacking."
(Knieps et al. 1982, p. 213)

Standards play a prominent role in many systems that are characterized by interaction or interrelatedness. In information systems such as software environments or Intranets standards provide for compatibility and are a prerequisite for collaboration benefits. More generally speaking, standards can constitute networks (e.g., supply chains, the "network" of users of certain software products, corporate intra- and extranets). Inherent in standards, the commonality property deriving from the need for compatibility implies coordination problems. From a theoretical perspective, the existence of network effects as a form of externality that is often associated with communication standards renders efficient neoclassical solutions improbable (Weitzel et al. 2000). The externality property deriving from network effects (and thus the multifaceted dynamics behind the diffusion processes of standards) makes standardization problems complex and interesting to solve.

Based on important findings from network effect theory and diffusion theory, we present in this paper a framework for network analysis. It is anchored in an agent-based simulation model that discloses decision behavior in terms of the selection of standards and the diffusion of technological innovations in networks.

STANDARDS IN NETWORKS: ECONOMIC APPROACHES TOWARD NETWORK ANALYSIS

A Brief History of Standardization

Among the first consciously set standards, language played an important role. The development of language from the monosyllabic grunts and growls used by hunters and cave dwellers through symbols and pictograms to what we now understand as written language is a perfect example of the standardization process. On the Indian subcontinent, in the Indus Valley, decimally subdivided length scales of the ancient Mohenjo-daro or Harappa civilization, dating back as far as 3500 B.C., have been unearthed (Verman 1973, 4). Kindleberger (1983) has described the evolution of monetary standards.

The French Revolution is considered to be an important step in the history of man's conscious evolution of standardization, with the responsibility for standardization given to scientists by the state. The advent of mass production that brought the necessity of interchangeable parts is another step (Verman 1973, p. 8). One can also find interesting cases of failed standardization efforts. When changing the weights and measures of the ancien régime to a metric system, some changes were successful, like money. But the decimalization of time widely failed. Year one of decimal time began on September 22, 1794. It consisted of twelve months of thirty days each, a week was ten days, and a day had ten hours of 100 minutes. While the decimal year system lasted ten or twelve years, decimal days did not survive even two years (Kindleberger 1983, 389–390; Carrigan 1978).

A very often cited example of historic standardization problems is the standard railway gauge of 4 feet and 8-½ inches, which is believed to be the "width of a hind end of a Norfolk mule used to pull coal wagons on wooden rails" and was set by the British Parliament as a standard for all railroads in the Gauge Act of 1846 (Kindleberger 1983, 384). Companies using other widths, like Great Western, of course opposed the standard width and said that five feet between the rails provides smoother and more stable rides; they used different locomotive axles and transshipped cargo at certain stations before finally adopting the standard gauge in the 1890s. Railway gauge problems were also known to exist between Germany and Russia:

> [T]he Germans for a time shifted one track inward on sleepers as they conquered Russian territory in World Wars I and II, and then adopted locomotive and wagon axles with an extra wheel to fit the wider size to make transfers possible without relaying track. In Australia each state kept to its own gauge until after the middle of the [twentieth] century, forcing most interstate cargo to be carried by sea between settlements along the coast, and interstate shipments by rail to be reloaded from one system to the other. (Kindleberger 1983, 384–385)

In World War I, Britain is reported to have had twenty-four different voltages and ten different frequencies produced by electricity generating companies (Plummer 1937, 21). Another well-known historic (non) standardization case is a fire in Baltimore on February 7, 1904. Firefighters from Washington could not help extinguish the huge fire because their hoses would not fit the

Baltimore hydrants. This sad incident resulted in over 1,000 burnt houses and damage valued at $125 million (Warren and Warren 1983, 125; Hemenway 1975, 3).

In the late nineteenth and early twentieth centuries, and with World War I eventually becoming a substantial driving force, the focus of most standardization efforts was improving national productivity. Standardization was seen as a means of reducing the heterogeneity of products and processes in order to obtain production-side economies of scale. A prominent example of early standardization efforts (already addressing cross-user compatibility) to reap compatibility benefits was the United States and the United Kingdom harmonizing the pitch of the screw thread between them during World War II to make screws exchangeable (Kindleberger 1983, 392).

After World War II the standardizers' goals slowly started to change, giving way to compatibility standards. This new dynamic first peaked with the release of the papers of McGowan and Fisher (Fisher et al. 1993) concerning the antitrust lawsuits versus IBM in the 1970s. Building on this, the influential works of Farrell and Saloner (1985) and Katz and Shapiro (1985) can be said to have opened standardization as an area of research of its own. The general problem associated with standards is their commonality property, which gives rise to a coordination problem, since standardization decisions therefore exhibit externalities. While it is common in many markets that the buying decision of one consumer influences the decisions of others (e.g., bandwagon, snob, and Veblen effects are broadly discussed in economic literature; see Leibenstein 1950, Ceci and Kain 1982), a discussion has emerged about whether some markets are determined by strong demand-sided economies of scale. These are often called positive network effects, deriving from the need of product compatibility as, for example, in software markets. The network effects in these markets mainly originate from two different areas, the need for compatibility to exchange information or data and the need for complementary products and services.

Leibenstein (1950) anticipated parts of the phenomenon, stating that demand curves are more elastic when consumers derive positive value from increases in market size. Parallel with the growth of the telecommunication and information technology (IT) markets in recent years, the discussion has gained considerable momentum. Especially in terms of the implications of demand-side returns to scale on market coordination and overall efficiency, it became obvious that these effects merited more research.

Network Effect Theory as Theoretical Foundation

Network effects have been defined as "the change in the benefit, or surplus, that an agent derives from a good when the number of other agents consuming the same kind of good changes" (Liebowitz and Margolis 1995; see Thum 1995, 5–12, for different sources of network effects).

The externality property implies coordination problems in markets subject to network effects, which are said to be endemic in high-tech industries in particular—". . . such industries experience problems that are different in character from the problems that have, for more ordinary commodities, been solved by markets" (Liebowitz and Margolis 1995). Network effects are primarily discussed in the literature on standards, in which a primary concern is the choice of a correct standard, and in the literature concerning path dependencies, in which patterns of diffusion, that is, standards adoption processes, are a focus. Thus, discussions about the use of standards or the diffusion of technological innovations are often based upon the theory of positive network effects (see Katz and Shapiro 1985, Farrell and Saloner 1985). Therefore, network effects imply demand-side economies of scale in the adoption of technology and make otherwise autonomous decisions of agents (about the use of technologies subject to network effects) interdependent, creating a coordination problem that is often called *the standardization problem*

(Wiese 1990, 1, Besen and Farrell 1994, 118). Throughout most parts of the literature, the term network effect describes *positive* effects. Of course, there are negative externalities, too (Roever, 1996).

Katz and Shapiro (1985, 424) differentiate between *direct network effects,* in terms of the direct, "physical effects" of being able to exchange information (as in the case of telephones) and *indirect network effects,* arising from interdependencies in the consumption of complementary goods (Braunstein and White 1985; Chou and Shy 1990; Church and Gandal 1992; Teece 1987). Examples are computer operating systems and available application software, or videocassette recorder systems and the format of the tapes. This relation is sometimes called the *hardware-software paradigm* (Katz and Shapiro 1985, 424). Other sources of indirect network effects can be the availability of after-sales services (e.g., popular automobile makes will probably have a higher availability of different services than rare models [Katz and Shapiro 1985, 425; 1986, 823]), learning effects, and uncertainties about future technology availability or the existence of a market for used goods (Glanz 1993, 31; Thum 1995, 8–12).

Complementarity can formally be described by negative cross-price elasticity ($\frac{\partial x_1}{\partial p_2} < 0$). Cabral (1987) states that processes subject to positive feedbacks (due to network effects or learning by doing) are analytically similar to learning processes. Arthur (1989, 116) emphasizes "learning by using" effects (see also Habermeier 1989, Rosenberg 1982). According to Braunstein and White (1985, 339), the more intense the network effects, the higher the converting and standard switching costs, the more long-lived the good, and the higher the stack of complementary goods (e.g., data files in a certain format), the more a common standard is important. Kindleberger (1983) describes free-rider problems due to the public good properties of standards. Arthur (1989) shows that technologies subject to increasing returns (in contrast to constant and decreasing returns) exhibit multiple equilibria and will finally lock in to a monopoly with one standard cornering the entire market. Since this standardization process is non-ergodic (or path dependent), the ultimate outcome is not predictable. Analogously, Besen and Farrell (1994) show that tippiness is a typical characteristic found in networks, describing that multiple incompatible technologies are rarely able to coexist and that the switch to a single, leading standard can occur suddenly.

An important distinction is to be made between *sponsored* and *unsponsored* networks: in sponsored networks, there are agents in possession of property rights concerning the standard of choice. Particularly, the possession of those rights enables internalization strategies by means of pricing. If you own a technology you can determine a price for it. This is not possible with open standards like XML, for example. In contrast, unsponsored technologies are not subject to proprietary means of control and accordingly might suffer more strongly from the externality property associated with standards. Some researchers distinguish between unsponsored *de facto* standardization processes and diffusion in sponsored networks: a quite commonly adopted terminology differentiates between the market-mediated diffusion processes of compatibility standards (leading to *de facto* standards [Saloner, 1990]) and *de jure* standards resulting from either political ("committee") or administrative procedures. *De facto* standards can either be sponsored (with certain actors holding property rights and the capability of restraining the use of the standard) or unsponsored (no actors with proprietary interests) (Arthur 1983; David and Greenstein 1990, 4). This distinction principally resembles the two institutional settings developed in the standardization gap and practical applications sections below, with centrally coordinated networks requiring a "sponsor" capable of influencing the agents' decisions.

The pattern of argument for standardization processes is always the same: the discrepancy between private and collective gains in networks under increasing returns leads to possibly

Pareto-inferior results, i.e. undesired standardization outcomes or more generally to market failure. With incomplete information about other actors' preferences, *excess inertia* can occur, as no actor is willing to bear the disproportionate risk of being the first adopter of a standard and then becoming stranded in a small network if all others eventually decide in favor of another technology. This start-up problem prevents any adoption at all of the particular technology, even if it is preferred by everyone. On the other hand, *excess momentum* can occur, for example, if a sponsoring firm uses low prices during early periods of diffusion to attract a critical mass of adopters (Farrell and Saloner 1986). In the case of complete information on the part of all actors concerning their symmetric preferences for a certain standard, a *bandwagon* process will overcome the coordination problem, with actors who stand to gain relatively high stand-alone utility or private benefits from adoption (as compared to network effects) starting the adoption process. Nevertheless, in the case of heterogeneous preferences, Farrell and Saloner (1986) show that due to strategic behavior, even perfect communication might not be able to overcome excess inertia or momentum. In the case of sponsored technologies the situation is somewhat different. Here there is a possibility of internalizing the network gains, which would otherwise be more or less lost, by strategic intertemporal pricing, for example (Katz and Shapiro 1986). There are private incentives to providing networks that can overcome inertia problems; however, they do not guarantee social optimality per se.

In contrast to *network effect theory* focusing on compatible technologies constituting networks, *diffusion theory* analyzes relational and structural interaction patterns to explain the diffusion of innovations (see Lilien and Kotler, 1983; Mahajan and Peterson, 1985; Mahajan et al., 1990; Weiber, 1993). Besides these essentially economic research approaches, many (mostly empirical) studies of network phenomena in the form of diffusion processes can be found in various research areas such as anthropology, early sociology, rural sociology, education, medical sociology, communication, and so on (for an early overview, see Rogers and Shoemaker, 1971, 44–96). For *geographical network* analysis, see Haggett et al. (1977); for *sociological network* analysis see Jansen (1999). Other related areas include *actor network theory* emphasizing the social construction of networks (see Callon 1991, Giddens 1986, Rosenberg 1982, Timmermans and Berg 1997), contributions concerning the dispersion of the Internet (see David and Steinmueller 1996, Drake 1993, Lehr 1995), policy issues in networks (see Branscomb and Kahin 1995, Braunstein and White 1985, Carlton and Klamer 1983, David 1995, Lemley 1996, Liebowitz and Margolis 1996, Trebing 1994), and intertemporal coordination problems when building infrastructures (Thum 1995).

Recently, deficiencies of traditional network effect theory and disciplinary network research approaches have been discussed. In Weitzel et al. (2000) it is argued that traditional approaches addressing network effects offer great insights to general problems concerning the diffusion of standards and thereby some of the evolutionary mechanisms behind networks but that they fail to explain the variety of diffusion courses in today's dynamic information and communication technology (ICT) markets. As a consequence, important determinants of network behavior and individual agents, such as agent size, decision sequence, network topology, and individual heterogeneous network effects, need to be modeled to increase the explanatory scope of the models and also their applicability to real-world networks.

THE STANDARDIZATION GAP

The network research framework described below was developed by incorporating some of the findings summarized above. It was especially designed to both abstractly model the situation of individual agents within their neighborhood (i.e., the particular informational and economical environment of all network agents, especially their heterogeneous costs, benefits, and information sets available) and to be applicable to real-world problems. Thus, in the model, costs and benefits associated with standardization are modeled generically. Typically, standardization costs include the costs of hardware, software, switching, introduction or training, and operations. Furthermore, the interdependence between individual decisions to standardize occasioned by network effects can yield coordination costs of agreeing with market partners on a single standard (Kleinmeyer 1998, 130). Standardization benefits can be direct savings resulting from decreased information costs due to cheaper and faster communication (Kleinmeyer 1998, 63) and also more strategic benefits, such as avoiding media discontinuities and allowing the automation and coordination of different business processes, for example, enabling just-in-time production (Rogers and Shoemaker, 1971) and hence bringing about stock reductions, and so forth. In addition, standardization can enhance the exchange of information so that more and better information can be exchanged between partners and it can result in fewer converting and friction costs (Braunstein and White, 1985; Thum 1995 14–15). See the practical applications section of this chapter for empirical data and sources of costs and benefits associated with standards.

Using a computer-based simulation model rather than an analytical approach implies associated disadvantages like smaller analytical transparency and results that cannot be presented in the form of an equation. But these shortcomings are compensated for by the ability to analyze more complex and dynamic structures and discrete choice scenarios as typically found in networks. See Tesfatsion (2002) for the paradigm of computational economics. Thus, in order to incorporate the individuality of incentives and disincentives in terms of standards adoption (i.e., network participation), an individual valuation of network effects and network costs is crucial. The basic concept of the standardization models is summarized below. See Buxmann (1996) for the centralized standardization model and Westarp et al. (2000) for the decentralized standardization model, a diffusion model, and their fusion.

A Basic Model

If K_i is the standardization costs of agent i and c_{ij} are i's costs for the exchange of information between agent i and j that can be saved by mutual standardization, then the standardization condition of agent i is described by

$$\sum_{\substack{j=1 \\ j \neq i}}^{n} c_{ij} - K_i > 0$$

Equation 1: Standardization condition of agent i

However, given autonomous agents and the availability of a realistic information set, it is not clear that all partners actually standardize. Each agent i then needs to anticipate the behavior of the other agents j ($j \in \{1, \ldots, n\}$; $j \neq i$). If it is assumed that all agents i know K_j and the communication costs directly associated with him (i.e., c_{ij} and c_{ji}) but no further data, like the information costs between other agents, the standardization problem is mainly a problem of anticipating the partners' strategic standardization decisions. We assume that the agents are risk-neutral decision makers and propose an approximation of their anticipation calculus according to Equation 2.

$$\mathrm{E}[\mathrm{U(i)}] = \sum_{\substack{j=1 \\ j \neq i}}^{n} \frac{c_{ji}(n-1) - K_j}{c_{ji}(n-1)} c_{ij} - K_i = \sum_{\substack{j=1 \\ j \neq i}}^{n} p_{ij} \, c_{ij} - K_i$$

*Equation 2: Expected utility (*ex ante*)*

p_{ij} describes the probability with which agent *i* believes that *j* will standardize. If $E[U(i)] > 0$, then agent *i* will standardize. Given the assumptions about the availability of data outlined above, p_{ij} can be heuristically computed as in Equation 2 using all data presumed available to the deciding agent. The numerator describes the net savings possible through the standardization for node *j*, assuming that all nodes standardize and that the edge <*ji*> is representative of all of node *j*'s communications relationships. The denominator normalizes the fraction for nonnegative K_j as a value from 0 to 1. Should the fraction have a value less than 0, that is, c_{ji} $(n-1) < K_j$, then $p_{ij} = 0$ holds. We call this the *decentralized standardization model* since it focuses on describing the individual perspective of agents deciding on adopting standards by determining local costs and benefits associated with that decision as, for example, in corporate Intranets by autonomous business units.

As long as the individual agents are unable to influence the standardization decisions of their communications partners (as in the unsponsored networks described in the previous section), they can do no more *ex ante* than estimate the probability that their partners will standardize. *Ex post* of course, the communications costs either remain or are no longer applicable. The decentralized model allows the prediction of standardization behavior in a network, thereby creating a basis for predicting the effects of various concepts of coordination. Such measures for influencing the decision to introduce standards also generally apply to influencing the development of expectations regarding the future spread of standards (installed base) or to forms of cooperation that would allow partners to jointly reap the profits of standardization through the partial internalization of network effects (either by information intermediation or a redistribution of the standardization costs and benefits among the participants).

Thus, the decentralized standardization model determines the outcome of network agents tied together by an externality known as *direct network effect* when there is no coordination among the agents. To determine the efficacy of solution strategies, as a diametrical concept the centralized standardization model by Buxmann (1996) is used as a benchmark of the maximum possible coordination quality, assuming that agency or coordination costs are resolved (at zero cost) and that there is a central manager who can determine and implement the optimum result networkwide and, most importantly, who is accredited with the resulting costs and benefits.[1] Therefore, the first best allocation of standards in a network, given there is an all-knowing planner, can be determined using the mixed integer problem formulation in Equation 3. The binary indicative variable x_i takes on a value of 1 if agent *i* has standardized, and 0 if not. The binary variable y_{ij} equals 0 if both nodes *i* and *j* are standardized ($x_i = 1$ Ù $x_j = 1$). For a multiperiod multistandard extension of the centralized standardization model, see Buxmann (1996).

$$OF = \sum_{i=1}^{n} K_i \, x_i + \sum_{i=1}^{n} \sum_{\substack{j=1 \\ j \neq i}}^{n} c_{ij} \, y_{ij} \quad \rightarrow \quad Min!$$

s.t.:

$$\mathrm{x_i} + \mathrm{x_j} \geq 2 - \mathrm{M\,y_{ij}} \quad \forall i, j; i \neq j$$

$$\mathrm{x_i}, \mathrm{x_j}, \mathrm{y_{ij}} \in \{0,1\} \quad \forall i, j; i \neq j$$

Equation 3: The basic standardization model in centralized networks (Buxmann, 1996)

Simulating Standardization Problems in Networks

Simulation Design

All simulation results were generated using Java 1.4 applications. For data analysis, SPSS 10.0 was used. Individual benefits, E_i, to agent i ($i \in \{1, \ldots, n\}$) from implementing a standard are:

$$E_i = \sum_{\substack{j=1 \\ j \neq i}}^{n} c_{ij} \cdot x_j - K_i$$

Equation 4: Individual ex post *benefits (*$\mathrm{E_i}$)

GE denotes aggregate networkwide savings resulting from standardization, that is, the horizontal aggregation of all individuals' benefits.

$$GE = \sum_{i=1}^{n} E_i = \sum_{i=1}^{n} \sum_{\substack{j=1 \\ j \neq i}}^{n} c_{ij} \cdot \left(1 - y_{ij}\right) - \sum_{i=1}^{n} K_i \cdot x_i = \underbrace{\sum_{i=1}^{n} \sum_{\substack{j=1 \\ j \neq i}}^{n} c_{ij}}_{\text{ex ante costs}} - \underbrace{\left(\sum_{i=1}^{n} K_i \cdot x_i + \sum_{i=1}^{n} \sum_{\substack{j=1 \\ j \neq i}}^{n} c_{ij} \cdot y_{ij} \right)}_{\text{ex post costs}}$$

Equation 5: Networkwide ex post *savings as the sum of all individual net savings*

The transformation in Equation 5 enables deduction of *GE* from *ex ante* costs (before standardization) and *ex post* costs. As before, y_{ij} takes a value of zero if both agents, *i* and *j*, have standardized. The interpretation of aggregate savings, *GE*, is not unproblematic in a decentralized network but it measures overall decision quality in decentrally coordinated networks, especially in contrast to the potential coordination efficiency that is achievable in centrally coordinated networks.

During the simulations, first a network is initialized assigning approximately normally distributed random values for K_i (K~ND(K_i| μ, σ^2)) to all agents *i* and c_{ij} (c~ND(c_{ij}|μ, σ^2)) to all communications relations <*ij*>.[2] Having generated a network, the centralized solution is determined according to the centralized model. For this purpose, a linear program with all network data is formulated and solved using Java-packages drasys.or by DRA Systems (www.opsresearch.com) and lp.solve 2.0 by M. Berkelaar (www.cs.wustl.edu/~javagrp/help/LinearProgramming.html).

The unimodularity of the basic (one standard) centralized standardization problem guaranteeing that the solution to the relaxation is also the solution to the integer program has recently been proven in Konstroffer (2001, 35–39). Still, the computational complexity of the centralized model becomes clear when we see that the number of variables (x_i for all agents and y_{ij} for all communication relations) and restrictions is polynomially dependent upon the problem size n as described by Equation 6.

$$\text{number of variables} = \underbrace{n}_{(agents)} + \underbrace{\sum_{1}^{n-1} i}_{(edges)} = \sum_{1}^{n} i = \frac{n \cdot (n+1)}{2} = \frac{n^2 + n}{2}$$

$$\text{number of restrictions} = n + 4 \cdot \sum_{i=1}^{n-1} i = \frac{(n-1) \cdot n}{2} \cdot 4 + n = 2n^2 - n$$

Equation 6: Complexity of the standardization problem (apart from nonnegativity conditions)

That is why the simulations use a network consisting of 35 agents corresponding to 630 variables and 2,415 restrictions. Other network sizes and parameter distributions have yielded analogous results. Although $c_{ij} = c_{ji}$ is not required in the course of the simulations, both directed edges can be considered for the linear program using one variable, $y_{ij,}$ by connecting the sum of both costs in the objective function of Equation 5. That does not make any difference because individual savings are irrelevant to the centralized solution.

After determining the centralized solution, the decentralized decisions are computed. In the one-period setting, the process stops after one period; later the agents can reconsider their decisions using additionally available information about their partners' previous decisions according to the relevant decision scenarios up to T periods. The whole simulation process is repeated fifty times before reducing $\mu(K)$ by 125 and then starting anew. On average, the following figures consist of 4,500 simulation runs each.

The Standardization Gap

Centralized and decentralized standardization decisions are compared using mean standardization costs that vary between 45,000 and 0. The number of agents standardizing is denoted with *no_stan*(z) (centralized) and *no_stan*(dz) (decentralized). *GE* describes total savings. Standardization costs are varied and assumed to be normally distributed with a standard deviation of $\sigma(K) = 1{,}000$; information costs are also normally distributed with $\mu = 1{,}000$ and $\sigma = 200$.

To compare the quality of decision making in both extreme forms of coordination, Figure 4.1 shows the results from randomly generated networks according to the parameter values described in Table 4.1. Cost savings for the entire network are graphed against decreasing expected values $\mu(K)$ on the abscissa. Structurally equivalent phenomena result from varying information costs instead (Wiese, 1990).

Table 4.1

Simulation Parameters (basic standardization problem)

μ(C) = 1,000	σ(C) = 200	μ(K) = *var.* (*Δ = 125*)	σ(K) = 1,000
n = 35	T= 1	B = 0.0	Q = 1

Figure 4.1 **Standardization Gap**

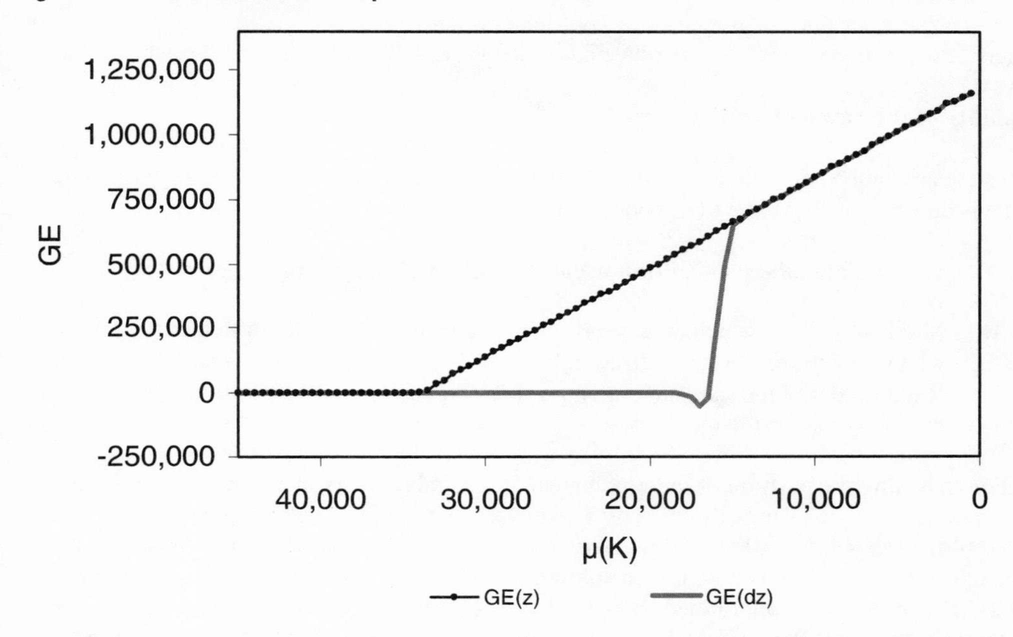

In a centrally coordinated network, all agents standardize if $\mu(K) \leq 34{,}000$. Here, the mean sum of standardization costs is smaller than information costs. In a decentrally coordinated network, agents standardize much later,[3] that is, only at significantly lower standardization costs do they consider standardizing to be an advantageous strategy. Uncertainty about their partners' standardization behavior and thereby their ability to reap network effects implies a start-up problem or excess inertia, since no agent is willing to bear the disproportionate risk of being the first adopter of a standard. All actors perceive an incentive to wait and see which standard prevails in order to avoid the risk of a premature and possibly unfavorable decision. At lower K ($\mu(K)$=[19,000; 16,700]), some agents decide in favor of standardizing, but not all of their expected partners do, which results in negative savings subsequently (i.e., wrong decisions *ex post*). In contrast, wrong decisions are impossible under centralized coordination, as the *ex post* results cannot deviate from the *ex ante* planned results. Measured against centralized coordination, too few actors standardize.

For $\mu(K)<14{,}000$, decentralized decisions equal those in centrally coordinated networks. Thus there is an intuitive discrepancy between centralized and decentralized networks that takes on the form depicted in Figure 4.1 for the basic standardization problem. In the course of this chapter, this discrepancy will be looked at in much more detail. We call this perpendicular distance between GE(z) and GE(dz) the *standardization gap* quantifying the magnitude of the standardization problem. Examples of standardization gaps are manifold and include, for example, EDI networks. Generally, it can be said that given decentralized coordination, the frequency of standardization *ceteris paribus* increases with c_{ij} or a growing installed base, and decreases with K_i. The risk of incorrect decisions under decentralized coordination leads to less willingness to standardize within the moderate range of values. Measured in cumulative, networkwide costs, the accuracy of the solution achieved in the centralized model cannot be attained by the decentralized network. On the other hand, there are no coordination costs in the decentralized model. Networkwide savings attainable through centralized coordination determine the critical value for the costs of coordination above which a centralized solution is no longer advantageous. This value corresponds to the (vertical) size of the standardization gap.

Stability of the Standardization Gap

The standardization gap is determined by the parameters $\mu(C)$, $\sigma(C)$, and $\sigma(K)$. For further analysis, it is described using three $\mu(K)$ coordinates:

- A: Left border of the standardization gap (i.e., the maximal μ(K) with centralized standardization)
- B: Maximal μ(K) at which at least one agent standardizes in a decentralized network (i.e., when decentralized standardization begins)
- C: Right border of the standardization gap (i.e., the maximal μ(K) of all agents standardizing in both coordination forms)

For analyzing the position of these points and their stability, six different network sizes (n = {5; 15; 25; 35; 45; 55}) and different cost parameters ($\mu(C)$ = {1000; 2000; 3000}, $\sigma(C)$ = {200; 400; 600}, $\sigma(K)$ = {500; 1000; 2000}) were used. Since in all simulations described above centralized coordination showed no mixed solutions, exchanging accuracy for simulation runs, the centralized results were determined using the heuristic that all agents standardize if $\sum c_{ij} \leq \sum K_i$ or no agents, otherwise. Possible deviations from the real optimum at very high $\sigma(K)$ and $\sigma(C)$ are possible but would only slightly change the position of A. As one could expect, the position of points A, B, and C is mostly determined by n and $\mu(C)$.

A: First Centralized Activities

A could always be explained by $(n - 1) * \mu(C)$. At small $\mu(C)$, increases of $\sigma(K)$ raised A slightly by up to 2,000 toward higher $\mu(K)$ values, mostly independent of n. Due to the obvious multiplicative properties, regression analysis is not appropriate here. The correlation between $\mu(K_A)$ and the mean deviations was close to 0 and not significant (to 0.05) while there was a significant correlation (0.01 level) between $\mu(K)$, $\mu(C)$, and n with $r(\mu(K), \mu(C)) = 0.54$ and $r(\mu(K), n) = 0.78$.

B: First Decentralized Activities

B showed similar correlations but also a systematic influence of both deviation parameters. An increase of both deviations implied moving the abscissa values of B toward higher $\mu(K)$ values. A formalization of these dependencies is not easy due to the nonadditive relationships. For large networks ($n \geq 35$) in which the influence of deviation values decrease, the relation can be approximated by

$$\mu(K) = \frac{n \cdot \mu(C)}{2}$$

with deviations of less than 10 percent in 94 percent of all cases.

C: Right Border of the Standardization Gap

The position of **C** is dissected not in its absolute position but relative to B, that is, those constellations where there are standardization activities in a decentralized network but no centralized solution quality is attained. Again, as well as the movement of B toward higher $\mu(K)$ values, a systematic dependency on $\sigma(K)$ and $\sigma(C)$ is found, expanding the gap with increased deviation. This can be explained as follows: since every agent has to anticipate his partners' decisions and since this anticipation implies estimating the partners' information costs to the partners' partners, a decrease in $\sigma(C)$ also lowers uncertainty because known c_{ji} become more similar and thus the estimations improve, thereby closing the gap between B and C.

The effect of different $\sigma(K)$ affects the aggregate network: the smaller the differences in standardization costs, the more similar the agents' decisions. With huge deviations of standardization costs, some agents standardize even "earlier," others always "later." The aggregate effect is an extension and flattening of both the *GE* and the *no_stan* graph.

Figure 4.2 summarizes the findings concerning the fundamental coordinates determining the standardization gap. In the next section, a multiperiod analysis of the standardization gap shows the dynamic aspects of standardization processes.

The Multiperiod Standardization Gap

In this section, a dynamic extension of the basic standardization model shows the influence of broadening the decision horizon to T periods and especially allows us to identify the number of periods before stable equilibria can be reached, that is, no additional agent standardizes.

It is assumed that an agent can decide to implement a standard only once and that after this decision he is tied to it. In other words, he can choose not to standardize until—if at all—he finds it advantageous at any one time. This is a common setting in network effect models, for example, Arthur (1989). Therefore, in this constellation, an agent cannot de-install or change a standard ($Q = 1$). Incomplete but perfect information is assumed. If an agent can see that a partner has standardized, the uncertainty about this partner's action vanishes ($p_{ij} = 1$). Thus, the state of the network (as binary $1*n$-vector consisting of all agents' x_i) and therefore the available information set can change up to $(n - 1)$ times; no later than in period n, all agents will eventually have made a decision in favor of standardization or they will no longer do so. Figure 4.3 shows the development of *GE* in the first and last period and over time (magnified).

The centralized solution is obviously the same for each period and thus only depicted once (background). One can see that the negative values of $GE(\text{dz}, t = 1)$ are neutralized over time. Uncertainty for later adopters is reduced by the costly standardizations of a few early adopters in period one. Then, they also standardize. The first movers' additional costs are neutralized and later yield benefits. This phenomenon is often called the *penguin effect* in network effect literature (Farell and Saloner 1986, 943).

Figure 4.2 **Changes of A, B, C When Varying Cost Parameters**

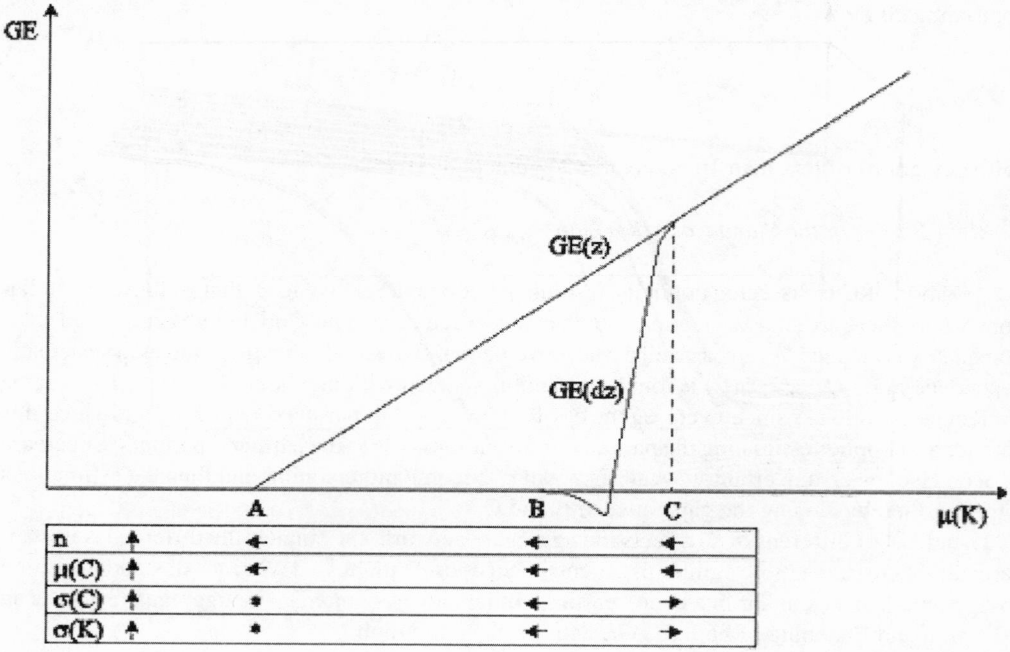

Table 4.2

Simulation Parameters (multiperiod basic standardization problem)

μ(C) = 1,000	σ(C) = 200	μ(K) = *var.* (*Δ* = *125*)	σ(K) = 1,000
n = 35	T = 10	B = 0.0	Q = 1

Figure 4.3 gives a detailed impression of the dynamics behind the penguin effect: the area between points B and C of the standardization gap shows the "speed" of the standardization process toward the centralized equilibrium. The figure shows only seven periods because afterward there was no longer any network activity. The graph in the background is the centralized solution. The penguin effect is very apparent, since the network reacts quite quickly to the actions of the first movers. As early as period three, there only are marginal discrepancies with the stationary graph.

First results of an extension of the model to *Q* standards show a sudden quite surprising second standardization gap at very low standardization costs, probably resulting from a locally persistent inefficient heterogeneity of standards.

PRACTICAL APPLICATION

Empirical research has shown that the parameters used in the standardization model are principally retrievable. For example, a survey among the largest 1,000 enterprises in the United States

Figure 4.3 **Standardization Gap Over Time** (Penguin Effect)

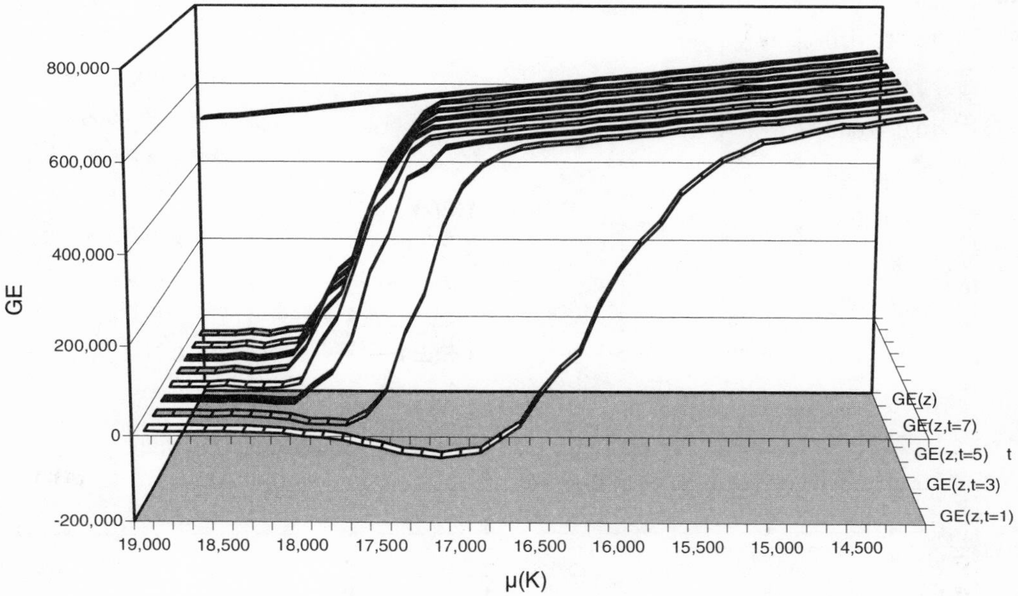

(and Germany) concerning the use of EDI revealed average annual K_i of \$457,000 (\$175,000 for Germany) and Σc_{ij} of \$3,218,000 (\$208,000 for Germany). A case study with 3COM revealed savings per business document amounting to \$36.65 (Wiese 1990).

In corporate standardization problems, this model has been successfully used to explicate the interdependencies between network agents. The model has therefore served as a network planning and controlling tool, as described in a case study that deals with the decision to use a common X.500-based directory service as an electronic phone directory among six German banking and insurance companies. Here, the magnitude of the value of standardization as well as of the standardization gap became clear. Using the directory, the six enterprises realized profits from the directory due to time savings, improved data administration and consistency, and print cost savings. Assigning the overall gains to the particular companies shows their standardization benefits. At the same time, the difference between the centralized solution (cooperative, i.e., all of the companies introduce the directory in a single centrally orchestrated effort) and the decentralized solution (each company introduces a directory due to sufficient stand-alone benefits, but there are no coordination and integration efforts) shows a concrete standardization gap in the amount shown in Table 4.3 and depicted in Figure 4.4. See Weitzel et al. (2001) for the full study.

The empirical data from EDI networks and an X.500 case study exemplify the possible value of standardization. At the same time, the problems of finding adequate coordination designs are obvious. The reasons include an asymmetric distribution of standardization benefits and costs, frequently resulting from different firm sizes. The associated problems are often discussed in the context of small- and medium-sized enterprises (SMEs) and their integration into value chains; see Beck et al. (2002) for empirical evidence.

An important area of further research from the perspective of standard users is thus the

Figure 4.4 **X.500 Costs, Genefits, and Standardization Gap** (DEM)

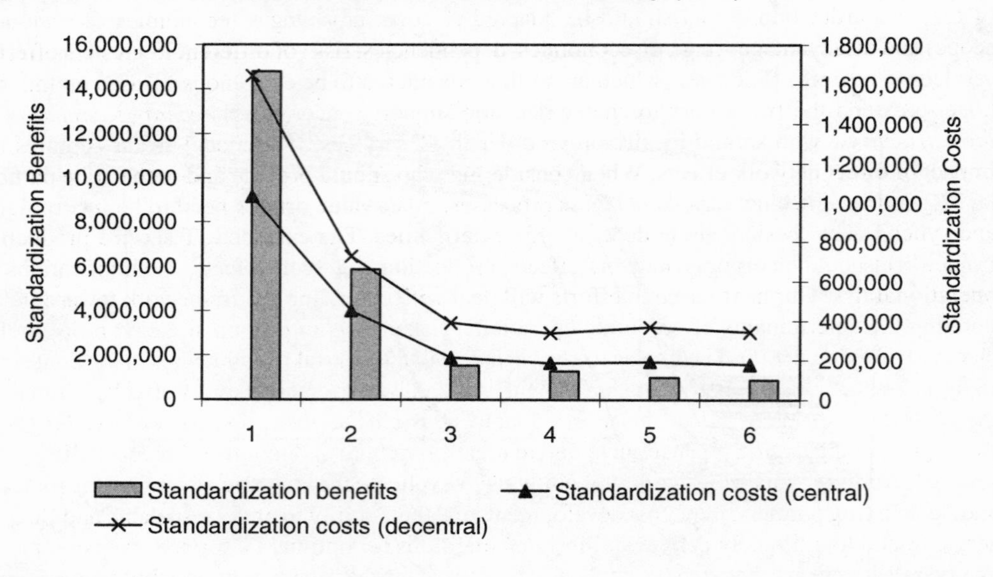

Table 4.3

Standardization Gap per Company (€)

	1	2	3	4	5	6	
€	180,000	71,000	18,500	15,500	12,500	11,000	Σ = 308,500

development and evaluation of solution strategies to the standardization problem. This could be done using and adapting the findings from larger parts of the literature on game theory, controlling and organization theory, and option price theories, to name but a few. One approach could be using the model to analyze the influence of local coalitions in networks: agents such as the firms from the X.500 case could make binding agreements with their most important (e.g., biggest c_{ij}) one, two, or more partners, imitating centralized decision behavior within their individual clusters. If coordination costs increase with the number of partners forming the coalition, we can expect to find an optimum number of internalization partners.

Empirical data concerning the cost development of the coordination costs compared to K_i, for example, could provide especially valuable assistance in evaluating coalitions as such. Standardization domains suitable for retrieving empirical data and for testing the results are, as shown, EDI networks. In this context, "fair" mechanisms should be discussed again. No distribution or cost allocation is fair per se; rather, they should meet certain requirements like those, for example, proposed by Shapley values describing power distribution between agents. See Güth et al. (2001, 100) for an experiment suggesting "that fairness concerns should be built into behavioral models of economic organizations."

FURTHER RESEARCH: SMART SOURCING OF IS INFRASTRUCTURES

Standardization is one important efficiency driver of information systems (IS) infrastructures. But in order to develop a general framework for optimal IS infrastructures there are other influences that need to be incorporated. Therefore, quite comparable to the X.500 case, the costs and benefits of the standardization model should be adapted to cover advantages (economies of scale and scope) and disadvantages (e.g., diseconomies, dependencies, risk) of different IS clusters offering services to business processes (which are at first considered to be exogenous). Based on this, we hope to extend the framework to enable decision support concerning the *smart sourcing of IS infrastructures:* who should ideally provide which IT services? The model so far captures the impact of direct network effects. When considering who should provide and orchestrate particular IT services enabling various business processes, other value drivers need to be incorporated and synchronized besides these demand-side externalities. The extended IT service production framework should incorporate network effects, production-side scale effects, and implications on operational risk. Our next research efforts will deal with extending the framework toward incorporating the determinants of corporate operational risk and its impact on strategic process efficiency (Bromiley, 1991). The goal is to derive and evaluate risk-taking strategies in the context of IS infrastructure outsourcing and trade-offs with standardization and scalability effects. Ultimately, the abstract vision is to select the most advantageous clusters of (principally) modular (ICT) services, forming *ad hoc* super services and to identify optimal institutions for orchestrating these services. Applying this framework will allow us to explicate the strategic situation of insourcing and outsourcing partners, their cost development, and their ability to provide scalable and flexible services, and to ultimately derive equilibrium conditions for optimal IT service provisioning.

Overall it appears that standardization and network problems are a reasonably new research domain of extraordinary magnitude. The main challenge for future standardization research is providing building blocks for a theory of networks that is common to a variety of academic disciplines and can be used to derive conscientious and deliberate managerial and policy proposals. Standards play a prevalent role in a modern society. As Shri C. Rajagopalachari, the first governor general of India, acknowledged after independence in 1948: "Standards are to the industry as culture is to society" (Rajagopalachari 1949, 11).

ACKNOWLEDGMENTS

The authors are grateful to the German National Science Foundation (DFG) for their support.

NOTES

1. Thus the individual implications of standardization decisions are irrelevant from the centralized perspective. In a game theoretical equilibrium analysis it becomes clear that the centralized solution is a Kaldor-Hicks optimum determining the biggest savings yet to be (re)distributed (Weitzel et al., 2003).
2. No negative cost values are used.
3. *Later* in this context does not describe a later period in time regarding one particular diffusion process, of course, but rather at parameter constellations farther to the right of the abscissa (as mostly lower *K*). Since the relevant scenario is always clear, this use of language makes a discussion of the results easier.

REFERENCES

Arthur, W.B. Competing technologies and lock-in by historical small events: The dynamics of allocation under increasing returns. Laxenburg, Austria: International Institute for Applied Systems Analysis Paper WP-83–92 (Center for Economic Policy Research, Paper 43, Stanford), 1983.

———. Competing technologies, increasing returns, and lock-in by historical events. *The Economic Journal* 99, 394 (1989), 116–131.

Beck, R.; Weitzel, T.; König, W. The myth of WebEDI. Proceedings of IFIP I3E 2002, Lisbon.

Besen, S.M., and Farrell, J. Choosing how to compete: Strategies and tactics in standardization. *Journal of Economic Perspectives* 8, 2 (1994), 117–310.

Branscomb, L.M., and Kahin, B. 1995. Standards processes and objectives for the national information infrastructure. In B. Kahin and J. Abbate (eds.), *Standards Policy for Information Infrastructure.* Cambridge, MA: MIT Press, 87–106.

Braunstein, Y.M., and White, L.J. Setting technical compatibility standards: An economic analysis. *Antitrust Bulletin* 30, 2 (1985), 337–355.

Bromiley, P. Testing a causal model of corporate risk taking and performance. *Academy of Management Journal* 34, 1 (1991), 37–59.

Buxmann, P. *Standardisierung betrieblicher Informationssysteme.* Wiesbaden: Gabler, 1996.

Cabral, L.M.B. On the adoption of innovations with "network" externalities. Center for Economic Policy Research Technical Paper Number 97, Stanford University, May 1987.

Callon, M. Techno-economic networks and irreversibility. In J. Law (ed.), *A Sociology of Monsters: Essays on Power, Technology and Domination.* London: Routledge, 1991, 132–161.

Carlton, D.W., and Klamer, J-M. The need for coordination among firms, with special reference to network industries. *University of Chicago Law Review* 50, 2 (1983), 446–465.

Carrigan, R.A., Jr. Decimal time. *American Scientist* 66, 3 (May–June 1978), 305–313.

Ceci, S.J., and Kain, E.L. Jumping on the bandwagon: The impact of attitude polls on polling behaviour. *Public Opinion Quarterly,* 46 (Summer 1982), 228–242.

Chou, D., and Shy, O. Network effects without network externalities." *International Journal of Industrial Organization* 8, 2 (1990), 259–270.

Church, J., and Gandal, N. Network effects, software provision, and standardization. *Journal of Industrial Economics,* 40, 1 (1992), 85–103.

David, P.A. Standardization policies for network technologies: The flux between freedom and order revisited. In R. Hawkins, R. Mansell, and J. Skea (eds.), *Standards, Innovation and Competitiveness: The Politics and Economics of Standards in Natural and Technical Environments.* Northampton, MA: Edward Elgar, 1995, 15–35.

David, P.A., and Steinmueller, W.E. Standards, trade and competition in the emerging global information infrastructure environment. *Telecommunications Policy* 20, 10 (1996), 817–830.

David, P.A., and Greenstein, S. The economics of compatibility standards: an introduction to recent research. *Economics of Innovation and New Technology,* 1 (1990), 3–41.

Drake, W.J. The Internet religious war. *Telecommunications Policy* 17, 9 (1993), 643–649.

Farrell, J., and Saloner, G. Standardization, compatibility, and innovation. *Rand Journal of Economics,* 16 (Spring 1985), 70–83.

———. Installed base and compatibility: Innovation, product preannouncements, and predation. *The American Economic Review* 76, 5 (1986), 940–955.

Fisher, F.M.; McGowan, J.J.; Greenwood, J.E. *Folded, Spindled, and Mutilated: Economic Analysis and U.S. vs. IBM.* Cambridge: MIT Press, 1993.

Giddens, A. *The Constitution of Society. Outline of the Theory of Structuration.* New York: Blackwell, 1986.

Glanz, A. *Ökonomie von Standards: Wettbewerbsaspekte von Kompatibilitätsstandards dargestellt am Beispiel der Computerindustrie,* Frankfurt am Main: Peter Lang, 1993.

Güth, W.; Königstein, M.; Kovács, J.; Zala-Mezõ, E. Fairness within firms: The case of one principal and multiple agents. *Schmalenbach Business Review,* 53 (April 2001), 82–101.

Habermeier, K.F. Competing technologies, the learning curve, and rational expectations. *European Economic Review* 33, 1989, 1293–1311.

Haggett, P.; Cliff, A.D.; Frey, A. *Location Models,* Volume I and II, 2nd ed., London: E. Arnold, 1977.

Hemenway, D. *Industry wide voluntary product standards.* Cambridge, MA: Ballinger, 1975.

Jansen, D. *Einführung in die Netzwerkanalyse,* Opladen: Leske und Budrich, 1999.

Katz, M.L., and Shapiro, C. Network externalities, competition, and compatibility. *American Economic Review* 75, 3 (June 1985), 424–440.

———. Technology adoption in the presence of network externalities. *Journal of Political Economy* 94 (August 1986), 822–841.

Kindleberger, C.P. Standards as public, collective and private goods. *Kyklos International Review for Social Sciences* 36, 3 (1983), 377–396.

Kleinemeyer, J. *Standardisierung zwischen Kooperation und Wettbewerb.* Frankfurt: Peter Lang, 1998.

Knieps, G.; Müller, J.; Weizsäcker, C.C.v. Telecommunications policy in West Germany and challenges from technical and market development. *Zeitschrift für Nationalökonomie* (Supplement), 2 (1982), 205–222.

Konstroffer, M. Solving planning problems with noisy objective functions—a comparison of genetic algorithms, simulated annealing, and Tabu search, and the effect of noise on their performance. Dissertation, Goethe University, Frankfurt, 2001.

Lehr, W. Compatibility standards and interoperability: Lessons from the Internet. In B. Kahin and J. Abbate (eds.), *Standards Policy for Information Infrastructure.* Cambridge, MA: MIT Press,1995, pp. 121–147.

Leibenstein, H. Bandwagon, snob, and Veblen Effects in the theory of consumer demand. *Quarterly Journal of Economics* 64, 2 (1950), 183–207.

Lemley, M.A. Antitrust and the Internet standardization problem. *Connecticut Law Review,* 28 (1996), 1041–1094.

Liebowitz, S.J., and Margolis, S.E. Are network externalities a new source of market failure? *Research in Law and Economics* 17 (1995), 1–22.

———. Should technology choice be a concern of antitrust policy? *Harvard Journal of Law and Technology* 9, 2 (1996), 283–318.

Lilien, G.L., and Kotler, P. *Marketing Decision Making. A Model Building Approach.* New York: Harper and Row, 1983.

Mahajan, V.; Muller, E.; Bass, F.M. New product diffusion models in marketing: A review and directions for research. *Journal of Marketing,* 54 (January 1990), 1–26.

Mahajan, V., and Peterson, A.P. *Models for Innovation Diffusion.* Thousand Oaks, CA: Sage Publications, 1985.

Plummer, A. *New British Industries in the Twentieth Century.* London: Pitman, 1937.

Rajagopalachari, C. Inaugural address at conference on standardization and quality control (February 1948 in Calcutta). *ISI Bulletin,* 1 (1949), 8–14.

Roever, A. Negative Netzwerkexternalitäten als Ursache ineffizienter Produktwahl. *Jahrbuch für Nationalökonomie und Statistik,* 251 (1996), 14–32.

Rogers, E.M., and Shoemaker, F.F. *Communication of Innovations,* 2nd ed. New York: Free Press, 1971.

Rosenberg, N. Technological interdependence in the American economy. In N. Rosenberg (ed.), *Inside the Black Box: Technology and Economics.* Cambridge: Cambridge University Press, 1982, pp. 55–80.

Saloner, G. Economic issues in computer interface standardization: The case of UNIX. *Economics of Innovation and New Technology,* 1 (1990), 135–156.

Teece, D.J. Capturing value from technological innovation: Integration, strategic partnering, and licensing decisions. In B.R. Guile and H. Brooks (eds.), *Technology and Global Industry: Companies and Nations in the World Economy.* Washington, DC: National Academy Press, 1987, pp. 65–95.

Tesfatsion, L. Agent-based computational economics. 2002 (available at www.econ.iastate.edu/tesfatsi/ace.htm).

Thum, M. *Netzwerkeffekte, Standardisierung und staatlicher Regulierungsbedarf,* Tübingen: J.C.B. Mohr, 1995.

Timmermans, S., and Berg, M. Standardization in action: Achieving local universality through medical protocols. *Social Studies of Science* 27, 2 (1997), 273–305.

Trebing, H.M. The networks as infrastructure: The reestablishment of market power. *Journal of Economic Issues* 28, 2 (1994), 379–389.

Verman, L.C. *Standardization—A New Discipline.* Hamden, CT: Archon Books, 1973.

Warren, M.E., and Warren, M. *Baltimore—When She Was What She Used to Be, 1850–1930.* Baltimore: Johns Hopkins University Press, 1983.

Weiber, R. Chaos: Das Ende der klassischen Diffusionsforschung? *Marketing ZFP,* 1 (1993), 35–46.

Weitzel, T.; Beimborn, D.; König, W. Coordination in networks: An economic equilibrium analysis. *Information Systems and e-Business Management* (ISeB) 1, 2 (2003), 189–211.

Weitzel, T.; Son, S.; König, W. Infrastrukturentscheidungen in vernetzten Unternehmen: Eine Wirtschaftlichkeitsanalyse am Beispiel von X.500 Directory Services. *Wirtschaftsinformatik* 4 (2001), 371–381.

Weitzel, T.; Wendt, O.; Westarp, F.v. Reconsidering network effect theory. In *Proceedings of the 8th European Conference on Information Systems.* ECIS, 2000, pp. 484–491 (available at http://www.wiwi.uni-frankfurt.de/~tweitzel/paper/reconsidering.pdf).

Westarp, F.v.; Weitzel, T.; Buxmann, P.; König, W. The standardization problem in networks—a general framework. In K. Jakobs (ed.), *Information Technology Standards and Standardization: A Global Perspective*. Hershey, PA: Idea Group Publishers, 2000, pp. 168–185.

Wiese, H. 1990. *Netzeffekte und Kompatibilität,* Stuttgart: Poeschel, 1990.

PART II

EMPHASIS ON CONSUMERS AND CUSTOMIZATION

CHAPTER 5

EXTENDING CUSTOMERS' ROLES IN E-COMMERCE

PROMISES, CHALLENGES, AND SOME FINDINGS

STEFAN KLEIN, FRANK KÖHNE, AND CARSTEN TOTZ

Abstract: *In theory, e-commerce facilitates new models of division of labor that encompass a higher level of involvement on the customer, specifically consumer, end. The notion of prosuming reflects the double role of customers as consumers and (co-) producers. Product and service customization or configuration and individualization or personalization are popular attempts to increase the attractiveness of Web applications for consumers. From a supplier's point of view, these strategies are attractive: they yield further information about (valued) customers and are efficient if large numbers of customers take over self-administration or self-service functions.*

This chapter provides classifications for different models and varying degrees of prosuming, with a focus on the telecommunication industry. Based on an analysis of drivers of acceptance and underlying customer tradeoffs, we will discuss strategic options and managerial implications for suppliers. In addition to decisions about services design and design of the configuration environment, we will highlight the role of relationship management.

Keywords: *Individualization, Prosuming, Relationship Management, Service Configuration, Telecommunication, User Acceptance*

CONSUMER PARTICIPATION IN BUSINESS TRANSACTIONS

Economic value generation has been closely linked with varying models of division of labor within and across firms (Smith [1776] 1981). The emergence of a service society has coincided with extended consumer self-service (see Bell 1974, Gershuny 1978). Authors like Toffler (1972) have extended this notion to include the consumer as part of the value chain and introduced the idea of consumers as co-producers, the so-called prosumer (see also Ramirez 1999, Tapscott 1996). In a related view, the economic analysis of households (Becker 1976, Lehmer 1993) has shown that household production is quite significant and, moreover, the patterns of division of labor within households (and, more importantly, between households and the official economy) are changing, depending on factors like household income, cost of labor (including taxes), and so forth.

Given the increasing level of price competition in almost every part of retail operations, companies have explored models of "mobilizing the customer" (Normann and Ramirez 1993), that is, enabling consumers to voluntarily take over parts of the value generation—such as picking, transporting, and assembling furniture—in return for price incentives, increased flexibility, and probably time savings. The Swedish furniture chain IKEA is one of the most prominent and successful examples of this idea. Retail banks where customers get their cash at automatic teller machines and print their account statements at printer terminals are another example of extended self-service functions.

The proliferation of the Web has opened up a rich new field of consumer self-service support (Hanekop et al. 2001). The almost universal access to the Web in homes, offices, cafés, and increasingly in mobile environments, combined with the browser as a uniform, easy-to-use interface and assumed customer benefits, such as extended availability, control, and documentation, have encouraged and enabled companies to put the following functions online.

- Private account and portfolio management, home banking (major banks)
- Administration of customer profiles (airlines)
- Access to current billing status (telecommunication companies)
- Access to insurance status and contract history (insurance companies)
- Ticketing (German Rail)
- Customer decision support systems (McEachern and O'Keefe 1998)

From Self-Service to Service Configuration

However, the vision of service configuration tasks carried out in a prosuming mode is far more extensive. It may even become the litmus test for the future success of e-commerce applications: only if companies succeed in finding new forms of division of labor with their customers will they be able to develop more advanced and complex online services (Wittke 1997). At the same time, careful *customer segmentation* is needed in order to separate "power users" with a high level of involvement and commitment from those who just want plain and simple online services. Our empirical findings indicate that prosuming preferences vary even within demographically homogeneous groups (Köhne et al. 2003).

This prosuming vision of configuration covers different aspects of consumer participation throughout the product and service life cycle (Kleinaltenkamp et al. 1996), including:

- in the innovation or design process, e.g., in consumer labs (Hippel 1988),
- in market research (Leenders and Blenkhorn 1988),
- in the selection and combination of components (customization) as part of the requirements specification process (Pine 1993), as well as
- in an ongoing selection and combination of product or service properties, in order to adjust the systems' properties to environmental parameters, contingencies, customers' preferences (personalization or individualization) or intentions. As far as the supplier is involved in this process, the customer relationship turns into a (mutual) learning relationship (Quinn 1992). Suppliers learn from customers' requirements, preferences, and willingness –to pay and involve them as co-designers. Customers are trained by suppliers to better understand and make better use of their products and services.

Classification of Modes of Customer Involvement

Table 5.1 gives a summary of supplier and customer activities and interactions related to service configuration and self-service. Activities and roles are structured along the transaction phases (or the customer buying cycle).

Table 5.1

Configuration and Self-Service Elements Throughout the Business Transaction Phases

	Information	Negotiation	Fulfillment	After sales
Supplier	Signaling (future) service options, expectations of management, involving customers as market research	Default settings vs. versioning, defining the solution space and configuration options, dominant design	Customizing services and products (build-to-order production model) and designing self-service environments	Monitoring customer behavior, CRM, engaging with customers in a mutual learning relationship, managing complaints
Customer	The (transparent) customer as *co-innovator:* Identifying and signaling of preferences and/or requirements	Customer as *configurator/ co-designer:* Comprehending and navigating in the solution space (price configuration, willingness-to-pay for combinations of features)	The *self-service* customer: selecting from available service options/levels and taking over administration activities	The persistently *active customer:* Ongoing configuration of service parameters, self-administering reinterpretation and recontextualization of services, problem-solving with FAQs or in communities

low — relationship potential — high

The examples reflect a mature form of e-commerce that requires a high quality of Web design as well as well-established customer relations and advanced customer segmentation. The level of consumer involvement varies significantly across different customer groups.

In our research we have focused on the latter (after sales) type of consumer configuration. It reflects the increasing complexity and versatility of products and services, such as intelligent homes or advanced telecommunication services (e.g., unified messaging), for which an initial configuration (customization, setting of defaults) is not sufficient, because it would limit the scope of functionality. Further, we are assuming that neither the producer (service provider) nor the product or service themselves are in a position to fulfill the configuration task without the consumer's participation. Even though intelligent systems can sense environmental conditions or mobile services can determine a consumer's location, they are not in a position to anticipate customers' intentions, plans, and wishes. In this scenario, the prosumer can only individualize and appropriate increasingly complex and versatile services through the execution of configuration tasks. At the same time, consumer configuration becomes a precondition for the suppliers and service providers to make the full potential of their services available. However, the earlier stages of identification of needs and preferences, initial configuration, and self-care are preconditions for the ongoing configuration and part of the prosumer role.

Figure 5.1 classifies the different options for customer participation in the telecommunication industry. The configuration activities are boxed.

SUPPLIERS' STRATEGIC RATIONALES

While the Web has been heralded on one hand as a medium for total customer care (Reinecke et al. 1998) and personalization (or more precisely individualization), it has been perceived on the other hand as a medium for offering services at a significantly lower cost for companies. While extended self-service, self-care, or self-administration features are indicative of a low-cost strategy, the notion of configuration is geared toward extending services while at the same time realizing cost advantages for the suppliers because of the higher involvement of customers.

We will focus our analysis on the telecommunication industry; however, we assume that our findings will be applicable to other industries as well. Telecommunication offers a rich field of research opportunities because "digital services" are more flexible than, for example, mass-customized products, and it is a context-dependent service with a large number of customers, which facilitates the deployment of individualization and self-service offers alike. In the widely saturated communication market, differentiation and customer retention move into strategic focus. The observed trend toward increasingly complex services in the telecommunication industry reflects competitive pressures as much as opportunities in an industry that has enjoyed an abundance of service innovations, which have often been difficult to market because of the prevailing network externalities. The extension of mobile services (3G and WiFi) opens a new range of location- and time-sensitive services. Figure 5.2 gives a summary of drivers of service individualization and, hence, emerging configuration needs in the telecommunication industry.

Despite a strong rationale for extended consumer configuration, which has been recently confirmed in a Delphi study (Köhne and Klein 2003), the industry is moving only slowly toward configurable services. We are seeing the proliferation of self-service portals, but the more extended configuration services are either prototypes (e.g., Hampe 1998) or niche offerings for specialized market segments (see, for example, www.daybyday.de/ or www.tenovis.de). Exist-

Figure 5.1 **Options for Telecommunication Customer Participation and Configuration**

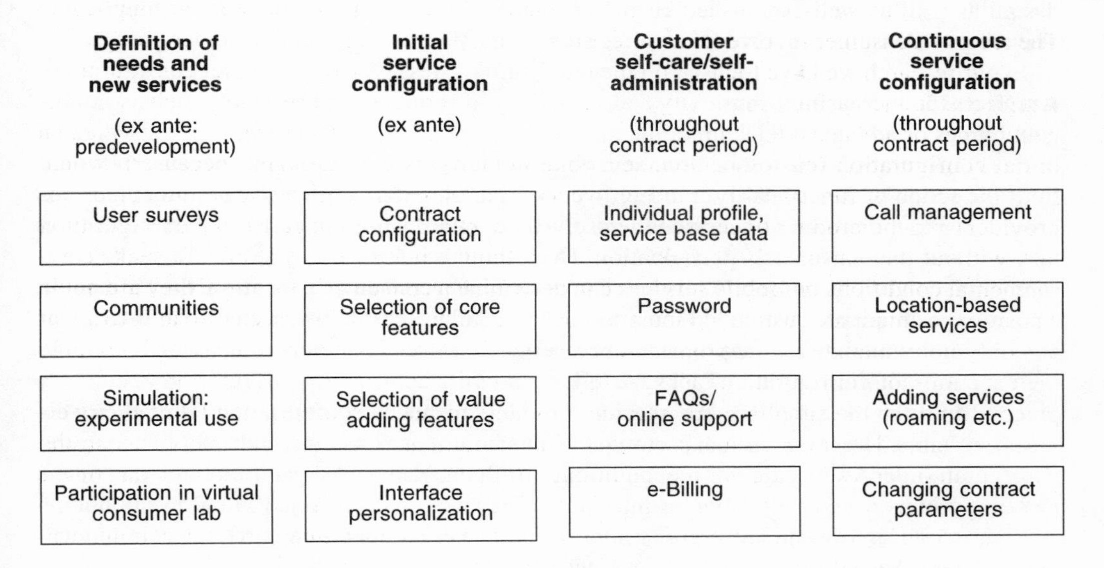

Figure 5.2 **Drivers of Service Configuration in the Telecommunication Industry**

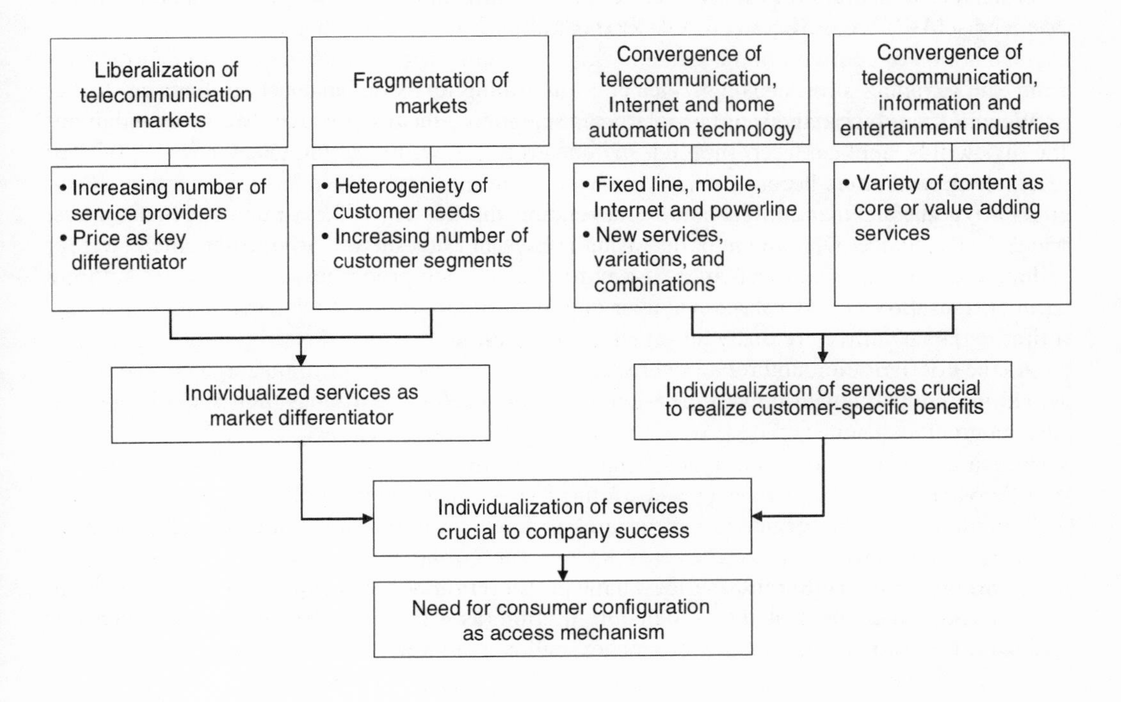

ing obstacles and barriers to acceptance from the consumer side have been studied (Klein and Totz 2004, Köhne and Totz 2002). However, the managerial implications for the suppliers or service providers have hardly been addressed.

Empirical Research Findings

1. In collaboration with a German mobile service provider we examined customer interaction with their Web-based self-service portal. Using critical incident methods and follow-up focus group discussions, the usability of representative self-service features was evaluated in 2001 and 2003. The overall negative customer feedback that was received can be largely attributed to poor Web interface quality, in particular the process evidence, which led most test subjects to prefer the call center as an interaction environment. The implemented self-service features fit into the category of self-care/self-administration in Table 5.2 (Klein and Totz 2004).
2. In order to test customers' response to more advanced configuration features, we developed an experimental prototype of a location-based recommender service for pubs. In order to use this service, an initial profile needed to be specified. Several student groups tested two different interfaces. Feedback was collected via a questionnaire-based survey and focus group interviews. The experiments captured the role of interfaces as well as joy of use, flow, and uncertainty (Köhne and Totz 2002).
3. Preferences for future service designs were collected by using an adapted version of conjoint analysis with a student group (Köhne et al. 2003).
4. A Delphi study was conducted in order to capture current thinking about the role of configuration in the telecommunication industry and among business and academic experts (Köhne and Klein 2003).

MANAGEMENT OF SERVICE CONFIGURATION

From the suppliers' perspective, service configuration is an extended aspect of their product or service policy, which targets certain customer segments. Because service configuration affects the division of tasks between supplier and customer, we will examine characteristics of their relationship and interaction.

We hypothesize that configuration and relationship design will have an influence on customers' acceptance, which is regarded as an important outcome of a market-oriented strategy (Klein and Totz 2004). Acceptance of a bundle of service properties, configuration options, and configuration interfaces as a whole or in parts primarily reflects customer preferences and attitudes. Hence, there are different levels of acceptance.

As the configuration and relationship designs are the outcome of managerial decisions, we would like to distinguish three dimensions of management and discuss their scope as well as their interdependencies:

- *Service innovation and design* address the need—in a turbulent competitive environment—to identify future service properties and, reflecting a trend toward increasing complexity and integration of service elements, service configuration.
- *Multichannel coordination* reflects the fact that services increasingly consist of mobile- or Web-based elements and that the configuration (as well as various after sales services) is offered via multiple channels (branches, call centers, the Web, etc.).

Figure 5.3 **Determinants of Service Configuration**

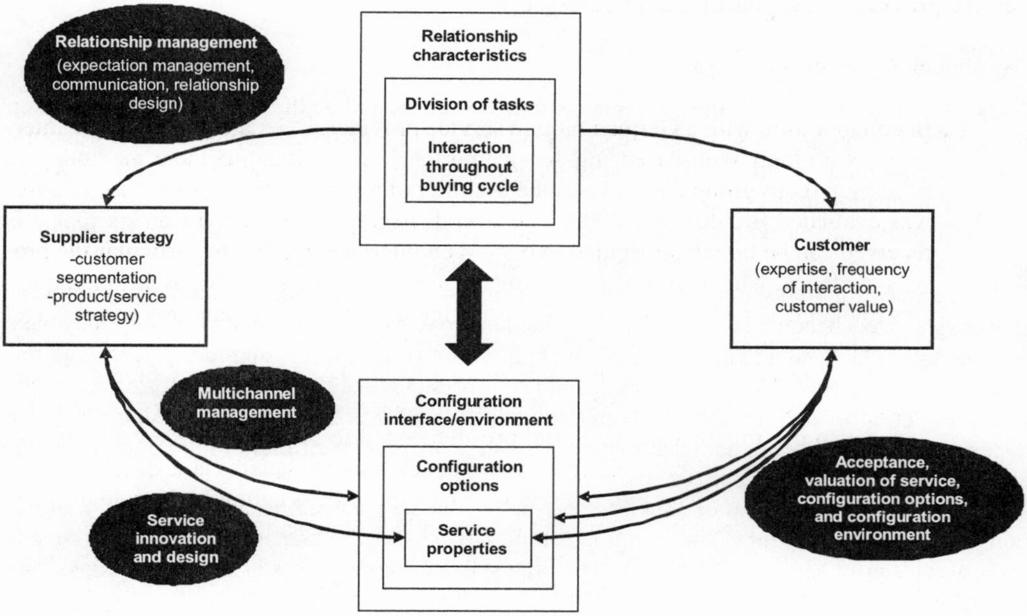

Relationship management (expectation management, communication, relationship design)
Relationship characteristics
Division of tasks
Interaction throughout buying cycle
Supplier strategy -customer segmentation -product/service strategy)
Customer (expertise, frequency of interaction, customer value)
Multichannel management
Configuration interface/environment
Configuration options
Service properties
Service innovation and design
Acceptance, valuation of service, configuration options, and configuration environment

- *Relationship management* addresses the relationship setting within which the selection and use of services (and related configuration tasks and channels) takes place. Suppliers are in a position to shape the interaction environment with their customers and to manage expectations about services, configuration options, and available channels. A major challenge of relationship management is that individual consumer capabilities determine service quality. Coaching and tutoring of consumers is thus of strategic relevance.

Figure 5.3 presents a framework of the main determinants of service configuration.

Service Innovation and Design

Service innovation and design reflect the strategic task to (re-)define the business (Abell 1980). The service provider must ask: which customer problem is addressed, with what technology, and which customer segment is targeted? Telecommunication services are a network business in three ways:

- There are positive network externalities for the customers (Katz and Shapiro 1985); hence, the challenge is to identify services that will be used (and paid for) by a reasonably high number of customers.
- Most services are made available across existing telecommunication infrastructures and by conforming to the technical standards that are available across those platforms.
- Increasingly, services are offered in collaboration with multiple players, such as specialized content providers or distribution partners.

Hence, service properties have to be defined within the range of those possibilities and restrictions.

Service Complexity and Configuration Needs

As we have indicated above, there is a major trend toward extending the range of communication modes and combining those modes (e.g., e-mail forwarding or broadcasting news to a mobile phone) across multiple, increasingly multifunctional devices (e.g., mobile handset, PC, PDA, or car communication unit, etc.).

Consequently, the need for managing the emerging complexity, defining and modifying preferences and filters, and individualizing the services interfaces is rising.

Using preconfigured settings or defaults is no longer functionally adequate as the communication devices have become increasingly embedded into day-to-day living and working. They have become individualized and appropriated symbols of life style, culture, and identity. Mobile settings are adjusted according to time, place, and contingencies, such as specific information needs or the intention to play or identify people or objects within a defined range. People become dependent on—some even addicted to—the way they organize their daily life around the availability of communication services.

As a result, configuration options become the crucial access mechanism to the wealth of options and parameter settings. The resulting complexity needs to be managed partly by the suppliers or service providers and partly by the customers, in a widening range of devices, versions, and skill levels.

However, for every trend there is a countertrend: examples from retailing (low-cost retail chains such as Aldi) or air transport (no-frills airlines) suggest that there is a market for simple, straight forward, low-price services. In the information and communication technology (ICT) field, Don Norman (1988; see also www.jnd.org) is a strong advocate for simple designs and invisible technology. Although we are aware of alternative service designs, we will focus here on the design and managerial implications of complex service designs.

Configuration Options

The different modes of configuration are driven by different motives: While the self-service mode is driven by an attempt to reduce cost, the involvement of customers in the early or late stages of business transactions aim at a more authentic participation of the customer in the value creation processes. The basic decision between an efficiency focus or extended service properties is also reflected in the design of configuration options. Configuration options might focus on

- the selection of the (default or situational) service level, which addresses, for example, the needs of high-intensity/ high-volume customers who may be particularly qualified for self-service because of their expertise and time preferences, yet, as most-valued customers might also expect special care and additional, customized service offerings if needed;
- the reduction of service cost by adjusting the division of tasks, for example, accepting self-administration tasks; or
- the extension of the scope of configuration options in order to increase customer utility and to deepen the customer relationship.

Promises and challenges of dynamically configured services can be illustrated by Negroponte's example of an individualized news service:

> What if a newspaper company were willing to put its entire staff at your beck and call for one edition? It would mix headline news with "less important" stories relating to acquaintances, people you will see tomorrow, and places you are about to go to or have just come from. It would report on companies you know. In fact, under these conditions, you might be willing to pay the Boston Globe a lot more for ten pages than for a hundred pages. . . . Call it The Daily Me. On Sunday afternoon, however, we may wish to experience the news with much more serendipity, learning about things we were interested in, being challenged by a crossword puzzle, having a good laugh with Art Buchwald, and finding bargains in the ads. This is The Daily Us. The last thing you want on a rainy Sunday afternoon is a high-strung interface agent trying to remove the seemingly irrelevant material. (Negroponte 1995, 153–154)

Our findings support Negroponte's comment that customers are concerned about their control over available service features and content that is displayed to them. While this may be partly attributed to a lack of familiarity (once customers are in a position to assess the quality of machine-generated recommendations they might be more inclined to accept them), the notion of serendipity, that is, finding something by accident, is prevailing.

The higher involvement of customers has to be reflected by appropriate economic incentives: suppliers who pursue a strategy of value-based pricing typically try to reduce customers' (perception of) uncertainties, encourage long-term relationships, and share with the customers cost savings that result from a better integration with them (see, e.g., Berry and Yadav 1996). However, the telecommunication industry has a long tradition of cross-subsidizing services. Prices often appear quite arbitrary in relation to the underlying cost structures. In particular, long distance and international calls have been charged far beyond the underlying costs, while local calls have been regularly subsidized. Largely as a result of changing regulation and increasing competition, prices for long distance calls have been significantly reduced and, where legally possible, call-by-call providers still undercut the incumbent players. In the long run, differential pricing is critical to be able to address the needs of attractive, profitable customer segments (Clemons and Weber 1993).

Configuration Options and Configuration Environment

Configuration options can be distinguished across a broad range of dimensions and properties, such as:

- Whether configuration options are mandatory or optional. Whether defaults are available.
- What the average frequency of changes is.
- What the required level of expertise to set parameters is.
- What the importance of the related service for the customer is and if it is a critical function.
- Whether the customer owns the service processes so that he or she is held responsible and does he or she have to take the initiative, and so forth.

If we collapse those configuration dimensions to bivariate complexity, we can assess the comparative advantages of computer-mediated versus human interfaces (Table 5.2). In particular, the challenges to support complex configuration tasks in a computer-mediated environment will hamper acceptance. However, if properly designed and embedded in a communication strategy, companies and customers might even detect benefits over human-mediated configuration.

Table 5.2

Configuration Environment Design Options

	Configuration environment	
	Human interface/call center	Computer-mediated environment: Web interface, mobile access to an automated phone system.
Configuration task complexity: High	*Advantage:* Typically handles uncertainty, need for confirmation, need for advice well	*Advantage:* Precise and well documentable interaction, 24/7 availability, high level of customer control
	Disadvantage: Costly, may not be (immediately) available when needed	*Challenge:* Need to manage complexity on a Web interface. Options to reduce complexity of service? Ways to compensate for the lack of human flexibility and confirmation needed. Needs to be embedded in a consistent communication strategy. Functional equivalent of "money-back guarantee" in order to build customer confidence.
Low	Acceptable, if customers pay for the service and/or the contact, can be used for additional functions such as cross-selling or market research	*Advantage:* Efficiency of Web-based self-service/ administrative tasks *Challenge:* Functional and interface design to maximize customer efficiency and satisfaction

As we assume that at least a part of the ongoing, after sales service configuration (see Table 5.1) takes place in a computer-mediated environment, we are facing a specific "click and brick" scenario (Gulati and Garino 2000, Steinfield et al. 2001): traditional (brick) services are administered and configured online (click). Customers increasingly live and work in a multidevice environment where they have to spend a considerable amount of attention to synchronize various devices. As mobile devices become more advanced, the need for a separate configuration environment, such as a PC with online access, becomes less important.

Multichannel Coordination

For the foreseeable future, customers will be able to use multiple touch points, that is, typically a branch office, call center, Web access, or an automated phone system, to communicate with the supplier. From the supplier's point of view, this raises numerous issues about the positioning and coordination of their channels (or customer touch points). This comes on top of design issues for the respective channels, some of which we have addressed in the previous section.

We have identified three major challenges:

- Signaling to the customer which functions are available via which channel. As the new channels have not been subject to the formation of social conventions that channel customer expectations, there is an opportunity and a need to shape those expectations.
- Coordinating the internal information flow across the channels. This is a precondition for professional customer service and it provides the opportunity to build a comprehensive picture of the customer interaction.

- The notion of value-based pricing is also applicable, with respect to different service and support channels. The prices (or incentives/ disincentives) should reflect underlying cost structures. This leaves room for preferential treatment of preferred customers, whose service fees could be waived.

Relationship Management

Innovation and change lead to an unfreezing of established relationships, expectations, and roles. This will inevitably lead to uncertainty. The challenge for the suppliers is to manage the transformation process, that is, to (gradually) explore new forms of interaction and models of collaboration, to involve customers in this process, and to shape the relationship with them. Even though relationships emerge out of the interaction among individuals or institutions, we assume that companies can and do actually shape the relationships with their customers. We can distinguish relationship characteristics that are part of a company's identity and image, as Quinn (1992, 138) observed at FedEx ("[I]t is FedEx's uncommon attention to people and motivation that gives the company much of its uniqueness") from those that are specific to customer segments.

The interaction between companies and their customers is primarily defined by product characteristics and channel parameters. However, in times of transformation the relationship dimension becomes more prominent. It makes explicit what is otherwise implicit in the design of products and sales channels: if the company understands their customers' needs, whether it cares and pays attention, and if it manages expectations well and lives up to its promises. The tone of communication across the various channels matters. Relationship characteristics in mass markets are like the (emotional) environment within which the interaction takes place.

Matching Relationship Types and Customer Segments

Our emphasis on consistent communication does not suggest that all companies should have a close relationship with their customers or that they should treat all customers in the same way. On the contrary, we propose that companies reflect on the type of relationship that would suit them and their customers (or specific customer segments) best and then design customer communication, channels, products, and so forth, accordingly. If a company is selling a low-involvement commodity, there is no reason to establish a close relationship; however, the expected service level and support infrastructure should be clear. Most likely, it does not make sense for a utility company to build a customer portal and populate it with content of general interest in order to attract traffic to their Web site. Hence, we propose a triangulation between (1) value propositions and product characteristics, (2) business transaction attributes, and (3) relationship attributes within a computer-mediated environment (Figure 5.4).

Interaction and Learning Throughout the Buying Cycle

A company's image is created and developed throughout various episodes of interaction. With a focus on configuration, we will look particularly into the early and the late stages of the buying cycle and the related opportunities for learning.

Understanding Customer Needs

Technologies in general and specific services do not determine their own usage. Rather, they provide combinations of features that, appropriated into various settings, can be molded into

Figure 5.4 **Triangulation between Product, Process, and Relationship Characteristics**

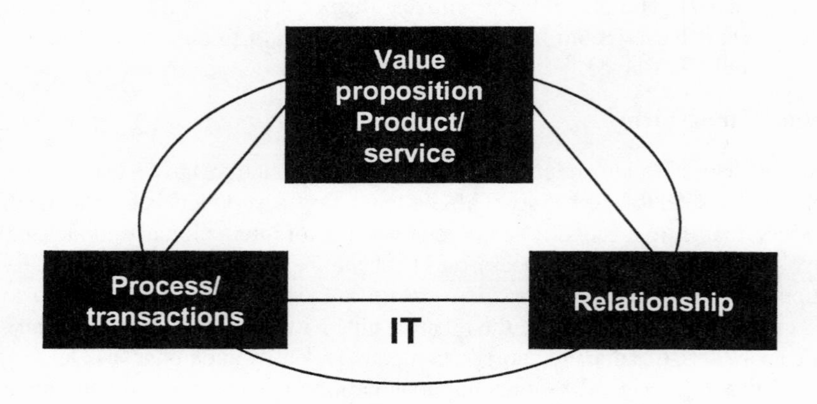

different types of usage. Hence, companies are trying to get a sense of potential uses; scope of appropriation; and the range of needs, wishes, and preferences that innovative services might fulfill.

Marketing provides a broad range of methods for determining customer preferences, such as conjoint analysis, focus group analysis, user laboratories, or trend scouts. Yet, the supplier has to decide about the type and intensity of customer involvement in this.

Hippel's (1988) notion of customer participation in innovation processes presupposes not only willing and able customers but also companies that take the trouble to involve customers in a sincere and credible manner.

The Notion of a Learning Relationship

The notion of a learning relationship between suppliers and customers (Quinn, 1992) refers to the after sales phase, when customers actually use products or services. Ideally, suppliers support their customers to make the best use of their products, for example, car companies providing driver training and giving drivers feedback based on the driving patterns and behaviors that they have monitored. At the same time, the supplier learns by observing their customers in a real-world usage situation and gains a lot of feedback.

However, to set up such tutoring and monitoring environments does not only require financial investment, but even more importantly, a relationship investment. Mutual trust has to be built as a precondition of revealing potentially sensitive insights.

Division of Tasks

Prosuming is about innovative ways of division of tasks between suppliers and customers (Meyer et al. 1999). It can be designed to be primarily substitutive, meaning service elements are "outsourced" to customers and hence are turned into self-service or complementary features. One example could be that extended service features are offered only in an electronic self-service environment.

The division of labor between suppliers and customers is a key topic in service marketing. Corsten (1999) describes the design of services as a strategic trade-off between customer and service provider activity, facilitating externalization or internalization of activities (see Figure 5.5).

Figure 5.5 **Strategic Options in Service Design**

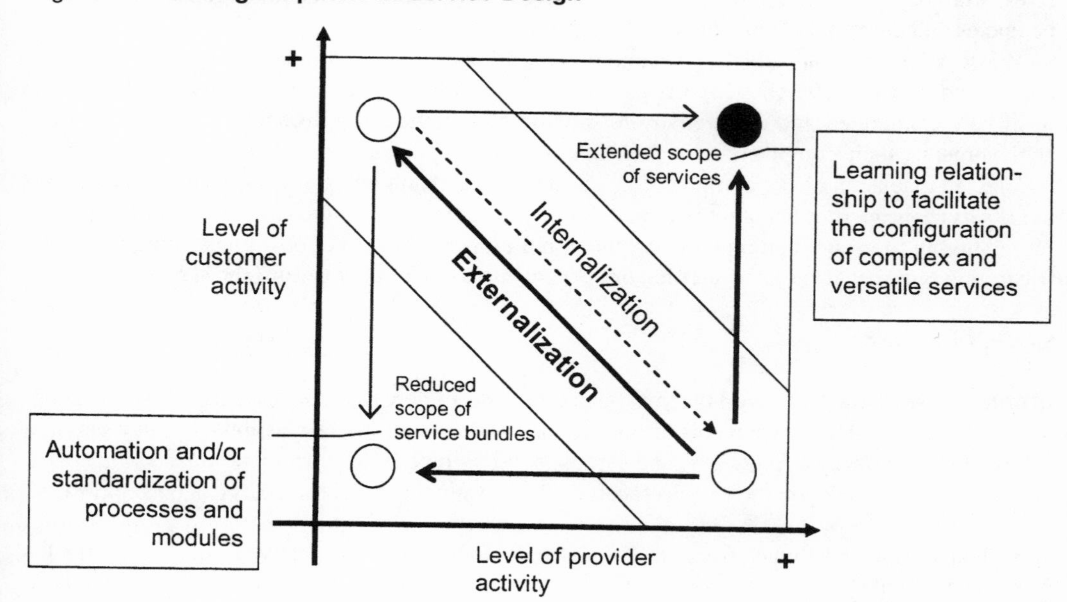

Externalization is not limited to a mere redistribution of labor but also affects the division of initiative and responsibilities in the interaction of customers and service providers. Externalization can be considered equivalent to substitutive prosuming. However, there are two variations of the pure strategies:

- If externalization is geared at involving and mobilizing customers in a broader way, then service providers have to invest in customer relations, build an infrastructure to support the customers (configuration environment), monitor usage, study usage patterns, and engage in a mutual learning relationship.
- Internalization can lead to a lower level of service provider involvement, if progress can be made in terms of automating tasks and processes.

Both strategies reflect dynamic processes in which value propositions need to be reinvented time and again.

Mobilizing the Customers and Getting Incentives Right

"Increasingly, the companies that survive and thrive are those that look beyond their immediate boundaries to the social and business systems in which they are enmeshed and discover new ways to reconfigure those systems in order to reinvent value for their customers . . . " Normann and Ramirez (1993, 74). Normann and Ramirez have studied successful examples of prosuming. They have found that it is not only about service design and reconfiguration of the value chain, but also about involving the customers emotionally. "Concessionaires have learned to master the design and management of interconnected, co-productive offerings. They have learned how to mobilize value creation in their customers and partners by reconfiguring roles, relationships, and structures. And they have learned the art of perpetually reinventing value in a dialogue between competencies and customers" (Normann and Ramirez 1993, 77).

While we have briefly addressed economic incentives, other, emotional incentives, need to be considered as well. The challenge is to design the division of tasks so that the customers are positively challenged and emotionally rewarded and satisfied and probably proud about their achievements, their competence, or their learning progress. Insofar as communication devices become an extension of our competencies, mastering them and being able to extend the range of value service properties becomes personally rewarding. However, there is a delicate balance, as a futile attempt to master certain tasks or functional properties may not only cause a high level of frustration but may also draw (justified or not) the customer's anger toward the service provider.

CONCLUSIONS

In order to assess the likelihood that customers will accept new roles and extended configuration tasks in economic terms, we resort to transaction cost economics. The attributes of uncertainty, information asymmetry, frequency, and asset specificity determine customers' transaction costs, that is, the costs to take on the various facets of the prosumer role. These costs can be kept low if:

- Transactions take place frequently—hence the focus on the respective customer segment.
- No or small partner-specific investments (asset specificity) are required. By using standard equipment and standardized interfaces, suppliers can keep these costs low. Partner-specific investments include learning or integration costs. These aspects reinforce the suppliers' dilemma between service differentiation and standardization in order to achieve positive network externalities.

Uncertainty and information asymmetry refer to the implications of a changed customer role. If suppliers or service providers invest in a consistent and comprehensive communication strategy that takes consumers' concerns and perceived risks into account and manages their expectations, they will make the prosumer role more attractive.

This chapter has distinguished different types of prosuming and configuration. It has structured the action parameters in particular from the suppliers' perspective and has argued for an alignment between services and configuration design on one side and relationship design on the other.

ACKNOWLEDGMENTS

Research for this chapter has been funded by the Deutsche Forschungsgemeinschaft (DFG). PROSUMER is a joint research project between the IOS research group at the Department of Information Systems (University of Muenster) and the Sociological Research Center (SOFI) at the University of Goettingen. The experiments were designed and executed jointly. We gratefully acknowledge the support of our Goettingen colleagues Heidemarie Hanekop, Andreas Tasch, and Volker Wittke in setting up the experiments and providing helpful insights.

REFERENCES

Abell, D.F. *Defining the Business—The Starting Point of Strategic Planning.* Englewood Cliffs, NJ: Prentice Hall, 1980.

Becker, G.S. *The Economic Approach to Human Behavior.* Chicago: University of Chicago Press, 1976.

Bell, D. *The Coming of Post-Industrial Society. A Venture in Social Forecasting.* New York: Basic Books, 1974.

Berry, L.L., and Yadav, M.S. Capture and communicate value in the pricing of services. *Sloan Management Review,* 1,4 (June 22, 1996), 41–51.

Clemons, E.K., and Weber, B.W. Using information technology to manage customer relationships: Lessons for marketing in diverse industries. In J.F. Nunamaker Jr., and R.H. Sprague Jr. (eds.), *Proceedings of the 26th Hawaii International Conference on System Science,* Vol. IV. Los Alamitos, CA: IEEE Computer Society Press, 1993, pp. 860–866.

Corsten, H. 1999. Der Integrationsgrad des externen Faktors als Gestaltungsparameter in Dienstleistungsunternehmen—Voraussetzungen und Möglichkeiten der Externalisierung und Internalisierung. In M. Bruhn and B. Stauss (eds.), *Dienstleistungsqualität: Konzepte—Methoden—Erfahrungen.* Wiesbaden: Gabler, 1999, 161f.

Gershuny, J. *After Industrial Society? The Emerging Self-Service Economy.* London: Prometheus Books, 1978.

Gulati, R., and Garino, J. Get the right mix of bricks & clicks. *Harvard Business Review* (May–June, 2000), 107–114.

Hampe, J.F. 1998. NOVICE: A solution for the awareness problem of mobile workers. In *Proceedings of the 3rd Int. Workshop "Teleworking Environments."* Turku, Finland, 1998, pp. 364–369.

Hanekop, H.; Tasch, A.; and Wittke, V. "New Economy" und Dienstleistungsqualität: Verschiebung der Produzenten- und Konsumentenrolle bei digitalen Dienstleistungen. *SOFI-Mitteilungen,* Nr. 29 (June, 2001), 73–92.

Hippel, E. von. *The Sources of Innovation.* Oxford: Oxford University Press, 1988.

Katz, M.L., and Shapiro, C. Network externalities, competition, and compatibility. *American Economic Review* 75, 3 (1985), 424–440.

Klein, S., and Totz, C. Prosumers as service configurators—vision, status and future requirements. In H. Bouwman, B. Preissl, and C. Steinfield (eds.), *E-Life after the DOT.com bust.* Berlin: Springer, 2004, 119–135.

Kleinaltenkamp, M.; Fließ, S.; and Jacob F. (eds.) *Customer Integration: von der Kundenorientierung zur Kundenintegration.* Wiesbaden:Gabler, 1996.

Köhne, F., and Klein, S. *Prosuming in der Telekommunikationsbranche: Eine Dephi-Studie.* IS Department, University of Muenster, Working Paper, 2003.

Köhne, F., and Totz, C. Personalization in mobile information services. In *Proceedings of the BITA/B4U Workshop on Business Models.* TU Delft, Netherlands, 2002.

Köhne, F.; Totz, C.; and Wehmeyer, K. Consumer preferences for location-based service attributes—A conjoint analysis. In *Proceedings of mBusiness 2003,* Vienna, 2003.

Leenders, M.R., and Blenkhorn, D.L. *Reverse Marketing—The New Buyer-Supplier Relationship.* New York: Free Press, 1988.

Lehmer, G. *Theorie des wirtschaftlichen Handelns der privaten Haushalte-Haushaltsproduktion und Informationstechnik im Wechselspiel.* Bergisch Gladbach: Josef Eul, 1993.

McEachern, T., and O'Keefe, B. *Re-Wiring Business—Uniting Management and the Web.* New York: Wiley, 1998.

Meyer, A.; Blümelhuber, C.; and Pfeiffer, M. Der Kunde als Co-Produzent und Co-Designer. In M. Bruhn and B. Stauss (eds.), *Dienstleistungsqualität: Konzepte—Methoden—Erfahrungen.* Wiesbaden: Gabler, 1999, 58ff.

Negroponte, N. *Being Digital.* New York: Alfred Knopf, 1995.

Norman, D.A. *The Psychology of Everyday Things.* New York: Basic Books, 1988.

———. Emotion and design: Attractive things work better. *Interaction Magazine* 9, 4 (2002), 36–42.

Normann, R., and Ramirez, R. From value chain to value constellation: Designing interactive strategy. *Harvard Business Review* (July–August, 1993), 65–77.

Pine, B.J. II. *Mass Customization—The New Frontier in Business Competition.* Boston: Harvard Business School Press, 1993.

Quinn, J.B. *Intelligent Enterprise—A Knowledge and Service Based Paradigm for Industry.* New York: Free Press, 1992.

Ramirez, R. Value co-production: Intellectual origins and implications for practice and research. *Strategic Management Journal,* 20 (1999), 49–65.

Reinecke, S.; Sipötz, E.; and Wiemann, E-M., eds. *Total Customer Care. Kundenorientierung auf dem Prüfstand.* Vienna: Ueberreuter, 1998.

Riemer, K., and Totz, C. The many faces of personalization: An integrative overview of mass customization and personalization. In *Proceedings of the 1st World Congress on Mass Customization and Personalization.* Hong Kong, 2001.

Smith, A. *The Wealth of Nations.* Harmondsworth: Penguin Books, 1981 [1776].

Steinfield, C.; Bouwman, H.; and Adelaar, T. Combining physical and virtual channels: Opportunities, imperatives and challenges. In *Proceedings of the 14th Bled Electronic Commerce Conference.* Bled, Slovenia, 2001, pp. 783–796.

Tapscott, D. *The Digital Economy. Promise and Peril in the Age of Networked Intelligence.* New York: McGraw-Hill, 1996.

Toffler, A. *The Futurist.* New York: Random House, 1972.

Totz, C., and Riemer, K. The effect of interface quality on success—An integrative approach on mass customization design. In *Proceedings of the 1st World Congress on Mass Customization and Personalization,* HongKong, 2001.

Wittke, V. *Online in die Do-it-yourself-Gesellschaft?-Zu Widersprüchlichkeiten in der Entwicklung von Online-Diensten und denkbaren Lösungsformen.* In R. Werle and C. Lang (eds.), *Modell Internet?* Frankfurt/Main: Campus (1997), pp. 93–112.

CHAPTER 6

HUMAN FACTORS AND E-COMMERCE

DENNIS F. GALLETTA

Abstract: *Many Web sites have been built hastily and without regard for the user. Extensive research on pre-Web user interfaces could have prevented such poor designs. It appears that both Web developers and Web users are less experienced than developers and users of other software applications. One of the most important guidelines provided by the literature is that of testing, which should be mandatory for any site to enable revision and retesting. There are several specific areas of understanding in usability that are also described, along with implications for Web designers. These areas include Fitts' Law, site organization, difficulties of user search, ill effects of page loading delay, trade-offs between site depth and breadth, options for what is seen by the user in inputs and outputs, and problems with users' mental models. Tools such as storyboards, checklists, and evaluation models are also described to prevent design errors. Once designers become aware of these guidelines, usability problems, and tools, Web site design quality might begin to catch up to that of systems sold in the mass market.*

Keywords: *E-Commerce, Fitts' Law, Human–Computer Interface, Human-Computer Interaction (HCI), Human Factors, Usability, Web Site Design*

THE PROBLEM

The scenario is perhaps all too familiar but, nevertheless, surprising each time: In an attempt to gather some comprehensive information, compare prices, and purchase a product, a user becomes frustrated with various sites and gives up in frustration. One online store was very sluggish, using an elaborate video introduction and unnecessarily large photos on each page. The second site was filled with garish graphics, contained little useful information, and triggered a pop-up window that said "Call Sales at (555) 555–1234." The third used unfamiliar terminology to categorize the information on the site and lacked a search function.

It is somewhat surprising and somewhat discouraging that most people reading this scenario will probably have experienced at least two of those three real situations. Although many might have trouble understanding why sites like these are created and why they still exist, some might chalk it up to unrealistic expectations of a shopper's ability, patience, and motivation to keep trying. However, there are more fundamental reasons that can explain the widespread nature of these problems.

Why does this occur? One likely reason is that Web site designers have been using a technique Negroponte (1988) calls "designer introspection," where the designer builds the system according to his or her own taste. To combat this tendency, McCracken and Wolfe (2004) recommend that a designer tape a large sign to the wall above the workstation that says "You Are Not Your User" (p. 37). This paper describes Web usability problems and offers methods of avoiding them based on decades of research in human–computer interaction (HCI).

Web Usability Problems

Brinck et al. (2002) describe common usability problems on the Web:

- Human perception problems, caused by allowing the physical storage of information to dictate the design or by allowing artistic style to dominate usability.
- Navigation disorientation, caused by inadequate logical architecture, insufficient indicators of the current location, or a mismatch between the site's language and organization and the user's needs.
- Human memory limitations, when too much is required of the user, over a long time frame, or when something must be memorized among other items that are very similar. A useful example: needing to remember an account number on a second screen after the first screen has disappeared.
- Database integration, where information on the screen becomes out of synch with information in the database (such as when prices change or items go out of stock), or when status information is not shown (so users might accidentally order multiple items).

Why do these problems exist? Perhaps Web designers and users are quite inexperienced.

Designers Are Inexperienced

Decades of research and experimentation on user interface design have been adopted by two design communities to varying degrees of success: those designing general use, mass market packages and, perhaps to a lesser degree, those designing high-visibility customized applications in organizations.

About a decade ago, some of the largest organizations provided software with puzzling messages, pre-installation steps, and mysterious questions. Documents were stored in folders tucked away with the applications and users often had trouble finding where they "went." Some applications were very creative, redefining the user's experience to the extent that they were placed on a bookshelf for future experimentation that never occurred. Although the user's path was obviously unpleasant then, going back even another ten years paints a sadistic picture of software designers.

In contrast, today's software mass market is close to maturity in designing applications. We have finally reached the point where the installation of a new high-market share software package (or even an operating system upgrade) provokes few puzzling questions, and, in most cases, can be accomplished in a nearly unattended short session. Today's situation might even be called uninterestingly reliable. Programs and documents are assigned by default to standardized locations, there are consistent menu and icon schemes, and most dialog boxes are standardized (for example, in most modern applications, opening and saving files will invoke the same dialog boxes). The standardization is at such an extreme that a user will not have much trouble moving from applications on one operating system to another. That is quite an accomplishment!

Custom applications used in organizations by smaller groups of users have improved as well. With a smaller set of potential users, lack of incentives to win market share, and dramatically smaller budgets, there are fewer opportunities to achieve the usability demonstrated by the mass market. While custom applications will probably always lag behind the mass market, they have also come a long way over the years.

What has changed over the years to improve usability so much? Obviously, today's mass market and corporate application designers have benefited from decades of experience in constructing complex applications. This experience has brought with it:

1. graphic user interfaces assembled with visual programming languages and oriented around objects and events,
2. interface standards recommended (or even imposed) for the operating system by the vendors,
3. high-level tools that allow creation of standard system components (such as pull-down lists, dialog boxes, and file management) with little programming,
4. published research describing usability standards and practices,
5. tools that allow users to critique quick prototypes of systems,
6. more involvement of users in defining requirements, and
7. planning for incremental improvements and other iterative processes.

It is somewhat curious that many Web designers do not seem to avail themselves of these helpful resources. One likely explanation is that Web designers come from a community that is less experienced with software design than those who design mass market and custom software in organizations.

At least in smaller firms, it might unfortunately be quite descriptive of practice to use the common joke that a firm does not have to pay thousands of dollars for building a Web site if the CEO has a computer-savvy teenager at home. For larger firms, it is common to relegate the design completely to outside consultants who self-proclaim what is often self-taught skill. In some firms, design is done in-house by computer-literate members of the marketing department. While such individuals, even the teenager, are likely to be quite creative, few of them are likely to have usability skills or even be aware of the products of experience listed above.

Unfortunately, the difficulties are not only on the developer side. There are also some difficulties caused by the inexperience of a large number of users.

Users Are Inexperienced

Decades of reductions in costs, new applications, and the Web browser have led to a larger computer market than ever before. Long gone are the days in which only computer professionals or selected personnel used computers. The most recent statistics reveal that 81.4 percent of all workers have access to a personal computer at work when omitting agriculture and manufacturing from the industries examined, and that 71 percent of all computer use at work is Internet related (Hipple and Kosanovich, 2003). According to the most recent study by Nielsen/Netratings (2003), about 168.1 million people in the United States (about 60 percent of the population) have Internet access. It is quite obvious that people from a variety of backgrounds are online.

With a small group of fervent experts, the quality of the interface is important. With a large, heterogeneous population of potential users, the quality of the interface is *crucial.* For example, an expert user might avoid using double or single quotes in text boxes, knowing that it can cause some systems to report an error message. A server's error message that warns of illegal content in the order form could cause a novice user to become very confused or frightened. They might wonder who broke the law. Another novice might try to choose multiple radio buttons at the same time and become frustrated.

The only effective remedy to reduce problems with inexperienced users is training. Such a remedy cannot cover all possible Web sites, and might even be unrealistic for a moderate number of sites, because people do not generally wish to spend as much time as would be needed to shift from "interacting with the technology [to] interacting with information, tasks, and other people *via* the technology" (Furnas 2002, 53). The desire for technology that is transparent places a large burden on the developer. The burden is to become aware of methods for improving the transparency, or usability, of systems, so that they are no longer a task, but facilitators of our tasks.

WHAT WE KNOW ABOUT IMPROVING THE USABILITY OF SYSTEMS

Unfortunately, three statements might make Web designers who are reading this throw up their hands in frustration:

- There is no ideal design for a system.
- There are no universal guidelines for every aspect of an interface.
- Sites must differ in meaningful ways or the online world will bore the user.

Fortunately, many design principles and approaches that have been adopted in the software industry can provide some help.

Design Principles

Quite some time ago, Gould and Lewis (1985) studied and wrote about three simple principles of design. A subsequent study provided a more detailed demonstration of the principles in practice (Gould et al. 1987).

The principles aim at building both usefulness and ease of use, and are as follows:

- Early focus on users and tasks (to understand them very well).
- Empirical measurement (observe actual users doing actual tasks with a candidate design or simulation).
- Iterative design (redesign as necessary and try again).

According to Gould and Lewis, using these principles is all that is necessary to achieve ease of use and usefulness. The assumption is that flaws in an early design will become obvious and will eventually be eliminated. Gould et al. (1987) demonstrated the process in a very successful design of an early voicemail system for the 1984 Olympics that had to operate in multiple languages and be used by novices who could not undergo training. The story reveals a surprising number of changes to the system as they went along.

Testing and iteration certainly helps. Based on an analysis of thirteen software development cases, Nielsen and Landauer (1993) provided some estimates of the benefit-to-cost ratio for additional iterations of usability evaluation. In Figure 6.1, the benefit-to-cost ratio beyond one iteration jumps dramatically until it reaches five iterations. Landauer (1995) provides the observation that the "benefit-to-cost ratios are rather large . . . [and he knows of] no other software engineering

Figure 6.1 **Value of Usability Assessments**

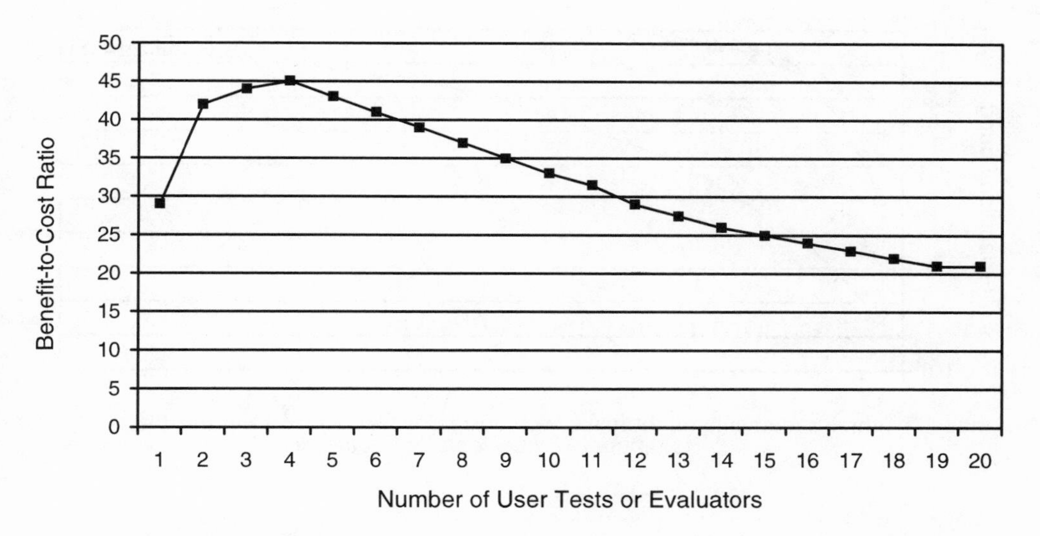

Source: Adapted from Nielsen and Landauer (1993).

techniques with anything approaching these payoffs" (p. 304). Landauer estimates that such testing is worth 500 times its cost for large systems and five times its cost for small systems.

Subsequent testing is clearly considered to be valuable, but the value decreases slightly with each test. Clearly this is dependent on the particular set of users and the system under scrutiny. Nielsen and Landauer provide the corollary of Figure 6.1 in Figure 6.2, based on the same thirteen cases. The figure shows the proportion of interface problems found in each subsequent test. In this view, the curves are subdivided into those systems with high, medium, and low detectability of problems.

Naturally, the better the initial system, the fewer iterations that would be needed, so researchers did not stop with these three principles; they continued to study and invent other useful design guidelines.

The Smith and Mosier Guidelines

At the other extreme in terms of the amount of detail offered is the classic 478-page set of guidelines from Smith and Mosier (1986). Based on a comprehensive review of the literature of that time, and not anchored to any particular technology, most of the guidelines are still quite relevant today and deserve careful attention by designers. The 948 guidelines are arranged into the following categories:

- *Data Entry* (for example, "Provide prompting for the required formats and acceptable values for data entries," p. 23)
- *Data Display* (for example, "The wording of displayed data and labels should incorporate familiar terms and the task-oriented jargon of the users, and avoid the unfamiliar jargon of designers and programmers. When in doubt, pretest the meaning of words . . . to ensure there is no ambiguity," p. 101)

Figure 6.2 **Finding Usability Problems**

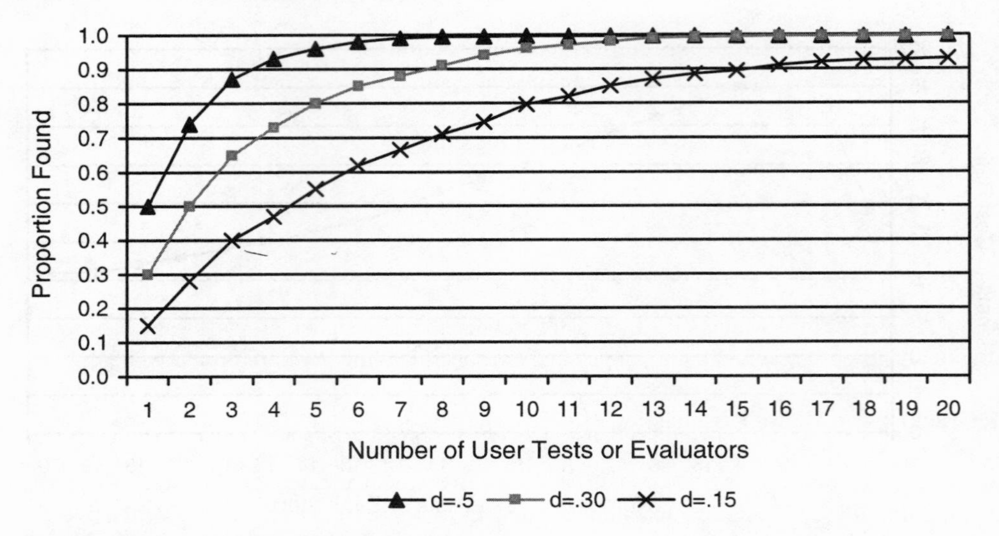

Source: Adapted from Nielsen and Landauer (1993).

- *Sequence Control* (for example, "If a command entry may have disruptive consequences, require the user to review and confirm a displayed interpretation of the command before it is executed," p. 262)
- *User Guidance* (for example, "When the computer detects an entry error, display an error message to the user stating what is wrong and what can be done about it, [such as] 'enter two letters then three digits' [rather than] 'invalid input,'" p. 316)
- *Data Transmission* (for example, "Allow users to defer the transmission of prepared messages, to be released by later action," p. 358)
- *Data Protection* (for example, "When a password must be entered by a user, ensure that password entry can be private; password entries should *not* be displayed," p. 385)

The guidelines do overlap to some extent, perhaps for the sake of completeness; the example chosen for the "sequence control" category above also appears in "data protection." Also, each category provides a very useful narrative introduction that includes design objectives. Nearly all include the following objectives:

- Consistency (of entry, display, actions, procedures, or transmission);
- Efficiency, minimizing user actions;
- Minimal memory load on the user;
- Compatibility with other tasks;
- Flexibility for greater user control.

A designer would do well to, at the very least, keep those five objectives in mind when developing systems.

Shneiderman's "Eight Golden Rules"

Shneiderman (1998) proposed "Eight Golden Rules" for designing interfaces, which he says were "derived from experience," and "should be validated and refined" (74):

1. Strive for consistency (in procedures and terminology).
2. Enable frequent users to use shortcuts.
3. Offer informative feedback (for every user action).
4. Design dialogs to yield closure (allowing people to know their progress and when they are finished).
5. Offer error prevention and simple error handling.
6. Permit easy reversal of actions.
7. Support internal locus of control (allowing users to feel they control the computer, not the other way around).
8. Reduce short-term memory load.

The eight rules offer valuable yet general guidance to the designer. However, they are intended to serve all systems in general. Guidelines that are specific to the Web are discussed below.

McCracken and Wolfe's Heuristics

Taking into account the special properties of the Web, McCracken and Wolfe (2004) specify several guidelines for designing usable Web sites. Each of the following is represented by a chapter in their book:

- Know the user. Learn who the users are, analyze their tasks, determine their surroundings, and determine how to measure quality.
- Organize content in a meaningful way. This will be discussed later in this article in more detail, but in general, if the content has a natural structure familiar to the users, then use that structure. If not, perhaps another structure (alphabetical, geographical, or chronological) is more useful.
- Organize the screen in a meaningful way. Proximity, alignment, and consistency suggest a relationship among items; contrast suggests that items are different.
- Build a prototype of key screens, test the prototype on real users, and redesign based on user feedback.
- Use colors based on their physical and perceptual aspects to make sure that text contrasts with its background and is in harmony with it.
- Become familiar with basic typography, to avoid fonts that are difficult to read. Use a basic font, use 10- or 12-point type, avoid extended use of bold, italics, or uppercase text, use 2 points of leading between lines, use cascading style sheets to facilitate changes, use left alignment, use dark text against a light background unless you are willing to enlarge the font size, and never use underlining for emphasis.
- Use multimedia sparingly, and only when it is the only way to convey important information.
- Design the site with due consideration to users with sight or motion impairments. Such impairments are discussed in the next section.
- Learn about global differences in language, text (such as date formatting), colors, icons, and images to extend the site's reach and avoid conveying the wrong ideas.
- Learn to build trust by suppression of personal information, judicious personalization, limiting of personal information collected, certification, and references.

There are more sets of principles and guidelines, but those offered above are likely to provide a good head start. It is perhaps becoming evident that there is no shortage of system design guidance at nearly any level of abstraction. Some of that guidance now addresses Web sites specifically. For example, a new book by Koyani, Bailey, and Nall (2003) has identified 187 guidelines focused on Web design. The book presents and rates each on relative importance and the strength of the underlying research evidence.

It would probably be useful for a Web designer to become familiar with several sets of guidelines for creating the first iteration of a site. Then, using Gould and Lewis's (1985) iterative approach, a final design will involve less iteration.

One additional set of guidelines is quite important yet underutilized. These are guidelines to improve the accessibility of sites to people with impairments, a topic we now turn to.

Web Site Accessibility Guidelines

Millions of people have impairments. The World Health Organization (WHO 1997) estimates that 180 million people worldwide have visual impairments and 121 million people have hearing impairments. Paciello (2000) reviews several strategies to assist those with mobility impairments.

IBM (2005) recommends producing accessible Web sites because:

- Everyone should be able to access a Web site.
- An e-commerce firm will enjoy a larger customer base.
- Worldwide regulations are emerging.
- Benefits can help everyone. Making a site accessible actually seems to make it more understandable and usable for everyone, even those without physical challenges.

The Web Accessibility Initiative (WAI) has created fourteen Web Content Accessibility Guidelines (W3C, 1999), mainly to ensure that documents "transform gracefully" to the medium that is needed (for example, to voice for vision-impaired individuals) and to make content understandable and navigable:

1. Provide equivalent alternatives to auditory and visual content.
2. Don't rely on color alone.
3. Use markup and style sheets, and do so properly.
4. Clarify natural-language usage.
5. Create tables that transform gracefully.
6. Ensure that pages featuring new technologies transform gracefully.
7. Ensure user control of time-sensitive content changes.
8. Ensure direct accessibility of embedded user interfaces.
9. Design for device independence.
10. Use interim solutions.
11. Use W3C (World Wide Web Consortium) technologies and guidelines.
12. Provide content and orientation information.
13. Provide clear navigation mechanisms.
14. Ensure that documents are clear and simple.

Finally, a very popular software tool called "Bobby" (Watchfire.com) allows for automatic analysis of the conformance of any given Web page to detailed accessibility guidelines.

Synthesis: How to Design

It seems very clear that design for usability requires testing and iteration. The entire development process might benefit from being restructured and made to revolve around usability. Brinck et al. (2002) recommend a "Pervasive Usability Process," where evaluation takes place at every stage. The stages of design include (1) requirements analysis, (2) conceptual design, (3) mock-ups and prototypes, (4) production, and (5) launch. At each stage, the results of evaluation can divert the team back to an earlier stage for additional work. For example, if a user reviews a mock-up that emerged from misunderstandings in the requirements analysis phase, the project can revisit that phase to make appropriate adjustments.

In any event, it is important to move beyond our current meager state of the art in Web development. Lest the reader believe that designers are being criticized with little mercy, it is important to look more deeply into the environment faced by a firm attempting to advance as either an offensive or a defensive move.

E-commerce touches many specialized areas in a firm. For example, in a firm such as Wal-Mart, recent moves to plan for future implementation of RFID (radio frequency identification) for inventory control can have implications on at least four independent functions: marketing, strategy, accounting, and supply chain management.

Providing adequate representation from all functions is not a trivial process. Communication barriers can be found at nearly every turn, and conflicts over resources do not help. It is important that an authority provide more strategic, objective assessment of relative importance over needs to make sure reasonable understanding of a broad variety of users is developed. For obvious reasons, identifying the users with greater accuracy would be an important early step in kicking off a testing program.

Maxwell (2002) describes a maturity model for human–computer interaction (HCI), where level 1 occurs with achievement of basic usability; level 2 is achieved when devices and software support a person's role, collaboration, and organizational needs; and level 3 provides individualized and holistic interaction. Level 3 describes an idealized future environment, where people take advantage of embedded and pervasive devices, electronic agents, and virtual presence. Let us agree that with many sites we are still chasing the pot under the level 1 rainbow in e-commerce. However, there are several cases where organizational needs have been served well in spite of poor usability, and we are prototyping on a grander scale, approaching usability after discarding earlier, immature products.

Beyond general guidelines, we know a great deal about individual interactions with software and devices; several well-known studies have been pivotal in shaping our understanding of HCI. It would be very useful for a Web designer to be aware of these theories, rules, and findings.

HCI THEORIES, RULES, AND FINDINGS

There are several perspectives in the literature that will help build usability during the design, development, or testing phases in a Web project. We will describe each one briefly to provide the interested designer or researcher with a head start.

The areas will be subdivided into those that allow understanding of human reactions to design and those that help in the design process.

Understanding Human Reactions to Design

Humans often have what seem to be unpredictable reactions to systems and their design features. After producing a "masterpiece," a designer might be extremely disappointed to find that users are not happy with the usability of the site.

A large number of studies of user acceptance have established the need for usability. In the Technology Acceptance Model (TAM), Davis et al. (1989) show that ease of use and usefulness are the two critical antecedents of behavioral intentions. Dozens of studies have provided results that are consistent with that model. Interestingly, the most recent incarnation of TAM, called UTAUT (Unified Theory of Acceptance and Use of Technology [Venkatesh et al. 2003]) modified the causal links by predicting and demonstrating that effort and performance expectancies, along with social influence and facilitating conditions, have important impacts on behavioral intentions and usage. In any event, with either model, usability is clearly an important antecedent to sustained and committed system usage.

Fitts' Law

Decades ago, Fitts (1955) discovered, in a noncomputer context, that difficulty of pointing to a target increased as the distance from the target increased and as the size of the target decreased. That is, a large target that is close is much easier to reach than a small target that is far away. The difficulty is actually based on information theory, and can be modeled in the following equation. The index of difficulty is measured in bits, but can be converted to time, as illustrated by MacKenzie (1992).

$$\textit{Index of Difficulty} = \log_2\left(\frac{2 * \textit{Distance}}{\textit{Width}}\right)$$

Jones (2003) studied Fitts' Law as one variable in an Intranet context, by providing different icon sizes (as well as colors and shapes) for an Intranet (purchasing) site. As predicted, icon size was a strong predictor of icon pointing performance, and in turn, performance was a significant predictor of attitudes about the Web site. Icon size also interacted with color and shape in predicting performance. That is, if using different colors and/or shapes of icons, the contribution of icon size is diminished.

Implications of Fitts' Law for Web design include:

- Icons should be larger, rather than smaller.
- If screen space is at a premium, the most frequently used icons should be larger than the least frequently used icons.
- Provide differentiation of icons through colors and shapes and provide icons that are easier to reach through larger size.

Navigation Behavior

Web sites are similar to menu-based systems. People hunting for a particular page will scan keywords in the hyperlinks and choose the one that sounds most promising along the "trail" to finding the desired page. Because this hunting behavior is similar to that of an animal searching for some food, it is often referred to as "information scent" (Paciello 2000). Some trails provide additional clues and stronger scent, and some trails do not, requiring the user to turn around and backtrack to find another more promising turn.

The ability to find an item depends on the categorization scheme and the user's familiarity with that scheme. The goal of the search is also important. A firm might employ different product lines, each with a particular category that is unfamiliar to the user or unrelated to the goal of the search. For example, Sony, the most popular brand of camcorders, subdivides camcorders into several categories, including Digital 8, DV, and Mini-DV. If a user is searching for a TRV-350 thanks to the recommendation of a good friend, but has no idea which of the formats is represented by that model, he or she will need to search every category until the TRV-350 appears. If the goal is merely to find the most inexpensive item, this categorization scheme will again be completely useless.

From research on menu design, we know that familiar categorization schemes can be powerful forces in leading a user to the goal extremely quickly (Norman and Chin 1988, Robertson et al. 1981). If users are unlikely to be familiar with the scheme, but know the target of what they need, it might be more effective to arrange the content in alphabetical order. For example, in searching an encyclopedia site for an opossum, many people will not know to look for mammals, then marsupials. It might be more efficient for most people to either search for the term, or, lacking a search facility, use an alphabetic set of links.

A promising option is to provide multiple paths. In the opossum case, providing both schemes will allow the zoologist to quickly move to the correct page by using the natural categorization scheme, and will also allow the grade school student to use the alphabet and browse the resultant groupings. Browsing might be the only option if the exact spelling of "opussom" is unknown.

A creative designer might arrange items into unusual but highly effective categories. For example, for children, there might be a set of categories such as "wet creatures," "dry creatures," and "flying creatures." Further subdivision in each category can include "smooth creatures," "furry creatures," and "feathered creatures." A child might be so delighted with such a scheme that he or she might browse eagerly through dozens of listings.

To sum up:

- The site designer should not assume that the user understands the firm's official categorization scheme, and should use more familiar terms if possible.
- The designer should provide search facilities if at all possible.
- The designer should provide multiple paths to important content.
- The designer may find that creative paths can be particularly effective.

Searching

However useful, search engines are not a panacea. Research has shown that novice users are confused with search engines (Marchionini 1995). Queries are often difficult to formulate, and results often include too many hits (false positives) or too few hits (false negatives). Brinck et al. (2002) and Dumais (1988) each paint a gloomy picture:

> Most people are relatively poor at searching. They use terms that are too broad or too narrow. They overconstrain the search. They don't consider synonyms. They don't know how to filter out documents that are irrelevant (Brinck et al. 2002, 169). It is clear that even the best formal query languages pose problems for users. (Dumais 1988, 675)

Users' mental models are often incorrect when they search. They often have little experience with Boolean expressions and make errors when they use AND and NOT operators (Jansen et al.

2000). They provide more information to the search engine, thinking that will result in more hits, but the result is usually the opposite of what they expect and the search becomes surprisingly more constrained by the extra terms.

In a study by Jansen et al. (2000), a surprising number of actual search engine queries failed. Fully 50 percent made errors when using the AND expression and 28 percent made errors when using OR. Interestingly, only 19 percent made errors with NOT and AND together, but a negligible number of subjects were brave enough to even try it.

To try to help solve these problems, Brinck et al. (2002) recommend several search engine capabilities, such as:

- Fuzzy search, where related items are also found;
- Spell-correction, where the engine is tolerant of less than perfect spelling;
- Alternate spellings, where the engine finds words spelled in equally acceptable ways;
- Synonyms, resulting in hits for words that mean the same as the one entered by the user;
- Stem words, where hits will be found with or without a suffix or prefix (for example, for singular and plural forms);
- "Stop words" that are not indexed, such as "and" and "to."

User searching involves five phases (Shneiderman and Plaisant 2005, 566):

- Formulation of the search expression,
- Initiating Action (submitting the expression or triggering the search),
- Review of results,
- Refinement of the expression if necessary,
- Use of the expression by various means, and for future reuse and modification.

Finally, Wildemuth (2005) provides a review of studies that focus on the design of search interfaces and shows how practice has already been influenced by those findings. Particularly interesting is the adoption by many engines of the implicit AND when multiple terms are entered. In her studies, Wildemuth showed that the most frequently used strategies were the simplest, using AND. In contrast, OR was very seldom used.

Implications of the work on search engines are as follows:

- Do not assume that users are highly skilled at searching.
- When an operator between terms is absent, assume AND.
- It would be more helpful to provide additional search features, so that users are not restricted to the use of one particular word that is spelled one way.
- Support all four phases of the entire search process, especially allowing a user to refine the search.

Response Time

Perhaps the most troublesome aspect of Web navigation is the delay imposed when moving from page to page. Several recent studies have determined that delay is one of the worst threats to e-commerce (McKinney, Yoon, and Zahedi 2002, Rose et al. 2001, Torkzadeh and Dhillon 2002, Turban and Gehrke 2000), seriously interfering with a site's usability (Dellaert and Kahn 1999, Straub et al. 2002). Delays have many causes (Nah 2002), and it is not likely that they will disap-

Figure 6.3 **An Example of Declining User Reactions with Longer Delays**

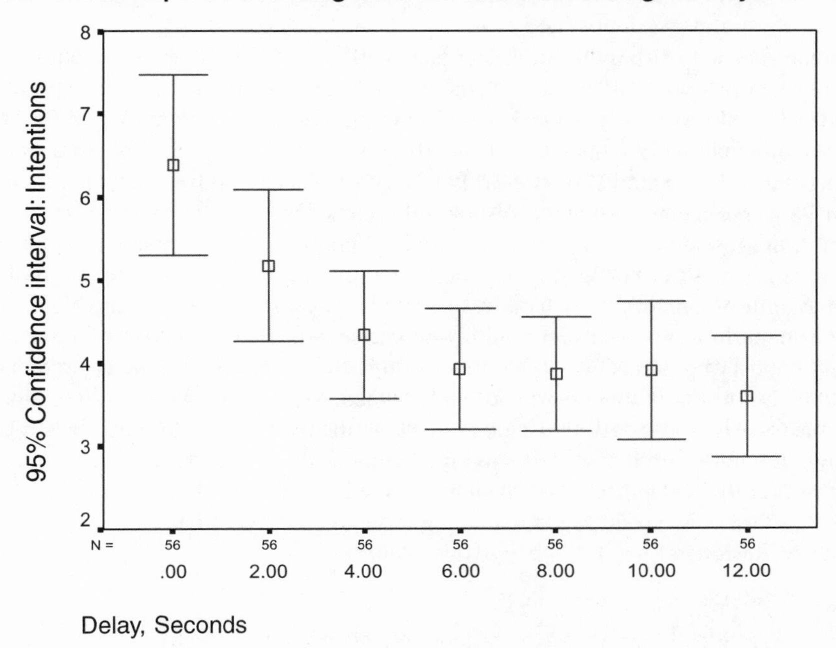

pear any time soon. The weakest link dictates the delay, whether it be the user's connection speed, congestion at the server, or server misconfiguration.

Several decades ago, Miller (1968) suggested that a response time longer than two seconds makes the interchange between user and computer less conversational. Galletta et al. (2004) reviewed the literature and found several different recommendations for maximum delay, ranging from Miller's two seconds to twelve seconds and greater. Zona Research's (2001) claim is the most intriguing of all: Web sites that match or exceed a delay of eight seconds are so often abandoned by users that the cost to the economy is estimated to be about $21 billion.

Improving page load speed from eight seconds and higher to between two and five seconds has doubled the traffic of some sites (Wonnacott 2000). Further, an analysis of the most popular sites led Nielsen (1999) to conclude that the enhanced usability of a fast site leads to increased usage.

An empirical study by Galletta et al. (2004) found evidence that user attitudes, behavioral intentions, and performance all exhibited a pattern similar to that found in Figure 6.3. Large declines in the outcome (behavioral intentions as shown in Figure 6.3) occurred immediately for subjects who experienced even a two-second delay, and outcomes of subjects in treatments with longer and longer delays continued to show lower values, but at a declining rate. The study indicated that delay is not tolerated very well, except in the case of a site with familiar organization, where there is some evidence that users are somewhat more tolerant of delay.

Lessons for the designer are as follows:

- A user's patience wears thin very quickly, so make the page load as quickly as possible.
- A user will have more patience when the site uses familiar categorization schemes in following hyperlinks to the goal.

Depth and Breadth of a Site

A designer can choose to display few links per page with several levels, or a large number of links per page, with fewer levels. The most well known studies on site depth have been performed by Miller (1981), Snowberry et al. (1983), Kiger (1984), and Jacko and Salvendy (1996). These and other studies show us that a constant number of menu nodes can be decomposed into several different structures. For example, sixty-four items can be placed into two items per menu for six levels, four items per menu for three levels, or eight items per menu for two levels.

In general, the research indicates overwhelming support for broad menus with many items. However, Larson and Czerwinski (1998) found, in applying depth versus breadth trade-offs to the Web, that limits to breadth are desirable. Designers were advised to be aware of the complexity of a list of hyperlinks and consider both layout and semantics on a page to minimize the need for scanning the list of potential links. As mentioned before, a "scent" can be offered that makes the trail more obvious, as if a person could "sniff" where to go next, like a hunting dog.

A deep site is usually less desirable because it forces the user to click through the structure and suffer many page loads and their accompanying, inevitable delays. Galletta et al. (2005) found an interaction between site depth and delay. When a site is deep, the ill effects are not as serious when delay is short. When a site is slow, making it broad (less deep) helps.

In summary, designers should therefore:

- Design broad, rather than deep, sites;
- Organize the links into meaningful, easily scanned sets;
- Deepen a site only when delay is short.

Visualization of Information

Understanding how users visualize information is multifaceted and crucial. Some of the research has addressed how information should be entered on forms that are organized into sections. Some studies address the layout of reports on the screen. Other research examines how to allow a person to browse such a large number of items that not all links to those items can fit on the screen at once. Finally, research has provided guidelines for displaying results of data analysis.

Forms are often problematic. Poor forms make use of inappropriate controls, provide inadequate feedback, or do not work at all. Good forms are short, identify required fields, provide an explanation of the purpose of each form and field, and provide a clear understanding of how to submit the information from the form (Brinck et al. 2002).

Reports can be provided in text and/or graphical format. Research has shown consistently that the choice of tabular or graphical output should focus on matching the representation to the task, making for "cognitive fit" (Vessey and Galletta 1991). The primary thrust is that there should be consonance among three factors: the user's cognitive skills, the task, and the representation of the task (as presented to the user). If there is a match, the proper mental representation will be formed, and proper solution of the problem will be possible.

Cognitive factors and aesthetics combine in Preece's (1993) guide for usability. Preece recommends:

- Only providing information that is necessary.
- Grouping information by color coding, locations and borders, or boldfacing.
- Highlighting important information so users do not have to hunt for it or draw incorrect conclusions.

- Standardizing screen displays so that users do not become confused.
- Presenting text in readable format, especially by using upper- and lowercase, using left-justification, and making sure that the space between lines is equal to or slightly greater than the characters themselves.
- Using graphics that match the user's task.
- Providing icons that work in a consistent manner.
- Using realistic colors to represent real objects and symbolic colors to represent common interpretations (for example, red would mean stop), or, lacking meaning, to differentiate objects (without overloading the user). (70–77)

Tullis (1998a, b) provides heuristics for evaluating the design of a textual screen, as well as a program that calculates an overall evaluation that correlates highly with users' subjective evaluations. The software evaluates five measures when provided a text file containing the screen layout as input:

- Ratio of uppercase characters to total characters
- Overall density (number of characters filling the screen as a percent of total spaces)
- Local density (average number of filled spaces in a five-degree visual angle around each character, weighted by distance from the character)
- Grouping (number of groupings that are made evident by calculating distances among the characters)
- Layout complexity (whether or not information appears in neat columns and/or rows)

Another view is concerned primarily with aesthetics. Many Web designers have technical backgrounds but have little training in visual design and typography.

McCracken and Wolfe (2004, 83) propose four principles of visual organization of a Web page:

- Proximity (A designer should know that when people see a small distance between items, they infer that there is a relationship.)
- Alignment (Place related items along an imaginary line.)
- Consistency (Make related items look similar.)
- Contrast (Make unrelated items look different.)

McCracken and Wolfe also point out that the printed page should not be a definitive guide for design of a Web page, and review characteristics of font size, shape, alignment, color, and other characteristics that apply to Web design. In general:

- Legibility is aided by several characteristics of the typeface, such as large size, variation in case, and high contrast with the background color.
- Many aspects are not in the control of the designer, such as the monitor's resolution, the window's size, text size, condition of the monitor, and available fonts.

It is often difficult to squeeze a large amount of information onto a small screen. Yet people want to have a large number of choices immediately at hand. There are many innovative strategies that have been proposed. Borges et al. (1997) provide a very specific list of recommendations for Web page layouts, for main ("home") pages as well as subordinate pages. With a series of usability tests, they evaluate and adjust their recommendations. Shneiderman (1998) reviews ways in which information that is not at the center of focus can be made into an abstract representation. He describes techniques such as color coding, location coding, a movable image of a magnifying glass with magnified text inside and a large amount of tiny text outside, using pinpoints on the screen, using markings in a 3-D representation of a navigable room, or shrinking into progressively smaller and smaller fonts until they collapse into lines and dots (fisheye display).

These disparate studies and visualization elements lead to the following implications:

- Provide short forms with clear explanations, labeling, and feedback.
- Provide output that matches the user's skills and the task.
- Several heuristics can enable a user to understand what is on a screen, such as simplification, grouping, and consistency.
- Case, location, density, and complexity can provide strong cues about grouping.
- Consistency and contrast are tools to indicate whether items are related or not.
- Many aspects of legibility are under the designer's control, but many others are not.
- Tools such as color coding, 3-D displays, and fisheye displays can help users wade through a large amount of information.

Mental Models

Occasionally, users have surprisingly inaccurate mental models. Such models have been studied in several fields, especially physics (Mayer 1988). Inaccuracies in understanding physics become dangerously obvious when drivers point their steering wheel in the wrong direction when slipping on ice, just as inaccuracies in understanding terminology result in searches that are irrelevant or incorrect.

Mayer (1988) categorizes knowledge into that which is syntactic (knowledge of elements and how they are combined), semantic (knowledge of meaning), schematic (knowledge of approaches to problem solving as a single "chunk"), and strategic (knowledge of how to devise and monitor solution plans).

Galletta (1985) performed an experiment to build first-time e-mail users' schematic knowledge by providing informal sketches of a hotel messaging system; such a sketch was intended to invoke their "schemata" about such systems and then infer the need for and role of corresponding functions of the e-mail system. The group members who were presented with the sketches and a five-minute explanation were able to recall more elements, capabilities, and procedures of the e-mail system than the group not presented with the schematic aid.

The lack of proper mental models can provide sometimes humorous situations, as seen in common experiences of multiple computer companies. Many computer company help lines have received photocopies of floppy disks in the mail (Carlton 1994) and calls asking "Where is the 'any' key?" Some resources have compiled such stories. *Computerworld* magazine has a "Shark Tank" column on the final page that reveals many misconceptions of technology. Rinkworks (2005) has a "Computer Stupidities" site that organizes the stories by topic. To prevent the expansion of these resources, it is rather clear that some heuristics should be followed:

- Do not make any assumptions about the Web shopper's knowledge or experience.
- Make instructions very clear and explicit.
- Build schematic knowledge whenever possible by employing useful analogies.

Table 6.1

Average Time Requirements for Selected Actions (average typist)

Symbol	Act	Time required (seconds)
K	Keystroke	0.2
P	Pointing to a target with a mouse	1.1
M	Mental preparation for a physical act	1.4
H	"Homing" the hands on the keyboard	0.4

Source: Card, Moran, and Newell 1983.

Designing the Site

Once the designer has built a reasonable level of understanding of trade-offs and user knowledge, the system is designed, built, and tested. There are several tools available to the designer.

Storyboards and Checklists

Movie directors have found that, before creating the actual product, it is very important to sketch a list of scenes in the story's sequence. Likewise, Web developers have found that the Web pages and their structure can be sketched informally, providing easier visualization of the Web site to be built. The resultant "storyboards" can be tacked up or placed on overheads and discussed by a design group. Software is also available to allow storyboard creation and manipulation. However they are developed, it is easier to make adjustments of the design on the storyboards before building the site, rather than make adjustments of the design after building the site.

Checklists are useful in complex tasks such as auditing and aviation to make sure no steps have been omitted inadvertently. Design goals and tasks can be listed, and, for each development task, a checklist can be completed to determine if any important steps have been skipped.

An illustration of the design and usage of storyboards and sets of sample checklists are available in Brinck et al. (2002).

GOMS and the Keystroke Model

No model has been more influential than the GOMS model developed by Card, Moran, and Newell (1983). GOMS stands for Goals, Operators, Methods, and Selection Rules, which are used to drive design and evaluation of a system. Rather than a single technique, GOMS represents a family of techniques that are positioned at various levels of granularity. However, most researchers have used the "Keystroke Model," which allows a designer to estimate the specific subtasks (such as typing, inserting text, and removing text) needed to accomplish a task (such as producing a document or executing a transaction) by an expert user. These subtasks can be further decomposed into micro-level acts, such as individual key presses, repositioning of the hand to the mouse or back to the keyboard, or simply having to think. From those acts, the designer can use standard estimates of time required for those acts, and then can estimate how long it would take to perform the given task.

Estimates of time required by expert users for common acts, from Card, Moran, and Newell (1983), can be found in Table 6.1.

Although the original Card et al. book describes in detail the entire family of models, many other researchers have focused on both methods and applications of GOMS. Kieras and John have studied a variety of methodological issues (see John 1996a, b; Kieras 1988) and proposed a notation. Gray et al. (1992, 1993) applied the Keystroke Model to a proposed system for use by telephone operators at NYNEX. The results underscore the importance of testing a design. The new system was designed following several principles of good design, making use of a fancy graphical interface, animations, and special keys for repetitive command combinations. However, the new system would have cost $2.4 million *extra* if deployed. After decomposing some benchmark tasks to the bottom-level acts needed, it was found that the new system had needlessly eliminated acts that occur during slack time, and paradoxically moved one keystroke from a slack period to the critical path. Using project management software to perform what they call CPM-GOMS, the researchers predicted the results of three months of testing, and the new system was not adopted.

The GOMS model is perhaps the most mature of all of the models available in the literature, and scores of empirical and conceptual studies still cite it. An e-commerce perspective certainly has concern for issues not included in the model, such as site visitation by intermittent or one-time users, the attitudes of the users, intentions to return to a site, or actual purchases. However, useful implications for the Web designer can still be drawn, such as:

- Usage can be modeled, minimizing expenditures of user time.
- Time required is a useful surrogate for effort and clumsiness of a design.
- Following principles alone might not be enough.

CONCLUSIONS

Given the extensive set of findings for enhancing usability of pre-Web software applications, poor Web designs can be prevented. Many pre-Web recommendations are also quite useful for designing Web applications.

This article has asserted that both developers and users are less experienced in Web applications than developers and users of the organizational applications of yesterday. The lack of user experience dictates that organizations make usability *more,* not *less* of a priority today, unfortunately at a time when designers seem to be less experienced as well. Furthermore, the task of Web design has an impact on several functions within an organization, so there is need for wide input and collaboration across those functions.

One of the most important guidelines provided by the literature is that of testing. Users and their tasks should be identified and target users should test the system for additional adjustments, if necessary. In some organizations, making testing a routine practice would require a dramatic change in organizational culture. Developers also would need to be prepared to make changes quickly and then test again, repeating the process as needed until adequate levels of usability have been achieved.

To provide quicker arrival at an adequate design, several areas of understanding and several tools are available. It is helpful to build awareness of Fitts' Law, impacts of terminology used in organizing a site, searching limitations, ill effects of page loading delay, trade-offs between site depth and breadth, options for what is seen by the user in inputs and outputs, and problems with users' mental models. The use of storyboards, checklists, and evaluation models can be instrumental in preventing design errors, such as overloading a site with graphics, failing to provide useful information, and confusing the user.

Stated another way, there is no longer an excuse for a site that confuses a user, requires more steps than is necessary, or fails to provide explicit prompts. If we merely become aware of interface design research that has been conducted over the last few decades, we will undoubtedly embark on the road to better Web design. Application of the findings of that research will help us arrive.

REFERENCES

Borges, J.A.; Morales, I.; and Rodriguez, N.J. Page design guidelines developed through usability testing. In C. Forsythe, E. Grose, and J. Ratner (eds.), *Human Factors and Web Development.* Mahwah, NJ: Lawrence Erlbaum Associates, 1997, pp. 137–152.

Brinck, T.; Gergle, D.; and Wood., S.D. *Designing Web Sites That Work: Usability for the Web.* San Francisco: Morgan Kaufmann Publishers, 2002.

Card, S.K.; Moran, T.P.; and Newell, A. *The Psychology of Human-Computer Interaction.* Hillsdale, NJ: Lawrence Erlbaum Publishers, 1983.

Carlton, J. Computers: Befuddled PC users flood help lines, and no question seems to be too basic. *Wall Street Journal* (March 1, 1994), B1.

Davis, F.D.; Bagozzi, R.P.; and Warshaw, P.R. User acceptance of computer technology: A comparison of two theoretical models. *Management Science,* 38, 8 (1989), 982–1003.

Dellaert, B.G.C., and Kahn, B.E. How tolerable is delay? Consumers' evaluations of Internet Web sites after waiting. *Journal of Interactive Marketing,* 13, 1 (1999), 41–55.

Dumais, S. Textual information retrieval.In M. Helander (ed.), *Handbook of Human-Computer Interaction.* Amsterdam: North-Holland, 1988, 673–700.

Fitts, P.M. The information capacity of the human motor system in controlling amplitude of movement. *Journal of Experimental Psychology,* 47 (1955), 381–391.

Furnas, G.W. Design in the MoRAS. In J.M. Carroll (ed.), *Human-Computer Interaction in the New Millennium.* New York: ACM Press, 2002, 53–73.

Galletta, D.F. A Learning model of information systems: The effects of orienting materials, ability, expectations, and experience on performance, usage, and attitudes. Unpublished PhD dissertation, University of Minnesota, 1985.

Galletta, D.; Henry, R.; McCoy, S.; and Polak, P. Sensitivity to web delays: A contingency analysis of users' tolerance for slow web sites, *Journal of AIS.* Volume 5, Issue 1, Article 1, 2004.

———. When the wait isn't so bad: The interacting effects of Web site speed, familiarity, and breadth. Working Paper, University of Pittsburgh, Pittsburgh, PA, 2005.

Gould, J.D.; Boies, S.J.; Levy, S.; Richards, J.T.; and Schoonard, J. The 1984 Olympic message system: A test of behavioral principles of system design. *Communications of the ACM,* 30, 9 (1987), 758–769.

Gould, J.D., and Lewis, C. Designing for usability: Key principles and what designers think. *Communications of the ACM,* 28, 3 (1985), 300–311.

Gray, W.D.; John, B.E.; and Atwood, M.E. The precis of Project Ernestine or an overview of a validation of GOMS. In *Proceedings of the SIGCHI Conference on Human Factors in Computing Systems.* Monterey, California: Association for Computing Machinery, 1992, pp. 307–312.

———. Project Ernestine: Validating a GOMS analysis for predicting and explaining real-world performance. *Human-Computer Interaction* 8, 3 (1993), 237–309.

Hipple, S., and Kosanovich, K. Computer and Internet use at work in 2001. *Monthly Labor Review,* 126, 2 (2003), 26–35.

IBM. Accessibility at IBM. (2005). International Business Machines (available at www-3.ibm.com/able/access_ibm/reasons.html).

Jacko, J., and Salvendy, G. Hierarchical menu design: Breadth, depth, and task complexity. *Perceptual and Motor Skills,* 82 (1996), 1187–1201.

Jansen, B.J.; Spink, A.; and Saracevic, T. Real life, real users, and real needs: A study and analysis of user queries on the web. *Information Processing and Management* 36 (2000), 207–228.

John, B.K., and Kieras, D.E. Using GOMS for user interface design and evaluation: Which technique? *ACM Transactions on Computer-Human Interaction,* 3, 4 (1996a), 287–319.

———. The GOMS family of user interface analysis techniques: Comparison and contrast. *ACM Transactions on Computer-Human Interaction,* 3, 4 (1996b), 320–351.

Jones, B. Assessing The effect of Web-site control differentiation on single step navigation. Unpublished PhD dissertation, University of Pittsburgh, 2003.

Kieras, D. 1988. Towards a practical GOMS model methodology for user interface design. In M. Helander (ed.), *Handbook of Human-Computer Interaction.* Amsterdam: Elsevier Science Publishers, 1988, pp. 136–157.

Kiger, J. The depth/breadth trade-off in the design of menu-driven user interfaces. *International Journal of Man-Machine Studies,* 20 (1984), 201–213.

Koyani, S.; Bailey, R.W.; and Nall, J.R. *Research-Based Web Design & Usability Guidelines.* Washington, DC: National Cancer Institute Publication No. 03–5524, 2003 (available at http://usability.gov/guidelines).

Landauer, T.K. *The Trouble with Computers.* Cambridge, MA: The MIT Press, 1995.

Larson, K., and Czerwinski, M. Web page design: Implications of memory, structure, and scent for information retrieval. In *Proceedings of the SIGCHI Conference on Human Factors in Computing Systems.* Los Angeles, CA: Association for Computing Machinery, 1998, pp. 18–23.

MacKenzie, I.S. Movement time prediction in human-computer interfaces. In *Proceedings of Graphics Interface '92.* San Francisco, CA: Association for Computing Machinery, 1992, pp. 140–150.

Marchionini, G. *Information Seeking in Electronic Environments.* Cambridge: Cambridge University Press, 1995.

Maxwell, K. The maturation of HCI: Moving beyond usability toward holistic interaction. In J.M. Carroll (ed.), *Human-Computer Interaction in the New Millennium.* New York: ACM Press, 2002, pp. 191–209.

Mayer, R.F. From novice to expert. In M. Helander (ed.), *Handbook of Human-Computer Interaction.* Amsterdam: North-Holland, 1988, pp. 569–580.

McCracken, D.D., and Wolfe, R.J. *User Centered Website Development.* Upper Saddle River, NJ: Pearson Prentice Hall, 2004.

McKinney, V.;Yoon, K.; and Zahedi, F. The measurement of Web-customer satisfaction: An expectation and disconfirmation approach. *Information Systems Research,* 13, 3 (2002), 296–315.

Miller, D.P. The depth/breadth trade-off in hierarchical computer menus. In *Proceedings of the Human Factors Society 25th Annual Meeting.* Santa Monica, CA: Human Factors and Ergonomics Society, 1981, pp. 296–300.

Miller, R.B. Response time in man-computer conversational transactions. In *Proceedings of AFIPS Fall Joint Computer Conference Proceedings.* Montvale, NJ: AFIPS Press, 1968, pp. 267–277.

Nah, F. Study of Web users' waiting time. In V. Sugumaran (ed.), *Intelligent Support Systems Technology: Knowledge Management.* Hershey, PA: IRM Press, 2002, pp. 145–152.

Negroponte, N. Invited Lecture, J.J. O'Hare. Keynote address, SIGCHI Conference on Human Factors in Computing Systems. Association for Computing Machinery. Washington, DC:, June 15–19, 1988.

Nielsen, J. 1999. "Who Commits the 'Top Ten Mistakes' of Web Design?" (available at www.useit.com/alertbox/990516.html.

Nielsen, J., and Landauer, T.K. A mathematical model of the finding of usability problems. In *Proceedings of INTERCHI'93, ACM Conference on Human Factors in Computer Systems.* New York, NY, 1993, pp. 206–213.

Nielsen/Netratings. Global internet population grows an average of four percent year-over-year. Nielsen Net Media, 2003 (available at www.nielsen-netratings.com/pr/pr_030220_hk.pdf).

Norman, K.L., and Chin, J.P. The effect of tree structure on search in a hierarchical menu selection system. *Behaviour and Information Technology,* 7 (1988), 51–65.

Paciello, M.G. *Web Accessibility for People with Disabilities.* Lawrence, KS: CMP Books, 2000.

Pirolli, P. Computational models of information scent-following in a very large browsable text collection. In *Proceedings of CHI 97: Conference on Human Factors in Computing Systems.* Atlanta, GA: Association for Computing Machinery, 1997, pp. 3–10.

Preece, J., ed. *A Guide to Usability: Human Factors in Computing.* Wokingham, England: Addison-Wesley Publishers, 1993.

Rinkworks. Computer stupidities (available at http://rinkworks.com/stupid/).

Robertson, G.; McCracken, D.; and Newell, A. The ZOG approach to man-machine communication. *International Journal of Man-Machine Studies,* 14 (1981), 461–488.

Rose, G.M.; Lees, J.; and Meuter, M. A refined view of download time impacts on e-consumer attitudes and patronage intentions toward e-retailers. *International Journal on Media Management,* 3, 2 (2001), 105–111.

Shneiderman, B. *Designing the User Interface,* 3rd ed. Reading, MA: Addison Wesley Longman, Inc., 1998.

Shneiderman, B. and Plaisant, C. *Designing the User Interface*, 4th ed. Boston, MA: Pearson Addison Wesley, Inc., 2005.

Smith, S.L., and Mosier, J.N. *Guidelines for Designing User Interface Software,* EDS-TR86 –278. Bedford, MA: The MITRE Corporation, 1986 (available at http://dfki.de/~jameson/hcida/papers/smith-mosier.pdf).

Snowberry, K.; Parkinson, S.R.; and Sisson, N. Computer display menus. *Ergonomics,* 26, 7 (1983), 699–712.

Straub, D.W.; Hoffman, D.J.; Weber, B.W.; and Steinfield, C. Measuring e-commerce in net-enabled organizations: An introduction to the special issue. *Information Systems Research,* 13, 2 (2002), 115–124.

Torkzadeh, G., and Dhillon, G. Measuring factors that influence the success of Internet commerce. *Information Systems Research,* 13, 2 (2002), 187–204.

Tullis, T.S. Screen design. In M. Helander (ed.), *Handbook of Human-Computer Interaction.* Amsterdam: Elsevier Science Publishers, 1988a, pp. 377–411.

———. A system for evaluating screen formats. In H.R. Hartson and D. Hix (eds.), *Advances in Human-Computer Interaction.* Norwood, NJ: Ablex, 1988b, pp. 214–286.

Turban, E., and Gehrke, D. Determinants of e-commerce Web sites. *Human Systems Management,* 19 (2000), 111–120.

Venkatesh, V.; Morris, M.G.; Davis, G.B.; and Davis, F.D. User acceptance of information technology: Toward a unified view. *Management Information Systems Quarterly,* 27, 3 (2003), 425–478.

Vessey, I., and Galletta, D.F. Cognitive fit: An empirical study of information acquisition. *Information Systems Research,* 2, 1 (1991), 63–84.

W3C (World Wide Web Consortium). Web Content Accessibility Guidelines 1.0, 1999 (available at www.w3.org/TR/WCAG10/).

Watchfire.com. Bobby (available at www.watchfire.com/products/desktop/bobby/default.aspx).

Windemuth, B.M. Evidence-based practice in search interface design. *Journal of the American Society for Information Science and Technology* (in press, 2005).

WHO. Health Report 1997 Executive Summary. World Health Organization, 1997 (available at www.who.int/whr2001/2001/archives/1997/exsum97e.htm).

Wonnacott, L. When user experience is at risk, tier 1 providers can help. *Infoworld,* November 6, 2000. p. 76.

Zona Research. The need for speed II. *Zona Market Bulletin.* Redwood City, CA: Zona Research, Issue 5, April 2001 (available at www.keynote.com/downloads/Zona_Need_For_Speed.pdf).

CHAPTER 7

BUNDLING AND UNBUNDLING OF ELECTRONIC CONTENT

NEVENA T. KOUKOVA, P.K. KANNAN, AND BRIAN T. RATCHFORD

Abstract: *New technologies are enabling firms to market traditional products such as books and newspapers in different forms (e.g., print and electronic), and to sell these different forms either as separate products and/or as a bundle. Additionally, the electronic products can be easily unbundled and the unbundled components can be rebundled with the traditional print products. For example, the publisher of the* Wall Street Journal *currently offers the following subscription options—the print version,* WSJ Online, *and a bundle of the two. Theoretically, the publisher can also sell separate sections or articles of* WSJ Online, *and the unbundled electronic units can be rebundled with the print version as well (e.g., subscription to the print version and the financial section in electronic form).*

The objective of this chapter is to provide preliminary insights into the issue of bundling of electronic content with print content, and the unbundling and rebundling of electronic content. We use choice-based conjoint analysis to obtain estimates of customer valuations of the different product options and thereby obtain useful insights. Our results show that when the same content is offered in two different forms (paper book and electronic book) and as a bundle (paper book and electronic book together), a significant number of consumers choose the bundle option, indicating that even though the content is the same, the forms tend to be viewed as imperfect substitutes or even complements. Print form still has the highest market share and has much lower own price elasticity than the bundle. Second, when the same content is offered in different forms and is also unbundled (electronic chapters), consumers become more price sensitive than in the case when the content is fully bundled. The electronic chapters option is the one with the highest market share and the lowest own price elasticity, thus cannibalizing the print book option sales. We provide managerial implications of our findings and outline areas for further research.

Keywords: *Bundling, Conjoint Analysis, Customer Valuation, Digital Products, E-Commerce, Market Share, Price Elasticity*

INTRODUCTION

New technologies are enabling firms to market traditional products such as books and newspapers in different forms (e.g., print and electronic), and sell these different forms either as separate products or/and as a bundle. Additionally, the electronic products can be easily unbundled, and the unbundled components can be rebundled with the traditional print products. For example, the publisher of the *Wall Street Journal* currently offers the print version, WSJ Online, and the bundle of the two subscription options. Theoretically, the publisher can also sell separate sections or articles of WSJ Online, and the unbundled electronic units can be rebundled with the print version as well (e.g., a subscription to the print version and the financial section in electronic form). Electronic information products are unique in that the marginal cost of reproducing and distributing them is often much lower than the cost of the print form. Consequently, the seller might be interested in selling the electronic product by itself or together with the conventional product to get additional revenue. However, many consumers may switch also from traditional print products to unbundled electronic products, leading to product cannibalization. Therefore, companies need insights on how to design and price product lines consisting of products in different forms in order to increase their total revenues.

Not surprisingly, companies selling information products are looking at bundling as a strategy to increase revenues and market shares. Bundling is the strategy of marketing two or more products and/or services as a package at a special price (Guiltinan, 1987). Two common approaches are pure bundling, whereby only the product bundle is offered, and mixed bundling, in which the bundled items are also sold separately. There can be variations in the composition of the bundle: selling multiples of the same product as a bundle (price bundling) or selling different products in a bundle (product bundling) (Estelami 1999, Stremersch and Tellis 2002).

The objective of this chapter is to provide preliminary insights into the issue of bundling of electronic content with print content, and the unbundling and rebundling of electronic content. The issues can be summarized as follows.

- How do consumers perceive electronic products relative to print products? How do they evaluate them on various attributes such as image quality, layout, browsing, convenience of use, and archival quality? How important are these attributes when making a choice?
- Is the bundling of electronic with print products attractive for consumers? What is the impact of changes in price on the purchase likelihood for the individual products and the bundle?
- Is the electronic unbundling of content and rebundling it with traditional print products attractive from a consumer point of view? What is the impact of changes in price on the purchase likelihood for the individual forms and the bundle?

In our study we use choice experiments and choice-based conjoint analysis to obtain estimates of customer valuations of the different product forms. We present respondents with hypothetical choice situations in which product offers and prices are varied to determine how choice varies with offer and price changes. Then we fit a multinomial logit model to the choice shares. Our results show that when the same content is offered in two different forms (paper book and electronic book) and as a bundle (paper book and electronic book together), a substantial number of consumers choose the bundle option, although the paper book option still has the largest market share. Changing the price of the print book has a relatively small effect on its own market share, while changing the price of the bundle offer has a very strong effect on its own market share. When the same content is offered in different forms and is also unbundled (electronic chapters), consumers become more price sensitive. The pattern of results in the case of unbundling is similar to the results when there is no unbundling, with one exception: the electronic chapters option is the one with the highest market share and the lowest own price elasticity. In general our results indicate that it may be best to maintain a relatively high price for the print book, and to set a relatively attractive price for the bundle. Also, they indicate that it may be best to unbundle the electronic content.

This chapter is structured as follows. First, we review the related literature and position our study. Second, we present our empirical results and elaborate on their implications. Third, based on our preliminary investigation and the extant literature, we suggest issues that need further investigation.

RESEARCH BACKGROUND

The extant literature in the area of bundling deals with bundling of *products* or *product components* while in the present research we study (in the first part) bundling of *product forms* (defined as marketing two or more forms of the same product together as a package). Although our focus is somewhat different, we can still derive implications for our research from the literature in the area of bundling. In this section we briefly discuss this stream of research and position our study.

The bundling research can be grouped in two broad categories, namely, sellers' motives for bundling and consumers' reaction to bundling.

Sellers' Motives for Bundling

Hanson and Martin (1990) provide an excellent overview on this stream of research. Some of the studies focus on the demand-side incentives that make bundling profitable: negative correlations in reservation prices (Schmalensee 1984, Stigler 1963), complementarity in consumption (Telser 1979), and uncertainty in the valuations of the quality of the goods (Kenney and Klein 1983). Mixed bundling is more beneficial than pure components or pure bundling, and it is the optimum bundling strategy when there is asymmetry in the reservation prices for the bundle components (Adams and Yellen 1976, McAfee et al. 1989, Schmalensee 1984). Other studies discuss supply-side incentives for bundling, focusing on digital and information goods. Bakos and Brynjolfsson (1999, 2000) demonstrate that large-scale bundling of information goods can be very profitable because it can create economies of aggregation when their marginal costs are very low. Chuang and Sirbu (1999) argue that mixed bundling is optimal for large bundles of digital information goods, and that pure unbundling can outperform pure bundling if consumers positively view only a subset of the bundle components.

Another group of studies focusing on the sellers' incentives to bundle comes from the marketing domain and uses an applied economic approach to bundling. Guiltinan (1987) integrates the theoretical rationales from the economic literature and provides a normative framework to bundling with important practical implications. Later studies focus on bundling and unbundling of industrial systems (Wilson et al. 1990), determining bundle prices and composition (Hanson and Martin 1990), and optimal bundle pricing (Venkatesh and Mahajan 1993). Recently Stremersch and Tellis (2002) examine the optimality of bundling under various conditions. They argue that bundling (either mixed or pure) yields higher revenues than unbundling if conditional reservation prices are asymmetric, and that mixed bundling is more profitable than pure bundling only when the reservation prices vary across consumers (in all other cases pure bundling yields at least the same revenues).

Finally, some articles discuss contingent valuations in bundling decisions, contrasting interrelated from independently valued products in a bundle (Guiltinan 1987, Venkatesh and Kamakura 2003). For example, Venkatesh and Kamakura (2003) model the optimal bundling and pricing strategies for interrelated products under monopoly. They suggest that moderate or strong substitutes should be offered separately; the same is applicable for complements if the marginal costs are moderate relative to the market's maximum willingness to pay. Also, the seller would gain by mixed bundling for weak substitutes/complements if the variable costs were not too high.

In sum, the above stream of research identifies the conditions for profitable bundling and specifies the optimal bundling strategies in various situations. Sellers are motivated to bundle because, on the demand side, it can help them extract consumer surplus, and, on the supply side, it can increase producer surplus or lead to cost savings. Our study extends this stream of research by examining bundling of interrelated products in the context of product forms, which is a very interesting and managerially relevant application. The unique characteristic of the above problem is that the product forms can range from being perceived as substitutes to being perceived as complements to each other. Consequently, the predictions of the marketing literature in terms of optimal bundle composition and pricing may not be applied directly. We study how consumers perceive electronic versus conventional print products, provide some preliminary results on how demand fluctuates with changes in price and product offer (e.g., print, electronic, bundle), and suggest future research that can extend the knowledge in this area. Furthermore, we also outline a choice-based conjoint methodology that can be used to estimate demand for product offers at various price levels and, as a result, recommend optimal product line design and pricing.

Consumers' Reactions to Bundling

These studies come from the consumer behavior literature and focus on the psychology of consumer judgment and choice behavior. Most of the research is grounded in prospect theory (Kahneman and Tversky 1979) and mental accounting (Thaler 1985). Research on mental accounting and related framing effects predicts that the integration (bundling) vs. segregation (debundling) of gains and losses for otherwise equivalent prospects influences evaluation and choice (Johnson et al. 1999). Specifically, individuals prefer to segregate gains and integrate losses (Thaler 1985). The mental accounting principles prevail in the absence of percentage-based frames (Heath et al. 1995), but mental accounting principles, price perception, and reference dependence are sensitive to the ways deviations from reference states are framed.

In terms of evaluation process, there is evidence that buyers average or balance the evaluations of the individual items when evaluating product bundles (Gaeth et al. 1990), or use anchoring and adjustment (Yadav 1995). The evaluation of a bundle depends on the price leader as well (Yadav 1995). With respect to price information, more positive evaluations result from integrating price information and segregating discount information (Johnson et al. 1999), and savings offered directly on the bundle have a greater relative impact than savings offered on the individual items (Yadav and Monroe 1993). Moreover, the partitioned presentation of multicomponent bundle prices raises evaluations and choice proportions relative to consolidated presentation of an equivalent total price (Chakravarti et al. 2002). Some of the latest studies on consumer reactions to bundling focus on questions such as the effects of price bundling on postpurchase consumption behavior (Soman and Gourville 2001), bundling of options (Hamilton 2003), and price discount framing (Janiszewski and da Cunha 2004).

In sum, the prospect theory and the principles of mental accounting have been very helpful in describing the reactions of consumers to bundling. Although they have been extended into various contexts, there are still interesting issues and areas that need further investigation. Most of the behavioral studies so far focus on bundles composed of complements (e.g., computer and printer) and investigate how consumers evaluate such bundles and the optimal strategies for price and discount information presentation. In our study we focus on different forms of the same product (interrelated products that can be seen as either substitutes or complements) and evaluate how consumers perceive the forms and/or the product form bundle and how likely they are to make a purchase. Moreover, we study the attractiveness of unbundling of content in digital form and rebundling it with print products from a buyer's point of view. The unbundling and rebundling of content has important implications in the area of personalization of product offering and customization, especially when applied to electronic products.

Although many publishers provide content online, others (e.g., marketers of full-length books, reference materials, music, and videos) are still cautious in distributing content in digital form over the Internet. While there are good reasons for such a cautious approach, namely piracy of content and bandwidth constraints, it is clear that technological solutions are emerging that will enable these publishers to sell and distribute content freely on the Internet, in addition to providing content in traditional forms such as print books, newspapers, and CDs (Kannan and Jain 2003). Our study is an important step in providing preliminary insights in the area of bundling of print and electronic products, and in the area of unbundling of electronic content. Furthermore, the application in the book category can be easily extended to other categories such as magazines, newspapers, and music.

METHODOLOGY

Choice-Based Conjoint Analysis

We use a conjoint analysis that has been proven successful in understanding consumers' reactions to and evaluations of predetermined attribute combinations that represent potential products or services (Hair et al. 1995). The choice-based conjoint is a relatively new type of conjoint analysis and is considered to better approximate actual decision processes as compared to the traditional ratings or rankings-based conjoint analyses.[1] Consequently, more realistic aggregate-level estimates are expected. Moreover, choice-based conjoint analysis provides quantitative estimates of the interaction between price and other factors considered important (Hair et al. 1995).

Study Design

We designed a conjoint study with the following characteristics. The subjects were presented with a situation (Situation 1) in which they would consider the purchase of a reference book relevant to their occupation (see Table 7.1 for situation description). The book was offered in two alternative forms, a hard cover print-and-bound book and an electronic (PDF) book, and the subjects could buy a single form or a bundle of the two forms. They were also informed that a hard cover print-and-bound book of similar subject material and content generally sells for around $100. Then, the subjects were presented with sixteen choice sets with three options in each set—two randomly selected product offers and the "no choice" option. The two product options were drawn from three possible product forms (print book, electronic book, and bundle) with three price levels each (high, medium, low) for a total of nine product options. Additionally, we did not allow the same product option to be presented at two different price levels in the same choice set—for example, print book at the low price and print book at the medium price—but two different product options were allowed to be at the same or different price levels (e.g., print book at the high price and electronic book at the low price in the same choice set, or print book at the high price and electronic book at the high price in the same choice set). The medium price level of a print or electronic book was set at $100, and the low and high price levels were calculated 25 percent lower or higher, respectively (see Table 7.2 for price information). The medium bundle price was computed as 40 percent less than the sum of the print and electronic book prices, and the other two bundle price levels were derived using several assumptions.[2]

Table 7.1

Situation Descriptions

Situation 1	Situation 2
You are considering the purchase of a book, which is very well written, up-to-date, and relevant to your occupation. You have used this book before and know that it's valuable. You are confident that you will use it as a reference book in the future. It will be nice to have it in your personal library. The book is offered in two alternative forms: a hard cover print-and-bound book and an electronic (PDF) format. A hard cover print-and-bound book form of similar subject material and content generally sells for around $100.	You are registered for a class at the University of Maryland. The class is relevant to your major requirement or occupation. There is one required book for the class. It has a total of ten chapters. From the syllabus, you realize that you will be required to use only five chapters from the book. The average retail price of books with similar content and subject material is around $100 (hard cover print-and-bound book). The book is offered in hard cover print-and-bound form as well as in electronic (PDF) form. In addition, you could buy any five chapters of the book in electronic (PDF) form for a special price.

Table 7.2

Product Offers with Price Levels for Situation 1

	Price ($)		
Product offer	High	Medium	Low
Print book	124.99	99.99	79.99
Electronic book	124.99	99.99	79.99
Print book and electronic book	157.49	142.99	129.99

After finishing the first task, the subjects were presented with a second task (Situation 2) in which they would consider the purchase of a book required for a class they were planning to take. While in Situation 1 the respondents considered a reference book and were uncertain about the specific content or when in the future they are going to use it, in Situation 2 their task was made relatively certain. The book had a total of ten chapters, and the subjects were told they would need to study five chapters from the book for the class they would be taking the next semester (see Table 7.1 for situation description). The subjects could buy any of the following five product options: (1) print book, (2) electronic book, (3) any five chapters of the book in electronic format, (4) print book and electronic book as a bundle, or (5) print book and any five chapters in electronic format as a bundle. They were also informed that a hard cover print-and-bound book of similar subject material and content generally sells for around $100. Then, the subjects were presented with sixteen choice sets with three options in each set—two randomly selected product offers and the no choice option. The two product offers were drawn from the fifteen possible combinations of product forms (print book, electronic book, electronic chapters, print book and electronic book bundle, print book and electronic chapters bundle) and price levels (high, medium, low). Similar to Situation 1, we did not allow the same product option to be presented at two different price levels in the same choice set, but two different product options could be at the same or different price levels in the same choice set. As in Situation 1, the medium price level of a print or electronic book was set at $100, and the low and high price levels were calculated 25

Table 7.3

Product Offers with Price Levels for Situation 2

Product offer	Price ($)		
	High	Medium	Low
Print book	124.99	99.99	79.99
Electronic book	124.99	99.99	79.99
Electronic chapters	73.49	69.99	66.89
Print book and electronic book	157.49	149.99	142.89
Print book and electronic chapters	142.89	135.99	129.49

percent lower or higher, respectively (see Table 7.3 for price information). The medium bundle price was computed as 33 percent less than the sum of the print and electronic book prices, and the other two bundle price levels were derived using several assumptions.[3]

After finishing the second task, respondents are asked to compare electronic (PDF) format with traditional print format using several attributes: image quality, layout, ease of browsing, convenience of use, and archival quality (using a 1–7 Likert scale, with higher numbers indicating print is better than electronic format for the specific attribute). Additionally, they evaluated the importance of each of the above attributes when making a choice (using a 1–7 Likert scale; the higher the number, the more important the attribute). Finally, respondents stated what they considered to be a fair price for an electronic book, given that the print book cost $50, and whether they perceived print books and electronic books as substitutes for each other, complements to each other, or unrelated products. Several questions dealing with demographic information were included as well.

Modeling Consumer Preferences

We fit a multinomial logit model to the conjoint data (separately for Situation 1 and Situation 2) to estimate consumers' choice probabilities for the different product options and the market share of these options. Specifically, we used the latent class approach developed by Kamakura and Russell (1989) to control for consumer heterogeneity. The above approach uses the observed purchase histories (in our study these are the stated choices in the sixteen-choice sets in each situation) to classify consumers into a small number of segments, each characterized by a vector of mean preferences and a single price sensitivity parameter. Then, a consumer's choice probability was expressed in terms of the choice probabilities corresponding to the various segments. The probability of choosing option *j*, conditional on consumer *k* being a member of segment *i*, is expressed as:

$$P_j(u_i, \beta_i, X_{kt}) = \exp(u_{ji} + \beta_i X_{jkt}) / (1 + \Sigma \exp(u_{ji} + \beta_i X_{jkt})) \quad (1)$$

where u_{ji} is the intrinsic utility of option *j* for segment *i*, β_i is the price parameter for segment *i*, and X_{jkt} is the available price of option *j* for consumer *k* in time *t*. The term 1 in the denominator is the utility contribution of the "no choice" option (exp(0)), and the corresponding probability of the "no choice" is given by:

$$P(\text{no choice}) = 1 / (1 + \Sigma \exp(u_{ji} + \beta_i X_{jkt})). \quad (2)$$

The relative sizes of the homogeneous consumer segments is expressed as:

(3) $$f_i = \exp(\lambda_i) \Big/ \sum_{i'} \exp(\lambda_{i'}).$$

As f_i is the likelihood of finding a consumer in segment i, the unconditional probability of choice for option j by consumer k can be computed as:

(4) $$P_j(u, \beta, X_{kt}) = \sum_i f_i P_j(u_i, \beta_i, X_{kt}).$$

We use LogitMix (Kamakura and Russell, 1989) to estimate the model. The parameters are estimated by the method of maximum likelihood.

Elasticity Structure

After estimating the intrinsic preferences for the options, the coefficients for price, and the market share of the options, we calculate the price elasticities as follows (Kamakura and Russell, 1989):

(5) $$\eta_i(own) = \beta_i(1 - S_{ij})X_j \text{ and } \eta_i(cross) = -\beta_i S_{ij'} X_{j'}$$

where β_i is the regression coefficient of price for segment i, S_{ij} is the share of product offer j in segment i, and X_j is the price of option j. The own elasticities show the percentage change in a product option's share after a percentage change in the price of this particular product option. The cross elasticities show the percentage change in a product option's share after a percentage change in the price of any of the other product options.

Study Participants

Forty-five full- and part-time MBA students who were enrolled in graduate-level marketing courses participated in our study. They were not offered any compensation to participate in the study.

RESULTS

The descriptive statistics of our sample are as follows: 82.2 percent were in the 26–40 age group, 66.7 percent were male, 55.6 percent were full-time students, all of them reported using computers for more than five years, and 86.6 percent used computers for more than twenty hours per week. In terms of income, 44.4 percent reported yearly income below $20,000 and 40.0 percent reported yearly income above $55,000.

Perceptions of Electronic vs. Print Format

The results are presented in Table 7.4. We used a one-sample t-test to compare each attribute rating with a test value of 4, which is the anchor of the scale (electronic format perceived as equal to print format in this attribute). On average, respondents perceived electronic (PDF) form as

Table 7.4

Perceptions of Electronic vs. Print Books

Attribute	Electronic vs. print format		t-stat (p-value)	Importance weight	
	Mean	SD	test value = 4	Mean	SD
Image quality	4.91	1.38	4.433 (0.000)	4.93	1.77
Layout	4.69	1.47	3.134 (0.003)	4.60	1.47
Browsing	3.11	2.10	–2.863 (0.007)	4.41	1.72
Convenience of use	4.32	1.52	1.387 (0.173)	4.91	1.44
Archival quality	3.38	2.11	–1.975 (0.055)	4.48	1.56

better than print in terms of browsing ($M = 3.11$, $p < 0.05$) and archival quality ($M = 3.38$, $p < 0.055$), while print form as better than electronic in terms of image quality ($M = 4.91$, $p < 0.05$) and layout ($M = 4.69$, $p < 0.05$). In terms of convenience of use, the two forms were perceived as equally good ($M = 4.32$, $p > 0.05$). The importance ratings of the above attributes are between 4.48 and 4.93 and are not significantly different from each other at $p < 0.05$.

With regard to whether the print and electronic books were considered substitutes, complements, or unrelated products, our results show that 62.2 percent of the respondents perceived them as complements, 26.7 percent as substitutes, and 11.1 percent as unrelated products. Therefore we can conclude that consumers are more likely to perceive the print and electronic books as complements rather than substitutes or unrelated products (chi-square value = 18.53, $df = 2$, $p < 0.05$). Additionally, our respondents considered an average price of \$24.48 ($SD = 9.24$) as a fair price for an electronic book, given that the print book was priced at \$50.

Situation 1

We systematically varied the number of segments and used Aikake's information criterion to select the number of segments that represent the data the best (Kamakura and Russell 1989). On the basis of choosing the segment representation with the minimum AIC, we selected the single segment representation. The results are presented in Table 7.5.

Parameter Estimates

The price was negatively related to the probability of buying (–0.061). When the items were bundled, the probability of buying decreased (–4.881). When there was a print book or electronic book in the offer (single item or as a part of a bundle), the probability of buying increased (8.498 and 5.713, respectively).

Market Shares

The print book option had the highest market shares (84 percent, 76 percent, and 55 percent in the low, medium, and high price levels, respectively), followed by the bundle option (9 percent, 12 percent, and 17 percent), and the electronic book option (5 percent, 5 percent, and 4 percent). The market shares of the "no choice" option were 2 percent, 7 percent, and 24 percent in the low, medium, and high price levels, respectively. When the prices increased, the market shares of the print book and electronic book options decreased, while the market shares of the bundle option and the "no choice" option increased.

Table 7.5

MNL Results, Market Shares, and Elasticities, Situation 1

Model Statistics

Log likelihood function	–537.351
Log likelihood for choice model	–537.351

Log–Lf	R–sqrd	R–sqrd Adj
–998.132	0.462	0.460

Variable	Coefficient	SE	b/SE	IP[IZI>z]
PRICE	–0.061	0.005	–11.442	0.000
BUNDLE	–4.881	0.397	–12.300	0.000
PB	8.498	0.628	13.525	0.000
EB	5.713	0.526	10.862	0.000

Market share

	Exp(Sum Bi*Xi)			Market share (%)		
	Low	Medium	High	Low	Medium	High
BUNDLE	3.866	1.741	0.715	8.93	12.44	17.26
PB	36.176	10.601	2.286	83.59	75.74	55.18
EB	2.234	0.655	0.141	5.16	4.68	3.41
NOTHING	1.000	1.000	1.000	2.31	7.14	24.15
SUM	43.277	13.996	4.142			

Own/cross elasticities

	BUNDLE			PB			EB		
	Low	Medium	High	Low	Medium	High	Low	Medium	High
BUNDLE	**–7.265**	**–7.684**	**–7.997**	0.713	1.092	1.669	0.713	1.092	1.669
PB	4.104	4.648	4.233	**–0.805**	**–1.489**	**–3.438**	4.104	4.648	4.233
EB	0.253	0.287	0.261	0.253	0.287	0.261	**–4.656**	**–5.850**	**–7.410**

PB = print book
EB = electronic book

Elasticities

The own and cross elasticities are presented in Table 7.5. The bundle option had the highest own price elasticity (–7.3, –7.7, and –8.0 in the low, medium, and high price levels, respectively), followed by the electronic book option (–4.7, –5.9, and –7.4) and the print book option (–0.8, –1.5, and –3.4). Consequently, changing the price of the print book option had a relatively small effect on its own market share (e.g., one dollar increase in the price of the print book in the low price level led to a 0.8 percent decrease in print book's share), while changing the price of the bundle option had a relatively strong effect on its market share (e.g., one dollar increase in the price of the bundle in the low price level led to a 7.3 percent decrease in the bundle's share). The cross elasticities of the print book option were between 4.1 and 4.6, showing that a one-dollar increase (decrease) in the price of the electronic book or bundle options resulted in a more than 4 percent increase (decrease) in the share of the print book. The cross elasticities of the electronic book option were between 0.25 and 0.29, and the cross elasticities of the bundle option were between 0.7 and 1.7. Consequently, changing the price of the other two options did not have a strong effect on the market shares of the electronic book and the bundle options.

Situation 2

The results are presented in Table 7.6.

Parameter Estimates

The price was negatively related to the probability of buying (–0.074). When the items were bundled, the probability of buying decreased (–7.599). When there was a print book, an electronic book, or electronic chapters in the offer (single item or as a part of a bundle), the probability of buying increased (9.398, 8.167, and 7.366 respectively).

Market Shares

The two bundle options had negligible market shares and their shares increased slightly with increases in prices. At the low price level, the print book option had the highest market share (59 percent), followed by the electronic chapters (20 percent) and electronic book (17 percent) options. At the other two price levels, the electronic chapters option had the highest market share (44 percent and 70 percent, respectively), followed by the print book (37 percent and 12 percent) and electronic book (11 percent and 4 percent) options. The market shares of the "no choice" option were 2 percent, 5 percent, and 10 percent in the low, medium, and high price levels, respectively.

Elasticities

The two bundle options had the highest own price elasticities (between –9.4 and –11.4), followed by the electronic book option (between –4.9 and –8.9) and the print book option (between –2.4 and –8.1). The electronic chapters option had the lowest own price elasticity (–3.9, –2.8, and –1.3 in the low, medium, and high price levels, respectively). Consequently, changing the price of the electronic chapters option had a relatively small effect on its own market share, changing the price of the print book and electronic book options had a bit stronger effect on their own market shares, and changing the price of the bundle options had a relatively strong effect on their own market

Table 7.6

MNL Results, Market Shares, and Elasticities, Situation 2

Model statistics		
Log likelihood function		–467.565
Log–L for choice model		–467.565
Log–L f	R–sqrd	R–sqrd Adj
–1290.067	0.638	0.636

Variable	Coefficient	St. E	b/SE	lP[lZl>z]
PRICE	–0.074	0.006	–12.687	0.000
BUNDLE	–7.599	0.425	–17.879	0.000
PB	9.398	0.675	13.916	0.000
EB	8.167	0.604	13.527	0.000
EC	7.366	0.479	15.376	0.000

Market share

	Exp (Sum Bi*Xi)			Market share		
	Low	Medium	High	Low	Medium	High
PBEB	0.568	0.336	0.193	1.00%	1.63%	1.93%
PBEC	0.684	0.423	0.255	1.21%	2.05%	2.54%
PB	33.161	7.592	1.202	58.67%	36.76%	12.00%
EB	9.690	2.218	0.351	17.15%	10.74%	3.51%
EC	11.414	9.083	7.017	20.20%	43.98%	70.04%
NOTHING	1.000	1.000	1.000	1.77%	4.84%	9.98%
SUM	56.517	20.653	10.019			

(continued)

Table 7.6 *(continued)*

Own/cross elasticities

	PBEB			PBEC			PB		
	Low	Medium	High	Low	Medium	High	Low	Medium	High
PBEB	**–10.427**	**–10.876**	**–11.385**	0.106	0.180	0.224	0.106	0.180	0.224
PBEC	0.115	0.205	0.268	**–9.430**	**–9.819**	**–10.265**	0.115	0.205	0.268
PB	3.460	2.709	1.106	3.460	2.709	1.106	**–2.437**	**–4.661**	**–8.108**
EB	1.011	0.792	0.323	1.011	0.792	0.323	1.011	0.792	0.323
EC	0.996	2.269	3.794	0.996	2.269	3.794	0.996	2.269	3.794
PBEB	0.106	0.180	0.224	0.106	0.180	0.224			
PBEC	0.115	0.205	0.268	0.115	0.205	0.268			
PB	3.460	2.709	1.106	3.460	2.709	1.106			
EB	**–4.885**	**–6.579**	**–8.890**	1.011	0.792	0.323			
EC	0.996	2.269	3.794	**–3.935**	**–2.890**	**–1.623**			

PB = print book
EB = electronic book
EC = electronic chapter
PBEB = print book and electronic book bundle
PBEC = print book and electronic chapters bundle

shares. Overall, the cross elasticities of the print book and electronic chapters options were between 1 and 4, showing that a one-dollar increase (decrease) in the price of the other options resulted in a 1 percent to 4 percent increase (decrease) in the share of the print book or electronic chapters option. The cross elasticities of the electronic book and the bundle options were between 0.1 and 1. Consequently, changing the price of the other two options did not have a strong effect on the market shares of the electronic book and the bundle options.

To summarize, consumers view electronic (PDF) form better than print in terms of browsing and archival quality, and print form better than electronic in terms of image quality and layout. With respect to convenience of use, the two forms are perceived as equally good. Additionally, consumers consider image quality, layout, browsing, convenience of use, and archival quality equally important when making a choice between print and electronic forms. The two book forms are more likely to be perceived as complements rather than substitutes or unrelated products. When the same content is offered in two different forms (paper book and electronic book) and as a bundle (paper book and electronic book together), although the paper book option is the predominant choice and has the largest market share, still a substantial number of consumers are choosing the bundle option. Changing the price of the print book has a relatively small effect on its own market share, while changing the price of the bundle offer has a very strong effect on its own market share. When the same content is offered in different forms and is also unbundled (electronic chapters), consumers become more price sensitive. Overall, the pattern of results in the case of unbundling is similar to the results when there is no unbundling of electronic content. The only difference is that the electronic chapters option is the one with the highest market share and the lowest own price elasticity.

DISCUSSION

Our preliminary results point at several interesting issues that are worth further elaboration. The first one is related to whether the bundling of electronic with print products is attractive for consumers. Although print books are still the predominant choice, bundling print with electronic content seems a viable strategy. Consumers are likely to derive utility from owning an electronic product together with the print product as the electronic products are superior to print products in terms of browsing and archival quality, while the print products are superior in terms of image quality and layout. The more dissimilar the two forms are considered regarding these important attributes, the more likely consumers are to buy the bundle. Consequently, content providers may focus on stressing the superior attributes of both forms in their promotional strategies, thus increasing the utility of owning both forms and boosting bundle sales.

The second interesting issue is the question of pricing of print and electronic products as separate items and as bundles. Our results suggest that print books have a relatively low own price elasticity, while bundles have a relatively high own price elasticity. Consequently, marketers may find it optimal to price the print products at a relatively high level while keeping the bundle price relatively low and attractive. If the print book prices are high, consumers may be willing to spend a little bit more and upgrade to the bundle. The additional benefits that the digital form in the bundle provides may come into play and outweigh the higher price they pay for switching from print book to bundle. Thus, although the number of consumers who do not buy at the high price level is substantial (24 percent), content providers may be able to make up for these lost sales by more bundle sales and be better off with such a pricing strategy.

The third interesting question is related to what consumers perceive to be a fair price for electronic content. The marginal cost of reproducing and distributing digital products is lower than that for print products, and consumers are probably considering this when making purchase decisions. Our results suggest that electronic products should be priced much lower than traditional print products (50 percent less), and companies may take this perceived fair price into account. Sellers may focus on initiatives that increase the perceived value of the electronic products in order to be able to charge higher prices, or suggest usage situations in which the electronic products are more appropriate and thus increase their sales. Nevertheless, consumers will be sensitive to the costs of the products (Bolton et al. 2003) and they will perceive a lower price for electronic products as more fair because of the associated lower production costs.

Another interesting discussion point is whether to unbundle electronic content and rebundle it with traditional print products. Our results suggest that consumers become more price sensitive when offered electronic chapters and switch from print book to electronic chapters. Still, it may be beneficial for publishers to offer unbundled content if it can generate sales from consumers who would not buy otherwise. In our second experiment the percentage of consumers who did not buy was much smaller than in our first experiment, when there was no unbundling of content. Future studies should try to provide companies with advice on whether to unbundle electronic content or not, and if yes, how to price it.

A final point is related to the single segment representation in our study. We used MBA students for our data collection, and our sample seems quite homogeneous. These are highly educated business professionals who use computers extensively and are probably well familiar with digital products. Consequently, it is not surprising that the single segment representation fits the data the best.

RESEARCH ISSUES

Although our study gives initial insights on how to market products that exist in both print and electronic form, it has several limitations. First, we did not consider the supply side—the costs associated with the various options that the sellers can market. Second, we focused on two usage situations only, while in real life consumers may consider a large number of substantively different usage situations when making purchase decisions. Third, the two usage situations we manipulated are different on several dimensions and we cannot easily compare the results across the two situations. Fourth, we used a highly homogeneous sample in our study and our results may not be applicable for other consumer segments. Additional research is needed in order to make our preliminary results generalizable and provide guidelines on optimal product and pricing strategies that sellers should consider. In this section we suggest feasible studies that can help practitioners and academicians get a better understanding on how to market electronic products such as books and magazines.

Product Line Design and Pricing

The first possible extension is to develop a method for determining optimal product line design and pricing strategy for an item available in both print and electronic forms by considering a representative sample of consumers and usage situations. Researchers can design choice experiments and use choice-based conjoint analysis to obtain estimates of customer valuations of the different product forms. Given a representative sample of respondents and usage situations, respondents can be presented with hypothetical choice situations in which product offerings and prices are varied to determine how demand fluctuates with offering and price changes. The electronic content can be unbundled and rebundled with print products as well. The resulting segment option shares, elasticities, and some financial information provided by book publishers can be used as input to find the optimal product and pricing mix.

Max = Sum (S_{sj} * MR_j), where S_{sj} is the share of product offer j in segment s, and MR_j is the marginal revenue of product offer j.

Constraints

They can be derived from the MNL output of the segment-level model (the segment share of each product option and its own and cross elasticities). Constraints for the marginal revenue (revenues minus costs) can be derived using cost information provided by companies.

In sum, the contribution of such a study will be outlining a methodology that companies may use in designing optimal product line and pricing strategies.

Substitutability/Complementarity between Print and Electronic Products

Another possible area for future research is to study how the perceived substitutability and complementarity between the print and electronic products is related to the likelihood of buying the single products and the bundle. Moreover, it will be interesting to see if these perceptions can be affected by marketing communications. Harlam et al. (1995) found that bundles composed of complements have higher purchase intent versus bundles of similar or unrelated products. Consequently, the more complementary consumers view print and electronic products, the more likely they will be to buy them as a bundle. One way to affect the perceived complementarity is to cue consumers with different usage situations in which the products are differentially appropriate. The logic behind our argument is that when each product form has distinctive usages—one product form is more appropriate for one usage situation and the other product form is more appropriate for another situation—consumers will be less likely to perceive them as direct substitutes (vs. unrelated products or even complements), and consequently, will be willing to purchase them as a bundle. For example, we expect consumers to be more likely to subscribe to both the print *Wall Street Journal* and *WSJ Online*, if the two journal forms are appropriate in different usage situations (e.g., print newspapers for keeping up with the daily news vs. electronic newspapers for doing research) versus being used interchangeably in the same usage situations (e.g., electronic newspapers for both keeping up with the daily news and for doing research).

Another way to increase the perceived complementarity between print and electronic products is to stress the superior attributes that they have. For example, in our study consumers viewed electronic (PDF) form as better than print in terms of browsing and archival quality, and print form better than electronic in terms of image quality and layout. Through marketing, communications companies may be able to further increase these differential perceptions of attributes and make the different forms more valuable because of these superior attributes. Consequently, consumers may be willing to buy the print and electronic products as a bundle because they value different product attributes.

NOTES

1. For an excellent review and empirical comparison between ratings-based and choice-based conjoint models see Elrod, Louviere, and Davey (1992).
2. In order to have realistic pricing, we calculated the bundle price with the following assumptions:
   - High price level (print book and electronic book) < 2*Low price level (book)
   - Low price level (print book and electronic book) > High price level (book)

3. In order to have realistic pricing, we calculated the bundle price with the following assumptions:
   - High price level (print book and electronic book) < 2*Low price level (book)
   - High price level (print book and electronic chapters) < Low price level (book) + Low price level (electronic chapters)
   - Low price level (print book and electronic chapters) > High price level (book)
   - Low price level (book) > High price level (electronic chapters)

REFERENCES

Adams, W. J., and Yellen, J. L. Commodity bundling and the burden of monopoly. *Quarterly Journal of Economics,* 90 (August 1976), 475–498.

Bakos, Y., and Brynjolfsson, E. Bundling information goods: Pricing, profits and efficiency. *Management Science,* 45, 12 (1999), 1613–1630.

———. Bundling and competition on the internet: Aggregation strategies for information goods. *Marketing Science,* 19, 1 (2000), 63–82.

Bolton, L.E.; Warlop, L.; and Alba, J. Explorations in price (un)fairness. *Journal of Consumer Research,* 29 (March 2003), 474–491.

Chakravarti, D.; Rajan, K.; Pallab, P.; and Srivastava, J. Partitioned presentation of multi-component bundle prices: Evaluation, choice and underlying processing effects. *Journal of Consumer Psychology,* 12, 3 (2002), 215–229.

Chuang, J., and Sirbu, M. Optimal bundling strategy for digital information goods: Network delivery of articles and subscription. *Information Economics and Policy,* 11 (1999), 147–176.

Elrod, T.; Louviere, J.J.; and Davey, K.S. An empirical comparison of ratings-based and choice-based conjoint models. *Journal of Marketing Research,* 29 (August 1992), 368–377.

Estelami, H. Consumer savings in complementary product bundles. *Journal of Marketing Theory and Practice* (Summer 1999), 107–114.

Gaeth, G.; Levin, I.; Chakraborty, G.; and Levin, A.M. Consumer evaluation of multi-product bundles: An information integration analysis. *Marketing Letters,* 2 (1990), 47–57.

Guiltinan, J.P. The price bundling of services: A normative framework. *Journal of Marketing,* 51 (April 1987), 74–85.

Hair, J.F.; Anderson, R.E.; Tatham, R.L.; and Black, W.C. *Multivariate Data Analysis,* 5th ed. Upper Saddle River, NJ: Prentice Hall, 1995.

Hamilton, R.W. Bundling options: Increasing consumer satisfaction by constraining choice. Working paper, University of Maryland at College Park, Department of Marketing (2003).

Hanson, W., and Martin, R.K. Optimal price bundling. *Management Science,* 36, 2 (1990), 155–174.

Harlam, B.A.; Krishna, A.; Lehmann, D.R.; and Mela, C. Impact of bundle type, price framing and familiarity on purchase intention for the bundle. *Journal of Business Research,* 33 (1995), 57–66.

Heath, T.B.; Chatterjee, S.; and France, K.R. Mental accounting and changes in price: The frame dependence of reference dependence. *Journal of Consumer Research,* 22 (June 1995), 90–97.

Janiszewski, C., and da Cunha, M.V.M. Jr. The influence of price discount framing on the evaluation of a product bundle. *Journal of Consumer Research,* 30 (2004), 534–546.

Johnson, M.D.; Herrmann, A.; and Bauer, H.H. The effects of price bundling on consumer evaluations of product offerings. *International Journal of Research in Marketing,* 16 (1999), 129–142.

Kahneman, D., and Tversky, A. Prospect theory: An analysis of decision under risk. *Econometrica,* 47 (1979), 163–191.

Kamakura, W., and Russell, G.J. A probabilistic choice model for market segmentation and elasticity structure. *Journal of Marketing Research,* 26 (November 1989), 379–390.

Kannan, P.K., and Jain, S. Pricing product lines of digital content: A normative model based decision support system. Working Paper No. 20742, University of Maryland at College Park, Department of Marketing (2003).

Kenney, R.W., and Klein, B. The economics of block booking. *Journal of Law and Economics,* 26 (1983), 497–540.

McAfee, R.P.; McMillan, J.; and Whinston, M. Multiproduct monopoly, commodity bundling, and correlations of values. *Quarterly Journal of Economics,* 104, 2 (1989), 371–383.

Schmalensee, R. Gaussian demand and commodity bundling. *Journal of Business,* 57, 1 (1984), S211–S230.

Soman, D., and Gourville, J.T. Transaction decoupling: How price bundling affects the decision to consume. *Journal of Marketing Research,* 38 (February 2001), 30–44.

Stigler, G.J. *United States v. Loew's, Inc.:* A note on block booking. *Supreme Court Review,* 153 (1963), 152–157.

Stremersch, S., and Tellis, G.J. Strategic bundling of products and prices: A new synthesis for marketing. *Journal of Marketing,* 66 (January 2002), 55–72.

Telser, L.G.A. Theory of monopoly of complementary goods. *Journal of Business,* 52, 2 (1979), 211–230.

Thaler, R. Mental accounting and consumer choice. *Marketing Science,* 4, 3 (1985), 199–214.

Venkatesh, R., and Kamakura, W. Optimal bundling and pricing under a monopoly: Contrasting complements and substitutes from independently valued products. *Journal of Business,* 76, 2 (2003), 211–231.

Venkatesh, R., and Mahajan, V. A probabilistic approach to pricing a bundle of products or services. *Journal of Marketing Research,* 30 (November 1993), 494–508.

Wilson, L.O.; Weiss, A.M.; and John, G. Unbundling of industrial systems. *Journal of Marketing Research,* 27 (May 1990), 123–138.

Yadav, M.S. How buyers evaluate product bundles: A model of anchoring and adjustment. *Journal of Consumer Research,* 21 (September 1994), 342–353.

———. Bundle evaluation in different marketing segments: The effects of discount framing and buyers' preference heterogeneity. *Journal of the Academy of Marketing Science,* 23, 3 (1995), 206–215.

Yadav, M.S., and Monroe, K.B. How buyers perceive savings in a bundle price: An examination of a bundle's transaction value. *Journal of Marketing Research,* 30 (August 1993), 350–358.

CHAPTER 8

CURRENT AND FUTURE INSIGHTS FROM ONLINE AUCTIONS

A RESEARCH FRAMEWORK

CHARLES A. WOOD

Abstract: *Internet technology can alter business models within organizations. Nowhere is this more evident than in online auctions. Participation in business-to-consumer (B2C) auctions has vastly increased over the last several years, and the number of companies participating in business-to-business (B2B) "reverse auctions" has also risen significantly each year for the last several years. In this article, a research framework based on public research is presented that describes how the research of online auctions has progressed and what areas still need to be examined in future research.*

Keywords: *Auction Design, Auction Research Framework, E-Commerce, Online Auction, Reverse Auction, Selling and Buying Strategy*

INTRODUCTION

Information technology, specifically the Internet, has significantly changed the way people exchange information and participate in business transactions. The advent of electronic commerce (e-commerce) has allowed for business models whose definition and scope are unattainable in traditional markets. Furthermore, these electronic markets are still growing at a phenomenal rate. Of all business models that have been impacted by the Internet, *online auctions* and business-to-business (B2B) *reverse auction exchanges* have had some of the largest impact.

Online auctions, in particular, exemplify a huge growth rate that was made possible by Internet technology. EBay, the premier online auction retailer, with over 80 percent of the online auction market, boasts that, on any given day, they have more than 12 million items listed across 18,000 categories. In the second quarter of 2003, eBay reported record net revenues of $509.3 million, up 91 percent from the same period in 2002. This massive sales and growth resulted in a record operating income of $168.7 million, up 109 percent from 2002. Users, too, have flocked to eBay, with 34.1 million active users (the number of users on the eBay platform who bid, bought, or listed over the trailing twelve months) in the second quarter of 2003, a 57 percent increase over the 21.8 million active users for the same period in 2002.[1]

In conventional auctions, the "host" of the auction is the *seller,* who is auctioning *assets* to bidders, and the *highest* bid wins. However, in *reverse auctions*, the host of the auction is the *buyer,* who is auctioning *production contracts* to the bidders, and the *lowest* bid wins. Reverse auction exchanges grew at an incredible rate during the 1998–2000 period. The "dot-com bubble burst" that occurred in 2000–2001 resulted in flat or reduced demand for B2B services, as many of the B2B providers went out of business or switched strategies to implement a more feasible business model (Tulder and Mol 2002). However, in 2002, B2B e-commerce once again found favor with businesses, and as a result also saw tremendous growth. According to figures from the European Commission, 90 percent of European online sales occur in the B2B space.[2] A study from the Institute for Supply Management and Forrester Research reveals that 84 percent of large companies now use the Web to purchase materials and services, and that the overall percentage of B2B online purchasing (by large and small companies) increased steadily during 2002.[3] Much of the B2B activity is done through reverse auction exchanges, where buyers place contracts online so that suppliers can bid on them, with the lowest bidder often winning the contract. Such exchanges have led to some extremely high initial savings. For example, General Electric Transportation Systems, one of the world's leading suppliers to the railroad, transit, and mining industries, now processes its approximately 100,000 invoices through Global eXchange Services and projects an annual savings of $900,000 because of the move.[4] In another example, Covisint, a relatively new online exchange for automobile manufacturers, projects savings for its members that range from 5 percent to 30 percent, and has over 103,000 member businesses with 4,800 auctions.[5]

As with the explosive growth of activity in online auctions, there has been a corresponding explosive growth in research on online auctions and exchanges as researchers and professors try to understand this relatively new phenomenon at a deep level. This chapter examines the current state of online auction research to examine two research questions:

- What topic matter is being examined in online auction research?
- How can these topics be characterized in the context of online auctions?
- What auction topics, behaviors, and designs need further examination?

These questions are examined through an intense literature review. Each article in the review is categorized on the basis of topic and behavioral traits examined. A framework is developed that shows what topics seem to be of great interest, in that certain topics are being researched intensely, and which topics could use further study in the future.

CHARACTERIZING SELLER AND BIDDER INTERACTION IN ONLINE AUCTIONS

In online auctions, research is dedicated to examining how *sellers* and *bidders* interact through the online auction market structure. As such, auction research can be characterized as typically concentrating on one of the following three auction characteristics: *seller behavior*, *bidder behavior*, and *auction design.*

Seller behavior. Research on seller behavior includes set-up strategies, seller opportunism (such as shilling, which is the act of bidding on your own item to drive up the price other bidders pay), and seller comments left in an online reputation system.

Bidder behavior. Research on bidder behavior includes the price a bidder pays, the bidding strategy employed by a bidder, buyer comments left in an online reputation system, buyer opportunism (such as colluding with each other when bidding), and factors that can cause a bidder to pay more or less for the same item. Note that, in auctions, sellers don't set the price (although they do set the starting bid), so most research that examines the price paid in an auction is investigating a bidder behavior, not a seller behavior.

Auction design. Research on online auction design typically involves the use of an analytical model that describes an optimal design of an entire online auction or some facet of an online auction, such as the optimal design of a reputation system.

This section describes how articles are selected for this review, and describes a grid framework that groups articles by topic and auction characteristic. This framework is intended to show areas of research that researchers find interesting, and areas that have not, as of yet, received much attention.

Rules for Article Selection

To develop an online auction research framework, rules were established upon which topics are relevant to this study, and which must be excluded from this study. This research includes any article that lists online auctions as of primary interest, through mentioning online auctions in the title, the abstract, or the keywords. This research excludes research that discusses auctions in general, but not primarily online auctions. For instance, there are many articles, especially from the economics literature, that discuss auction theory in general (e.g., Milgrom 1989, Riley and Samuelson 1981, Vickrey 1961). While these articles are important in the understanding of auction theory as it relates to online auctions, they are not specifically concerned with online auctions per se, and thus are not included in this sample.

Similarly, research is excluded that discusses topics that may affect online auctions, but are not specifically about online auctions. For instance, there are many articles that discuss reputation systems in general and are important to the understanding of how reputation systems can affect online auctions (e.g., Dellarocas 2002, Resnick et al. 2000, 2003). However, while these studies often bring up online auctions as a predominant beneficiary or implementer of reputation systems, the thrust of the articles is *primarily* concerning general online reputation systems and *not primarily* concerned with auction reputation systems, as noted by the lack of the word "auction" (or related words, like eBay, OnSale, etc.) in the title, abstract, or keyword listing. Conversely, there are those who specifically study auction-based reputation systems (e.g., Dellarocas 2003, Resnick and Zeckhauser 2002, Wood et al. 2003). Thus, these studies are included in our sample. In this vein, meta-research topics (e.g., Beam and Segev 1998), where the research is primarily concerned with other online auction research (similar to this article), are excluded from this study.

We also excluded B2B research that dealt only with electronic data interchange (EDI) through the Web without specifically dealing with an exchange. EDI and electronic purchasing are important for cost reduction, specifically with the implementation of XML as a vehicle for transmitting data from one corporate database to another. However, these articles are not specifically about reverse auction exchanges and thus are excluded from this research.

Finally, research was not included when it discussed auction houses without specifically dealing with the *process* of the auction. For example, research dealing with legal liability of online auctions houses (e.g., Antonelli et al. 2001) and similar topics were discarded.

The resulting collection of research included seventy-nine articles that deal specifically with online auctions. Journals articles, conference proceedings, and working papers were among the articles examined in this research.

Framework for Online Auction Research

In the literature review for this article, four main areas of research emerged as the primary focus of online auction research. These topic areas are:

- *Auction bids, winner's curse, selling prices, and bundling.* This topic area is primarily con-

Table 8.1

Online Auction Research Framework

	Articles on host behavior	Articles on bidder behavior	Articles on auction design	Total articles
Auction bids, winner's curse, selling prices, and bundling	2	13	1	16
Selling and buying strategies and decision processes	7	8	5	20
Auction fraud, opportunism, reputation systems, and trust	7	11	6	24
B2B reverse auction exchanges	7	2	10	19
Total	23	34	22	79

cerned with the price that is received in an online auction. Included are articles that describe nonreputation factors that cause a bidder to bid more or less for the same item; literature on the winner's curse, where a buyer pays more than market value for an item and later feels remorse that so much was paid; and the effect that bundling or debundling items has on the price received for those items within an auction. Note that there were enough articles on pricing behavior due to seller reputation and trust that trust and reputation systems were split into their own topic.

- *Selling and buying strategies and decision processes.* This topic area is primarily concerned with bidding and selling strategies employed by online auction bidders and sellers. Included are articles about bidder types and economic motivations for bidding techniques.
- *Auction fraud, opportunism, reputation systems, and trust.* This area is concerned with seller fraud, buyer collusion, misrepresentation or low-quality service, the effect of reputations systems (especially when new reputation system designs are proposed), and the effect of trust within an online auction.
- *B2B reverse auction exchanges.* In this area, we concentrate on reverse auctions typically used within a B2B framework. This includes buyer behavior and strategies with suppliers, supplier strategies with buyers, supply chains that incorporate a reverse auction, and B2B exchange design.

Table 8.1 describes the online auction research framework proposed by this article, and shows how the three aforementioned auction characteristics (*host behavior, bidder behavior*, and *auction design*) are juxtaposed against these four topics of discussion.[6] In Table 8.1, we show how the number of articles selected from our literature review fit within our framework, shedding light on those areas that appear to be of great interest and those where more research is suggested. In the next section, we describe these topics of discussion in detail, and discuss work that has been done in these areas as well as areas that still need investigating.

Table 8.2

Auction Bids, Winner's Curse, Selling Prices, and Bundling in Online Auction Research Framework

Host (seller) behavior	Bidder behavior	Auction design
Bajari & Hortacsu 2003b	Ariely & Simonson 2003	Lucking-Reiley 2000
Kung et al. 2002	Eaton 2002	
	Kauffman & Wood 2005	
	List & Lucking-Reiley 2000	
	List & Lucking-Reiley 2002	
	Lucking-Reiley 1999	
	Lucking-Reiley et al. 2000	
	Massad & Tucker 2000	
	Oh 2002	
	Stafford & Stern 2002	
	Ward & Clark 2002	
	Wilcox 2000	
	Yin 2002	

AUCTION RESEARCH FRAMEWORK APPLIED TO ONLINE AUCTION RESEARCH

In this section, we describe various articles as they apply to the topic matter shown in the framework in Table 8.1.

Work on Auction Bids, Winner's Curse, Selling Prices, and Bundling

One of the primary topics in online auction research is the investigation of how much a bidder is willing to pay for an item. Table 8.2 lists the research done in this area.

Much online auction research deals with factors that affect price.[7] Kauffman and Wood (2005) track individual bidders in online auctions and point out that items typically sell for less than the real-world counter, and find a *weekend effect* that was not found in Lucking-Reiley (1999), though both articles agree on other factors that affect price in online auctions. List and Lucking-Reiley (2000, 2002) discuss the effect of bundling in online auctions, while Ward and Clark (2002) describe how bidders pay an "insurance premium" in order to win their auction. Stafford and Stern (2002) investigate participation in online auctions from a technology acceptance perspective. Eaton (2002) also looks at factors that affect price, especially concentrating on the effect that additional information (provided by the seller) has on the bid level. Massad and Tucker (2000) find the surprising result that online auctions exceed in-person auctions in price. Yin (2002) finds that the Nash-equilibrium predictions regarding the winner's curse are accurate in online auctions. Oh (2002) explores how the winner's curse affects different bidder types, and also examines how product value, information asymmetry, and type of auction affect the occurrence of the winner's curse. Ariely and Simonson (2003) find that bidders *undersearch*, and therefore *overpay* in online auctions, and that online auctions yield high prices only when competing products are not available.

Notably lacking from this topic area are discussions on seller behavior. Although many factors at the auction level that affect buyers are controlled by sellers, there still seem to be few articles on seller strategies (other than reputation) that can be employed to gain higher prices. Included in

Table 8.3

Strategies, Techniques, and Decision Processes in Online Auction Research Framework

Host (seller) behavior	Bidder behavior	Auction design
Bapna et al. 2002	Bajari & Hortacsu 2003a	Bapna 2003
Beam & Segev 1998	Bapna et al. 2000	Bapna et al. 2003a
Dans 2002	Bapna et al. 2001a	Happel & Jennings 2002
Gilkeson & Reynolds 2003	Bapna et al. 2001b	Liu et al. 2003
Halstead & Becherer 2003	Bapna et al. 2003b	Rafaeli & Noy 2002
Heck & Vervest 1998	Easley & Tenorio 2003	
Wang et al. 2002	Roth & Ockenfels 2002	
	Wilcox 2000	

this area would be the effects of advertising or other marketing promotion, the choice between online auction and traditional markets, and the effect of online auction competition. Of all the articles in this survey, only Kung, Monroe, and Cox (2002) discuss brand loyalty, packaging, and promotion as they apply to online auctions, and Bajari and Hortacsu (2003b) discuss how the winner's curse can be affected by the starting bid set by the seller. More research in this area could help shed light on business practices and strategies that could be employed by online auction sellers to become more profitable in this new channel.

Also underresearched are online auction design mechanisms that maximize or minimize the price that a bidder pays in an online auction. Part of the reason for this lack is that traditional, nononline auction literature covers this topic extensively (e.g., Vickrey 1961). However, as technology for online auctions has become more sophisticated and more advanced, online auction mechanisms that can affect price could be developed. While Lucking-Reiley et al. (2000) don't suggest new auction designs, they do track and discuss online auction mechanisms from before the World Wide Web up to the current incarnations.

Work on Strategies, Techniques, and Decision Processes

How sellers and bidders behave inside the online auction mechanism has long been an area of interest in economics research. Table 8.3 shows research on the strategies, techniques, and decision processes used within online auctions.

The area least researched is bidder strategies and techniques. This is in sharp contrast with research that examines the price paid by bidders, which continues to be examined quite extensively. Bapna, Goes, and Gupta are very prolific in this area, examining bidder types (Bapna et al. 2001a, b), economic theory as it relates to bidder strategies in online auctions (Bapna et al. 2000), and how bidding strategies are affected by the bid increment set by the seller (Bapna et al. 2003b). Roth and Ockenfels (2002) examine bid sniping and bid timing. Easley and Tenorio (2003) also examine bid timing and why it is economically feasible to "jump bid" by bidding higher than the minimum bid dictated by the bid increment. Wilcox (2000) also examines bid timing as it relates to bidder experience, and finds that sniping increases as experience also increases. Bajari and Hortacsu (2003a) discuss how structural estimates of online auctions, despite their assumptions, appear to predict behavior quite well.

Much interest has been shown in seller behavior and strategies in online auctions. Many authors discuss online auctions as a viable business strategy to supplement or replace the current

Table 8.4

Auction Fraud Opportunism Reputation Systems and Trust in Online Auction Research Framework

Host (seller) behavior	Bidder behavior	Auction design
Albert 2002	Ba & Pavlou 2002	Ba et al. 2003
Bywell & Oppenheim 2003	Brinkmann & Seifert 2001	Dellarocas 2003
Kauffman & Wood 2003	Dellarocas et al. 2003	Resnick & Zeckhauser 2002
Lansing & Hubbard 2002	Dewan & Hsu 2001	Snyder 2000
Sinha & Greenleaf 2000	Ederington & Dewally 2003	Wang et al. 2003
Standifird 2001	Houser & Wooders 2000	Yamagishi 2003
Wood et al. 2003	Lee 1998	
	Livingston 2002	
	Melnik & Alm 2002	
	Ow & Wood 2003	
	Resnick et al. 2003	

method of sales within a company (e.g., Beam and Segev 1998, Dans 2002, Heck and Vervest 1998). Bapna et al. (2002) show analytically and empirically that sellers often set up auctions that do not deliver the the highest selling price. Gilkeson and Reynolds (2003) illustrate the importance of setting a proper starting bid price to attract more bidders and make an auction successful. Halstead and Becherer (2003) point out how diversification and cost leadership are still present in online auctions, creating market friction and allowing price differences. Wang, Wang, and Tai (2002) discuss online auction strategies as they relate to the auction market structures in Taiwan.

There are many studies that examine the role of auction structural design in motivating different seller and buyer behaviors. Bapna (2003) examines new auction design mechanisms for eliminating the detrimental effect of bidder sniping (bidding at the last possible minute), while Bapna, Goes, and Gupta (2003a) use empirical results to design optimal bid increments inside auctions. Happel and Jennings (2002) discuss the design for a workable futures market to be used to speculate on future prices in online auctions. Liu, Wang, and Fei (2003) discuss how auctions typically use unicast communication by only communicating about one seller auction at a time, and they show how multicast auctions will perform better than unicast auctions. Rafaeli and Noy (2002) found that adding social facilitation elements, such as those found in face-to-face communication, to online auctions will cause bidders to stay longer on the auction site and that they prefer these auctions to traditional online auction designs.

Work on Auction Fraud, Opportunism, Reputation Systems, and Trust

Many articles investigate the role that trust and fraud play within online auctions. Table 8.4 lists these articles within the research framework shown in Table 8.1.

Internet fraud has been a concern in online auctions since their inception, ranking the highest in the number of reported fraud cases compared to any other type of online auction enterprise. The Internet Fraud Watch (www.fraud.org) reports that, in 2002, online auctions accounted for 90 percent of online fraud cases. They reportedly received 33,122 online auction fraud complaints in 2002, close to *triple* the 11,105 online auction fraud complaints filed in 2001. Thus, fraud and trust have become important topics in online auction research. Kauffman and Wood (2003) and Wang, Hidvegi, and Whinston (2003) investigate *shilling,* a type of fraud where a seller secretly sets up another identity to bid on his own item, thus driving up the price for the final bidder. Sinha and Greenleaf (2000) discuss how bidder aggressiveness can lead to shilling, and how this is a particular problem within electronic markets. Lansing and Hubbard (2002) and Albert (2002) examine how fraud can be mitigated through regulation, while Bywell and Oppenheim (2001) suggest that bidders should be more aggressive in fraud complaints. Finally, Ederington and Dewally (2003) find that warranties do not seem to impact bid level, but that third-party certifications cause a significant price increase.

The converse of fraud in the online environment is trust. Lee (1998) examines AUCNET, the Japanese used-car online auction site. He finds that bidders are willing to pay *more* for used cars bought through AUCNET when compared to traditional used car lots because of procedures put in place by the AUCNET auction house that help ensure the sale of higher-quality used cars. Ow and Wood's (2003) research reaffirms Lee's reported trust effect with an analytical and empirical investigation and find, surprisingly, that more bidder experience leads to *higher* prices paid by bidders, since more experienced bidders are more likely to develop trust in the online auction market structure.

Most researchers find that a bad reputation can deter participation in an auction (e.g., Brinkman and Seifert 2001). However, there is some disagreement in the literature of the effect of reputation on price paid. Ba and Pavlou (2002), Dewan and Hsu (2001), Houser and Wooders (forthcoming), Livingston (2002), Melnik and Alm (2002), and Standifird (2001) show empirically that the seller's reputation score can increase the price paid in an auction, while Eaton (2002) and Kauffman and Wood (2003b) cannot find a significant effect of reputation on price despite relatively large data sets. Most probably, there are other factors that increase or reduce the effect of reputation on price, and these need to be researched in the future to resolve this disagreement. Yamagishi (2003) argues that the lack of a closed market among online traders benefits the reputation mechanism.

Many authors suggest auction designs that can minimalize fraud through reputation system design. Resnick and Zeckhauser (2002) examine in depth the current reputation design at eBay and find several flaws in the reputation system, including detrimental effects of reciprocated comments, and Pollyannaish assessments of reputation. Ba, Whinston, and Zhang (2003) suggest adding a *trusted third party* to the auction mechanism to reduce the chance of fraud, echoing Ederington and Dewally (2003), who show empirically that third-party certification can increase prices received in an auction by over 50 percent. With an assumption that sellers are opportunistic, Dellarocas (2003) finds, surprisingly, that the sanctioning effect of a reputation system to screen out opportunistic sellers cannot be improved by increasing the number of transactions reported. Snyder (2000) suggests that auction houses step up detection of online auction fraud to enhance the online auction marketplace.

Thus far, not much work has been done in the area of participation within reputation systems. Wood, Fan, and Tan (2003), and Resnick et al. (2003) both show about a 50 percent participation rate in the reputation rating systems of online auctions, while Dellarocas, Fan, and Wood (2003) show that buyer participation levels drop off in online auctions as reputation score increases.

Work on B2B Reverse Auction Exchanges

As mentioned in the introduction, B2B exchanges have seen significant growth in the last two years. EMarketer (www.emarketer.com) reported that worldwide B2B sales increased from $474.32 billion in 2001 to $823.48 billion in 2002 and were expected to exceed one trillion dollars in 2003. Despite this huge level of transaction, B2B reverse auctions, often used within B2B e-commerce for bidding on production contracts, has not been written on anywhere near as

Table 8.5

B2B Reverse Auction Exchanges in Online Auction Research Framework

Host (buyer) behavior	Bidder behavior	Auction design
Emiliani & Stec 2001	Bajari & Summers 2002	Arcelus et al. 2002
Emiliani & Stec 2002a	Jap 2003	Dias et al. 2002
Emiliani & Stec 2002b		Emiliani 2000
Jap 2000		Jap 2002
Kwoka 2001		Lightfoot & Harris 2003
Mullane et al. 2001		Lucking-Reiley & Spulber 2001
Tulder & Mol 2002		McAfee 2000
		Sairamesh et al. 2002
		Segev et al. 2001
		Wise & Morrison 2000

extensively as B2C auctions, such as those found on eBay.[8] Table 8.5 lists the articles that discuss B2B reverse auctions.

As can be seen in Table 8.5, the majority of research into reverse auctions is at the auction design level, with relatively little attention given to the bidder behavior inside these auctions. This is surprising, since bidder behavior is probably one of the most interesting factors to companies who participate in these B2B exchanges. Jap (2003) finds that reverse auction implementation increases the belief among bidders that the buyer is opportunistic, yet also finds the surprising result that, in reverse auctions, bidders seem more willing to make dedicated investments to transact with the buyer. Bajari and Summers (2002) discuss the possibility and detection of *bidder collusion*, where suppliers collude so that a higher bid can win a contract, via some mechanism such as taking turns.

More work has been done on buyer behavior and strategy in reverse auctions. Mullane, Peters, and Bullington (2001) and Tulder and Mol (2002) describe the costs and benefits of implementing a B2B reverse auction, while Tulder and Mol go on to describe how reverse auctions should fit within a business strategy. Jap (2000) issues similar cautions, noting that reverse auctions can save large amounts of money but can also undermine the supply base and probably should be coupled with at least some long-term sourcing contracts. Emiliani and Stec (2002a) continue this discourse and note that buyers, who host auctions in a B2B reverse auction mechanism, can save quite a lot when suppliers are forced to bid against each other for production contracts. However, these same authors also note that online auctions can cause divisiveness between seller and buyer and that buyers must take a long-term view of purchasing (Emiliani and Stec 2002b), with careful attention to ensure their technology choices fit with their business model (Emiliani and Stec 2001) to be ultimately successful. Kwoka (2001) investigates reverse auction exchanges in the automobile industry, such as Covisint (www.covisint.com), and notes how reverse auctions have raised questions about the impact of excessive buyer power and how these auctions can transform an industry.

The largest amount of research in B2B reverse auctions is in the area of reverse auction exchange design. Many pieces investigate the basic functionality of a reverse auction, especially as it relates to current economic theory (e.g., Emiliani 2000, Jap 2002, Lightfoot and Harris 2003, Lucking-Riley and Spulber 2001) or the design of a single B2B product, such as IBM's WebSphere Commerce Suite (e.g., Dias et al. 2002, Sairamesh et al. 2002). Some authors advocate new designs. For example, Arcelus, Pakkala, and Srinivasan (2002) advocate a two-price purchasing policy that alleviates the immediate negative impact of online auctions to suppliers by coupling the auctions with long-term supply contracts, and McAfee (2000) advocates a new peer-to-peer exchange format that reduces supply chain fees. Segev, Beam, and Shanthikumar (2001) model a reverse auction in terms of a Markov chain on a state space defined by the current price of the item and the number of bidders who have been previously "bumped," in an effort to optimize auction satisfaction and predict final ending bids. Finally, Wise and Morrison (2000) use examples of past acceptance of other technologies to try to predict how these new B2B technological structures will be accepted in the future.

CONCLUSIONS

Online auction research has seen a remarkable growth in the last several years. This article examines this research and categorizes it within an online auction research framework with the intention of helping researchers examine those areas that interest them, gauge the interest level among other researchers, and determine what areas need to be researched more intensely in the future.

Several insights have been gained from this study. In particular, some research areas need more investigation, especially bidder behavior in B2B reverse auctions, and online auction design that shows how technology can be incorporated into auction design to affect the price paid by bidders. Also, more seller-level analysis, especially in the context of marketing research, could be performed to show how seller-level behavior, such as promotion, market presence, and so forth, can affect the price paid in online auctions.

This study is limited by the vast amount of new working papers, conference proceedings, and journal articles that are being developed or have been published. Though an attempt was made to find and report on these articles, some relevant research is bound to be omitted from this study, despite efforts to be inclusive. Rather, this study should be looked at as an unbiased sample of current research so that researchers can glean levels of interest and areas of future research. Thus, this research should not be considered to be a substitute for a literature review, but instead can be used as a springboard to delve into new research topics in online auctions.

NOTES

1. Based on eBay's quarterly report.
2. See www.ecommercetimes.com/perl/story/31195.html for more information.
3. Reported in www.ecommercetimes.com/perl/story/20603.html.
4. From a GXS press release on October 28, 2002.
5. See covisint.com/.
6. Note that, in most auctions, the *host* is the *seller*, who sells some asset to the highest bidder. However, in reverse auctions, the *host* is the *buyer*, who lists a purchasing contract for suppliers to bid upon, and the lowest bid wins.
7. Articles whose primary focus is to discuss how reputation affects price are placed in a different category, discussed later in this article. However, many papers that list multiple factors that affect price, including reputation, are included in this section.
8. Sometimes, B2C (business-to-consumer) auctions like those listed on eBay are also referred to as P2P (peer-to-peer) auctions, since buyers can easily become sellers and sellers can easily become buyers.

REFERENCES

Albert, M.R. E-buyer beware: Why online auction fraud should be regulated. *American Business Law Journal,* 39, 4 (2002), 575–643.

Antonelli, M.; Kumar, C.R.; McCann-Ezring, B.; Peterman, C.; and Roberto, S. Online auction company immune from liability for sales of bootleg sound recordings. *Intellectual Property and Technology Law Journal,* 13, 1 (2001), 16–18.

Arcelus, F.J.; Pakkala, T.P.M.; and Srinivasan, G. A purchasing framework for B2B pricing decisons and risk-sharing in supply chains. *Decision Sciences,* 33, 4 (2002), 645–666.

Ariely, D., and Simonson, I. Buying, bidding, playing, or competing? Value assessment and decision dynamics in online auctions. *Journal of Consumer Psychology,* 13 (2003), 113–123.

Ba, S., and Pavlou, P.A. Evidence of the effect of trust building technology in electronic markets: Price premiums and buyer behavior. *MIS Quarterly,* 26, 3 (2002), 243–268.

Ba, S.; Whinston, A.B.; and Zhang, H. Building trust in online auction markets through an economic incentive mechanism. *Decision Support Systems,* 35, 3 (2003), 273–286.

Bajari, P., and Hortacsu, A. Are structural estimates of auction models reasonable? Evidence from experimental data. Working Paper, Palo Alto, CA: Stanford University Department of Economics. (2003a).

———. The winner's curse, reserve prices and endogenous entry: Empirical insights from eBay auctions. *The Rand Journal of Economics,* 34, 2 (2003b), 329–355.

Bajari, P., and Summers, G. Detecting collusion in procurement auctions: A selective survey of recent research. *Antitrust Law Journal,* 70, 1 (2002), 143–170.

Bapna, R. When snipers become predators: Can mechanism design save online auctions? *Communications of the ACM,* 46, 12 (2003), 152–158.

Bapna, R.; Goes, P.; and Gupta, A. A theoretical and empirical investigation of multi-item on-line auctions. *Information Technology and Management,* 1, 1 (2000), 1–23.

———. Comparative analysis of multi-item online auctions: Evidence from the laboratory. *Decision Support Systems,* 32, 2 (2001a), 135–153.

———. Insights and analysis of online auctions. *Communications of the ACM,* 44, 11 (2001b), 42–50.

———. Analysis and design of business-to-consumer online auctions. *Management Science,* 49, 1 (2003a), 85–101.

———. Replicating online Yankee auctions to analyze auctioneers' and bidders' strategies. *Information Systems Research,* 14, 3 (2003b), 244–268.

Bapna, R.; Goes, P.; Gupta, A.; and Karuga, G. Optimal design of the online auction channel: Analytical, empirical, and computational insights. *Decision Sciences,* 33, 4 (2002), 557–577.

Beam, C., and Segev, A. Auctions on the Internet: A field study. Working Paper 98-WP-1032, The Fisher Center for Management and Information Technology, Haas School of Business. University of California at Berkeley (1998).

Brinkmann, U., and Seifert, M. 'Face to interface': Zum Problem der Vertrauenskonstitution im Internet am Beispiel von elektronischen Auktionen *Zeitschrift für Soziologie (Journal for Sociology),* 30, 1(2001), 23–47.

Bywell, C.E., and Oppenheim, C. Fraud on Internet auctions. *Aslib Proceedings,* 53, 7 (July/August 2001), 265–272.

Dans, E. Existing business models for auctions and their adaptation to electronic markets. *Journal of Electronic Commerce Research,* 3, 2 (2002), 23–31.

Dellarocas, C. The digitization of word-of-mouth: Promise and challenges of online reputation mechanisms. Working Paper. Cambridge: Massachusetts Institute of Technology (2002).

———. The digitization of word-of-mouth: Promise and challenges of online feedback mechanism. *Management Science*, 49, (October 2003), 1407–1424.

———. Efficiency and robustness of eBay-like online feedback mechanisms in environments with moral hazard. Working Paper. Cambridge: Massachusetts Institute of Technology (2003).

———. Reputation Mechanism design in online trading environements with pure moral hazard. *Information Systems Research*, 16, 2 (June 2005), 209–231.

Dellarocas, C.; Fan, M.; and Wood, C.A. Reciprocity and participation in online reputation systems. Working Paper. Notre Dame, IN: University of Notre Dame, Department of Management (2003).

Dewan, S., and Hsu, V. Trust in electronic markets: Price discovery in generalist versus specialty online auctions. Working Paper. Seattle: University of Washington Business School, Department of Management Science (2001).

Dias, D.M.; Palmer, S.L;, Rayfield, J.T.; Shaikh, H.H.; and Sreeram, T.K. E-commerce interoperability with IBM's WebSphere commerce products. *IBM Systems Journal,* 41, 2 (2002), 272.

Easley, R.F., and Tenorio, R. Jump-bidding strategies in Internet auctions. Working Paper. Notre Dame, IN: University of Notre Dame (2003).

Eaton, D.H. Valuing information: Evidence from guitar auctions on eBay. Working Paper. Murray, KY: Murray State University (2002).

Ederington, L.H., and Dewally, M. A comparison of reputation, certification, warranties, and information disclosure as remedies for information asymmetries: Lessons from the on-line comic book market. Working Paper. Norman: University of Oklahoma (2003).

Emiliani, M.L. Business-to-business online auctions: Key issues for purchasing process improvement. *Supply Chain Management,* 5, 4 (2000), 176–186.

Emiliani, M.L., and Stec, D. J. Online reverse auction purchasing contracts. *Supply Chain Management,* 6, 3/4 (2001), 101–104.

———. Realizing savings from online reverse auctions. *Supply Chain Management,* 7, 1 (2002a), 12–23.

———. Squaring online reverse auctions with the Caux round table principles for business. *Supply Chain Management,* 7, 2 (2002b), 92–100.

Gilkeson, J.H., and Reynolds, K. Determinants of Internet auction success and closing price: An exploratory study. *Psychology and Marketing,* 20, 6 (2003), 537–566.

Halstead, D., and Becherer, R.C. Internet auction sellers: Does size really matter? *Internet Research,* 13, 3 (2003), 183–194.

Happel, S.K., and Jennings, M.M. Creating a futures market for major event tickets: Problems and prospects. *Cato Journal,* 21, 3 (2002), 443–461.

Heck, E.V., and Vervest, P. How should CIOs deal with Web-based auctions? *Communications of the ACM,* 41–42, 7 (1998), 99.

Houser, D., and Wooders, J. Reputation in auctions: Theory and evidence from eBay. *Journal of Economics and Management Strategy* (forthcoming).

Jap, S.D. Going, going, gone. *Harvard Business Review,* 78, 6 (November/December 2000), 30–31.

———. Online reverse auctions: Issues, themes, and prospects for the future. *Academy of Marketing Science Journal,* 30, 4 (2002), 506–525.

———. An exploratory study of the introduction of online reverse auctions. *Journal of Marketing,* 67, 3 (2003), 96–107.

Kauffman, R.J., and Wood, C.A. Doing their bidding: An empirical examination of factors that affect a buyer's utility in Internet auctions. *Information Technology and Management*, forthcoming (2005).

———. Why does reserve price shilling occur in online auctions? Paper presented at the International Conference on Electronic Commerce (ICEC '03), Pittsburgh, PA (2003).

Kung, M.; Monroe, K.B.; and Cox, J.L. Pricing on the Internet. *Journal of Product and Brand Management,* 11, 4/5 (2002), 274–287.

Kwoka, J.E. Automobiles: The old economy collides with the new. *Review of Industrial Organization,* 19, 1 (2001), 55–70.

Lansing, P., and Hubbard, J. Online auctions: The need for alternative dispute resolution. *American Business Review,* 20, 1 (2002), 108–116.

Lee, H.G. Do electronic marketplaces lower the price of goods? *Communications of the ACM,* 41, 1 (1998), 73–80.

Lightfoot, W., and Harris, J.R. The effect of the Internet in industrial channels: An industry example. *Industrial Management & Data Systems,* 103, 1/2 (2003), 78–84.

List, J.A., and Lucking-Reiley, D. Demand reduction in multi-unit auctions: Evidence from a sportscard field experiment. *American Economic Review,* 90, 4 (2000), 961–972.

———. Bidding behavior and decision costs in field experiments. *Economic Inquiry,* 40, 44 (2002), 611–619.

Liu, H.; Wang, S.; and Fei, T. Multicast-based online auctions: A performance perspective. *Benchmarking,* 10, 1 (2003), 54–64.

Livingston, J.A. How valuable is a good reputation? A sample selection model of Internet auctions. Working Paper. College Park: University of Maryland (2002).

Lucking-Reiley, D. Using field experiments to test equivalence between auction formats: Magic on the Internet. *American Economic Review* 89, 5 (1999): 1063–1080.

Lucking-Reiley, D. Auctions on the Internet: What's being auctioned, and how? *Journal of Industrial Economics,* 48, 3 (2000), 227–252.

Lucking-Reiley, D.; Bryan, D.; Prasad, N.; and Reeves, D. Pennies from eBay: The determinants of price in online auctions. Working Paper. Tuscon: University of Arizona, Department of Economics (2000).

Lucking-Reiley, D., and Spulber, D.F. Business-to-business electronic commerce. *Journal of Economic Perspectives,* 15, 1 (2001), 55–68.

Massad, V.J., and Tucker, J.M. Comparing bidding and pricing between in-person and online auctions. *Journal of Product and Brand Management,* 9, 5 (September/October 2000), 325–332.

McAfee, A. The Napsterization of B2B. *Harvard Business Review,* 78, 6 (November/December 2000), 18–19.

Melnik, M.I., and Alm, J. Does a seller's ecommerce reputation matter? Evidence from eBay auctions. *Journal of Industrial Economics,* 50, 3 (2002), 337–349.

Milgrom, P. Auctions and bidding: A primer. *Journal of Economic Perspectives,* 3, 3 (1989), 3–22.

Mullane, J.V.; Peters, M.H.; and Bullington, K.E. Entrepreneurial firms as suppliers in business-to-business e-commerce. *Management Decision,* 39, 5/6 (2001), 388–393.

Oh, W. C2C versus B2C: A comparison of the winner's curse in two types of electronic auctions. *International Journal of Electronic Commerce,* 6, 4 (2002), 115–138.

Ow, T., and Wood, C.A. The conflicting effect of experience on buying and selling in online auctions: An empirical examination of the effect of trust in electronic markets. Paper presented at the Conference for Information Systems and Technology (CIST '03), Atlanta, GA (2003).

Rafaeli, S., and Noy, A. Online auctions, messaging, communication and social facilitation: A simulation and experimental evidence. *European Journal of Information Systems,* 11, 3 (2002), 196–207.

Resnick, P., and Zeckhauser, R. *Trust Among Strangers in Internet Transactions: Empirical Analysis of eBay's Reputation System* (Vol. 11). Amsterdam: Elsevier Science, 2002.

Resnick, P.; Zeckhauser, R.; Friedman, E.; and Kuwabara, K. Reputation systems. *Communications of the ACM,* 12, 45 (2000), 43–46.

Resnick, P.; Zeckhauser, R.; Swanson, J.; and Lockwood, K. The value of reputation on eBay: A controlled experiment. Working Paper. Ann Arbor: University of Michigan. School of Information (2003).

Riley, J.G., and Samuelson, W.F. Optimal auctions. *American Economic Review,* 71, 3 (1981), 381–392.

Roth, A.E., and Ockenfels, A. Last-minute bidding and the rules for ending second-price auctions: Evidence from eBay and Amazon auctions on the Internet. *The American Economic Review,* 92, 4 (2002), 1093–1103.

Sairamesh, J.; Mohan, R.; Kumar, M.; Hasson, L.; and Bender, C. A platform for business-to-business sell-side, private exchanges and marketplaces. *IBM Systems Journal,* 41, 2 (2002), 242–252.

Segev, A.; Beam, C.; and Shanthikumar, J.G. Optimal design of Internet-based auctions. *Information Technology and Management,* 2, 2 (2001), 121–163.

Sinha, A.R., and Greenleaf, E.A. The impact of discrete bidding and bidder aggressiveness on sellers' strategies in open English auctions: Reserves and covert shilling. *Marketing Science,* 19, 3 (2000), 244–265.

Snyder, J.M. Online auction fraud: Are the auction houses doing all they should or could to stop online fraud? *Federal Communications Law Journal,* 52, 2 (2000), 453–472.

Stafford, M.R., and Stern, B. Consumer bidding behavior on Internet auction sites. *International Journal of Electronic Commerce,* 7, 1 (2002), 135–150.

Standifird, S.S. Reputation and e-commerce: eBay auctions and the asymmetrical impact of positive and negative ratings. *Journal of Management,* 27, 3 (May/June 2001), 279–296.

Tulder, R.V., and Mol, M. Reverse auctions or auctions reversed: First experiments by Philips. *European Management Journal,* 20, 5 (2002), 447–458.

Vickrey, W. Counter-speculation auctions and competitive sealed tenders. *Journal of Finance,* 16, 1 (1961), 8–37.

Wang, K.; Wang, E.T.G.; and Tai, C. A study of online auction sites in Taiwan: Product, auction rule, and trading type. *International Journal of Information Management,* 22, 2 (2002), 127–142.

Wang, W.; Hidvegi, Z.; and Whinston, A.B. Shill bidding in English auctions. Working Paper. Atlanta, GA: Emory University, Department of Decisions and Information Analysis, Goizueta School of Business (2003).

Ward, S.G., and Clark, J.M. C2C versus B2C: A comparison of the winner's curse in two types of electronic auctions. *International Journal of Electronic Commerce,* 6, 4 (2002), 139–155.

Wilcox, R.T. Experts and amateurs: The role of experience in Internet auctions. *Marketing Letters,* 11, 4 (2000), 363–374.

Wise, R., and Morrison, D. Beyond the exchange: The future of B2B. *Harvard Business Review,* 78, 6 (November/December 2000), 86–99.

Wood, C.A.; Fan, M.; and Tan, Y. An examination of the reputation systems for online auctions. Working Paper. Notre Dame, IN: University of Notre Dame, Department of Management (2003).

Yamagishi, T. The role of reputation in open and closed societies: An experimental study of Internet auctioning. Working Paper, Hokkaido University, Graduate School of Letters (2003).

Yin, P. Information dispersion and auction prices. Working Paper. Palo Alto, CA: Stanford University, Department of Economics (2002).

PART III

MANAGEMENT OF MOBILE AND INFORMATION TECHNOLOGY INFRASTRUCTURE

CHAPTER 9

PEER-TO-PEER TECHNOLOGIES FOR BUSINESS-TO-BUSINESS APPLICATIONS

FU-REN LIN, KAI FISCHBACH, AND MICHAEL J. SHAW

Abstract: *Peer-to-peer (P2P) networking has been attracting increasing attention in the business community. With the growing demand for business entities to automate business processes through Web services, P2P technologies may contribute to the flexibility and robustness of workflow connectivity. There may be interesting implications to general corporate information technology strategies, such as the decentralized management of resources and, especially, business-to-business (B2B) applications. This chapter evaluates the applicability of various P2P technologies to different B2B relations and brings insights to the future deployment of P2P technologies for B2B applications.*

Keywords: *Business-to-Business (B2B) Applications, E-Commerce, Industrywide Consortium, Peer-to-Peer (P2P) Technologies, Supply Chain Management*

INTRODUCTION

The possibility of using peer-to-peer (P2P) networking for interorganizational collaboration has recently been attracting increasing attention. The term P2P refers to the concept that, in a network of equals (peers) using appropriate information and communication systems, two or more individuals are able to spontaneously collaborate without necessarily needing central coordination (Barkai 2001, Schoder and Fischbach 2003). P2P extends our means of accessing and utilizing distributed resources, such as information, as well as bandwidth, storage, knowledge, files, and central processing unit (CPU) cycles. Ideally, the corresponding technologies and applications take advantage of fully decentralized architectures. Largely independent of central institutions, P2P computing appears to hold great promise with regard to information management, for example, it can accelerate communication processes, increase the exchangeability of up-to-date and decentralized information, reduce collaboration costs, exploite idle resources, and offer individual users a higher degree of emancipation (Barkai 2001, Oram 2001). Thanks to the continuously declining costs for storage and transport of digital information, together with the availability of 3G mobile networks, P2P computing is expected to become a "ubiquitous" part of our technical, economic, and social life (Cerf 2001).

A number of books and articles have been dedicated to the issue of P2P computing, from a technical as well as a social perspective (e.g., Barkai 2001, Foster 2002, Oram 2001). Although some authors have suggested P2P networks for (B2B) solutions (e.g., McAfee 2000, Parameswaran et al. 2001), very little in-depth research has been conducted in this field. Though it may be comparatively easy to envision its applications, the study of how P2P technologies benefit today's

Figure 9.1 **Classification of P2P Networks**

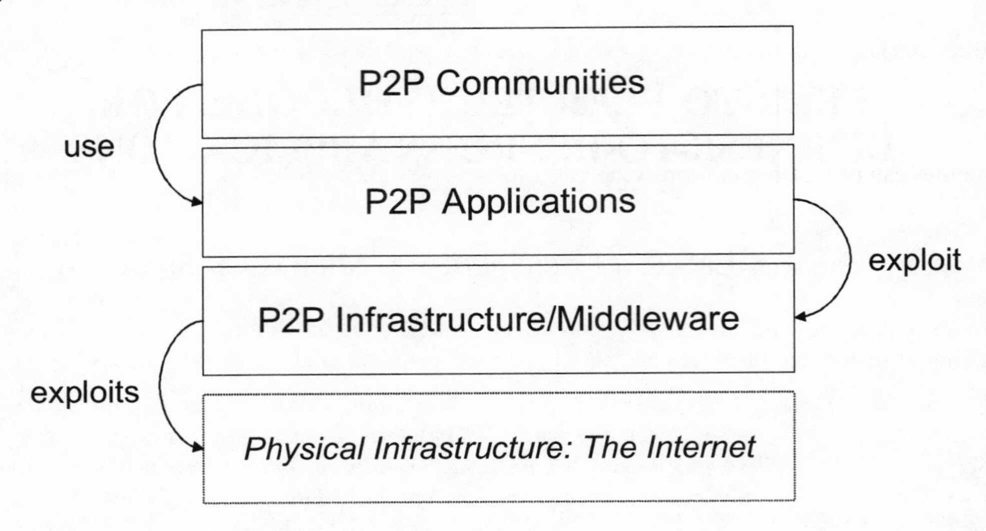

Source: Schoder and Fishbach, 2003.

highly dynamic and information-intensive business world is not a trivial task. In this study, we aim to analyze the applicability of various P2P technologies to business processes within different B2B relations, and to bring insight to the deployment of P2P technologies for B2B applications. In the next section, we provide an overview of P2P architectures and applications, which provides the basis for the follow-up analysis and discussions. Section 3 categorizes B2B relations with existing e-business models as the basis for the matching between B2B applications and P2P technologies. Section 4 addresses issues in applying P2P technologies to B2B applications, which leads to an analysis of business models to run P2P technologies for B2B applications. Section 5 describes and analyzes various business models that fit using P2P technologies for B2B applications well. Section 6 makes some conclusions and presents future research opportunities.

OVERVIEW OF P2P NETWORKS AND APPLICATIONS

Overview of P2P Networking

P2P networking can be analyzed from both technical and socioeconomic viewpoints. Unfortunately, various approaches have been subsumed under the label P2P in the past, which has led to much confusion within the different communities. To overcome this problem, Schoder and Fischbach (2003) introduced a conceptual framework that aims to provide a better understanding of different perspectives of P2P and to allow a differentiation between technical and socioeconomic aspects. According to this framework, P2P networks can be divided into four layers: physical infrastructure, P2P infrastructure, P2P applications, and P2P communities, as shown in Figure 9.1.

Starting from the bottom, the first layer represents the physical infrastructure underlying P2P networks. The physical infrastructure is, essentially, the World Wide Web. It includes computers and their operating systems, as well as the communication protocols and mechanisms (Barkai 2001). The second layer is called P2P infrastructure. It is located between the physical infrastructure and the applications. Its purpose is to facilitate the communication between P2P applications. Important approaches in this area are XML, SOAP, Jabber, or JXTA (Barkai 2001, Gong 2001, Miller 2001). The third layer represents end-user P2P applications like Napster, Groove, or ICQ. All these applications follow the P2P paradigm and make use of P2P infrastructures. The top layer represents P2P communities. The term "P2P communities" denotes virtual communities that consist of geographically separated members who make use of P2P applications. These communities can be realized in forms such as exchange-based B2B marketplaces, strategic alliances, or virtual organizations.

The Characteristics of P2P Technologies

The main characteristics of P2P technologies can be specified in the form of two attributes: the sharing of distributed resources and services on the one hand, and a decentralized and dynamic organization with various governing structures on the other.

Sharing of Distributed Resources and Services

The nodes of a P2P network can play different roles: they can be *clients*, when accessing resources, or *servers*, when providing resources or services to others at the same time. Apart from acting as clients or servers, peers within such a network can be *routers* (or cooperators; i.e., they transmit information through the network).

There are two categories of resource sharing technology: sharing of files and storage, and grid computing, which shares the computer processing power. File and storage sharing provides potential benefits in the form of dynamic information repositories, redundancy and fault tolerance, content-based addressing, enhanced load balancing, and improved searches. Storage sharing applications also provide alternatives to existing mass storage solutions by organizing disk resources at the edges of the Extranet or Internet. Well-known examples of networks for file and storage sharing are Napster, Gnutella, or Kazaa. They allow peers to access and download music, video, or any other type of files from other peers.

Grid computing, or distributed computing, systems aim to exploit the CPU processing power both in Intranet and Extranet environments. This can be realized by splitting computational problems into small independent parts (domain decomposition), which can be processed on nodes within the network (Foster 2002, Foster and Kesselman 1999). Grid computing has emerged as an important new field, distinguished from conventional distributed computing by its focus on dependable, consistent, and pervasive access to resources across heterogeneous platforms. Grid technology aims to make it easy to use diverse, geographically distributed, and locally managed and controlled computing facilities, as if they are formed in a coherent local cluster. Emphasis is placed on standardization and interoperability, with the aim of simplifying the creation of large networks. Its popularity is likely to increase, since it enables a user to participate in large-scale distributed computing networks and projects without the necessity of being a computer expert. Grid applications open up new dimensions of very high computer power, accessible from desktops.

Complementing the technological aspects described above, applications for sharing resources can be subdivided into two categories: *information sharing* and *process sharing*. Information sharing refers to the exchange of data between peers, for example, in the form of order information exchanged by two business partners, prototype specifications shared by a current design team, and domain documents shared by a professional community. Process sharing refers to the sharing of control flows to execute processes owned by counterparts. For example, the remote

Figure 9.2 **P2P Application Taxonomy**

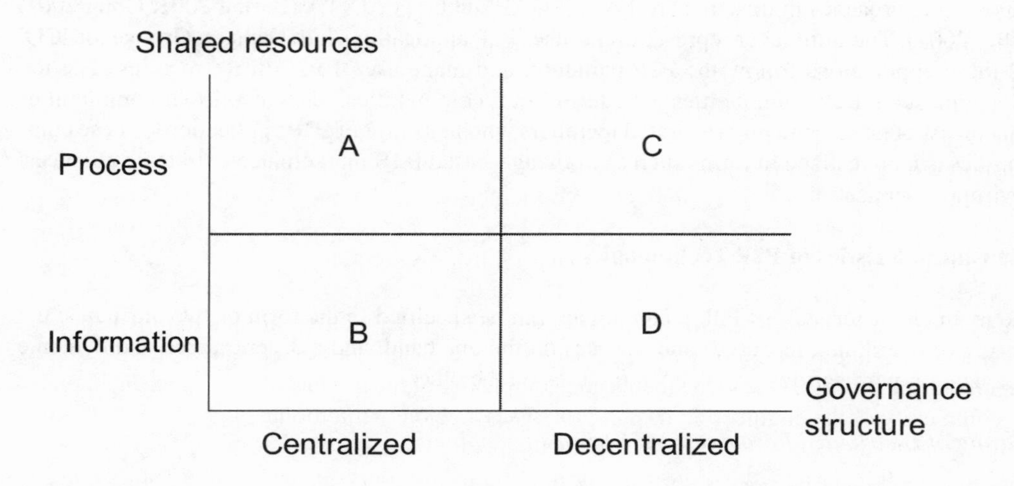

procedure call to trigger peers' processes and the control codes to coordinate workflow. In short, we can say that the former shares "what" and the latter shares "how."

Dynamically Organizing with Various Governance Structures

If it has been granted autonomous search and binding capabilities, a peer can connect with other peers to form various forms of organization governed by different mechanisms, such as centralized versus decentralized controls. An ideal P2P network is totally decentralized, which means that it does not need central coordination—each peer is autonomous. Autonomy refers to the level of control that can be exercised by the owner of a shared resource. Peers can decide whether they want to contribute to the network or not, and to what extent. However, total decentralization does not hold for every real-world implementation. This is the reason why many P2P networks are implemented in the form of hybrid architectures, in which some services are centrally coordinated and others follow the principle of decentralization. The choice between centralized and decentralized governances may depend on the organizational or interorganizational structures to which P2P technologies are applied.

In Figure 9.2, we draw P2P's characteristics in two dimensions: resource sharing and governance structure. Type A denotes the P2P architecture governed by the centralized authority to share processes between peers, and Type B shares information within a centralized governance structure. Peers in a Type C application framework share processes within a decentralized governance structure, and peers in a Type D framework organize themselves in a decentralized manner.

Why P2P Provides Benefits for B2B Applications

The implementation of P2P networks for B2B exchanges offers benefits like resource sharing and aggregation, lower cost of ownership, robustness, scalability and reliability, dynamism, and enhanced ad hoc connectivity and collaboration (Barkai 2001, Schoder and Fischbach 2003, Shirky et al. 2001).

Resource Sharing and Aggregation

P2P networks allow the aggregation and use of untapped resources like computing power or data storage. By aggregating those resources, the whole is made greater than the sum of its parts. Applications that benefit from the aggregation of these resources are compute-intensive simulations or distributed file systems. Application areas can be found in the financial, life sciences, transportation, telecommunication, or semiconductor sectors, where large computing problems occur. In a B2B scenario, two companies with large-scale computing infrastructures could exchange or resell their surplus capacity to each other over the Internet or a private network. This transfer can be mediated through a vendor that establishes standards and prices for the exchange.

Small- and medium-sized enterprises (SMEs) in the automotive industry may be a good example. SMEs are confronted with the need to take part in (temporary) collaborations with their customers (i.e., automakers) or with other suppliers during the design of a new product and its manufacturing process. Due to the increasing complexity of the products—and hence the increasing complexity of the engineering design process as a whole—traditional approaches to product design are not sufficient anymore. The applications of computer-aided design (CAD) and computer-aided engineering (CAE) are gaining importance not only for large, multinational enterprises, such as automakers, but also for SMEs along the supply chain in the automotive industry. In contrast to automakers, these SMEs do not have access to an adequate IT infrastructure comprising software and hardware.

The decentralized organization of certain types of P2P networks and the feature of possible "spontaneous" collaboration and utilization of services on demand make P2P technologies relevant in this context. In this context, the utilization of (unused) computing power allows SMEs to execute adequate analysis tools in distributed computational environments according to their actual needs. For example, in a parallel environment for high-performance computing, the outputs of the computation must be available in a given time span. Furthermore, the application of P2P networking to knowledge management promises a great potential because the characteristics, such as adaptability and flexibility, fit exceptionally well with those of informal communications processes within and between corporations. The process of designing a product involving various participants is an example of these informal communication processes. Organizations have always faced considerable difficulties when trying to aggregate and leverage their existing individual human expertise. P2P networking offers new possibilities for that purpose by facilitating an *ad hoc* knowledge exchange among connected peers, and thereby closely emulating the way humans interact in face-to-face communication.

The Reduced Cost of Ownership

Through the use of P2P infrastructure, the cost of ownership is reduced. A good example is the use of decentralized collaboration software like Groove Workspace or file and storage sharing applications, which reduce the cost of purchasing and maintaining expensive servers for storing data or group access.

Robustness

The distribution and replication of information objects reduces individual points of failure, and thereby enhances the robustness of a network. For example, P2P networks can facilitate the distribution of product catalogs of supply chain companies for the e-procurement process. The failure of the catalog server of a product provider will not cause severe consequences, since other partners store copies of the catalog for others to access.

Scalability

A system is scalable if none of the components become a bottleneck as the system grows through adding hosts, devices, users, and files. Scalability is often promoted as a key advantage of decentralized systems over centralized systems, although the reality is more complex. For example, a Gnutella network may become tangled due to too many search requests (Kan, 2001). Moreover, the nature of P2P's decentralization and leveraging of unused resources makes it more scalable than traditional client-server systems (Milojicic et al. 2002).

Dynamism or Intermittent Connectivity

P2P systems assume that the computing environment is highly dynamic. A node may not always connect to the network. The temporary exclusion of certain nodes of the network can have various reasons, ranging from purely technical (physical disconnection) to highly social (lurking) phenomena. Hence, P2P applications manage the temporary unavailability of a peer, or even the permanent loss of one or more peers, by using intelligent replication mechanisms or message queuing.

Related to intermittent connectivity is the notion of supporting *ad hoc* environments, where members come and go based on their current physical locations or their current interests. P2P applications fit these needs because they naturally take changes into account in the group of participants.

Challenges of P2P Technologies

Although it appears profitable to build information systems based on P2P architectures, the extent to which companies can take advantage of P2P technologies is still being debated (Schoder and Fischbach 2003). Practitioners at the forefront of corporate information management, especially those working in settings that extend beyond the boundaries of their own company, have raised a number of concerns, or, more discreetly formulated, have articulated the challenges to be met. Will decentralized control be able to cope with challenges regarding network control, security, interoperability, metadata, cost sharing, and intellectual property?

Network Control

Unlike traditional technologies, which favor a top-down design and planning approach, P2P facilitates a bottom-up approach in the sense of favoring emerging, self-organized networks or the communities using them. As a result, the development, size, and connections, as well as throughput and stability of P2P networks (in particular, those that extend beyond an individual company) can hardly be planned or predicted. The upside is that this facilitation of emergent coordination makes new application scenarios feasible.

Security

Due to the widely acknowledged threats to networked systems, effective security mechanisms constitute one of the most important requirements for a modern IT infrastructure. The implementation of P2P technologies creates additional challenges with respect to security, as their use frequently requires that third parties be allowed to access the resources of an internal system, for example, to share files or CPU running time (Barkai 2001, Udell et al. 2001). Use of an information system to communicate with or grant access to third parties can be accompanied by problematic side effects. During communication in P2P networks, conventional security mechanisms, such as firewall software, are frequently circumvented. An example is instant-messaging software, where communication without encryption creates another risk of company data being exposed. If P2P is for business use, techniques and methods for authentication, authorization, availability, data integrity, and trust have to be integrated.

Interoperability

Interoperability is the ability of an entity (device or application) to speak to, exchange data with, and be understood by any other entities. Today's world of P2P does not even begin to fulfill this requirement. Virtually all applications utilize specific protocols and interfaces. As a result, interoperability that extends beyond a single application or network is rare in current P2P networks. Although there are serious doubts about the feasibility and desirability of an "Übernetwork" (Wiley 2001) that would satisfy the needs of everyone, work aimed at creating a common infrastructure (middleware), with standardized interfaces for P2P applications, is in progress. The goal is to shorten development time and to enable applications to be implemented easily in existing systems. A platform for discussing suitable architectures and protocols for achieving this goal is the Global Grid Forum (www.gridforum.org).

Another promising development is the convergence of P2P and Web services (Shirky et al. 2001). The Web services concept is based on standards such as XML-RPC, SOAP, WSDL, and UDDI. Different Web services are designed to work together and interoperability is a fundamental goal. It can be expected that P2P and Web services will become increasingly symbiotic and that Web services will influence P2P standards.

Metadata

The implementation of P2P technology is accompanied by the problem of locating resources that may be significantly more difficult to identify than MP3 files within context-specific file-sharing systems. In order to convert raw data into usable information and make this available for efficient searches, suitable metadata concepts are required, such as those being discussed in connection with the Semantic Web and emerging XML standards (Berners-Lee 1999).

Cost Sharing

Free riders (or freeloaders), peers who take advantage of the available resources but do not contribute any in return, can present a considerable problem for P2P networks. This behavior undermines the P2P benefits because bottlenecks are created to restrict the availability of information and to reduce network performance. It also has a particularly negative effect on the willingness of people to make resources available. A possible solution is accountability, for example, keeping records on participants and introducing negative or positive incentives, such as charges or credits in the form of remuneration or user rights. Due to the absence of central authorities, this raises difficult questions with respect to the acceptability, enforcement, and privacy of the data usage.

Intellectual Property

The distribution of resources through P2P networks creates a dilemma in protecting intellectual property. On one hand, a company hopes to reduce the bottleneck of centrally distributing the original digital artifacts by adopting the P2P distribution approach. On the other hand, this company may lose profits from failing to protect its intellectual property. Therefore, the challenge faced by the business model of distributing intellectual property through P2P networks is how to gain the benefits from the network externality effect while protecting the intellectual property of knowledge contributors.

THE APPLICATION OF P2P TECHNOLOGIES TO B2B APPLICATIONS

B2B Structures and Applications

The B2B relationship can be viewed as having two attributes: *structure* and *relational ties*. Adopting Thompson's typology of interdependence between interorganizational units (Thompson 1967), we describe B2B relations as exhibiting three types of interdependence between organizations: *pooled, sequential,* and *reciprocal dependences*. Figure 9.3 illustrates the configuration of these three types of interorganizational interdependency. Organizations with pooled interdependency share and use common resources to conduct business processes. For example, firms in an electronic marketplace buy and sell things through e-hubs, which mediate the e-procurement process between buyers and sellers. The example structures can be Cisco's eHub and Wal-Mart's RetailLink®. Cisco has implemented a private exchange, called eHub, which provides a central point for integrating interenterprise manufacturing supply chain planning information and execution processes across its extended supply chain trading network. Ultimately, Cisco plans to include more than 2,000 of its suppliers, distributors, and contract electronic manufacturers in its private trading network (Grosvenor and Austin 2001). Wal-Mart's RetailLink® is also a private exchange to enable multienterprise supply chain synchronization by sharing their forecasts, production schedules, inventory levels, and real-time sales activity within their entire supplier base (Whitaker et al. 2001).

The sequential dependency cascades business activities across organizations, where the output from one organization becomes an input to another one. For example, for firms in a supply chain to deliver the final products to end customers, the sequence of activities for the order fulfillment process demonstrates this sequential interdependency. The example structures can be the HP printer supply chain and a textile/apparel supply chain. A printer supply chain consists of such stages of activities as print-circuit board and printer head design and manufacturing, printer assembly operations done at the factory and distributors, and distribution channel management, which relies on seamless coordination among supply chain partners across these stages. A textile/apparel supply chain involves the cooperation of different enterprises in the sequence of producing final products from fiber to retailing.

Organizations in reciprocal dependency iteratively receive input from and produce output to others. For example, for firms to form a strategic alliance or for a virtual organization to pursue a product development process, products are designed through the interweaving of product design activities among firms. The example structures can be industrywide consortiums, for example, Transora and Business Internet Consortium. Transora was created in June 2000 when many of the world's leading food, beverage, and consumer products companies joined forces to create the largest B2B e-marketplace for their industry (www.transora.com). Transora is an example of a single public exchange that provides exchange-to-exchange interoperability and end-to-end visibility for participants of the consumer products industry. It utilizes the Collaborative Planning, Forecasting, and Replenishment (CPFR) methodology developed by the Voluntary Interindustry Commerce Standards (VICS) Association to define processes and best practices for establishing and implementing collaborative relationships among trading partners.

Figure 9.3 **Topology of B2B Interdependence**

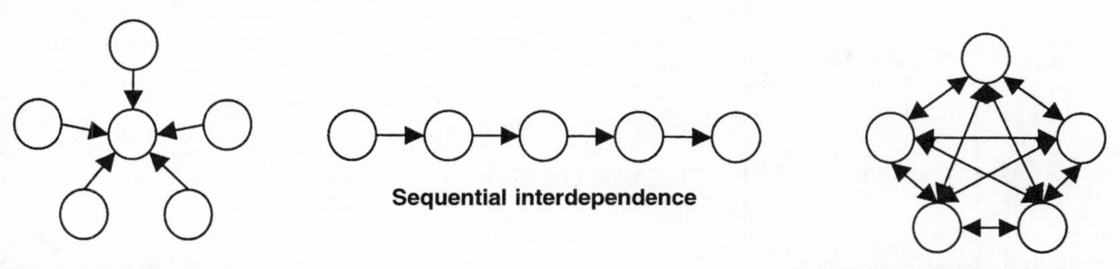

Business Internet Consortium is a nonprofit consortium aiming to be a "think tank" for generating technologies and business practices to help companies overcome the challenges of implementing e-business applications. It is composed of IT vendors such as Computer Associates International Inc., Dell Computer Corp., Hewlett-Packard Co., IBM, Intel Corp., Microsoft Corp., and SAP AG, and pioneer users such as Capital One Financial Corp., Charles Schwab & Co., and Ford Motor Co., which provide direct input on their e-business requirements to the new consortium. In addition, the consortium issues a series of reference designs and white papers on topics such as e-business architectural directions, interoperability technologies, and common business procedures. Work groups are being formed to address specific issues that include the use of XML and other technologies, integrating existing business systems with Web-based applications, and establishing secure online systems (Evans and Copeland 2000).

Since the complexity level of interdependence varies among these three configurations, it emphasizes different needs for coordinating their business processes. For example, three coordination mechanisms to handle these three types of interdependences have been suggested (Kumar and van Dissel, 1996; March and Simon, 1958). Coordination by standardization is appropriate for pooled dependency, where pooled business entities can interchange information through common protocols. For sequential interdependency, besides standard communication protocols, coordination by plan is needed to schedule activities to streamline a series of activities across organizations. The reciprocal interdependency calls upon mutual adjustment besides the aforementioned two coordination mechanisms in order to construct feasible business processes flexibly. The resulting interorganizational information systems demand various features. To handle pooled interdependency, an interorganizational system (IOS) requires interoperability on the data level. Common data interchange standards, such as EDIFACT or XML-based protocols, are essential to coordinate such loosely coupled business transactions. Besides data interchangeability, the interoperability of an IOS demands information sharing mechanisms to streamline the sequence of activities executed by different organizations to reach effective and efficient business processes in order to handle sequential interdependency. To handle reciprocal interdependency, the IOS should possess dynamic process formation and management capabilities, such as workflow creation, monitoring, and adaptation. Since tasks are tightly coupled among those participating organizations, coordination mechanisms augment the need for human intervention and contact, which increasingly demand interpersonal communication and collaboration facilitation.

The relational tie defines the degree of relations between two organizations. From social network analysis literatures, the defining feature of a tie is that it establishes a linkage between a pair of actors (Wasserman and Faust 1994). Pairs may maintain a tie based on one relation only or a multiplex tie based on many relations. Thus, a tie may contain characteristics like content, direction, and strength; however, a tie is often referred to as weak or strong. In B2B relationships, a tie

Figure 9.4 **B2B's Relations**

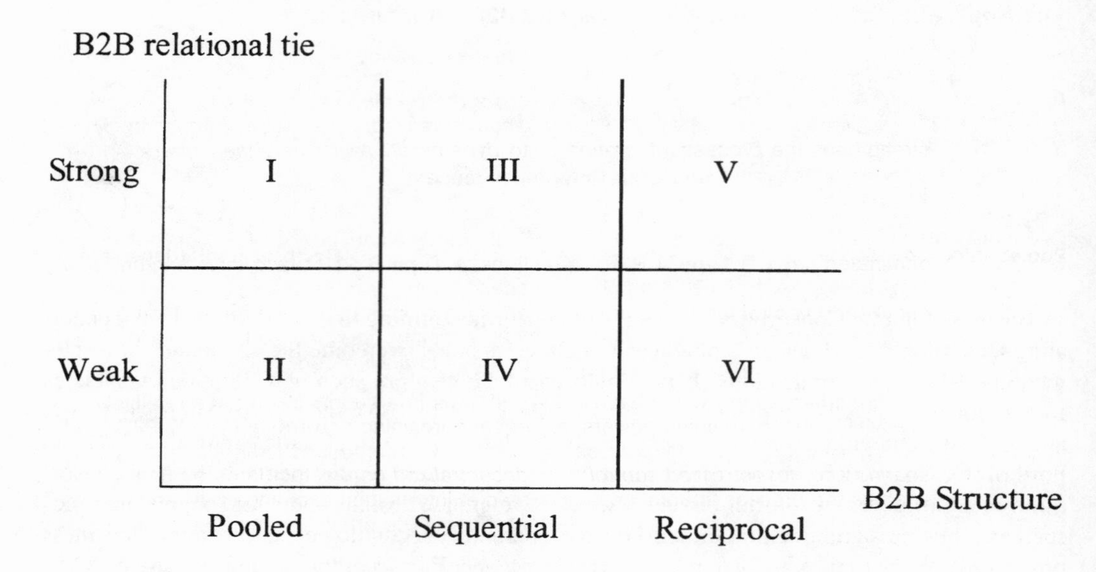

can be denoted as the transfer of resources (supply vs. demand), association (independent units vs. alliances), and interaction (spot vs. frequent communication).

Based on the two attributes of structure and relational ties, we have identified six types of B2B e-commerce relations for performing business processes between business entities (see Figure 9.4). We can elaborateon these variations with some major business processes, such as e-procurement, product development, distributed manufacturing/service, product/service distribution, and customer services. Taking e-procurement in a Type I relation (strong tie, pooled dependency) as an example, firms tend to build continuous replenishment to reduce inventory uncertainty by relying on their stable and strong relationship; nevertheless, firms tend to adopt e-hubs to source from e-marketplaces in a Type II relation (weak tie, pooled dependency). Firms in a Type III relation (strong tie, sequential dependency) may be able to seek time advanced information from neighboring peers in order to react agilely in the sequential interdependency because of their strong relational tie; however, with weak ties between firms in a Type IV relation (weak tie, sequential dependency), the level of information sharing may be restricted in the order level. In a Type V relation (strong tie, reciprocal dependency), the strong tie between peer firms enables direct communication for coordinating the procurement activities; however, the weak ties typical of Type VI relations (weak tie, reciprocal dependency) present an open e-market for peer firms to source materials or services. Other major business processes, such as product development, distributed manufacturing/service, product/service distribution, and customer services, can be differentiated by their relational ties as being governed either by e-market or e-hierarchy mechanisms.

The Contingency of Applying P2P Technologies to B2B Applications

The contingency of applying P2P technologies to B2B applications can be identified by enumerating potential consequences of using different types of P2P architectures for B2B processes under different relations. Table 9.1 shows the application of P2P technology to various B2B structures.

Table 9.1

The Application of P2P Technology to Various B2B Structures

	Strong tie relation	Weak tie relation
Pooled	**Type A P2P** platform with *process sharing and centralized control* strengthens the *process integration* between the dominated central peer and its supply peers.	**Type B P2P** platform with *information sharing and centralized control* allows the central peer to *dynamically switch* its supply peers.
Sequential	1. If a supply chain exists with dominated firms, a **Type A P2P** platform with *process sharing and centralized control* facilitates process integration for firms between tiers.	1. If a supply chain exists with dominated firms, a **Type B P2P** platform with *information sharing and centralized control* enables the dominated firms to acquire information from their neighbor tiers and go to market to find partners to fulfill orders.
	2. If firms in a supply chain have relatively equal bargaining powers, a **Type C P2P** platform with *process sharing and decentralized control* enables the process integration.	2. If firms in a supply chain have relatively equal bargaining powers, a **Type D P2P** platform with *information sharing and decentralized control* facilitates efficient market information exchange between tiers to coordinate the order fulfillment process.
Reciprocal	**Type C P2P** platform with *process sharing and decentralized control* mobilizes the process integration among involved partners in the consortium to form *virtual organizations* to capture business opportunities.	**Type D P2P** platform with *information sharing and decentralized control* facilitates information exchange to aggregate partners to form *strategic alliances* to capture business opportunities.

Type A P2P Deployment (Sharing Processes and Centralized Control)

Type A P2P deployment is centrally governed to share business processes, with a peer granting its capacity to serve its partner peers to execute tasks for accomplishing the shared business processes. Since the deployment of P2P technologies strongly integrates business processes among peers, partners with strong relational ties, such as strategic alliances, frequent supply demand, and collaborative product development further enhance their process coordination and integration. The deployment of P2P to Type I, III, and V B2B relations is relatively more applicable than to Type II, IV, and VI, since organizations in the former types have stronger relational ties than those in the latter types.

Type B P2P Deployment (Sharing Information and Centralized Control)

The level of resource exchange between peers is limited in terms of information, so that each peer retains full autonomy to react to information received from other peers. Although a P2P network is governed by a central peer, coordination is restricted to the information level, and process integration may be carried out in a loosely coupled manner.

Type C P2P Deployment (Sharing Process and Decentralized Control)

The level of resource exchange between peers on the process level includes process control information, and, due to decentralized control, the coordination process becomes more com-

Table 9.2

Issues of Applying P2P Techniques

B2B relation	Issues	Applications of P2P techniques
Pooled	Synchronization	Standard protocols to synchronize activities of business processes
Sequential	Quick response	Tier-wise information sharing to coordinate business processes
Reciprocal	Dynamic process formation	Industrywide collaboration networks to capture business opportunities

plicated. The process integration may foster dynamic business processes via forming virtual organizations.

Type D P2P Deployment (Sharing Information and Decentralized Control)

The level of resource exchange between peers is on the information level and, due to decentralized control, leaves individual peers to react to information autonomously. The coordination of business processes is loosely coupled to the formation of strategic alliances.

ISSUES OF APPLYING P2P TECHNOLOGIES TO B2B APPLICATIONS

The discussion of B2B applications in the previous section classifies three B2B relations—pooled, sequential, and reciprocal dependence—into three typical business practices: e-hub, supply chain, and industrywide consortium. Major issues raised by these different B2B relations and the corresponding techniques that can be adopted to tackle these issues are summarized as follows. Table 9.2 summarizes these issues and the corresponding P2P techniques.

Pooled Relation

A firm in the central position of the pooled relationship bears the role of synchronizing business activities among business partners. A company with exclusive products, processes, or market position is the ultimate candidate to develop such private exchange with the pooled relation, for example, Cisco's eHub, Wal-Mart's RetailLink®, and Taiwan Semiconductor Manufacturing Corporation's virtual factory. The pooled relation grants the company in the central position the possibility of aggregating information from surrounding partners, which in turn increases the visibility of all the pooled partners. Through information sharing and process synchronization, the collection of pooled partners collaborates to create e-B2B value.

Based on the taxonomy of the P2P search model in two dimensions, data versus index and centralized versus distributed, we can easily suggest that centralized index and distributed data are the most suitable for pooled B2B applications (Parameswaran, Susarla, and Whinston 2001). With P2P technology, the central peer is given a relatively light weighting compared with the client-server architecture. Companies with their unique product market and manufacturing status launch private exchange services by presenting pooled business directories to connected peers to share information and synchronize processes. Therefore, the application of P2P technology to the pooled relation can be viewed as the "Napsterization" of B2B relations in order to share process information guided by central directories. The involved business entities should comply with common protocols to exchange information. Depending on their relational tie, peers may have different degrees of autonomy. For example, companies with strong relational ties tend to share process control information, which automates process integration as a whole. Companies with weak ties may withhold their control power and share process status information.

Sequential Relation

Firms' interdependences in the sequential relation tend to be affected by the performance of upstream or downstream business partners. The bear game example illustrates the ripple effect on supply chain uncertainty that a small increasing of demand at the downstream customers of a supply chain may cause excess inventory at the upstream suppliers. The main issue in handling such effects on companies in the sequential relation, such as supply chain networks, is how to streamline business processes under conditions of uncertainty deriving from upstream and downstream partners.

P2P networks can be deployed between partners in a tier of a supply chain to facilitate supply allocation in a dynamic supply chain structure. A peer on behalf of a partner of a supply chain goes to market to seek possible suppliers through P2P networks. By virtue of P2P networks, content-based addressing, redundancy, and fault tolerance, business partners can efficiently search suitable suppliers to contribute to activities of business processes even without providing the centralized e-marketplace Web site. In order to reduce the risks of dynamically engaging peers in fulfilling business processes, trust is essential to evaluate partners' trustworthiness as suppliers. The strength of relational ties between partners determines the propensity to trust each other. Therefore, up-to-date information regarding partners' trustworthiness should be combined with current quotations issued by partners to select suppliers through P2P networks between supply chain tiers. The connection of tier-wise P2P networks can propagate business transactions in their sequential relations more smoothly by enlarging their supply chain visibility and responding to these changes more effectively and efficiently.

Reciprocal Dependences

The fully meshed connections of business partners through P2P networks allow companies to communicate directly when performing business process activities. Due to their reciprocal dependence, the chain effects from their decision making need efficient and direct responses from their counterparts. Therefore, P2P networks work most effectively when facilitating peer-wise negotiation and coordination. The main issue in managing peers' reciprocal dependence in B2B applications is how to build industrywide business process integration protocols so that peers can connect their services dynamically to streamline their activities of delivering value to customers. Dynamic process formation relies on sharing information between peers to increase supply chain visibility, and on utilizing core competences of peers in order to deliver value to customers.

An industrywide yellow pages, similar to a Web service registry accessible by UDDI protocol, adopts P2P's centralized index architecture to allow industry firms to search for potential partners. Individual peers can maintain their distributed knowledge about other peers' collaborative experience in selecting partners. A referral mechanism based on transactional memory is useful for directing partner selection, and the peer-wise negotiation capability enables the automated process formation.

DESCRIPTIVE ANALYSIS OF BUSINESS MODELS OF ADOPTING P2P TECHNOLOGIES TO B2B APPLICATIONS

After identifying issues in applying P2P networks to B2B applications, we are interested in knowing prospective business models for realizing P2P technologies with these applications. Since the

Figure 9.5 **P2P Networks for Pooled Relations**

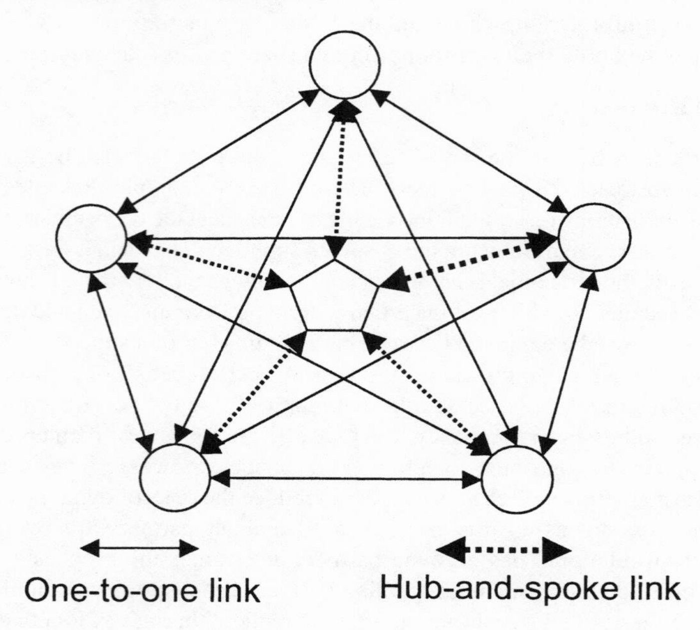

business model positions a company in the value chain, it is contingent on the company's mutual relations and roles playing for generating values. Based on that general principle, patterns of how P2P technologies may help enhance B2B relations emerge.

In pooled business relations, such as Cisco's eHub and Wal-Mart's RetailLink®, we expect that the application of P2P networks adopts a private exchange business model. The company in the central position holds the legitimate status to deploy the P2P network to its partners. The central peer will authorize the connection built between peers by providing an up-to-date centralized directory, so that the central company's role of synchronizing business processes among connected partners can be identified and executed. Therefore, the business model for the pooled business relation to apply P2P technologies is the single private exchange network. The centralized governing structure of the single exchange model enables the central company to coordinate business partners' activities by either sharing processes or information, depending on their mutual relation ties as specified in Figure 9.5. The private exchange business model enables the lightweight central peer to aggregate information and synchronize actions provided by its peers, which coordinate the material flow across fully meshed one-to-one links. In summary, we can generalize that a feasible business model using P2P networks for pooled business relations possesses such characteristics as information sharing and process synchronization. The central peer takes the legitimate role to deploy P2P networks.

In dealing with sequential relations, P2P technologies are mainly applied to supporting tier-wise supply chain partners' coordination and extending supply chain visibility in order to foresee and promptly respond to uncertainties across tiers. The prospective business model to deploy P2P networks is to build multiple exchanges to interconnect tier-wise business partners. Suppliers and customers in a tier of a supply chain can connect through an eHub as an exchange to streamline activities in a tier, and the connection between tiers can further coordinate activities across the whole supply chain. The reason for adopting a multiexchange model lies more in the incentive for

Figure 9.6 **P2P Networks for Sequential Relations**

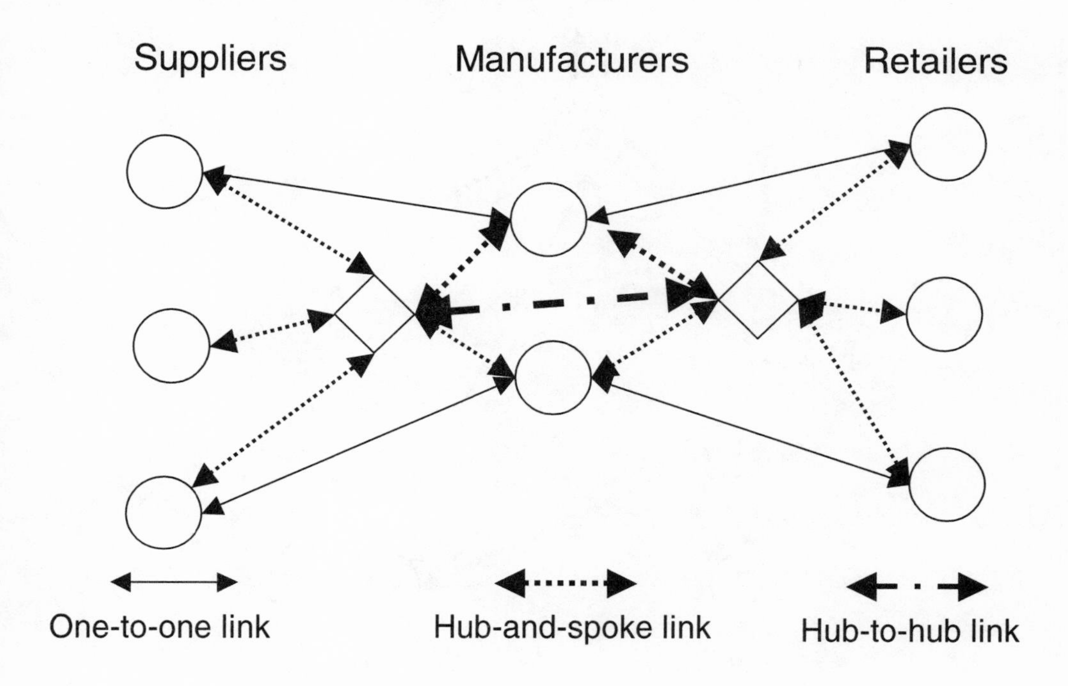

peers to build the connection solely on a tier-wise span rather than a multitier span. On the one hand, the centralized index of a P2P network in a tier serves as a directory for customers and suppliers to allocate their partners, and payload can be transferred directly through P2P networks. Tier-wise P2P shared resources can be information and processes depending on their relational ties. On the other hand, the governing structure can be decentralized, where P2P's content-based addressing allows peers to allocate pier-wise partners, which increases the adaptability of supply chain processes to cope with unpredicted events. Figure 9.6 illustrates the structure of P2P networks for supply chain applications.

In summary, we generalize that the business model for dealing with sequential relations using P2P networks should connect tier-wise activities to agilely respond to changes from neighboring piers.

The reciprocal dependence relation demands high connectivity between peers to search for partner peers, negotiate feasible workflows, and execute business processes due to the dynamics of peer interactions. Firms in an industrywide consortium can share information through P2P networks with common protocols. Depending on firms' relative roles in the business processes, P2P technologies enable firms in a consortium to share information or processes in delivering value to their customers. For example, participant companies in a consortium with relatively equal bargaining power tend to keep one-to-one linkages between firms under commonly acceptable P2P platforms. One or few companies whose importance dominates in a consortium tend to develop centralized P2P networks to coordinate business processes. Therefore, firms in a reciprocal dependence adopt P2P technologies to distributed and centralized governing structures depending on their relational ties. Figure 9.6 shows the potential P2P networks in an industry consortium.

Figure 9.7 **P2P Networks for Reciprocal Dependency**

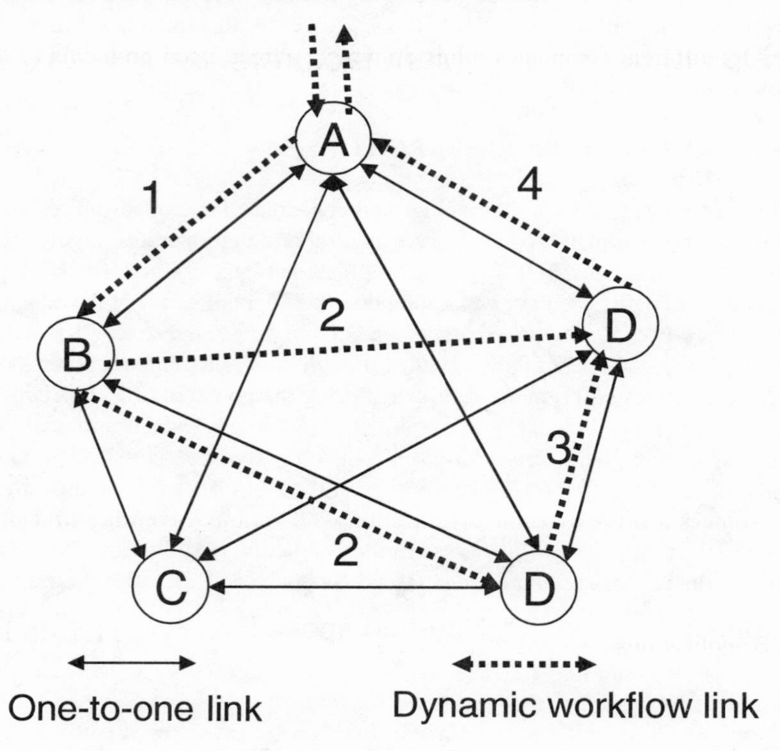

Figure 9.7 shows the potential P2P networks in an industry consortium. Peer-wise negotiation and coordination through P2P networks enable the formation of dynamic business processes in a reciprocally dependent community. In Figure 9.7, Peer *A* receives the order from its customer. From its P2P network, Peer *A* forwards the order to Peer *B*, which distributes the order to two partners, Peers *D* and *E*. Peer *E* finishes the process after receiving outcomes from Peer *D*. Peer *A* delivers the products to its customer after receiving outcomes from Peer *E*. Dynamic business processes can be realized by P2P networks to manage their reciprocal dependency.

In summary, the most suitable business models for managing pooled business relations are centralized P2P networks. Such networks take advantage of the central role of a peer in synchronizing business activities executed by its connected peers. However, they are vulnerable to the central peer's failure in coordinating the business processes. The most suitable business models for managing sequential relations are multiexchange models, which connect tier-wise partners across neighboring tiers to coordinate the upstream and downstream partners of a supply chain. The advantage of this type of P2P deployment lies in reducing bullwhip effects through information sharing across peer groups. However, the interoperability of P2P architecture for sequential relations across upstream and downstream ties may hinder the deployment of P2P networks. Finally, the most suitable business models for dealing with reciprocal dependency are to develop industrywide standards in order to enable quick and dynamic process formation.

Currently, many efforts are going into developing domain-specific ontology to facilitate the interchange of information across organizations. However, the interoperability between services offered by different companies relies on widely agreed upon protocols to dynamically connect business processes.

CONCLUSIONS AND FUTURE RESEARCH

P2P networking is concerned with the pooling and coordinated use of resources within distributed communities and is constructed as an overlay structure that operates largely independently from central institutions. Thus, P2P networking offers new possibilities for B2B systems and networks, including benefits such as aggregating distributed intelligence at the edge of networks, enhanced degree of integration, lower costs of ownership, improved scalability, fault-tolerance, and the ease of allowing *ad hoc* collaboration. Although the basic component technologies exist today, research challenges still remain in fully exploring the potential of P2P networking.

In this study, we surveyed the application of P2P technologies to B2B applications. We summarized P2P networking characteristics and introduced taxonomies for P2P technologies and B2B applications. We specified P2P technologies in the form of two attributes: the sharing of distributed resources and the dynamic organization with various governing structures. In addition, B2B relations can be viewed in two attributes: structure and relational tie. Based on this taxonomy, we identified the contingency and issues in applying P2P technologies to B2B applications. Finally, we presented a descriptive analysis of business models of adopting P2P networks to B2B applications.

We found that P2P technology becomes an important solution to certain inherent problems in B2B applications. This paper laid the foundation for future research in this broad and rich field. In future research, we can develop appropriate measures to capture the effects of applying P2P technology to B2B transactions. We can also adopt P2P systems, such as JXTA, Gnutella, or Groove, to implement B2B application systems in obtaining empirical experiences.

REFERENCES

Barkai, D. *Peer-to-Peer Computing, Technologies for Sharing and Collaboration on the Net*. Hillsboro, NC: Intel Press, 2001.

Berners-Lee, T. *Weaving the Web: The Original Design and Ultimate Destiny of the World Wide Web*. New York: Harper, 1999.

Cerf, V. Beyond the post-PC Internet. *Communications of the ACM,* 44, 9 (2001), 34–37.

Evans, J., and Copeland, L. Vendors, users setting up e-business think-tank. *Computerword,* November 29, 2000. Available at www.computerworld.com/managementtopics/ebusiness/story/0,10801,54493,00.html.

Foster, I. The grid: A new infrastructure for 21st century science. *Physics Today,* 55 (2002), 2.

Foster, I., and Kesselman, C. *The Grid: Blueprint for a New Computing Infrastructure*. San Francisco: Morgan Kaufmann, 1999.

Gong, L. JXTA: A network programming environment. *IEEE Internet Computing,* 5, 3 (2001), 88–95.

Grosvenor, F., and Austin, T.A. Cisco's eHub intiative. *Supply Chain Management Review* (July–August 2001), 28–35 (available at www.manugistics.com/documents/SCM0121cisco.pdf).

Kan, G. Gnutella. In A. Oram, (ed.), *Peer-to-Peer: Harnessing the Benefits of a Disruptive Technology*. Sebastopol, CA: O'Reilly & Associates, 2001, pp. 94–121.

Kumar, K., and van Dissel, H.G. Sustainable collaboration: Managing conflict and cooperation in interorganizational systems. *MIS Quarterly,* 20, 3 (1996), 279–300.

March, J.G., and Simon, H.A. *Organizations*. New York: John Wiley and Sons, 1958.

McAfee, A. The Napsterization of B2B. *Harvard Business Review,* 78, 6 (2000), 18–19.

Miller, J. Jabber—conversational technologies. In Oram, A. (ed.), *Peer-to-Peer: Harnessing the Benefits of a Disruptive Technology.* Sebastopol, CA: O'Reilly & Associates, 2001, pp. 77–88.

Milojicic, D.S.; Kalogeraki, V.; Lukose, R.; Nagaraja, K.; Pruyne, J.; Richard, B.; S. Rollins; and Xu, Z.. Peer-to-peer computing (March 8, 2002) (available at www.hpl.hp.com/techreports/2002/HPL-2002-57.pdf).

Oram, A., ed. *Peer-to-Peer: Harnessing the Benefits of a Disruptive Technology.* Sebastopol, CA: O'Reilly & Associates, 2001.

Parameswaran, M.; Susarla, A.; and Whinston, A.B. P2P networking: An information sharing alternative. *IEEE Computer*, 34, 7 (2001), 31–38.

Schoder, D., and Fischbach, K. Peer-to-Peerpeer-netzwerke für das Ressourcenmanagement. *Wirtschaftsinformatik*, 45, 3 (2003), 313–323.

Shirky, C.; Truelove, K.; Dornfest, R., eds. 2001 P2P networking overview. Sebastopol, CA: O'Reilly & Associates, 2001.

Thompson, J. *Organizations in Action.* New York: McGraw-Hill, 1967.

Udell, J.; Asthagiri, N.; Tuvell, W. Security. In Oram, A. (ed.), *Peer-to-Peer: Harnessing the Benefits of a Disruptive Technology*. Sebastopol, CA: O'Reilly & Associates, 2001, pp. 354–380.

Wasserman, S., and Faust, K. Social network analysis: Methods and applications. Cambridge: Cambridge University Press, 1994.

Whitaker, J.D.; Murphy, M.D.; Haltzel, A.H.; and Dik, R.W. Private exchange: The smart path to collaboration. *Supply Chain Management Review Global Supplement* (July–August, 2001), 8–11.

Wiley, B. Interoperability through gateways. In A. Oram (ed.), *Peer-to-Peer: Harnessing the Benefits of a Disruptive Technology*. Sebastopol, CA: O'Reilly & Associates, 2001, pp. 381–392.

CHAPTER 10

TOPOGRAPHICAL LEVERAGING OF SHARABLE SERVICES

THE CONCEPT OF CAPACITY PROVISION NETWORKS

XIANJUN GENG, RAM GOPAL, R. RAMESH, AND ANDREW B. WHINSTON

Abstract: *Internet service providers (ISPs) face exploding demand from business and consumers for service aspects such as quality-of-service, mobility, geographical reach, and seamless functionality integration. As their service capabilities are stretched thin, they often find it difficult to provide satisfactory services. In this paper, we introduce the notion of topographical leverage in providing Internet services and develop the concept of capacity provision networks (CPNs). A CPN enhances Internet service providers' service capabilities by pooling all providers' underused resources and supplying them as needed. Through several industry-specific examples we illustrate the viability and business value of the CPN concept. We further develop a model of business and market forces impacting business decisions to trade and collaborate among the various players in the Internet service industry. The business implications of a CPN are also discussed. In particular, we believe our research should give rise to several innovative business models in the Internet service industry, where the concepts of trading and collaborating as envisioned in CPNs are likely to become predominant in the future.*

Keywords: *Business Model, Capacity Provision Network (CPN), Internet Service Industry, Internet Service Provider (ISP), Quality-of-Service, Topographical Leverage*

INTRODUCTION

The provision and delivery of a variety of services over the Internet are both expanding and advancing at a rapid pace. The landscape of service offerings is continually evolving, with numerous types of new services that replace or augment existing services, for two primary reasons: to attain improved levels of cost-effectiveness and quality in service provisioning and delivery and to take advantage of new business opportunities that arise due to developments in technology, business environments, and markets. These developments can be broadly classified using four dimensions of the Internet service industry: *service types, communities of service providers and consumers, contractual business relationships among the various players,* and *service infrastructures and architectures.* The service types can be further classified into *core services, emerging managed services,* and *specific consumer value-adding services* (ISP-Market 2003a, b). The core services essentially pertain to connectivity and access to the Internet, caching/hosting content, and co-location of customer infrastructures. The emerging managed services include security, administration of infrastructures/architectures, messaging, and storage. The value-adding services are numerous, ranging from Web-based e-mail and spam filters to customer portal management.

As service types change and grow, the underlying communities of service providers and consumers also evolve. Typically, the core services pertain to a logical delivery path in the content supply chain—from content publishers to content distributors to Internet service providers (ISPs) to the end customers. As a result, a variety of business relationships and contractual agreements exist among these players. At each stage of this supply chain, a provider adds value to the content and its delivery process. The value is created by provisioning necessary and appropriate infrastructural and architectural components in the delivery path. A view of the entire content distribution process as a supply chain logically leads to the concepts of *vertical* and *horizontal integration* that have dominated the traditional supply chain domain till now. Furthermore, as in the traditional supply chains, the integrations in the content distribution industry can occur at various levels of business conglomerations. To name a few examples, content publishers can integrate separately with content distribution networks (CDNs); CDN providers can integrate independently with ISPs; ISPs can horizontally unite with each other for joint delivery services to the end customers; and large publishers can integrate with both CDN providers and ISP clusters to extend their reach into their customer base.

Concomitant with changes in the core services of the content distribution industry, a major revolution is currently under way in the managed services and value-added services areas. A range of technologies, from small to very large, is basically enabling these services. While the services under the *managed* category are targeted at business customers—from small to large business houses—those under the *value-added* category are targeted at both business and individual customers. The key technology enablers in the managed services are monitoring systems at all levels—networks, servers, content, and application. Storage area networks (SANs) are evolving into Internet storage infrastructures (ISIs), peer-to-peer (P2P) computing is evolving into more widespread grid computing architectures, and there are rapid advances in the security and virtual private network (VPN) domains. The parallel developments in the wireless area are essentially adding a new orthogonal dimension to these enablers. In the value-added category, some of the major technology enablers include the near-ubiquitous Web-based e-mail services, URL and content filtering with local cache management services, and customized content and portal services, to name a few.

Where do all these evolutions point to? First, we draw certain observations on the state and direction of the Internet service industry as follows:

1) customers—both corporate and individual—are increasingly discriminating on the quality of service,
2) customers are increasingly mobile and their needs for the variety of services are growing,
3) customer bases are rapidly expanding—both geographically and volume-wise,
4) content publishers have an increasing need to respond to these customer needs and reach out to their growing bases,
5) varieties of technologies at different levels of maturity, performance, and cost-effectiveness are arriving at the market to jointly facilitate the needs of both publishers and customers,
6) communities of different service providers are expanding toward more competitive environments in certain areas and shrinking toward large oligopolistic conglomerates in some others, and

7) while the existing communication infrastructure of the Internet is getting stretched thin due to the growing levels of activity, both alternate infrastructures, such as the wireless media, and unused capacities, such as the miles of dark fiber being implemented by many telecom providers, continue to grow.

These observations logically lead to the following inferences. First, the Internet service industry in the core area at a minimum, is getting more vertically integrated in order to respond effectively to the market externalities, supply/demand forces, and competition. Second, horizontal alliances—both independent and within vertical structures—will increase in all types of service. These alliances would be the outcomes of the instability, costs, and performance-effectiveness of new technologies; growth in market demands; and the constraints of time and space in value creation and service delivery. Third, the increasing competition in several service domains and the capability to leverage resources (such as bandwidth, server capacities, geographic advantages, etc.) that are either unused or potentially reserved for future use would create several market forces leading toward greater integration with different combinations of service providers.

Two natural outcomes of these trends in the Internet service industry are *leverage* and *resource trades.* Leverage is obtained from the strategic positioning of a service provider among other players in an Internet supply chain; resource trades with other players arise as a consequence. In order to derive the leverage, the availing service provider should possess a geographic advantage in a service operation that others may not have and the required infrastructural/architectural capabilities to realize the benefit. For instance, a service provider that has a bandwidth connection between two points could trade some of its bandwidth to another provider that needs this connection. Another, rather classical example, is that of the CDNs. A CDN provider strategically locates servers at different places on the *edge* of the Internet; a publisher that wishes to minimize the delays in the delivery of its content to a geographically distributed customer base could replicate its content Web site at the CDN servers and thus minimize the data traffic through the Internet *core.* A third example is that of an ISI service provider. ISI is typically an outsourced service for the strategic storage of enormously rich content—such as streaming media for instance—at the Internet edge. Several data centers across the world offer these services. ISI is a scalable economic service that typically uses a pay-as-you-go model employed to complement existing Web hosting and other service architectures, especially when service using an ISI solution is faced with considerable demand uncertainty. Several publishers of streaming media content avail themselves of this service.

The above analysis of some of the major Internet trends and the examples show that there will be increasing levels of leveraged resource trades among several service providers in the future. This can also be seen from the classical economic perspective: when service resources are limited and could be expensive to build, and when consumption externality occurs at a much faster rate than resource growth rates within the industry, several innovative resource pooling strategies will naturally arise with underlying economic trade mechanisms among different service providers. This behavior can clearly be seen in the telecom industry, where, after the deregulation act of 1997, the markets became highly competitive in almost all of the sectors; resource pooling through trade agreements has become central to the delivery of telecom services since consumption externalities are occurring at increasing levels. In the broader arena of Internet services, this phenomenon is occurring in different segments at different levels. Consequently, several novel business models involving vertical as well as lateral agreements for leveraged resource trades are in a process of evolution and implementation. The principal driving forces in this evolution are *externalities at different layers of resource consumption, economies of scale and scope,* and *increasing demands on the quality of service.*

Given this background, we introduce the notion of *capacity provision networks* (CPNs) consisting of various players in the Internet service industry that trade resources between each other using certain context-specific leverages in the service delivery process (Geng et al., 2003a, b, c, d). In particular, we focus on a specific type of leverage that arises due to a combination of the network topographical advantages and infrastructural/architectural capabilities of the availing service provider. In general, a CPN is a network of four broad types of participating firms in the Web: *content publishers, content distributors, service providers,* and *intermediary brokers.* In such a network, we can envision a node as representing a firm and an arc between a pair of nodes as indicating a business relationship between the two. The business relationship entails a contract, where one firm provides a service to the other; the revenue from the service provided could come either from the recipient node or elsewhere. The service can be viewed as a *commodity,* and could include providing infrastructural/architectural capacities, sharing of content and other abstract resources, and providing other administrative human services, in any combination. Central to this trade is the notion of *sharability:* a resource that is sharable among different constituents (such as content, bandwidth, or server capacity, for instance) yields a basis for trade. Accordingly, the commodity traded could be categorized into three types: *capacity, content,* and *other services.* We term such a network the *business-level CPN.* The business-level CPN establishes a basis for trade relationships from which specific business models involving a network of participating firms can be derived. The business-level CPN is a financial network, where the arcs could also be interpreted to indicate the flow of service value to a recipient from a provider, and also possibly the reverse flow of revenues from the trade to the provider.

A business-level CPN could assume several configurations in its implementation. For this purpose, we introduce the notion of a *technical-level CPN* as follows. At the technical level, a node can be envisioned to symbolize a service, and an arc from a node to another would indicate that the recipient service would access and utilize the resources contained within the provider service. For example, each node could represent a server farm; an arc could indicate that the recipient server farm utilizes some of the resources contained within the provider farm, such as CPU time, storage, and bandwidth, for instance. Clearly, each arc of the business-level CPN could subsume an underlying technical CPN; since each business entity could possess a network of its own services, an arc specifying a contract at the business level could translate into a full network of interconnected and mutually accessing services. Consequently, a *collection* of technical-level CPNs integrated together would describe the implementation of a business-level CPN. Furthermore, technical specifications of a CPN would occur at various levels of *granularity.* For example, assume that a server farm utilizes the cache servers at another farm for its content delivery processes. At the level of minimum granularity, each farm would perhaps be specified as a node in the technical CPN with an arc indicating the provisioning of the service. If the granularity were increased to the level of server farm architectural specifications involving specific servers, load balancers, and bandwidth connections, then this arc would expand into a more detailed connectivity and access path network. Hence, an implementation of a business-level CPN would take the form of several layers of technical CPN specifications with increasing levels of granularity.

In this research, we develop the underpinnings of CPN. Focusing on the network topographical leveraging of sharable resources, we develop a framework for modeling and analyzing the business and technical components of CPN. We note that any technical innovation should lead to viable business models, and the viability of a business model depends on its effective technical implementation. As a result, we observe a close coupling between the business and technical levels of CPN. The proposed CPN framework is described in terms of the following components:

- an ordered structure of the CPN elements,
- economic and market mechanisms driving the Internet service industry toward CPN formations,
- a classification of potential business models that could be developed from the CPN concept,
- the technical CPN architectures needed for these business models, and
- a layered structure of the technical-level CPN that could be used to derive design configurations for specific CPN business models.

The organization of this paper is as follows. Section 2 provides a brief analysis of the current state of the Internet service industry. Section 3 presents the concept of network topographical leverage with illustrations. Section 4 develops the proposed CPN framework and Section 5 presents the conclusions and directions for future research.

AN INDUSTRY ANALYSIS

In this section, we first investigate the current state of the Internet service industry as a whole, which leads to several important pointers for the emerging business- and technical-level CPN architectures. In particular, we focus on the ISP, CDN, ISI, and other related services.

The ISP Sector

Currently, there are in excess of 150 million subscribers to the Internet. Although the ISP industry has gone through several major changes in the past few years—especially the disappearance of several small players and the emergence of a few dominant service providers—currently there are about 6,000 ISPs in the United States alone, and only about thirteen of them have more than a million customers (ISP-Market 2003a, b). Clearly, the ISP sector continues to grow and the major market consolidations predicted by some have not materialized. ISPs continue to develop innovative business models in order to survive the forces of market consolidation, technological innovation in service provisioning and delivery, and increasing customer demands for quality of service and publisher demands for sustaining and growing their customer bases. As a consequence, the traditional ISP that normally provided only basic Internet access to its customers is now being transformed into a service center providing numerous other services—such as hosting and caching Web content, specialized streaming services for multimedia, management and monitoring of customers' specific Internet assets, intrusion detection and firewall services for these resources, and numerous other application services targeted at both corporate and individual customers. More specifically, the range of services offered by many ISPs today can be broadly classified into *access and connectivity, hosting/caching and collocation, customer resource management,* and *other specific value-adding services.* We synthesize some of the important characteristics of the ISP sector in the following discussion. This synthesis is based on extensive research in the trade literature, and significant parts of it are derived from the publications of ISP-Market LLC (2003a, b); the HTRC Group (2001a, b; 2003b); the Internet Research Group (IRG); Stardust.com, Inc. (Stardust.com, 2001a, b); and the North American Network Operators Group (www.nanog.org) (Claffy et al. 1996, Linton 2002, Mitchell 2002). In particular, we draw statistics from comprehensive field studies conducted by ISP-Market LLC in structuring and positioning the emerging ISP landscape.

Access and Connectivity

A major trend in this area that will dominate access and connectivity with significant growth both in the near and long terms is broadband access. In 2003, over 35 percent of the ISPs were offering broadband and wireless connectivity. This was a sharp increase from 2002 and a shift of focus from DSL services, although more than 50 percent of the ISPs still offer DSL. Currently, about 15 percent of ISPs offer both broadband wireless and DSL solutions, while an average ISP already connects over 20 percent of its customers with wireless access. While xDSL access is currently offered by over 30 percent of ISPs, less than 25 percent of the remaining ISPs (approximately 15 percent of the total market) are planning to introduce xDSL services. In this context, the ISP literature reveals that more than twice as many ISPs (roughly 31 percent) are planning to offer broadband wireless than those planning to add xDSL. Interestingly, 65 percent of ISPs still service 50 percent or more of their customer base with dial-up access. This could potentially be ascribed to connectivity constraints at the customer end rather than the ISPs' end. Further, more than 30 percent of U.S. ISPs currently offer virtual private network (VPN) services, and voice over IP (VoIP) services are a planned offering for more than 25 percent of them. Besides Internet access, the most requested network services from the ISPs by their customers are VPN and network-based storage services. However, only about 2 percent of the current ISPs offer the storage service, and it is therefore a potential market for ISPs to expand their offerings.

Hosting and Collocation

Hosting and collocation have been the predominant value propositions in the ISP sector after providing access and connectivity to customers. Being the first point of Internet access to the customers, the ISPs have a powerful network topographical advantage in delivering these services. Roughly, over 86 percent of U.S. ISPs avail themselves of this opportunity and offer hosting services, and nearly a third of the total ISP revenues come from this. In particular, collocation is the most widely offered hosting service. In collocation, customer-owned servers are housed with an ISP. Due to the proximity of the ISP to the Internet by way of its positioning on the Internet, and perhaps due to the backbone infrastructural capabilities of the ISP, customers would prefer to collocate for strategic reasons and for ensuring quality of service. Collocation services are currently offered by more than 70 percent of U.S. ISPs.

Hosting can be viewed at three levels: *shared hosting, virtual dedicated server hosting,* and *managed hosting.* In shared hosting, typically multiple hosting customers share the server and storage capacity of a server farm. In virtual dedicated server hosting, ISPs provide usually large customers with significant portions of their server farm and associated resources for the customers' exclusive use. As businesses grow globally, needs for large global bandwidths increase, and acquiring them could be prohibitively expensive. As a result, corporations leverage the edge positioning of the ISP data centers and acquire virtual dedicated server capacities both for their internal use as well as external commercial purposes. Virtual dedicated server services are offered by more than 50 percent of the ISPs. Stemming from basic hosting, *managed hosting* is a recent phenomenon. Managed hosting combines network management and monitoring with traditional hosting. As ISPs grow in their scope and scale, they develop into bigger data centers with managed hosting capabilities. Although relatively new, managed hosting is offered by about 31 percent of the ISPs.

Hosting is clearly a central component of the ISP business. Hosting occurs at the content publisher level, where a publisher could contract with an ISP to host its Web sites. At the other side of the spectrum, *caching* occurs at the level of the customers of an ISP who buy Internet access and connectivity. Almost all ISPs provide some level of local caching capability at their server farms in order to speed up content delivery to their customers. While hosting is an option in the set of value propositions of an ISP, caching is almost a necessity, in order to compete effectively in the ISP market. Currently, over 28 percent of ISPs include content delivery as an additional service to their hosting customers. In particular, Webcasting, content delivery, and mirroring are planned extensions for 25 to 35 percent of ISPs. Besides content delivery, Webcasting or streaming media delivery is the second most widely planned service. ISPs, big or small, now present as distributed networks of server farms with load-balancing capabilities and a variety of hosting services. More than 38 percent of the ISPs already offer state-of-the-art load balancing in their hosting environments.

Customer Resource Management

Customer resource management extends the managed hosting services described above to an entirely new and extended set of services offered by ISPs. Resource management in general pertains to managing and monitoring network devices and other services across a network. Broadly, these services can be grouped into three categories: *management services, security services,* and *application services.* Management services include all aspects of monitoring—networks, servers, Web sites, applications, and security. Security services include managed firewalls, intrusion detection and prevention, security consulting, and stress testing. Application services extend to partnerships with high-end application vendors, independent vendors, as well as custom application developers.

In the management services area, a key service is server monitoring, with over 51 percent of ISPs reporting to offer it. More than 22 percent of ISPs are planning to add security management, while 24 percent already include it in their service set. Each type of management service is offered by more than 20 percent of the ISPs, while Web site monitoring has the highest demand from the hosting customers. Server monitoring and Web site monitoring are rather closely coupled, and 77 percent of those who offer server monitoring also offer Web site monitoring.

In the security services area, all types of services are being planned by over 24 percent of ISPs, with intrusion detection being the most widely planned. Currently, about 39 percent of ISPs offer managed firewalls, 18 percent offer intrusion detection, and over 12 percent provide security consulting.

In the application services area, there is greater interest in the ISP community to partner with independent vendors rather than high-end vendors, although the customers of the ISPs seem to demand more application support from the high end. Currently, many ISPs partner with custom application developers; roughly 33 percent of the ISPs are planning to partner with independent vendors, and a gradual drift of the ISP industry toward the applications service provider (ASP) model is developing.

Customer Value-Adding Services

Several ISPs are continually innovating to develop and deliver specialized as well as universal value-adding services to sustain and grow their basic business propositions. As the ISP market becomes more competitive and with the forces of market consolidation looming large, innovative value additions have acquired a critical importance in the ISP business. Some of the important value-adding services include unsolicited commercial e-mail filtering, Web-based e-mail, URL and content filtering, and customized content delivery with portal management services. These add-on services are expected to have a revolutionary impact on the ISP industry as a whole in the future. Although 75 percent of the ISPs still consider providing consumer access as a primary business focus, almost 85 percent of ISPs with more than 50,000 customers offer specific value-adding services such as Web-based mail and spam filters. It is also anticipated that over 90 percent of ISPs with 5,000 or fewer subscribers will offer content filtering by the end of 2003.

ISP Peering Trends

Effective management of costs and provision of high quality of service to customers are two key strategic initiatives in the ISP sector. As the cost of transit connections comprise a majority of the operational costs, *peering contracts* among ISPs are becoming increasingly popular. *Peering* is basically a business relationship among ISPs where they agree to reciprocally provide access to their respective customers through privately established communication links. Peering has emerged as an alternative to the standard *transit* relationships, but not a substitute. In a transit relationship, an ISP typically provides an Internet access service for a fee to another ISP. In this case, the ISP buying the service would connect via a private line to the ISP that already has Internet access. The buying ISP would then obtain Internet access through the transit link for servicing its own customers.

A central theme in ISP peering is to enhance the quality of service (QoS) to the end users by bypassing certain traffic-intensive segments of the Internet when using transit services. Additionally, peering is expected to give ISPs more control over routing, yield redundant connections to the Internet, resulting in better fault-tolerance, and potentially enable aggregations of transit traffic to lower local loop costs. Besides the technical advantages, peering has also been expected to enhance business functionalities through closer relationships with other service providers and to serve as significant marketing collateral (Norton 1999, 2001, 2002). Some of the major trends in the peering area are as follows (Linton 2002, Metro Ethernet Forum 2002):

- Large ISPs and other network operators are setting up significant metro-level next generation peering centers,
- The arrival of the fast Metro Ethernet is a key driver in this process,
- The metro nets will be composed of both large NextGen high-speed peering centers and multipoint distributed switches,
- Large ISPs will essentially have significant shares of the metro connectivity and the NextGen peering centers,
- Mid-sized ISPs would peer at both points of connectivity depending on their needs and cost factors, and
- Smaller ISPs would start with Metro ether port for transit, add peering VLANs on the same port for cost savings, and use the Metro Ethernet as a bridge to the NextGen peering centers as they grow.

In conclusion, we draw the following general inferences about the ISP sector:

- The ISP industry continues to grow and remain competitive; market consolidations have not occurred as predicted although reorganizations are happening at increasing levels.
- The basic thrust of the ISP sector is access and connectivity; however, it has become imperative for ISPs to diversify by including a variety of additional services in order to stay in business and compete effectively.

Table 10.1

Business-Level Classification of CDNs

Enterprise CDNs	Extranet CDNs	Public CDN services
• Executive announcements	• Partner communications	• Common Web access to consumers
• Product demos	• Product development	• Customer relationships and training
• Technical training	• Supply chain management	• Product demos
• Soft-skills training	• Web seminars	• Marketing communications
• Policies/compliance		

Source: Adapted from Digital Pipe.

- ISPs continue to innovate in their service offerings. The model of providing only Internet connectivity that dominated the last decade is no longer valid. Currently, almost all ISPs bundle access and connectivity services with some focused value added services and offer packages of services to specific target customer groups.
- Hosting/caching and collocation have emerged as strong value propositions for all ISPs; however, customer resource management requires greater infrastructural and architectural capabilities with strong network topographical positioning advantages. Hence, resource management as a value proposition is yet to mature in the ISP industry.
- The growth in high-speed networking and fast Metro Ethernets will be key drivers in ISP peering; as a result, peering emerges as a major factor in cost-effective delivery of most of the value propositions of ISPs.

The CDN Sector

A CDN essentially contracts with a content publisher to provide a scalable distribution service for their content (Cooper et al. 2001). While the primary purposes of a CDN are to enable wider and possibly global reach for the publishers' content and protect Web site performance under flash events, several types of CDNs exist. Broadly, they can be classified into *hosting* and *relaying* CDNs, and the relaying type can be further classified as to location of receiving customer hits: whether to take the first customer hits from the origin servers or at their own servers (Rabinovich and Spatcheck 2002). The essential components of most CDNs include primary storage, caches, content distribution tools, request-routing capabilities (Barbir et al. 2003), IP multicast, and Edge Side Includes (ESI). An alternative, business-level classification of CDNs based on their applications is summarized in Table 10.1. The CDN technology has matured significantly over the last three years and a trend toward internetworked CDNs with contractual agreements for content sharing and hosting is developing (Day et al. 2001, Gilletti et al. 2002, Rzewski et al. 2003).

A study by the HTRC Group (2002b) indicates that enterprise CDNs could result in savings of up to 70 percent of training costs from traditional instructor-led education, and a savings of about 60 percent on companywide meetings, conferences, and events, by largely replacing them with CDN-based electronic communications. A similar study from Jupiter Communications (www.library.hbs.edu/go/jupiter.html) addresses the savings in network bandwidth costs as follows. WAN bandwidth costs roughly about $800 per megabit per second per month. If a T1 line (at 1.54 Mbps) were used, the cost would total about $1,250 per month. Comparatively, a $500 disk drive can deliver about 10 Mbps, and amortizing the fixed costs over thirty-six months, a disk drive costs $14 per month compared to $1,250 per month in bandwidth. Hence, it makes logical sense to employ locally accessible CDN services rather than lease private lines for enterprise applications. Similar characterizations of CDN services have been identified in the context of a variety of edge services offered by CDNs in several other studies (Stardust.com 2001a, b; HTRC Group 2002b). The Volera study (HTRC Group 2002b) focuses on the enterprise and service provider markets and yields several insights on the challenges facing the CDN industry, especially in the case of streaming media. The report shows that streaming in the corporate sector increased from 35 percent of the total streaming traffic on the Internet in 2001 to 42 percent in 2002, and this could be attributed to a correlation between implementing streaming services and CDN solutions within an enterprise. A HTRC report on the digital content network receiver service market (HTRC Group 2002a) indicates the bandwidth effect of applying the CDN concept in bundling access and connectivity with CDN-type content services. Their conclusion is that network service providers can generate significantly higher revenue from flexible service models with digital content network receivers using the bundling principle and not just providing basic bandwidth.

In conclusion, the studies by the Internet Research Group indicate three fundamental findings about the CDN industry: (1) content delivery will become more demanding, not less; (2) quality of service problems on the Internet will not disappear soon; and (3) data storage will continue to be cheap compared to data transmission. Coupled with the notion of different types of CDN services segmented along the dimensions of both content types and consumer types, and the possibility of offering innovative services by bundling content delivery with other types of services, we conclude that the CDN and CDN-related markets will evolve rapidly. A natural corollary to this thesis is that the strategic positioning of CDN servers along the edge of the Internet and of their networking bandwidths into the Internet, the ISPs' edge networks, and the publishers' sites will become critical to their success.

The ISI Sector

Internet storage infrastructure (ISI) has emerged as a possible solution to the enormous challenge of storing and distributing rich media content over the Internet. Although particularly targeted for the Internet entertainment industry and other multimedia streaming scenarios such as corporate video conferencing, for instance, the ISI technology offers reliable, flexible, and scalable solutions to a variety of distributed storage needs for corporate users. ISI is essentially an outsourced service that uses networks of storage clusters and server farms to store large databases. ISI is a complementary solution to existing Web-hosting architectures. Although ISI exists in the realm of unique providers of such services, it is a natural extension of the value propositions of ISPs, who already have sufficient computing, storage, and network infrastructures to begin with. The subscribers to ISI services are corporate customers, and according to the HTRC report (2003a), the subscribers are expected to spend over $2.7 billion in 2004. This forecast includes storage services only, and does not include the bandwidth costs. Therefore, ISI technologies have tremendous growth potential and, coupled with emerging technologies such as Web services, are likely to revolutionize the enterprise computing industry as a whole.

Most of the current ISI service providers offer a pay-as-you-go model of storage that mitigates the problems associated with demand uncertainty. Many rich-media-oriented Web sites are unable to forecast their demands with certainty. This is due to the fact that demand for streaming content is affected by competition, broadband availability, and other customer-specific demand behaviors. Consequently, building storage capacity for rich-media distribution is subject to trade-offs between the costs of overbuilding versus underbuilding, as in the classical news vendor problem. Typically, these costs are not small, since rich-media require specialized streaming servers, large-scale storage management, and a whole set of specialized software—for data compression and decompression and encryption and decryption, to name a few applications. Accordingly, given the market uncertainties, ISI has emerged as a viable, highly available, reliable, and scalable solution to this problem.

The central components of ISI are *storage area networks* (SANs) and *network attached storage* (NAS). A SAN is a storage-dedicated LAN with high-performance network connectivity to servers and storage resources. A NAS provides standards-based high-speed network access. Combining these two technologies with existing infrastructures, a new breed of service providers called storage service providers (SSPs) is emerging from the ISP industry. The HTRC report specifies a set of service requirements for ISI solutions, including fault-tolerance, service-level agreements (SLAs) between SSPs and their customers and management tools required for monitoring, security, scalability, interoperability, global access, and service support functions. Based on the existing literature on ISI, we synthesize the following observations on the future of this business:

- Storage capacity requirements for Web sites will nearly quadruple every year.
- Internet expertise does not scale well with demand; consequently, sites will outsource more IT functions.
- New Internet access technologies will drive more sophisticated high-bandwidth content.
- High-bandwidth content will increase demand for broadband and other high-speed access.
- The number of large Web sites will increase at a faster rate through 2004 and beyond.
- The growing number of online users will drive Web content publishers to further differentiate their products and services with increasing rich-media content.
- The use of online storage services for personal and professional use will increase significantly over time.
- Competition will decrease the cost of ISI services over time.

Some Key Web Services

Web services, defined typically as "loosely coupled, reusable software components that semantically encapsulate functionality and are programmatically accessible over the Internet (Devarajan 2003)," are gaining momentum in both business and consumer sectors. As this paradigm provides consumable services on an "as-needed" and "pay-only-for-what-you-consume" basis, the underlying economics are compelling. On the other hand, it radically increases the usage and dependence on the underlying infrastructure of the Internet to provide adequate "end-to-end" performance to the consumers of these services. CPN provides the market fundamentals to make this happen.

Entertainment industries, such as the music and movie industries, are radically affected by the digitization of their content. Unauthorized duplication of their content, termed digital piracy, is undermining the fundamental and long-term viability of the entertainment industry. The industry needs to fight back and retool their business models. Two broad fronts of the new strategy are streaming and interactivity.

Streaming

Delivering content in a streaming format as opposed to complete downloading of content prior to consumption helps significantly in reducing the levels of piracy. Viability of this strategy is critically dependent on the provision of a high quality of service to the customers. All the infrastructure elements (server capacity, bandwidth, storage, and cache capacities) need to be effectively leveraged and implemented to provide a compelling value proposition to the end consumers. Being the first and main conduit for consumers to the world of online entertainment, ISPs will likely emerge as key stakeholders in the new marketplace. In the world of digital entertainment, ISPs will serve the role of "local movie theaters."

Interactivity

Interestingly, while the music and the movie industries have fallen prey to the plague of digital piracy, the online gaming industry continues to thrive and prosper. The reasons for this are clear: while content can be pirated, interactivity is an experience, and experience cannot be pirated and duplicated. This underlying reasoning will drive the entertainment industry to embed interactivity as a key value-added component of their service offerings. ISPs will need to gear up, both technologically and business-wise, to effectively manage "two-way" data traffic. Consumption of such entertainment will entail both downloading and uploading from consumers, and this can place significantly more stress on the ISP resources.

Other Related Services

Several services either directly or tangentially connect with the above set of core services. Principal among them are *IP services* and *load balancing services.* We briefly discuss the emerging trends in these services below.

As discussed above, a common and strong trend in the Internet service industry is to bundle services into *sticky services,* in order to combat competition and sustain customer bases. Accordingly, integrated IP services is a common theme adopted by a large number of service providers. This integration includes, in general, *integrated voice and data applications, video conferencing, document storage and backup, outsourcing mission-critical applications, software rentals, unified messaging, computer/telephony integration, and network-based training services.* Combined with the core services, including Web hosting, peering, CDN, and ISI, this integrated set offers a rich set of value propositions for any business model in the Internet service industry. Most ISPs today use some combinations of these services and bundle them according to market needs and position themselves in the broader canvas of Internet service. However, several challenges still remain. For example, guaranteed quality of service, security, and providing on-demand consumption are still major problems. The pay-as-you-go revenue model has been proven to be good in many IP services. The enterprise customers will leverage the latest networked applications in an on-demand, pay-as-you-go format, with little incremental investment. Advanced IP services offer a viable and attractive outsourcing alternative to internal IT initiatives, which are usually capital and resource intensive. Small- and medium-sized enterprises, which previously could afford neither extensive internal IT departments nor high-end outsourcing, now could gain access to a range of valuable IP services. The HTRC Group proposes a three-partner model of IP services: *service portals–ASP–NSP.* They argue that this model will capture an increasing share of corporate IT spending by addressing the common requirements of guaranteed bandwidth, security, and on-demand service activation. The combination of services created by partnerships generates customer loyalty and reduces churn. This business model allows each player to focus on its core competency in turning the vision of advanced IP services into a reality.

Another important service in the effective delivery of Internet content is *load balancing.* Typically, Web content is distributed from server farms, which are a group of servers (of various configurations and capabilities) collocated at the premises of a service provider. In fact, large service providers maintain several such farms at several locations and internetwork them either through private lines or through a combination of localized backbones and Internet connectivity. The primary reasons for this architecture are scalability and availability. When demand for service increases beyond existing thresholds, service providers need either to upgrade their existing servers or add new servers. In many cases, it will be economical to add new servers. Consequently, server clusters together serving target customer communities have become commonplace. While adding new servers obviously is a scalable solution, it also enhances availability. However, with multiple servers clustered together at a site, the issues of load balancing interserver communication become important. The servers in a farm can be either loosely coupled, with back-end data sharing, or tightly coupled, as in symmetric multiprocessors. A load balancer is typically positioned as a front-end to the server farm and its IP address is used as a *virtual IP* address for the farm as whole. The purpose of a load balancer is threefold: (1) to maintain a common front-end access point to a set of collocated servers, (2) to ensure an equitable load distribution among the servers in order provide a high level of quality of service to the customers, and (3) to sustain availability by efficient request routing when servers go down or are faced with flash-crowd situations.

Based on the above description, we can clearly envision a load balancer at each server farm, and possibly coordinated by a *global load balancer* (GLB), when several geographically distributed farms are interconnected. The HTRC Group examines two kinds of GLB solutions: product-based GLB solutions, which are owned by a company and operated by its Web site professionals, and service-based GLB solutions, where all of the functions of a production solution are outsourced to a GLB provider, thus avoiding the heavy capital investment costs. Both of them offer advantages and disadvantages, depending on the prospective buyer. The GLB providers obtain real-time assessments of Internet traffic and server load conditions from several sources (such as other load balancers, routers, etc.) using both probing and broadcasting techniques. Performance metrics gathered throughout the Internet are used for both request-routing and content distribution.

Web site monitoring through global and local load balancing has emerged as a major service on the Internet. The HTRC Group claims that e-commerce Web sites lose an average of $16,200 in sales revenue for every hour the site is down. The chief causes of this downtime are problems with basic connectivity to the service provider, hardware failure at the primary servers, and network equipment and power outages. Further, downtimes due to bandwidth restrictions are still a major problem. Sites that do not outsource Web site hosting or collocate Web servers with a service provider are dependent on the local exchange carrier and ISP in order to maintain their own Web site Internet connection. According to the 1999 Content Delivery Service Study of the HTRC Group, Web site bandwidth increases an average of 8.4 percent per month. Web site owners provisioning additional capacity through data connections, rather than collocation facilities, are at the mercy of local exchange carriers (LECs) and ISPs for increased site availability. As a result of all these problems, sustaining availability through load balancing has become a viable and efficient solution.

TOPOGRAPHICAL LEVERAGE

The notion of topographical leverage introduced earlier could assume different forms in various contexts. The current state of the service industry analyzed above indicates that possibilities for such leverage are virtually unlimited. The underlying contexts for leverage are numerous, as the industry continues to expand and grow. Further, resource limitations, strategic situational advantages of certain firms with respect to some others, and some of the pressing needs for service performance cause leveraging contexts to arise frequently and rapidly; hence, trading resources of a variety of types could become a common practice in the evolving landscape. In understanding the structure of topographical leverage, we first need to specify a framework of analysis of trading contexts in general, so that we can derive specific contexts and their associated business models from it. We develop the following framework for this purpose.

Two important concepts that are central to the proposed framework are *service requirements* and *service capabilities* of a servicing agent. The service requirements are the objectives of a servicing agent that are specific to its business proposition. Typically, these requirements can be stated as performance metrics in real-time operations and business goals in the short and long runs. For example, access time and system availability are real-time service requirements, and scalability and reach into larger customer bases are short-to-long-run business goals of a service provider. In order to fulfill this proposition, a provider needs service capabilities, which can be specified at both infrastructural and architectural levels. Broadly, the capabilities translate into capacity (servers, storage, bandwidth, load balancers, etc.) and content (hosted, cached, or shared). As service requirements change and grow, the capabilities need to keep pace in order to sustain the business. It is precisely these dynamics that cause service providers to look for scalable solutions up front, scale up as and when necessary, or even contract or outsource when appropriate. When existing solutions do not scale well, service providers may have to undertake major upgrades or reconfigurations, which could be far more expensive than contracting services out. Under this premise, we raise the following critical questions that constitute our framework for analysis.

- Consider two firms A and B. Suppose that A has some service capabilities. How can B use these capabilities to meet its service requirements?
- Does A possess certain *unique* capabilities that B does not have (such as infrastructural, architectural, and administrative components; geographic advantages; etc.) that could enable or enhance the service obligations of B?
- If B were to acquire these capabilities by itself, would it be feasible, technically and business-wise?
- If feasible, would acquiring them be more expensive (in both the short and the long runs) than contracting with A for these services?
- If B were to contract with A, then are their incentives to buy and sell mutually compatible?

Using this framework as a guide, we illustrate topographical leverage through trading using some viable contexts in the following discussion.

Cache Trading

Consider an ISP. The key service requirements of the ISP are: *consumer's quality of experience; availability and accessibility of services; scalability—in terms of both services and the number of consumers that can avail themselves of these services;* and *reach—whereby the service or content providers can extend their geographic coverage.* The service capabilities in this case can be broadly specified in terms of the capacity and content described above. Figure 10.1 illustrates a high-level architecture of the linkages that could be established between two ISPs that agree to trade content and capacity for topographical leverage purposes.

The two ISPs can trade in cache services in two primary ways: *content level* and *capacity level.* We outline these trading mechanisms in the following discussion.

Figure 10.1 **Cache Trading ISPs**

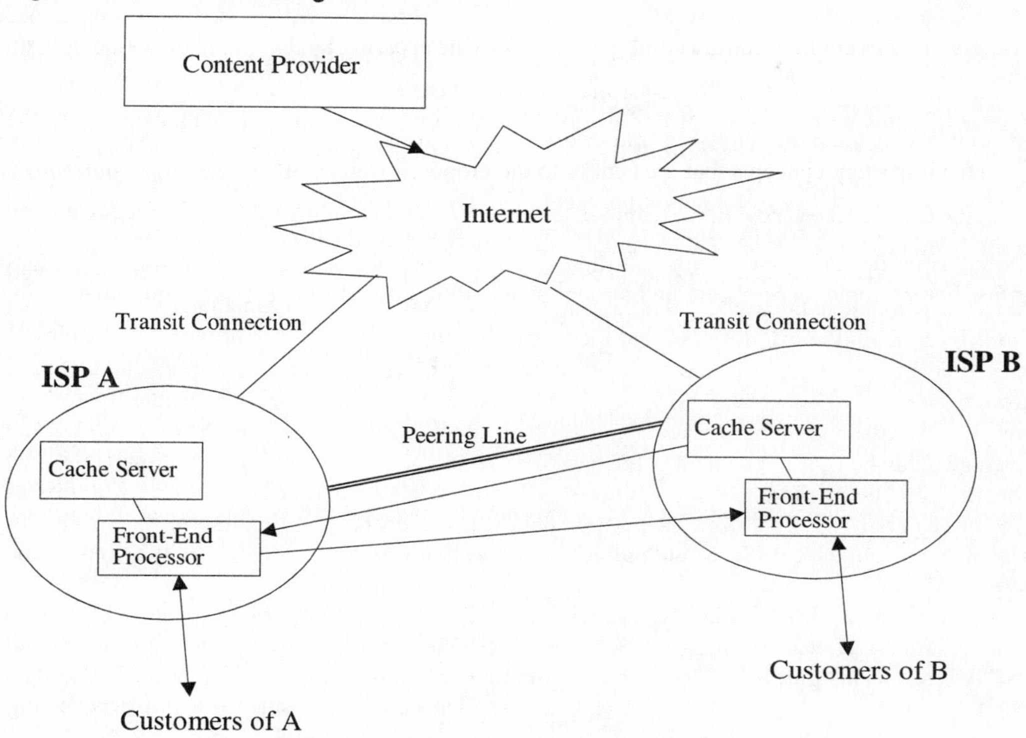

Content-Level Trading

Consider a contract between A and B as follows. If customers of A request certain Web objects and they are not available locally, the front-end processor of A could ask the front-end processor of B if the requested data are available and if it could handle the request to provide the Web objects. The trade contract is purely at the content level and ISP A has no control of what objects are cached at the cache server of B. This model of sharing is more applicable when the two sets of customers have similar Web access patterns. In this arrangement, ISP A might be able to provide good quality of experience to its customers, since the access times to ISP B could be much smaller than those from the content providers, especially when the two ISPs are peered. Further, the contract between A and B could provide for mutual support in the event of failures. For example, if cache server A fails, then the customers can be rerouted to server B. This is also a good scalable solution, since more customers could avail themselves of the caching services than if each cache server were operated independently. Note that the contract can be one-way access (where only A uses the cached content of B), or two-way (where A and B mutually use their respective caches). This model is applicable in the contexts of pure caching by pre-fetching mechanisms, or of remote hosting services, such as in CDNs or in specific collocation services offered by the ISPs in different situations. The ISP providing the service would enhance its revenue by content trading and would possibly increase its customer reach as well. Furthermore, the sharing agreement could integrate the servers as cooperating units, resulting in better load balancing at the individual level as well as the collective level.

Capacity-Level Trading

In this case, the contract could be specified as follows. ISP B allocates part of its caching resources for exclusive use of ISP A for the duration of the contract. With this, ISP A can ensure higher hit rates with the content that is cached at the remote site. This arrangement shifts the management of the remote cache to ISP A, who could use the remote capability for both real-time operational performance as well as scalability requirements. The topographical leverage arises from the fact that the access times from the cache servers at the trading partner site are lower than those from the origin server. This leverage can be modeled as follows.

A cache system works by responding to requests for Web objects from clients. If the requested object is available in the cache and is current, then it is immediately served. Otherwise, the object is retrieved from the origin server and then served to the client. The performance of caching is measured by *hit rate,* that is, the probability that the content a consumer requests can be found from the cache. To understand how hit rate relates to average access delay, consider the following. Let the average delay for accessing content directly from the origin server be t_0. Let the average delay be t_c, if the content is fetched from an ISP's local cache. By definition, $t_0 > t_c$. Let the hit rate be η. Then, with caching, a buyer will experience an average delay of $t_1 = \eta t_c + (1 - \eta)\, t_0$. Therefore the average delay, t_1, is a decreasing function of the hit rate, η. Given this result, a local ISP would prefer to build a large enough caching capacity to reduce the average delay.

In this scenario, ISP A could either build enough capacity locally or buy capacity from B so that the same level of access performance is achieved. The question is, how much capacity should ISP A buy for this purpose? The farther the remote cache, the more likely that retrieving data from it could be delayed. Let the average delay experienced by a customer of ISP A in accessing content from ISP B be t_r . Then by definition, $t_r > t_c$. Further, it should also be true that $t_r < t_0$, otherwise remote caching makes no sense. Now suppose that ISP A uses the remote cache for all its caching needs. The question now is, how large should the new hit rate, η', be, such that the average delay time is still $t_1 = \eta' t_r + (1 - \eta')\, t_0$? Comparing local caching with remote caching, we obtain $\eta' = (t_0 - t_c) / (t_0 - t_r)\, \eta > \eta$. Therefore, with remote caching, ISP A needs a larger hit rate to maintain the same average delay. Let the total amount of contents that the customers of ISP A request be Δ. Then: $\eta\Delta = ((t_0 - t_r) / (t_0 - t_c))\, \eta'\, \Delta$, where, $\eta\Delta$ and $\eta'\, \Delta$ are the capacities of the local and remote caches, respectively. To be exact, one unit of remote cache only equals $(t_0 - t_r) / (t_0 - t_c)$ units of local cache, which implies that remote cache is *discounted* by a factor δ. ., where δ. equals $(t_0 - t_r) / (t_0 - t_c)$. As a result, the topographical leverage is realized from this trade as follows: if ISP A needs x units of capacity to service its clients, then it could either set aside x units locally or buy x/δ units from ISP B. This will enable ISP A to service this need at the same level of quality in both scenarios. By acquiring x/δ ($> x$) units of capacity from ISP B, ISP A will cache more at the remote site than necessary locally; as a result, more content gets cached from the origin server. This results in a greater hit rate at the remote cache, leading to the same level of expected performance as with the local cache.

Leveraging in Content and Capacity Levels

An alternate characterization of the topographical leverage when caching preselected Web sites for specific customer requirements is as follows. Let C_1 and C_2 be the cache capacities available at ISPs A and B, respectively. Let the consumers of ISP A desire to use and access S_1 Web sites and, without loss of generality, let caching each Web site require one unit of capacity. Similarly, assume that the customers of ISP B wish to access S_2 sites. Now, suppose $S_1>C_1$ and $S_2< C_2$. In this case, ISP A has a shortfall and ISP B has excess capacity.

Let $r = 1, \ldots, R$ represent time periods under consideration such that in each time period, one Web site is accessed. The granularity of time can be chosen according to the requirements of a given context. Assume that the customers of ISP A would access any one of the S_1 Web sites randomly. Therefore, the expected response time in period $r = t_c(C_1/S_1) + t_0(S_1\text{-}C_1)/S_1$. Consider a contract where ISP A pays a penalty of b for every unit of time delayed over the promised response time to the customers. Assuming t_c is the promised response time to customers, the penalty paid each period is $(t_c(C_1/S_1) + t_0(S_1\text{-}C_1)/S_1\text{-}t_c)b$. Therefore, the total penalty cost of underprovisioning for R periods is $(t_c(C_1/S_1) + t_0(S_1\text{-}C_1)/S_1\text{-}t_c)bR$. Now, we illustrate the leverage in the above scenario with two specific cases, *content-level trading* and *content- and capacity-level trading,* as follows.

Content-Level Trading

Assume that among the S_2 sites specified by the customers of ISP B, fS_2 of these sites are also specified by customers of ISP A. In content-level trading, ISP B will agree to serve customers of A if any of these sites are needed. The expected response time for customers of A is now $t_c(C_1/S_1) + t_r(fS_2)/ S_1 + t_0((S_1\text{-}C_1\text{-}fS_2)/S_1)$. Hence, the total penalty cost to ISP A with content-level trading is $Rb(t_c(C_1/S_1) + t_r(fS_2)/ S_1 + (t_0(S_1\text{-}C_1\text{-}fS_2)/S_1)\text{-}t_c)$, which would be less than the penalty incurred without content sharing. The basic leverage in this case essentially arises out of the fact that $t_0>t_r>t_c$, and that t_0 could be significantly higher than t_r and t_c.

Capacity- and Content-Level Trading

In this case, assume that ISP B makes $C_2\text{-}S_2$ units of capacity available for use by ISP A. With this arrangement, there is capacity trading of $C_2\text{-}S_2$ units and content-level sharing of fS_2 Web sites. The total penalty cost with content and capacity trading is:

$$Rb(t_c(C_1/S_1) + t_r(fS_2)/ S_1+ t_r(C_2\text{-}S_2)/ S_1 + (t_0(S_1+S_2\text{-}C_1\text{-} C1\text{-}fS2)/S_1)\text{-}t_c).$$

The penalty savings provide the basis for trade between the ISPs and the consequential monetary values to each. The effectiveness of the trade increases as f increases and t_r decreases.

Cooperative Multimedia Streaming

As broadband connections become commonplace, customers increasingly demand high-quality streaming applications that encompass movies, video streaming of live concerts and other performances, and video conferencing. In the movie rental business, the current model of renting movies from bricks-and-mortar outlets is becoming increasingly cumbersome. Streaming such content online with low latency levels and jitter-free presentations is a major challenge for any service provider, as it requires enormous server, bandwidth, and storage capacities. High variability in customer demand and return on investment render these massive investments risky for any service provider. Therefore, topographical leveraging through cooperative multimedia caching is a viable option for many service providers. Figure 10.2 illustrates a high-level architecture of the linkages that could be established between two ISPs that agree to trade and stream multimedia content for topographical leverage reasons.

In typical streaming applications, each customer has a persistent TCP or UDP connection. Content is streamed initially from the content provider, then compressed and encrypted at the

Figure 10.2 **Cooperative Multimedia Streaming**

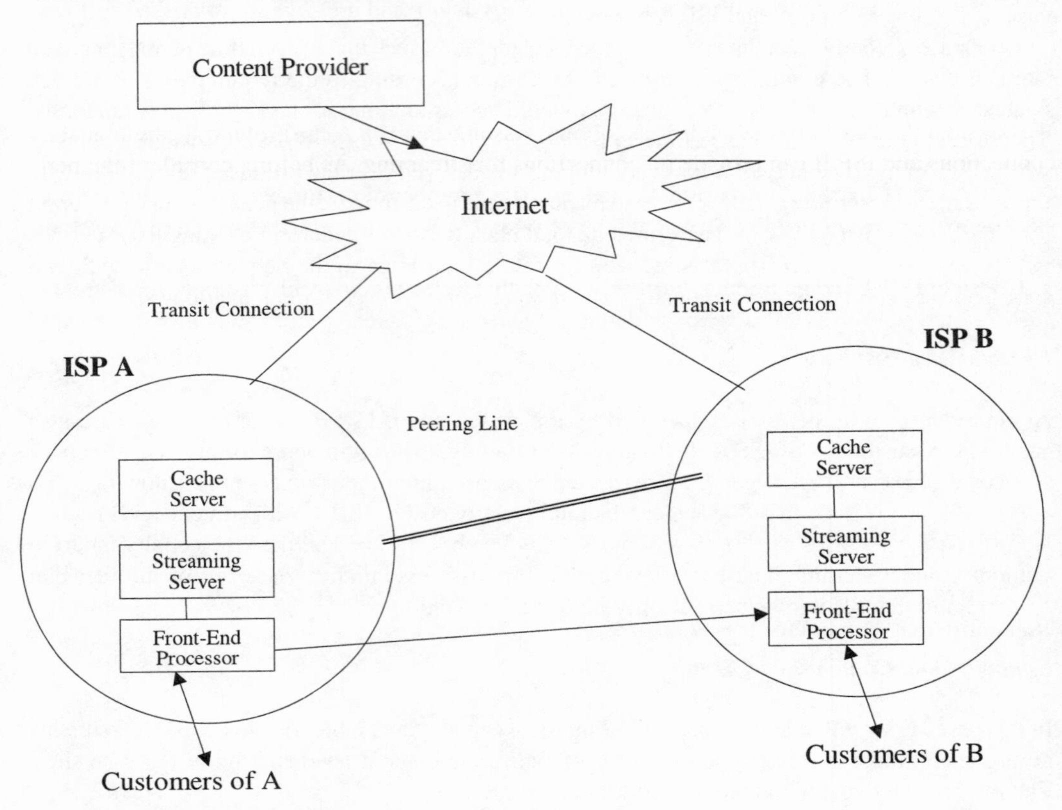

streaming server, and finally delivered to the client through the front-end edge server. The media player at the client end usually performs the decompression and decryption. Now, consider the following scenario. If ISPs A and B have a trade contract, then the customers of A would be routed to front-end processor B if:

1. The streaming server of A is overloaded and cannot accept any further persistent connections.
2. The streaming content that a customer requests is not available at ISP A, but is available at the cache server of ISP B. This provides a better quality of service to the customer, as the content is not streamed through the Internet. We can easily envision a scenario where, at a given time, a customer of A is serviced by the streaming server of B while at the same time a customer of B is serviced by the streaming server of A.

As a result of this trade, we could expect better quality of service (low latency and jitter), greater scale (as more customers could simultaneously avail themselves of the streaming services), and better load balancing and increased reach (as remote users could access the streaming server and cache resources of an ISP). The increased reach is especially beneficial for an ISP that has unique content (such as training videos for professional pilots, gardening shows) but geographically distributed markets where the ISP may not be present. We illustrate the leverage in the above scenario with two specific cases, *live streaming* and *non-live streaming,* as follows.

Live Streaming

We consider the case of live streaming as follows. Assume that ISP A can provide N_a simultaneous connections and ISP B can provide N_b connections for streaming. As before, consider time periods $r = 1, \ldots, R$. In each time period, the demand (i.e., number of customers, with each requiring one connection) is uniformly distributed between 0 and N. We consider the case where $N > N_a$ and $N > N_b$.

Consider ISP A and no trading. Further, assume that revenue from each customer for a streaming session is p. With a little algebra, and imposing integrality, the expected revenue with no trade is given by

$$(E_{no-trade}) = \frac{p(\sum_{1}^{N_a} i + (N - N_a)N_a)}{N}$$

Now, consider the situation where ISPs A and B agree that if ISP A needs extra connections, B will provide them as long as it has some open connections. Therefore, the probability that at least one customer of A is directed to ISP B = the probability that demand for A is N_a+1 or higher × probability that demand for B is N_b-1 or lower

$$= (1 - \frac{N_a + 1}{N}) * \frac{(N_b - 1)}{N}$$

The revenue generated by ISP A from a customer who is redirected to ISP B could be lower as that customer gets streaming content from a nonlocal ISP, which could involve higher latency and jitter. This could lead to lower quality of experience and, as a result, let the revenue from such a case be γp ($\gamma \leq 1$). Suppose that ISP A has a shortfall of k connections in this service. ISP B would then satisfy this shortfall depending on the number of connections available with it. If ISP B has k or more available, then all the k required connections could be provided. With some algebra, the expected revenue for ISP A with a shortfall of k is given by

$$E(k) = \frac{p\gamma(\sum_{1}^{k-1}(k - i))}{N} + \frac{(N_b - k)kp\gamma}{N}$$

Further, if the trade contract is such that ISP B agrees to satisfy at most K connections each time period, then the total expected revenue for ISP A from this agreement is given by

$$\frac{\sum_{1}^{K} E(k)}{N}.$$

The difference between the expected revenues when trading is possible with a scenario where no trade possibility exists provides the basis for leveraging topographical advantage in this case. Clearly, pricing is an important issue here, and the mechanisms of profit sharing would depend upon the negotiations between the two ISPs and equilibrium conditions. The above model presents a one-way usage of streaming services with a unique buyer and a unique seller. The incentive to trade in this case is straightforward. A similar example, where a two-way trade is conducted, can be envisioned. In this case, depending on the demand conditions and capacity availabilities, the trades would be conducted in the appropriate directions.

Non-Live Streaming

An example of this scenario is where the ISP maintains a library of content, such as movies. When a customer requests a movie, the ISP checks whether it is in the library. If it is available, then it is served from the local cache. This provides the highest quality of service to customers (q_c). If it is not in the local cache (or library), the request is routed to the streaming server of the provider. This option results in a lower quality of service (q_0) due to network latencies. If ISP B has a particular movie that a customer of A requests and is willing to provide it, then the quality of service (q_r) that is lower than q_c but higher than q_0 could be realized. Then, the revenues for ISP A from providing streaming content could be modeled as functions of pq_c, pq_r, or pq_0, depending on where the content is being served from. This scenario results in trade models very similar to the cache trading scenarios discussed above.

Internet Storage Infrastructures (ISIs)

The HTRC Group, in their report on ISI, indicates several benefits of subscribing to ISI services (HTRC Group, 2003a). In particular, they imply increases in scalability and reliability as well as a reduction in cost per megabyte stored. They compare cost models for in-house storage, outsourcing storage, and ISI services. They conclude from their analysis that: (1) the largest difference in storage costs between the three models are in terms of scalability in the number of simultaneous users and terabytes-on-demand for storage requirements; (2) the ISI solution is the cheapest, with subscribers having the largest growth capacity; (3) outsourcing offers medium cost performance; and (4) the in-house model offers the highest access performance, also at the highest cost. The ISI solution is cost-efficient because of two basic reasons: *no labor costs to the subscribers* and *lower per gigabyte per month storage cost* ($20 for the ISI solution vs. $44 for the outsourcing solution). These savings are quite remarkable. Nevertheless, the report does not provide any specific explanations as to why ISI solutions yield lower marginal storage costs than the outsourcing solutions. We consider three explanations, *economies of scale, pooling of uncertainty,* and *diminishing returns of content,* using the simple model below. Topographical leveraging can be combined with these three factors, and together they yield powerful incentives for ISI providers to deliver increasingly cost-effective services. To simplify the analysis, we use only a social planner's perspective, that is, we ignore individual incentive issues.

Consider two content publishers, 1 and 2, who need storage for their rich-media content. Assume that the storage demand, x_i, is a uniform random variable in [0, 1] for each publisher i (i=1, 2). We consider two possible scenarios as follows. In scenario 1, each publisher uses an in-house storage solution. In scenario 2, each publisher subscribes to its local storage service provider (SSP) (i.e., publisher 1 subscribes to SSP 1, and publisher 2 to SSP 2). Assume that both SSPs in turn belong to a uniform ISI so that they can exchange storage capacity as needed. In this example, we ignore the discount factor discussed above in the case of cache trading among the two

SSPs for simplicity, although the discount factor is equally relevant in this case as well. Consequently, each SSP i needs to decide on how much storage capacity to allocate. Let this be denoted as s_i. If we consider only pooling of uncertainty, then the analysis will be similar to the model presented in Geng et al. (2003d). In the following analysis, we illustrate economies of scale and diminishing returns of content using a simple model. We consider the special case of $\delta = 1$, where services can be provided from anywhere in the ISI network to any destination without losses in quality of service metrics. This assumption can be relaxed with d values less than 1 when such losses occur.

Economies of Scale

The SSPs always purchase storage capacity with a decreasing marginal cost. Let the cost of capacity s be $C(s)$, and $c(s) = C'(s)$. Then, we consider the case where $c(s)$ is a positive but decreasing function. Possible explanations include the dilution of fixed up-front cost, mass purchase discount, and the fact that larger storage devices have a smaller unit cost (e.g., a 60GB hard disk's marginal cost is smaller than that of a 20GB's).

Diminishing Returns of Content

Clearly, "all content is not created equal." A common practice in data processing/storage is to serve the most valuable content requirements first. As a result of this practice, we observe that the marginal value of content is the largest for the first unit of content, and the smallest for the last unit. Let the value of content of size x be $B(x)$, and marginal value of content be $b(x)$. Note that in the social planner's view, any penalty associated with an unsatisfied demand unit equals exactly the opportunity cost of servicing the requirement. Therefore, we have $b(x) = B'(x)$.

Let y_1 and y_2 denote the capacity the ISI allocates for publishers 1 and 2. Then, the total social welfare is

$$W = \int_0^d \int_0^d (B(y_1) + B(y_2)) dx_2 dx_1 - c(s_1 + s_2) \tag{1}$$

$$\text{s.t. } y_1 + y_2 \le s_1 + s_2 \tag{1a}$$

$$y_1 \le x_1 \tag{1b}$$

$$y_2 \le x_2 \tag{1c}$$

$$b(y_1) = b(y_2) \text{ if } y_1 < x_1 \text{ and } y_2 < x_2 \tag{1d}$$

$$b(y_1) \ge b(y_2) \text{ if } y_1 = x_1 \text{ and } y_2 < x_2 \tag{1e}$$

$$b(y_1) \le b(y_2) \text{ if } y_1 < x_1 \text{ and } y_2 = x_2 \tag{1f}$$

In the above model, constraint (1a) requires that supply cannot exceed capacity. Constraints (1b) and (1c) require that any excess supply is actually unnecessary and does not add value. The interesting conditions are (1d)—(1f), which show a load balancing property: unlike in traditional thinking, where local demand would always have the highest priority, here the remote demand may be more important because it is *serving more valuable content.* If we introduce the discounting factor due to geographical service performance differences, then the above model will have to be appropriately modified. However, the following key point still holds: the central planner has to carefully balance between the location issue (i.e., discount factor representing topographical leverage) and the issue of the importance of specific content. Using the above model, a central planner would realize the maximum social welfare between the two SSPs by taking advantage of economies of scale, diminishing returns of content, and topographical leverage in serving the customers.

THE CPN FRAMEWORK

We have already presented the notion of capacity provision networks (CPN) as a network of service providers trading resources and services among themselves. We develop this notion further in this section. Central to the proposed framework are the five key questions that should be answered in this conceptualization: *What commodities are traded? Why are they traded? Who are the trading partners? How are they traded? When are they traded?* Together, the answers to these questions yield sets of *trading contexts.* A trading context can be specified as a tuple (trading partners, trade contract). We present the structure of trading contexts using BNF notation in Table 10.2.

As can be seen from the above discussions and Table 10.2, a CPN could encompass a whole array of trading contexts. A business-level CPN is essentially a network-level specification of various trading contexts in a given environment. However, in order to make our presentation simpler, we structure the business-level CPNs so that a separate CPN can be envisioned for each context, although, in practice, a trading agreement could involve different commodities bundled together. Accordingly, we formally define a business-level CPN (BCPN) as follows. Let $T = \{P, C\}$ denote a trading context, where P represents the set of trading partners and C represents the set of contracts. Each contract $c \in C$ involves a set of partners $\{p\} \subseteq P$. If the contract is bilateral, then the set $\{p\}$ involves exactly two parties; otherwise it would include several. Let BCPN denote a hypergraph, where each node represents a firm $p \in P$ and each hyper-arc represents a contract $c \in C$ linking a set of firms $p_c \in P$. As a result, a BCPN is indicated as the network specification of a context T. In a simpler case, each arc represents a bilateral contract and hence links just two nodes. We denote such a network as a *bilateral BCPN.* In a bilateral *CPN*, we differentiate between sellers and buyers. Each arc is directed from a seller to a buyer node. In the rest of the discussion, we address bilateral BCPNs.

Each contract arc in a BCPN would entail a technical-level CPN. A technical-level CPN (TCPN) could assume various forms and be specified at different levels of granularity. At the highest level, let TCPN denote a bipartite graph B = (N, M, F), where N and M denote the two sets of nodes and F represents the set of arcs. Each node in this case represents a service and each arc denotes the trading of one service to another. Clearly, N represents the set of services offered by the seller and M represents the set of services of the buyer that utilize the seller services. This is indicated by the arcs. Note that while a BCPN is an abstraction of business relationships among the partnering firms, each arc of the BCPN maps onto a TCPN, which at the highest level of granularity is an abstraction of the technical implementation of the underlying contract.

The core of a TCPN is the specification of how a service employs another service in its delivery to the service consumers. To begin with, we illustrate the process of combining services in a TCPN using a simple example as follows.

Consider the case where two ISPs trade cache capacities. The BCPN consists of two nodes, ISP1 and ISP2, with an arc from 1 to 2. The arc specifies the contract as follows: <Cache capacity X, Encapsulated commodity trade>. At the abstract TCPN level, this translates to a two-node graph, where each node represents an ISP service, which in this case is the cache service to their respective clients. In order to implement this trade, we need to consider the following issues: How

Table 10.2

A BNF Formalism of CPN Contexts

<table>
<tr><td>Trading Context ::</td><td>= *<Trading Partners, Trade Contract>*</td></tr>
<tr><td>Trading Partners ::</td><td>= *<Service Provider>|<Content Publisher>|<Customer>|<Service Broker>|<Other>*</td></tr>
<tr><td>Trade Contract ::</td><td>= *<Trade Commodity, Contract Type, Contract Structure>*</td></tr>
<tr><td>Trade Commodity ::</td><td>= *<Capacity>|<Content>|<Services>*</td></tr>
<tr><td>Capacity ::</td><td>= *<Infrastructure>|<Architecture>*</td></tr>
<tr><td>Infrastructure ::</td><td>= *<Server Capacity>|<Storage Capacity>|<Bandwidth Capacity>*</td></tr>
<tr><td>Architecture ::</td><td>= *<Cache Architecture>|<Hosting Architecture>|<Other Storage Architecture>|<Application Architecture>|<Administrative Architecture>*</td></tr>
<tr><td>Content ::</td><td>= *<Web Content>|<Other Private Content>*</td></tr>
<tr><td>Services ::</td><td>= *<Web Services>|<Application Services>|<Administrative Services>*</td></tr>
<tr><td>Contract Type ::</td><td>= *<Trade Contract, Brokerage Contract>*</td></tr>
<tr><td>Contract Structure ::</td><td>= *<Bilateral>|<Multilateral>*</td></tr>
<tr><td>Trade Contract ::</td><td>= *<Bilateral Trade>|<Multilateral Trade>*</td></tr>
<tr><td>Bilateral Trade ::</td><td>= *<Encapsulated Commodity Trade>|<Shared Commodity Trade>*</td></tr>
<tr><td>Multilateral Trade ::</td><td>= *<Uncoupled Trade>|<Loosely Coupled Trade>|<Tightly Coupled Trade>*</td></tr>
<tr><td>Uncoupled Trade ::</td><td>= *<Individual Bilateral Trades>*</td></tr>
<tr><td>Loosely Coupled Trade ::</td><td>= *<Bilateral trades linked by some level of infrastructure and/or architectural sharing>*</td></tr>
<tr><td>Tightly Coupled Trade ::</td><td>= *<Bilateral trades linked by highly integrated infrastructure and/or architectural sharing>*</td></tr>
<tr><td>Brokerage Contract ::</td><td>= *<Trade facilitation only; no infrastructural or architectural support from a broker>|<Trade facilitation with infrastructural and/or architectural support from a broker>*</td></tr>
</table>

are the two ISP networks connected—via peering or through Internet transit? If peered, how is the peering point managed? At the server level, we consider the following questions: Assuming each ISP has a server farm with load balancers, how are the respective caches organized? How is the dedicated space from the seller to the buyer managed? How should the buyer distribute its contents among the local cache and the bought cache space ? How should the customer requests be routed? What are the load balancing issues? What additional application- and administrative-level services are needed to support this operation? The answers to these questions would lead to specific technical architectures implementing this trade in terms of network structures needed, server configurations and coordination mechanisms, content distribution and maintenance strategies, request routing protocols, accounting and billing, security, and other administrative services.

The process of linking services as in the above example can be viewed in terms of an architecture of service integration and delivery. We develop a component-based framework of this architecture as follows. The key components of integrated services are: *source components, service components, sources-to-services architecture, interservices architecture, destination components,* and *services-to-destination architecture.* In the above example, the source components include the origin server and network components with the publishers' content. The service components include the server farm architectures and Internet connectivities of the respective ISPs. The sources-to-services architecture specifies how the content is obtained, distributed, and maintained among the server farms of the two services, and how the billing and accounting functions underlying the business contract between the publishers and the contracting ISPs are implemented. The interservices architecture includes the communication protocols and coordination mechanisms between the two server farms. The destination components specify the clients and their last mile network connectivities to the servicing ISP farms. The services-to-destination architectures specify how the client requests are routed and serviced, and how the billing and accounting functions at the client level are implemented. Figure 10.3a illustrates the BCPN and Figure 10.3b shows the associated TCPNs in the above example. A high-level component-based architecture of the integrated TCPNs is shown in Figure 10.4.

The implementation of each component of an integrated TCPN can be further specified at five layers of realization: *network, server, application, administration/security,* and *content.* The network layer specifies how a component is connected to other networks with their underlying communication protocols. The server layer specifies the configuration of the server units, constituting the given component with protocols for interserver communication both within a component and among components. The application, administration/security, and content layers specify what is hosted on each server and how they are managed. The specifications at each layer would indicate the subcomponents of a given component and the mutual relationships among them. Some detailed technical specifications for request routing, distribution, and accounting in internetworking of CDNs can be found at the Request For Comments (RFC) of the Network Working Group. (www.ietf.org). Some of these architectures are equally applicable to CPN systems as well, and could be used to configure the various components of the integrated TCPN.

CONCLUSIONS

In this paper, we introduce the notion of topographical leverage in providing Internet services and develop the concept of capacity provision networks. We conclude our analysis with a model of business and market forces impacting business decisions to trade and collaborate among the various players in the Internet service industry. In particular, we organize the service industry along four dimensions: customers, content publishers, CDN/ISPs, and service brokers. Two intrinsic factors determining the behaviors in each of these dimensions are scale and reach. The scale factor in the customer dimension refers to the internal expansion within a given base, while the reach factor refers to the expansion in the base itself. The other dimensions react to this phenomenon in response: publishers, CDN/ISPs, and brokers scale and expand the reach of these services. The growth in scale and reach of the customer bases is due to the market externality force, while the reactive responses of the providers are due to the forces of supply/demand economics and competition. We synthesize the interactions among these forces in Figure 10.5. In fact, these interactions would give rise to several innovative business models in the Internet service industry where the concepts of trading and collaborating as envisioned in CPN are likely to become predominant in the future. Modeling and analysis of the economics of these business models, their technical implementations, and operational optimization issues together offer a rich agenda for future research on CPN systems.

Figure 10.3a **A BCPN Example**

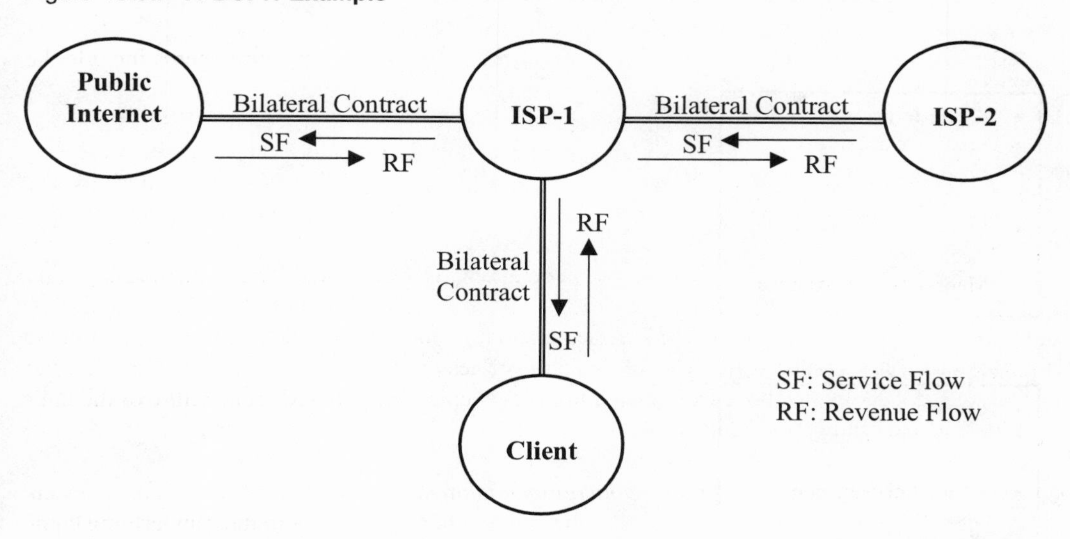

Figure 10.3b **TCPNs for the BCPN in Figure 10.3a**

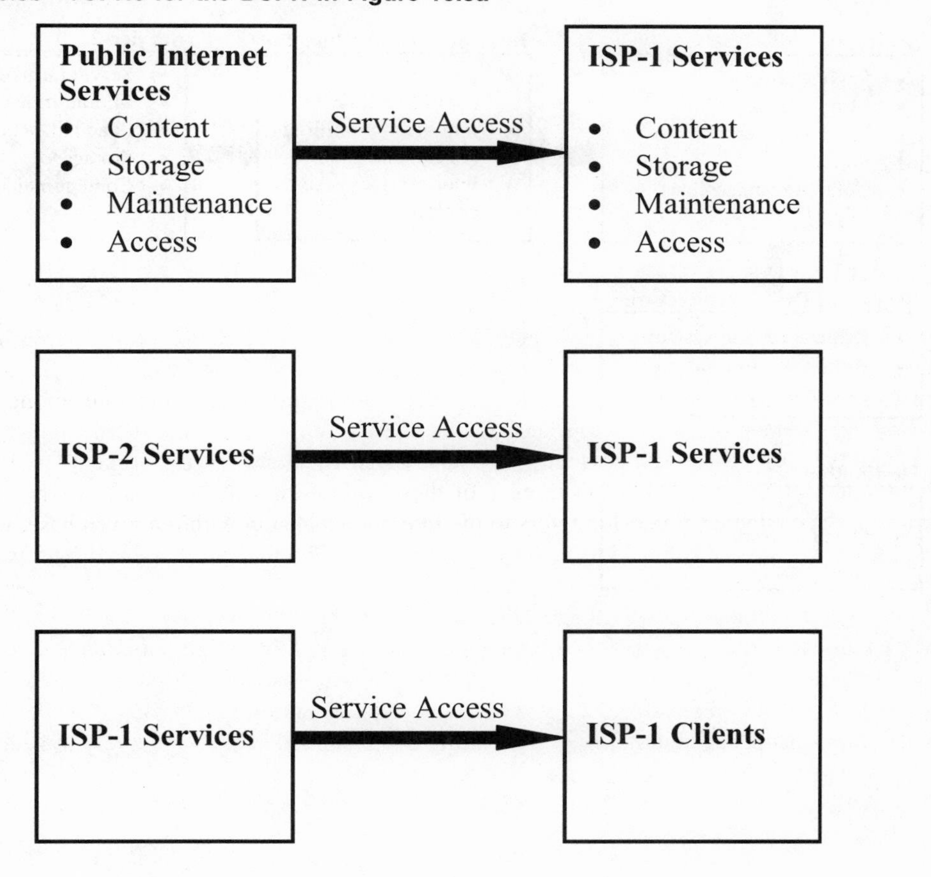

Figure 10.4 **A Component-based Architecture of TCPNs**

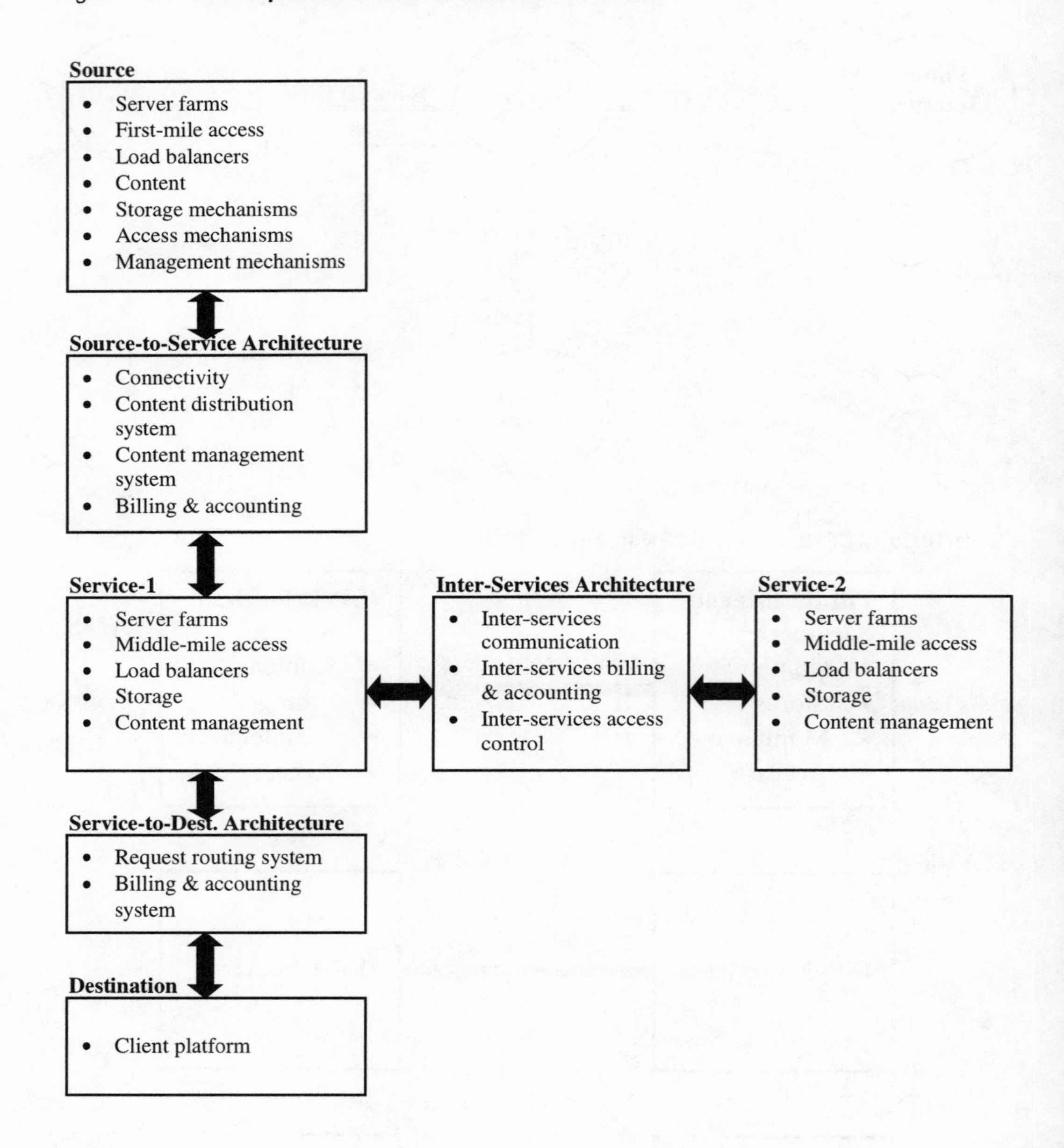

Figure 10.5 **A Model of Interactions Among the CPN Components** (influence diagram)

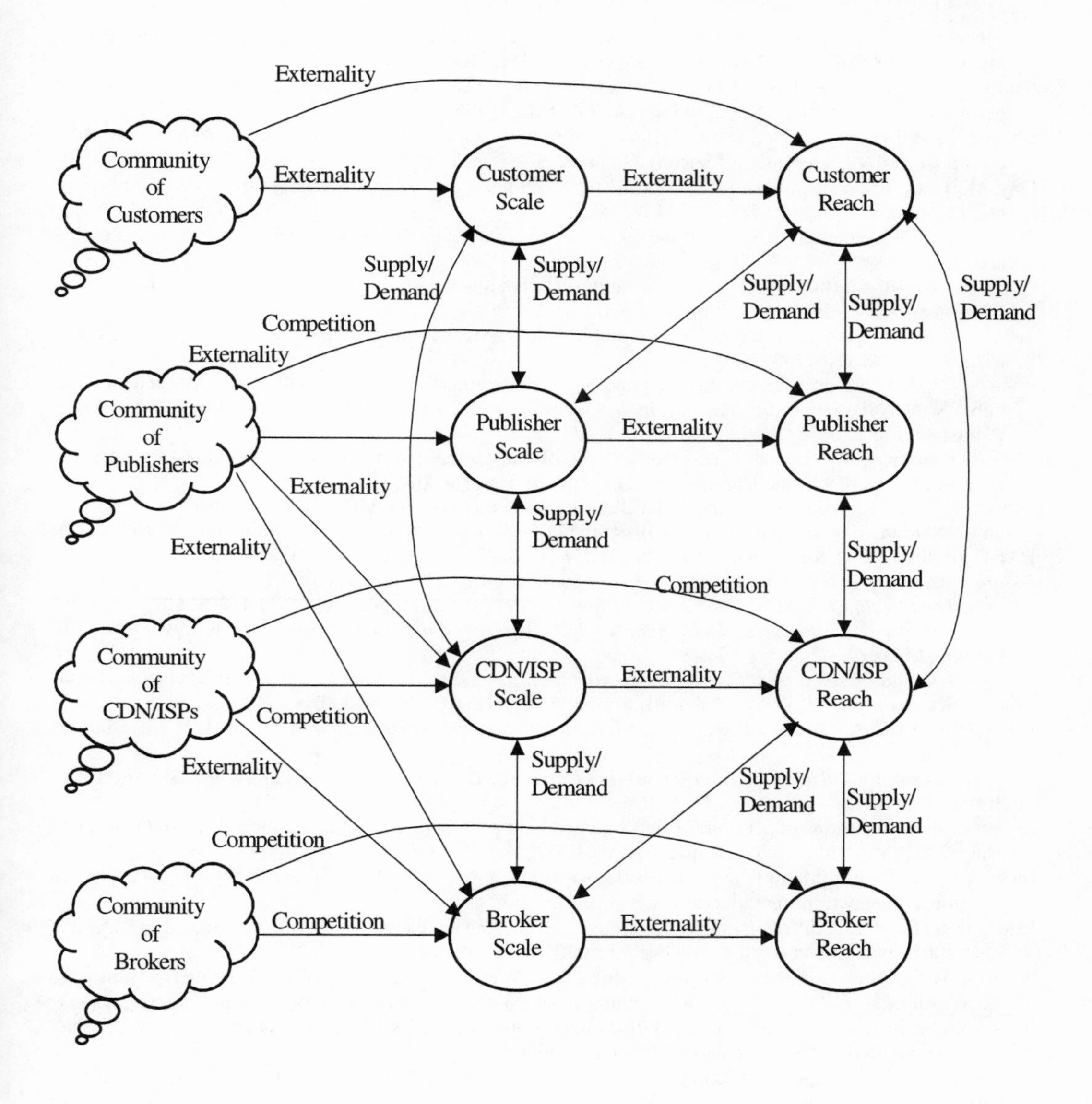

REFERENCES

Barbir, A.; Cain, B.; Nair, R.; and Spatscheck, O. Known content network (CN) request-routing mechanisms. *Network Working Group RFC 3568,* The Internet Society (July 2003).

Claffy, K.; Siegel, D.; and Woodcock, B. A common format for the recording and interchange of peering point utilization statistics. Presented at NANOG (May 1996).

Cooper, I.; Melve, I.; and Tomlinson, G. Internet web replication and caching taxonomy. *Network Working Group RFC 3040.* The Internet Society (January 2001).

Day, M.; Cain, B; and Tomlinson, G. A model for CDN peering. *Network Working Group draft-day-cdnp-model-04.txt.* The Internet Society (May 2001).

Devarajan, V. Introduction to web services. March 31, 2003. Available at www.developersdex.com/gurus/articles/569.asp.

Geng, X.; Gopal, R.; Ramesh, R.; and Whinston, A.B. Trading caches: Capacity provision networks. *IEEE IT Professional* (July/August 2003a). 30–36.

———. Capacity provision networks: A scalable web services architecture for web cache trading hubs. *IEEE Computer* (November 2003b).

———. Capacity provision networks: A technology framework and economic analysis of web cache trading hubs. In A. Nagurney (ed.), *Innovations in Financial and Economic Networks.* London: Edward Elgar Publishers Ltd., 2003c.

———. Capacity provision networks: Foundations of markets for internet caching. Working Paper. Center for Research in Electronic Commerce, University of Texas at Austin, 2003d.

Gilletti, D.; Nair, R.; Scharber, J.; and Guha, J. Content internetworking (CDI): Authentication, authorization and accounting requirements. *Network Working Group Internet Draft,* The Internet Society (August 2002).

HTRC Group, LLC. *Global Load Balancing Solutions.* San Andreas, CA: The HTRC Group, 2001a.

———. *Streaming in the Enterprise—the Market Opportunity.* San Andreas, CA: The HTRC Group, 2001b.

———. *The Digital Content Network Receiver Service Market.* San Andreas, CA: The HTRC Group, 2002a.

———. *Internet and Enterprise CDN Vendor Analysis: Volera's Velocity CDN.* San Andreas, CA: The HTRC Group, 2002b.

———. *The Emerging Internet Storage Infrastructure Market.* San Andreas, CA: The HTRC Group, 2003a.

———. *The Future of IP Services.* San Andreas, CA: The HTRC Group, 2003b.

ISP-Market, LLC. *ISP to xSP: Putting the Service in the Service Provider.* Walnut Creek, CA: ISP-Market, LLC, 2003a.

———. *Taking the Pulse of the Internet Service Provider Industry.* Walnut Creek, CA: ISP-Market, LLC, 2003b.

Linton, J. New directions in peering for tier-2 and content providers. Presentation slides, NANOG 24, February 2002 (available at www.nanog.org/mtg-0202/ppt/linton.ppt).

Metro Ethernet Forum. Metro ethernet networks—a technical overview. *MEF Research Report* (2002). http://www.metroethernetforum.org/metro-ethernet-services.pdf.

Mitchell, K. Economic differences between transit and peering exchanges. Presentation slides, NANOG 25, June 2002 (available at www.nanog.org/mtg-0206/ppt/keith.ppt).

Norton, W.B. Interconnection strategies for ISPs. White Paper. Equinix Inc., 1999 (available at morse.colorado.edu/~epperson/courses/routing-protocols/handouts/ISPInterconnectionStrategies2.1.pdf).

———. A business case for ISP peering. White Paper. Equinix Inc., 2001 (available at arneill-py.sacramento.ca.us/ipv6mh/ABusinessCaseforISPPeering1.2.pdf).

———. Internet service providers and peering. White Paper. Equinix Inc., 2002 (available at www.nanog.org/papers/isp.peering.doc).

Rabinovich, M., and Spatcheck, O. *Web Caching and Replication.* Boston, MA: Addison-Wesley, 2002.

Rzewski, P.; Day, M.; and Gilletti, D. Content internetworking (CDI) scenarios. *Network Working Group RFC 3570,* The Internet Society, July 2003.

Stardust.com, Inc. Content networking and edge services: Leveraging the Internet for profit. Stardust.com white paper (2001a) (available at whitepapers.zdnet.co.uk).

———. Edge services: the next wave of computing. Stardust.com white paper (2001b) available at whitepapers.zdnet.co.uk).

CHAPTER 11

MOBILE COMMERCE

A VALUE SYSTEM PERSPECTIVE

CHRISTER CARLSSON, BILL ANCKAR, AND PIRKKO WALDEN

Abstract: *Mobility, beyond simple convenience, means freedom, and freedom creates choice and value, which may revolutionize the way companies work, buy, sell, and collaborate. In this way, mobile commerce (m-commerce) may mark the start of a new era of innovation in business. The m-commerce products and services, which are being formed with the help of wireless technology, will drive the emergence of new business models at the same time as the products and services themselves will help shape new user contexts. The wireless products and services will reshape the world of the users and the routines they use in their everyday life, which in turn will change the way they perceive "how things should be," that is, their ideas of what is possible and valuable. (Take, for example, the Short Message Service [SMS], which replaced part of voice communications and offered an easier method of nonurgent communication than the phone.) These changes will drive the emergence of new value systems that will extend the way organizations conduct business—and change the relationships among companies, customers, suppliers, and partners.*

Keywords: *Business Model, Business Value Systems, Mobile Commerce (M-Commerce)*

INTRODUCTION

We have chosen a European perspective for our study of mobile commerce (m-commerce). There are several reasons for this. The growth in Global System for Mobile Communication (GSM) acceptance in Europe has been extremely fast, and the penetration of mobile phones reached 63 percent of the population of European Union (EU) nations in 2000, which translates to eleven times the number of users in 1995 and a total of 252 million users (Durlacher Research Institute, 2001). Therefore there is a fast-growing potential, large, and very significant market for products and services that use the GSM standard mobile platforms. This market has continued to grow at a rapid pace, despite some slowdown in 2002–3 due to the slowdowns and recessions in some key EU economies.

The Durlacher *UMTS Report* presents a scenario in which mobile voice communication is expected to reach a saturation level of 87 percent around 2005–6. In 2003 about 75 percent of the European population was expected to be using mobile phones (more than 300 million users). The saturation of mobile voice demand will shift the focus to mobile data communication, and this will drive the development of m-commerce products and services. The Durlacher study notes that the investment in Universal Mobile Telecommunications System (UMTS) licenses throughout Europe reached €120 billion, but makes the optimistic proposal that this will not slow down investments in the new mobile technology, which are estimated to reach €260 billion, because the initial license costs will be worked into the business models by 2005 and largely forgotten, as they are being covered by growing streams of revenues. This will put a viable infrastructure in place for data communication, which will grow to 350 million connections by 2005, running more than 3,000 applications.

The technologies and the markets grow in tandem, and it is important to realize that the development of the mobile markets will be evolutionary, that is, new products and services will have a backbone and a basis in the existing products and services. We cannot expect to stumble upon revolutionary new (killer) applications that will happen overnight with the introduction of the UMTS networks (even if this actually could happen). There were a number of first applications, which were introduced in the GSM networks and discarded because they were slow and cumbersome, which have now reappeared in the General Packet Radio Service (GPRS) networks and are gaining acceptance. The Wireless Application Protocol (WAP) was a failure in the GSM but is gaining increasing acceptance in the GPRS, and news, information, and entertainment services, which are built as WAP applications, are getting more and more acceptance. Common wisdom had it that the WAP would be replaced by the Japanese i-Mode, but the introduction of this standard has been very slow in the UK, Germany, and the Netherlands and will probably not become an alternative to WAP, GPRS, and UMTS.

Another common wisdom is that multimedia services will drive the acceptance of the new mobile technology and there is speculation as to what the advanced multimedia will be used for. The facts of technology do not support this—the GPRS networks cannot handle more than very limited video applications and the early UMTS networks will not provide the envisioned 2 Mbps capacity, which will be reached only around 2008–9 (throughout Europe, but of course with regional exceptions). It is interesting to note the visions voiced by senior representatives of the major mobile hardware vendors.

In a survey published in the Finnish daily *Helsingin Sanomat* on March 23, 2003, senior executives of Nokia Mobile Phones, Motorola, Samsung, Siemens, and Sony Ericsson were asked when they thought that the penetration of third generation (3G) services and applications would take place—all of them agreed that this would happen by 2006. In response to the question of what the most attractive 3G services are, the answers varied quite interestingly:

> *Nokia*: Multiple services that can be used simultaneously; most services emerge through evolution
> *Motorola*: Those services that are more useful, more valuable, and more fun if they can be used spontaneously, that is, through wireless
> *Samsung*: Multimedia, m-commerce, and localization-using services
> *Siemens*: Multimedia, entertainment, payment, and localization-using services
> *Sony Ericsson*: Video conferencing

Another interesting set of facts can be found in the TNS Telecoms 3G 2003 report on a survey (MobileInfo 2003) that was carried out in ten EU countries. It was found that 42 percent of European mobile phone users are interested in 3G services. An interesting observation was that a majority of the users were prepared to pay extra for 3G handsets and services. The average monthly invoice for a mobile phone user in Europe was 26 € in 2003 (20 € for prepaid and 37 € for contracts). Fifty percent of those interested in 3G services were willing to pay an additional 6–10 € per month for 3G services such as Multimedia Message Service (MMS), high-speed Internet, and e-mail. A majority of respondents across all countries surveyed were willing to pay up to 330 € for a 3G handset. The most-favored 3G applications were sending and receiving e-mail on mobile phones (77 percent) and using videophone handsets (77 percent). The least-favored applications were downloading music files (47 percent) and viewing video clips (40 percent).

These are visions and speculations, but the message the studies convey supports the evolutionary, gradual development of mobile services—users will work with applications they can incorporate into their everyday activities and then change to more advanced services as these become feasible and useful. It appears to be the exception that users jump to a service just because it has become technically available.

These fragmentary and quick sketches will serve as a background for working with the m-commerce arena both as a research area of conceptual constructs and theory formation and as a domain for empirical studies.

Our examination of value propositions will start from some simple observations, which are at the core of the applications built around the mobile, wireless technology:

- *Mobility:* Mobile phones are brought along as individual tools and instruments, which has significantly changed the everyday routines of communicating.
- *Availability:* Mobile phones allow their users to be continuously connected, which has changed the communication infrastructure in significant ways.
- *Ubiquity:* Network interconnectivity and roaming agreements allow mobile communication anywhere and at any time.

We will state as a proposal that any m-commerce service should show an evolutionary path of development from these three value-building features.

The conceptual discussion of m-commerce starts, in most of the cases, from the conceptual constructs of electronic commerce (e-commerce). It is probably only a coincidence, but e-commerce has not yet reached the explosive growth figures that were commonly predicted in the mid-1990s. These turned out to be as unrealistic as the early predictions of explosive growth for m-commerce in the foresight scenarios of 1999–2000. Partly as a consequence, scholars and industry representatives are turning their attention to the promise of electronic wireless media, envisaging that the next—or "real" phase—of e-commerce growth will be in the area of m-commerce (see, for example, Hampe et al. 2000, Kalakota and Robinson 2001, Li 2002, Varshney and Vetter 2001, Varshney et al. 2000).

Keen and Mackintosh (2001) define m-commerce as the extension of electronic commerce from wired to wireless computers and telecommunications, and from fixed locations to anytime, anywhere, and anyone. On the other hand, mobility in itself and mobile technology is not necessarily a value, but the *freedom* created and supported by the technology is the key issue. Freedom, Keen and Mackintosh say, makes a real difference to how m-commerce customers go about their day, to how companies build their options and design new business processes, and to how their staff mobilizes the organization's knowledge and communication resources. Freedom is about choices and value for customers and consumers. The choice has to translate to values that customers are willing to pay for and that companies can afford to provide. The very core of m-commerce is to make the user the center of the information and communication world, with relationships and business operations that create new freedoms.

May (2001) finds that when something is mobile it means that its primary usage environment is a mobile one, but goes on to define m-commerce as "electronic commerce using mobile devices such as cell phones as client devices." Paavilainen (2002) takes issue with this notion. He defines mobile business as "the exchange of goods, services and information using mobile technology," and notes that mobile business is a broad definition that includes communication, transactions, and different value-added services using various kinds of mobile terminals. Then he goes on to define m-commerce as "transactions with monetary value, conducted using the mobile Internet," which he recognizes to cover business-to-business (B2B), business-to-consumer (B2C), and consumer-to-consumer (C2C) transactions. Traditional voice calls are not included in m-commerce, but services using voice recognition to enable commercial transactions fall into this category. Paavilainen points out that the term "mobile e-commerce" is misleading, because the business models and the value chain are totally different from e-commerce. We agree, based on our empirical studies, that "mobile commerce is not a truncated form of e-commerce but a new, innovative way of conducting time-critical transactions regardless of location" (Paavilainen 2002, 2). Kalakota and Robinson (2001) place themselves somewhere in between May and Paavilainen with the notion that m-commerce is an evolution of the e-commerce paradigm from fixed networks to wireless data networks. They also recognize that m-commerce refers to business transactions conducted while on the move, and they expect the growth in m-commerce to be driven by users seeking to conduct business, communicate, and share information while away from their fixed-network connections. They do not, however, recognize that the paradigm evolution actually is a paradigm shift from e-commerce to m-commerce.

Kalakota and Robinson (2001) make the point that m-commerce is not about telecom infrastructure, operating systems, and software breakthroughs but about applications and solutions for everyday users in various contexts and locations. Nevertheless, it is helpful to recognize that m-commerce products and services are information systems constructs (software) (Carlsson 2002, Carlsson and Walden 2001, 2002a, b, c, d), and that the features referred to in the various definitions can be implemented as software designs. Bearing this in mind, it is possible to work out the designs of m-commerce products and services in terms of software modules, layers of software components, and bundles of modules, which make the features to be built for various categories of users in a variety of contexts as useful and as freedom-building as possible.

Although the mobile Internet appears to have much to offer as an instrument of commerce, little is known about consumers' willingness to adopt wireless electronic media and the factors that influence their adoption decisions and value perceptions of the products and services that form m-commerce (Pedersen et al. 2002, Urbaczewski et al. 2002). We are now gradually starting to understand the unique characteristics of the fixed Internet, but the wireless Internet raises many of the same questions in a new context (Guerley 2000, May 2001). Building successful strategies for the mobile marketplace begins with a recognition of the distinctive forces that drive the emergence of m-commerce (Senn 2000): on the Internet, firms can create value for customers in a manner that is different from that which has been achieved in conventional business (Han and Han 2001). Correspondingly, m-commerce is expected to possess unique characteristics in relation to e-commerce, and many statements on an impending m-revolution have been triggered by the assumption that the potential of m-commerce will involve lower barriers and greater benefits in comparison to both fixed e-commerce and traditional commerce. In view of that, the key question for m-commerce is to find some way to assess the value of mobile applications to prospective users (Carlsson and Walden 2002a, b, c, d), and to gain an understanding of the factors that may delay the penetration of the mobile Internet on a larger scale (Lee et al. 2002). Such insights are certainly needed to form the foundations for conceptual frameworks, systematic research, and an effective research methodology, but also to support investment decisions; find viable business models; and develop mobile devices, networks, and services that address and take the concerns/wants of consumers into consideration.

VALUE COMPONENTS AND ADOPTION DECISIONS

Although m-commerce still is an emerging phenomenon, a significant body of literature has, from the late 1990s onward, pointed out the factors that are likely to drive the diffusion of m-commerce in the B2C marketplace. In this area, most contributions—which are strongly dominated by intuition-based reasoning and conceptual analyses rather than empirical investigations—have primarily focused on establishing the value proposition of m-commerce from the consumer's point of view, pointing out such general concepts as *flexibility, ubiquity, localization, personalization,* and *mobility* as key adoption motivators (see, for example, Booz Allen Hamilton 2000, Herman and Neff 2002, Müller-Versee 1999, Vittet-Philippe and Navarro 2000). Such terms appear to be too general, technology-oriented, and abstract to provide a comprehensive explanatory understanding of the reasons for consumers' decisions to adopt mobile distribution channels. This is especially true if we look at the current situation or, in other words, the factors that drive adoption *today*. Most of the concepts listed above are understood in terms of the advanced features of the 3G, rather than the technology of the 2G or 2.5G networks, which are rather more modest.[1]

Moreover, it should be noted that not only the *benefits* offered by new mobile channels, but also—and in particular—the *barriers* to using mobile services need to be identified to build an understanding of the factors that affect adoption decisions by consumers. In the marketing literature, many studies have proposed or verified that *perceived customer value*[2] is an important determinant of consumers' purchase intentions and purchase decision making (see, for example, McDougall and Levesque 2000, Zeithaml 1988), and is valuable for understanding consumer behavior (see Parasuraman 1997). While value considerations are associated with a prepurchase assessment of the utility of a product, we argue that the core idea of the concept is equally relevant, as we examine the relative advantages of technological innovations, commercial media, or even electronic distribution channels (Anckar and D'Incau 2002, Han and Han 2001). In this context we argue, however, that the traditional view of the value equation as a trade-off between *benefits* and *costs* (or even a price–quality trade-off) is too simplistic in terms of building an understanding of the primary motivators and inhibitors to m-commerce adoption. Instead, the value concept should be interpreted as the trade-off between *benefits* and *barriers*—that is, get and give components described not only in monetary terms, but seen from a much broader perspective, addressing nonmonetary sacrifices as well (see Eggert and Ulaga 2002, Sweeney and Soutar 2001).

To date, many studies, primarily from the information systems (IS) discipline, on adoption decisions of information technology (IT) in fixed or mobile settings have built on the widely recognized and used technology acceptance model (TAM) by Davis (1989) (see, for example, Lee et al. 2001, Lee et al. 2002, O'Cass and Fenech 2003, Teo et al. 1999). Although a large body of research supports the TAM as a good model to explain the acceptance of IT tools and information systems it is questionable whether the model is applicable to consumers' choice of commercial channels. Adoption decisions in m-commerce are likely to be different from technology adoption decisions. First of all, what the consumer chooses to adopt in m-commerce is not merely a technology per se, but rather a new instrument of commerce. Second, m-commerce encompasses both transactional and nontransactional dimensions, which means that consumers' intentions to transact could be understood as multidimensional behavioral intentions (see Pavlou 2002). Then we need—in contrast to most technology adoption decisions—to distinguish between different *levels of m-commerce adoption* as we analyze consumer choices of electronic channels—fixed or mobile. Third, as pointed out by Eikebrokk and Sørebø (1998), TAM is usually applied as if every situation would be a single-target situation, building on the implicit assumption that only one specific technology is available for the potential users. The authors argue that it may be difficult to obtain valid predictions and explanations of technology acceptance with TAM when consumers actually are exposed to a multiple-choice situation where they can choose among several alternative technologies—or in this case—alternative channels. Fourth, TAM is, as argued and demonstrated by Malhotra and Galletta (1999), incomplete in the sense that it does not account for social influence in the adoption and utilization of new information systems, a limitation that seems particularly disturbing when adoption decisions relating to m-commerce are examined. Fifth, TAM assumes that usage is volitional, that is, there are no barriers that would prevent an individual from using an IS if he or she chose to do so, a fact that has drawn criticism from, for example, Mathieson et al. (2001), and that has influenced some authors (e.g., Lee et al. 2001) to extend the TAM with theoretical models that postulate perceived risk as a factor to be weighed into decisions to adopt m-commerce. Pavlou (2002) highlights the fact that the advent of the Internet has introduced uncertainty and risk in system adoption, and validates the need for integration of variables that capture such notions in existing models of technology adoption by showing that *trust* and *perceived risk* are guiding decisions to transact online (Pavlou 2003). Previous studies have shown that consumers' rejection decisions on household adoption of personal computers and nontransactional or transaction-based Internet commerce are based on perceived critical barriers more than on a perception of the associated benefits (Anckar 2002a, Venkatesh and Brown 2001). There is little doubt that the impact of various nonmonetary sacrifices should be included in any model or study relating to channel adoption decisions.

M-Commerce Adoption Drivers and Inhibitors

Perceived usefulness and *perceived ease of use* are general multidimensional constructs. On the other hand, our starting value propositions were based on three simple components—mobility, availability, and ubiquity—which should now be linked to the key benefits and barriers—the core get and give value components—that drive or inhibit consumer adoption of m-commerce today and in the future. This discussion will be guided by two research questions:

1. Are adoption decisions/intents driven to a greater extent by benefits or barriers?
2. Which benefits and barriers constitute important drivers/inhibitors to the adoption and use of mobile Internet and m-commerce in different consumer groups?

The potential set of benefits and barriers is large and not well understood, which is why we selected the benefits and barriers to be included in the study through an extensive review of work relating to m-commerce drivers and inhibitors. Based on the material, which consists of both anecdotal and empirical evidence, we selected the most frequently mentioned potential drivers and inhibitors to m-commerce adoption—and extended the list with some other plausible factors.

As the literature review will show, different authors and studies have underlined very different factors as key drivers/inhibitors to m-commerce adoption.

Gillick and Vanderhoof (2000) propose five possible inhibitors, all very broad in nature, to the widespread growth of m-commerce: *the technology itself, industry standardization, the business case, consumer expectations,* and *security and reliability.* Of these factors, the last-mentioned one is perhaps the most widely cited, with many authors having contended that lacking privacy and security could be a major stumbling block to the growth of m-commerce (see Langendoerfer 2002, Li 2002). Such contentions are partly supported by empirical evidence: in an empirical multimarket study conducted by e-Mori on behalf of Nokia Networks (Nokia 3G Market Research 2001), *the lack of perceived need, conservatism,* and *perceptions relating to the reliability and security of the technology* were the main barriers to m-commerce adoption, while *convenience* and *control* were found to be the key determinants of demand.

Drawing, for example, on data collected through expert interviews, Buellingen and Woerter (2002) highlight four critical success factors for the use of mobile services: *transmission rate, personalization, data security,* and *user-friendliness.* Findings from a UK-based survey by Strong and Old (2000) suggest that *the convenience of having Internet access at any time and place* will be the most important incentive for consumers to use mobile Internet applications. The authors found that significant barriers to a quick take-up of the mobile Internet in the very near future are the *lack of awareness of content and application, high operating costs,* and *the unfavorable comparison of the mobile Internet with the fixed line Internet* due to smaller screen sizes, fiddly input, poor searching facilities, poor connections, and so on. In contrast, many authors have argued that the overall volume of e-commerce may experience a significant growth with mobile technologies, as many consumers who are not yet Internet adopters now will access the Internet due to the lower costs involved and their familiarity with mobile devices (see Müller-Versee 1999, Ropers 2001, Vittet-Philippe and Navarro 2000).

Vittet-Philippe and Navarro (2000) and Green (2000), argue that *user-friendliness* will be the key for a wide adoption of m-commerce. In line with this, the constraints such as small screen size, limited bandwidth, and the *simplistic functionality* of mobile phones affect the design of effective user interfaces for m-commerce applications. Similarly, the results from an expert survey conducted in Finland (Carlsson and Walden 2002a, b, c, d) indicate that the *slow speed of service* and the *limited screen size* of mobile devices constitute the major barriers for a rapid m-commerce expansion. In contrast, Langendoerfer (2002) found that technological issues will not be the major problem for m-commerce, but that psychological aspects—especially privacy concerns —will be the reason why m-commerce will not take off.

Shuster (2001) speculates that *pricing* certainly will have an impact on adoption. Reporting on an online survey, Vrechopoulos et al. (2002) present a broad list of critical success factors for accelerating m-commerce diffusion in Europe: *improved mobile devices, user-friendly shopping interfaces, effective applications and services, reduced prices, secure transactions, high bandwidth,* and *network coverage.*

Findings from a consumer survey conducted in Finland (Anckar 2002b) indicated that m-commerce adoption mainly appears to be driven by a need for solutions that add *convenience and flexibility to daily routines* rather than excitement and entertainment. The survey also found that consumers perceive the ability to satisfy *spontaneous and time-critical needs* as the most important driver of m-commerce adoption.

As this review of previous research has shown, the main factors affecting m-commerce adoption decisions are associated with services and device features that go beyond the traditional use of a mobile phone, that is, person-to-person communication. Consumers will be driven toward m-commerce by the fact that the mobile phone will turn into a personal trusted device, through which all kinds of commercial activities and transactions can be managed. An alternative and plausible scenario is that the opportunities and benefits associated with new application areas of mobile phones will not serve as significant adoption drivers in the B2C segment. Instead, consumers will be persuaded by the value of *enhanced features and new dimensions* offered by smart phones and next-generation networks in *person-to-person communication,* and/or will be driven toward new mobile technologies as older networks and phones gradually are replaced by new, m-commerce facilitating ones. Curiosity, playful experimentation, and customization of the devices while using them for conventional purposes will eventually make the users realize the capabilities of new mobile technologies and the value of mobile services. As this line of argument suggests, our empirical investigation should not focus exclusively on possible adoption drivers for m-commerce services, but also on the benefits of advanced (3G) mobile devices and networks in person-to-person communication (acknowledging that this application area generally is excluded from definitions of m-commerce).

THE SURVEY

Since our research focus is to study different consumer groups in terms of m-commerce adoption, we decided to use noninteractive media to study consumer groups in terms of their *level of experience* with m-commerce.[3] With this approach, we were able to draw on two different dimensions of m-commerce adoption: *mobile Internet adoption* and *adoption of (transaction-based) m-commerce,* and thus to differentiate between important consumer groups when analyzing the data. The corresponding subsamples were defined as follows:

- *Mobile Internet adopters:* Respondents who have experiences with the mobile Internet, but who have not necessarily purchased products or services over a mobile device.
- *Intended mobile Internet adopters:* Respondents who have never used the mobile Internet, but who reported an intention to use the mobile Internet in the future.
- *Mobile Internet averse:* Mobile Internet nonadopters who reported that they have no intention to use the mobile Internet now or in the future.
- *M-commerce adopters:* Respondents who have made purchases over a mobile device (and thus have embraced transaction-based m-commerce).
- *Intended m-commerce adopters:* Respondents who have not made purchases over a mobile device, but who reported an intention to do so in the future.
- *M-commerce averse:* M-commerce nonadopters who reported that they have no intention to make purchases over a mobile device now or in the future.

The Survey Instrument

Data was collected using a four-page self-administered questionnaire that was mailed out to a sample of 1,000 Finnish consumers in March–April 2002, with two follow-up mailings to all nonrespondents in June. The sample was drawn from the electronic sampling frame provided by the Finnish Population Register Centre, based on a stratified sampling procedure where the sample was drawn, using a simple random-sampling method. The sampling frame used offered a complete representation of the target population, which was defined as the Finnish population ages 16–64 years.[4]

The survey instrument covered twenty questions relating to the consumers' perceptions and intentions relating to m-commerce, as well as their current experience with the mobile Internet and m-commerce. In this paper we primarily report on the questionnaire section in which the respondents were instructed to indicate how strongly they agreed or disagreed with a number of statements relating to their perceived importance/magnitude of different benefits of and barriers to m-commerce. For this, a five-point Likert scale was used (5 = strongly agree, 1 = strongly disagree). These data were used to identify the motivators and hindrances that constitute important/unimportant factors influencing consumer m-commerce adoption/nonadoption decisions.

In an attempt to motivate the respondents to complete and return the questionnaire, the drawing

Figure 11.1 **Sample Demographics and Subsample Sizes**

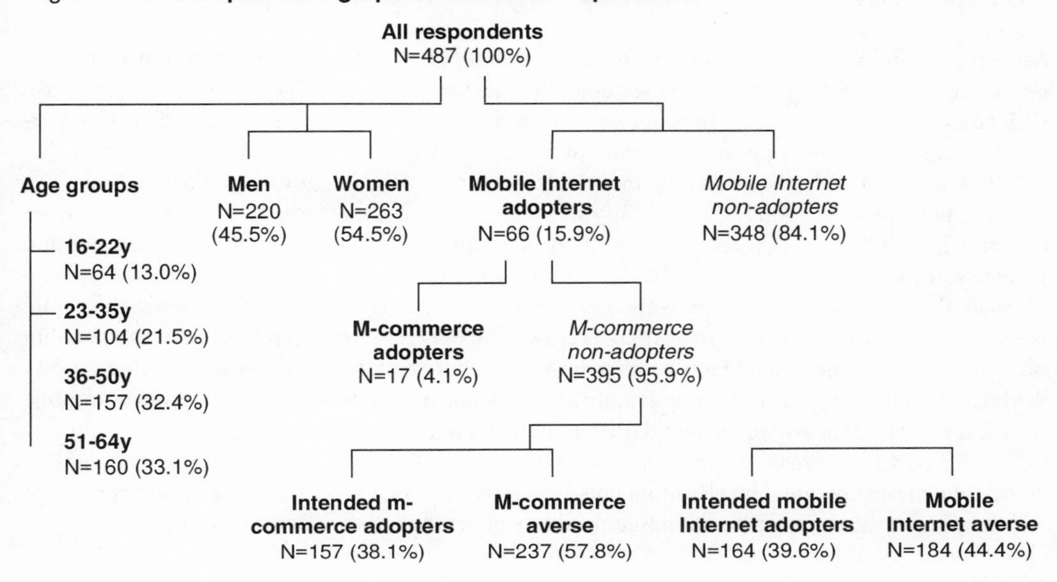

of a top-of-the-line mobile phone among all respondents was announced. Eight questionnaires were returned undelivered due to incorrect addresses. Four hundred eighty-seven completed and utilizable questionnaires were returned by the deadline, giving an effective response rate of 48.7 percent.

FINDINGS

Sample Demographics

Figure 11.1 shows the sample demographics with respect to general variables such as gender and age, and portrays the sizes and partial overlap of the subsamples used in this study. The demographics are used as a background description as we do not have the space (in this paper) for a complete statistical analysis of the respondents by age and gender groups. This analysis will appear in a forthcoming paper.

In the following we will work through a summary of the results, which have been organized into the benefits (the "get" value components) and the barriers (the "give" value components) seen from the viewpoints of adopters, intended adopters, and nonadopters of mobile Internet services and m-commerce.

Accessing the Internet by Computer and Mobile Device

The majority of the respondents had used the Internet via a computer (81.8 percent) but less than a sixth had used it via a mobile device (15.9 percent). The majority of the respondents seemed to be familiar with using a computer (75.1 percent). The biggest group of nonusers were in the age category 51 to 64, where 37.3 percent had not accessed the Internet via a computer. Purchasing via a computer was not unusual (34.8 percent), still, purchasing via a mobile device was extremely unusual (4.4 percent).

Mobile Devices in Use

Most people in Finland have a mobile device and 88.9 percent of the respondents used a mobile device. The great majority had a GSM device (77 percent) and some had several devices in use (7.8 percent). Only a few respondents had a communicator (0.8 percent) or a GPRS- (0.6 percent) or a WAP-enabled phone (2.7 percent). Only 11.1 percent of the respondents said that they did not use a mobile device. The mobile devices were used only or mainly for personal use by 72.8 percent of respondents and only or mainly for business use by 11.5 percent of the respondents, with 15.6 percent reporting that they divided use equally between personal and business purposes.

More than half of the respondents (63.6 percent) declared that they would change their mobile device within the near future, almost all of them within two years and 56.6 percent of them within one year. Most of the respondents were planning to change their mobile device to a new GSM device (50.2 percent). A rather big group (24.7 percent) did not know to what kind of mobile device they would choose to change. GPRS was found attractive by 9 percent and a communicator by 4.5 percent of respondents. Only 4.1 percent said that they would change their mobile device to a mobile phone with a color display. There were no statistical differences between male and female respondents and between the different age categories.

Who Is Paying for the Usage of the Mobile Device?

Most of the respondents said that they were paying for their own mobile device usage (69.7 percent), and only a few (12.5 percent) said that their employer was paying for the usage. Not too many (9.7 percent) were having a family member pay for the use of the mobile device. Taking care of the bills jointly with someone else was also a possibility (11.1 percent).

Benefits and Barriers of Mobile Services

Using a five-point Likert scale, we asked the respondents to indicate their degree of agreement or disagreement with benefits and barriers associated with the use of mobile services. We analyzed the data on an item-by-item basis (Figures 11.2 and 11.3). With regard to benefits, there were not too many differences between the opinions in the different age categories; flexibility in using the mobile services anywhere and anytime was seen by all as a benefit, as well as enhancing communication, convenience, and handiness. The younger respondents (age categories 16 to 22 and 23 to 35) had a more positive opinion than the older respondents.

When we analyze the responses about benefits according to gender, we find that flexibility in using mobile services is valued by women (chi-Square 12.1 Sig. 0.002). Although the majority of all respondents did not see being trendy/up-to-date when using a mobile service as a benefit, those who saw it as a benefit were mainly women (chi-Square 12 Sig. 0.002). Statistically more women also felt enhancing social status to be a benefit (chi-Square 8.5 Sig. 0.014).

When we consider the barriers associated with the use of mobile services, the profiles for different age categories differ. The profiles for the age categories 16 to 22 and 23 to 35 show rather similar patterns and the profiles for the age categories 36 to 50 and 51 to 64 show similar patterns. High initial costs and operating costs, limited capacity of the mobile devices, slow data connections, as well as the small screen size of the mobile devices were seen as major barriers in all categories, but with different magnitude. The complexity of using the mobile devices was a barrier for the respondents in the older age categories. Respondents in the younger age categories

Figure 11.2 **Mobile Services: Barriers**

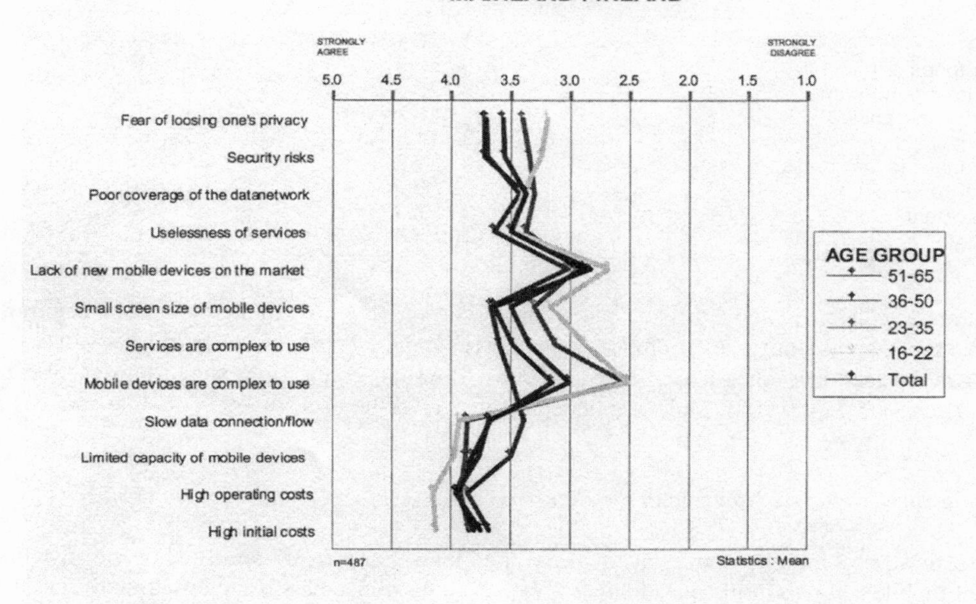

Figure 11.3 **Mobile Services: Benefits**

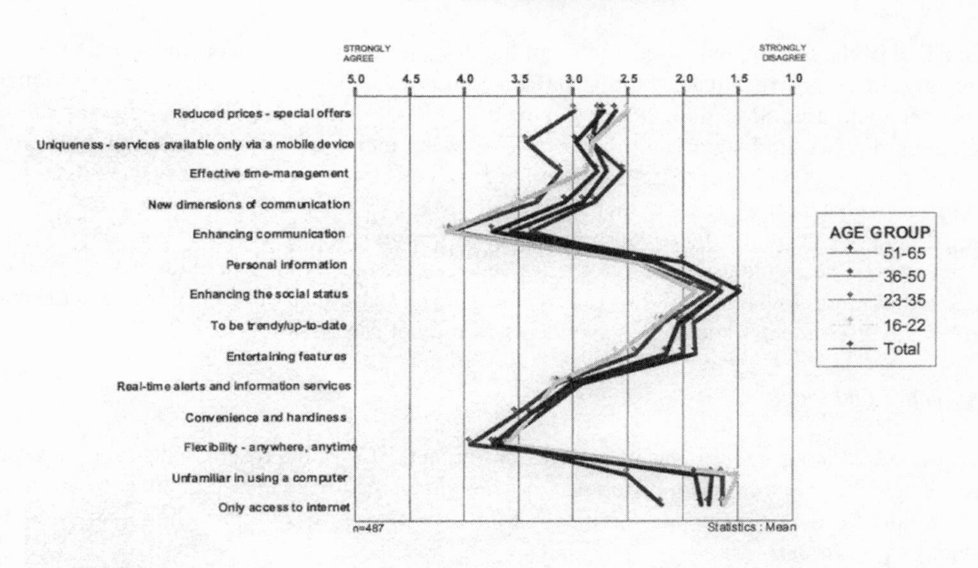

Table 11.1

Mobile Services: Distribution Between Users and Nonusers (%)

Users/non-users	Users	Non-users
SMS	375 / 90.1	41 / 9.9
Ring tones and icons	215 / 52.3	196 / 47.7
Entertainment, games	98 / 23.8	314 / 76.2
Routine m-banking	77 / 18.7	335 / 81.3
M-e-mail	49 / 11.8	365 / 88.2
Personalized information messaging	48 / 11.6	365 / 88.4
Ticket reservation	39 / 9.5	371 / 90.5
M-payment	31 / 7.5	381 / 92.5
Lottery	15 / 3.6	397 / 96.4

were not as concerned about privacy and security issues as are those in the older age categories.

We found some statistical differences in gender. High initial costs were a barrier for women in using mobile services (chi-square 12.4 Sig. 0.002). Slow data connections were a barrier for men (chi-square 9.5 Sig. 0.008). Male respondents considered the uselessness of mobile services a barrier (chi-square 6.18 Sig. 0.045).

Mobile Services in Use Now and in the Future

There are several mobile services available on the Finnish market. We specified twenty-five different mobile services in the questionnaire. We asked the consumers if they used these services currently and, if not, would they be interested in using them in the future. We will discuss some of the services that have a rather big share of users among the respondents and some that are often mentioned in connection with mobile services (Table 11.1).

Short Message Service (SMS)

Almost all of the respondents used SMS, but the distribution between male and female was significantly different (chi-Square 5.6 Sig. 0.018 (Asymp.Sig., 2-sided)). There were more female consumers who used SMS than there are male users. If we compare the results according to the age categories, we find significant differences between males and females ages 51 to 64 (chi-square 7.8 Sig. 0.005 (Asymp.Sig., 2-sided)). Female consumers in this category were the typical SMS users. In general we can say that the typical SMS user is a woman. Of those who were not using the service currently, there was only one male respondent in the age category 23 to 35 who did not know if he would use the service in the future; were older and most of them would not use SMS in the future. In the age group 51 to 64, there was a significant difference between the male and female respondents. The male respondents would not use SMS services in the future.

Ring Tones and Icons

Ring tones and icons are popular m-services in Finland. Half of the respondents used these services. There was no significant difference in general between male and female users, but in the age category 51 to 64, there was a significant difference: two-thirds of those who said they use the services were women.

Most of the respondents who did not use the service currently were within the age categories 36 to 50 and 51 to 64, and the majority definitely or probably would not use the services in the future. We did not find any significant differences between male and female responses to this question.

Mobile Entertainment Services: Games

We did not find a significant difference between male and female responses about use of mobile entertainment services and no differences between responses by age category.

The majority of those who did not use entertainment services would definitely or probably not use them in the future. There were no significant differences between gender or age categories.

Routine Mobile Banking

There were no significant differences overall in the responses of male and female users of routine banking services. There was a significant difference between male and female users in the age category 16 to 22: most of the users were female (chi-Square 5.76 Sig. 0.016 (Asymp.Sig., 2-sided)). The majority of the users said they would definitely or probably continue to use routine mobile banking.

Forty-nine percent of nonusers said they would definitely or probably use the service in the future, 20 percent did not know, and 31 percent said they would definitely or probably not use the service. There was no significant difference in opinions between male and female nonuser respondents in the different age categories.

M-E-Mail

There was a significant difference between male and female users of m-e-mail (chi-Square 6.4 Sig. 0.011 (Asymp.Sig., 2-sided)). Males used more m-e-mail than females did. There was a significant difference in the percentage of male and female users in the age category 23 to 35: most of the users were male (chi-Square 8.03 Sig. 0.005 (Asymp.Sig., 2-sided)).

Of those respondents who were not using m-e-mail, 42.8 percent of them said they would definitely or probably use it in the future, 26.6 percent ddi not know, and 30.6 percent said they would definitely or probably not use it in the future. No significant differences were found among gender or age categories.

Personalized Information Messaging

There was no significant difference overall between the male and female users of personalized information messaging. There was a significant difference between male and female users in the age category 23 to 35: most of the users were male (chi-Square 6.1 Sig. 0.013 (Asymp.Sig. 2-sided)).

Fifty-six percent of those who did not use personalized information messaging said they would not use it in the future, 20 percent said they would definitely or probably use it in the future, and 24 percent did not know if they would use it in the future. There was no significant difference in opinion among gender and age categories.

M-Ticketing Services

There was no significant difference in responses between male and female users of m-ticketing services for making reservations for movies, concerts, and so forth. Also, the age categories did not show any differences in usage.

Among those who were not using mobile ticketing services, 33.3 percent said they would definitely or probably not use them in the future, 20.9 percent said they did not know, and 45.8 percent said they would definitely or probably use them in the future. There were no significant differences among age categories or gender.

M-Payment

Very few of the respondents had used m-payment and no significant differences were to be found between male and female respondents. There was a difference in the age category 36 to 50: five men and one women used m-payment. Due to too few observations, no definite conclusions can be made.

Among those who were not using mobile payment services, there were differences in gender. In the age categories 16 to 22, 23 to 35, and 36 to 50, there were more women who said they would definitely or probably not use mobile payment services in the future. In the age category 51 to 64, there were more males that said they would definitely or probably not use mobile payment services. The differences were, however, not statistically significant. Those who would definitely or probably use the services in the future made up 48 percent of respondents, those who did not know made up 24 percent, and those who said they would definitely or probably not use the services made up 28 percent.

Lottery

Not very many of the respondents used the mobile lottery service, but there was a significant difference between male and female users (chi-Square 6.2 Sig. 0.012 (Asymp.Sig. 2-sided)). Most of the users of the lottery service were male.

Among those who were not using the lottery service, 46.5 percent said they would definitely or probably not use them in the future, 20.7 percent did not know, and 32.8 percent said they would definitely or probably use the services. There were differences among those who said they would not use the services in the future. The age category 51–64 differs from the rest: there were more males than females in this category, and the difference was significant. In the other three age categories, there were more females than males (chi-Square 10.6 Sig. 0.014 (Asymp.Sig. 2-sided)). In the age category 36 to 50, more women than men did not know about their future usage. In the other three age categories, more men than women did not know (chi-Square 7.8 Sig. 0.05 (Asymp.Sig. 2-sided)). We did not find any statistical differences in gender or age categories between those who said they would use the lottery service in the future.

Benefits: The "Get" Value Components

As shown in Table 11.2, the descriptive data analysis showed that three benefits of using mobile devices and services stood out as especially important for consumers in general: *enhanced communications features; flexibility with respect to the user's location and the time of the day;* and *convenience and handiness of small, wireless mobile devices.*

As noted, it has been commonly hypothesized that handheld devices will expand access to the Internet and increase the overall volume of e-commerce, as consumers are much more familiar with mobile devices than with PCs. However, the results of this study certainly did not support this view, as the associated benefits (the *mobile device being the only Internet connection,* and *lack of proficiency with computers*) were not seen as sources of attractiveness of m-commerce for

Table 11.2

Summary Statistics for Benefit Variables (N = 410–418)

Benefit	Mean	SD (%)	Agree[1] (%)	Disagree[2] (%)
Enhanced communication features	3.74	1.28	68.9	18.9
Flexibility (anywhere, anytime)	3.73	1.18	64.9	14.9
Convenience and handiness	3.40	1.29	55.4	25.7
New dimensions of communication	3.07	1.28	43.1	33.0
Reminder and information services in real time	3.01	1.31	41.4	36.4
Uniqueness: exclusively mobile services	2.98	1.31	41.9	36.1
More effective use of time	2.78	1.35	37.8	44.0
Lower prices/special offers	2.72	1.22	29.7	41.2
Personalized information and services	2.24	1.30	22.7	64.1
Entertaining features	2.15	1.21	17.7	65.5
Being trendy/ahead of my time	2.04	1.18	15.4	68.8
Lack of proficiency with computers	1.89	1.33	16.5	75.1
Only connection to the Internet	1.84	1.31	13.7	75.2
Accentuation of social status	1.65	1.00	8.4	81.3

[1]Percentage of consumers who responded *strongly agree* [5] and *agree* [4].
[2]Percentage of consumers who responded *strongly disagree* [1] and *disagree* [2].

the general public or for the subsamples constituting the "untapped" market (see Table 11.3).

Mean values for all of the benefits and barriers were calculated for all subsamples, and an analysis of variance, with subsequent *post hoc* tests, was employed to identify the main drivers and inhibitors of the adoption of mobile electronic channels. Comparing the stated importance of the benefits by the different consumer groups (Table 11.3), we can conclude that the two main drivers to early and intended adoption of the mobile Internet and m-commerce are clearly the *enhanced communication features* and *flexibility (anywhere, anytime)*. These benefits are, in contrast to nearly all of the proposed benefits, acknowledged even by the consumers who are Internet and m-commerce averse.

Interestingly, the consumer groups by far most convinced of the benefits offered by the mobile Internet and m-commerce were the intended adopters. These consumers reported the highest mean scores on most of the proposed benefits as well as on the aggregate benefit value. Based on basic statistical tests of differences between adopters and intended adopters, we did not find any benefits that would explain why intended adopters of mobile Internet and/or m-commerce have not already become adopters. An equally interesting and unexpected finding was that most of the proposed benefits were perceived as less important by the m-commerce adopters than by the mobile Internet adopters. This suggests that the key motivation for embracing transaction-based m-commerce does not lie in a greater appreciation of the benefits associated with commerce over wireless devices. Instead, the fact that some mobile Internet adopters have moved on to m-commerce is primarily explained by differences in perception of the barriers involved (see Table 11.5).

Barriers: The "Give" Value Components

As far as the "give" value components are concerned, nearly all of the proposed barriers were perceived as significant impediments to using mobile services today or in the future. Yet, the *cost-related* issues (*high operating costs, high initial costs*) stood out as the main barriers to using

Table 11.3

Perceived Importance of Benefits by Subsamples: Tests of Differences of Means

Benefit	Mobile internet adoption				M-Commerce adoption			
	Adopters	Intended	Averse	Significance	Adopters	Intended	Averse	Significance
Enhanced communication features	4.05	4.01	3.39	0.000[c]	3.47	4.11	3.49	0.000[c]
Flexibility (anywhere, anytime)	4.05	3.98	3.45	0.000[c]	3.94	4.12	3.43	0.000[c]
New dimensions of communication	3.50	3.49	2.54	0.000[b,c]	2.76	3.65	2.71	0.000[a,c]
More effective use of time	3.36	3.09	2.26	0.000[b,c]	2.53	3.36	2.41	0.000[a,c]
Convenience and handiness	3.27	3.76	3.10	0.000[c]	3.29	3.85	3.10	0.000[c]
Reminder/information services in real time	3.14	3.32	2.65	0.000[c]	3.18	3.42	2.74	0.000[c]
Uniqueness: exclusively mobile services	3.09	3.43	2.47	0.000[c]	2.71	3.48	2.67	0.000[c]
Lower prices/special offers	2.73	3.02	2.41	0.000[c]	2.53	3.12	2.46	0.000[c]
Entertaining features	2.00	2.47	1.82	0.000[c]	1.76	2.47	1.97	0.000[c]
Personalized information and services	1.91	2.46	1.98	0.001[c]	2.29	2.50	2.06	0.004[c]
Being trendy/ahead of my time	1.82	2.29	1.70	0.000[c]	1.47	2.34	1.87	0.000[a,c]
Only connection to the Internet	1.41	1.89	1.97	0.189	1.71	1.87	1.87	0.883
Accentuation of social status	1.41	1.74	1.48	0.027[c]	1.71	1.70	1.60	0.614
Lack of proficiency with computers	1.00	1.81	2.14	0.000[a,b]	1.65	1.82	1.94	0.516
Aggregate	2.62	2.91	2.39	0.000[c]	2.51	2.98	2.46	0.000[a,c]

[a]Significant differences ($p < .05$) between adopters and intended adopters (Sheffé).
[b]Significant differences ($p < .05$) between adopters and averse (Sheffé).
[c]Significant differences ($p < .05$) between intended adopters and averse (Sheffé).

Table 11.4

Summary Statistics for Barrier Variables (N = 395–413)

Barrier	Mean	SD	Agree[1] (%)	Disagree[2] (%)
High operating costs	3.95	1.13	73.7	13.4
High initial costs	3.81	1.22	69.5	18.6
Limited capacity of mobile devices	3.77	1.03	63.8	10.0
Slow connection and/or data transfer	3.68	1.06	54.2	10.4
Fear of privacy invasion	3.56	1.26	58.6	20.6
Security risks	3.55	1.24	57.9	22.6
Uselessness of services	3.50	1.11	52.9	18.9
Small screen size of mobile devices	3.50	1.25	59.7	25.2
Poor coverage of networks	3.37	1.10	48.4	20.9
Complexity involved in using mobile services	3.34	1.07	45.4	21.5
Complexity involved in operating mobile devices	3.01	1.21	37.1	36.4
Lack of new mobile devices on the markets	2.88	1.11	25.7	31.5

[1]Percentage of consumers who responded *strongly agree* [5] and *agree* [4].
[2]Percentage of consumers who responded *strongly disagree* [1] and *disagree* [2].

mobile services today or in the future. The limitations of the current technology (*limited capacity of devices, slow connection and/or data transfer*) were also seen as crucial, whereas the risks relating to *privacy and security* were not, interestingly, perceived to be equally critical as in the wired e-commerce environment (Anckar 2002a, Furnell and Karweni 1999).

When working out distinctions between different subsamples in terms of mobile Internet and m-commerce adoption, we found that the consumers' decisions and intents to take on mobile technologies appeared rational when observing their perceptions of the barriers. Overall, the adopters perceived the barriers to using mobile services as less significant than nonadopters, with the adopters of m-commerce even less concerned about the impediments than the mobile Internet adopters (when evaluating these results, it should be noted that we had significant results in only five cases). However, some important exceptions from this pattern can be found: First, three of the four barriers that were perceived as the most critical among the mobile Internet adopters (*slow connection/data transfer, limited capacity of mobile devices,* and *uselessness of services*) were not seen as equally important by the nonadopters, indicating that these particular barriers are real (in the sense related to actual use) rather than presumed. Second, the barrier *uselessness* of mobile services, which was rated as the most critical impediment by the m-commerce adopters, was not perceived to be equally crucial by the nonadopters.

Other important survey findings relating to the barriers were that *security risks* are not a major concern for Internet and m-commerce adopters, whereas nonadopters tend to be more sceptical in this respect; actual users of the mobile Internet and m-commerce are mainly troubled by the *limitations of networks and mobile devices;* and *high initial and operating costs* are the main inhibitors to m-commerce adoption.

CONCLUSIONS

Arguing that TAM constructs, such as perceived usefulness and perceived ease of use are multidimensional constructs that are too general to have significant explanatory power, we set out from

Table 11.5

Perceived Importance of Barriers by Subsamples: Tests of Differences of Means

	Mobile internet adoption				M-commerce adoption			
Barrier	Adopters	Intended	Averse	Significance	Adopters	Intended	Averse	Significance
Slow connection and/or data transfer	4.23	3.74	3.42	0.000[b,c]	3.76	3.83	3.58	0.080
Limited capacity of mobile devices	4.05	3.75	3.65	0.217	3.75	3.81	3.74	0.804
High operating costs	3.77	3.93	4.03	0.484	3.18	3.97	3.99	0.016[a,b]
Uselessness of services	3.68	3.40	3.56	0.292	3.76	3.34	3.59	0.054
The fear of privacy invasion	3.41	3.49	3.64	0.460	3.06	3.49	3.61	0.182
High initial costs	3.36	3.88	3.89	0.140	3.29	3.85	3.83	0.199
Security risks	3.14	3.58	3.61	0.237	3.06	3.47	3.64	0.109
Complexity of using mobile services	3.09	3.26	3.47	0.092	3.06	3.23	3.42	0.141
Poor coverage of networks	3.05	3.39	3.47	0.241	2.75	3.32	3.44	0.039
Lack of new mobile devices on the market	2.95	2.93	2.87	0.886	2.53	2.99	2.83	0.160
Small screen size of mobile devices	2.82	3.39	3.60	0.017[b]	3.41	3.46	3.54	0.804
Complexity of operating mobile devices	2.41	2.98	3.21	0.007[b]	2.29	2.87	3.14	0.005[b]
Aggregate	3.36	3.48	3.54	0.458	3.14	3.47	3.53	0.087

[a]Significant differences ($p < .05$) between adopters and intended adopters (Sheffé).
[b]Significant differences ($p < .05$) between adopters and averse (Sheffé).
[c]Significant differences ($p < .05$) between intended adopters and averse (Sheffé).
For meaning of symbols, see Table 11.3.

a perceived value-based view on adoption decisions with the objective to identify the key benefits and barriers—the core get and give value components—that drive or inhibit consumer adoption of m-commerce today and in the future.

As far as the first research question of this study is concerned, our study has shown that adoption/rejection decisions—and especially intents—relating to the mobile Internet and m-commerce appear to be determined to a greater extent by perceived benefits than by perceived barriers. More precisely, the main determinants of m-commerce adoption or rejection are not primarily related to a wide disagreement on the obstacles involved in using mobile services, but instead they originate from conflicting perceptions on a number of key benefits offered by mobility.[5] This finding contradicts the results of previous studies, which have shown that consumers' rejection decisions relating to PCs and e-commerce in a fixed environment are based on perceived critical barriers to a much higher extent than on a lack of appreciation of the associated benefits (Anckar 2002a, Venkatesh and Brown 2001).

It should, however, be noted that the recognition of the overall benefits was rather low in comparison to the perceived barriers in all consumer groups—even among the current users of the mobile Internet and m-commerce. The overall value of m-commerce is thus not seen as substantial, a fact that would suggest that the commercial prospects of m-commerce are not as bright as is often proclaimed. Likewise, the facts that the intended users paint a rosier picture of the promise of m-commerce, expecting to derive greater value from mobile technologies than the actual users report that they currently attain, and that almost 60 percent of the respondents reported that they have no intention to use mobile services in the future, certainly do not signal an imminent m-revolution. On the other hand, considering that m-commerce is a just-emerging phenomenon, the portion of the sample indicating an intention to use mobile services should by no means be seen as insignificant. Companies attempting to predict consumer interest in brand-new products or service concepts are often greeted with a disappointing show of interest from the end users (Yankee Group 2000), as their understanding of the associated benefits may be limited, and their assessment of the barriers involved may be exaggerated.

As far as the importance of the drivers/inhibitors are concerned, we found a clear divide between different consumer segments: *adopters* and *intended adopters* feel that the mobile Internet and m-commerce can offer a number of important benefits, especially with respect to *enhanced person-to-person communication* and *flexibility* (being able to use mobile services anywhere, anytime), whereas the *averse* consumers perceive nearly all of the proposed advantages as unimportant.

Mobile Internet adopters perceive greater barriers in terms of the *limitations of networks and mobile devices* than the nonadopters, indicating that these factors constitute significant barriers to mobile Internet usage today and thus likely also to an extensive use of mobile services in the future. For the current nonadopters, the *high initial and operating costs* were found to be the key factors that are influential in a nonadoption of mobile services.

"Mobility means freedom" was one of our starting points in this paper, and we noted that freedom creates choice and value, that is, freedom can contribute to the formation of our value system. Keen and Mackintosh (2001) described this as "freedom becomes value when it changes the limits of the possible in the structure of everyday life," which is also known as the *Braudel Rule*. The perceptions of benefits and barriers are formed by the value system, and as these perceptions drive the demand for m-commerce services, it is quite straightforward to propose that the value systems drive the demand for future mobile applications and that this demand will develop differently for different contexts, guided by different value systems. This is supported by our findings on both the actual demand and the reported perceptions of benefits and barriers. The three most-often-mentioned benefits are congruent with the three value propositions we identified for the mobile technology: *enhanced communication features* (mobility), *flexibility (anywhere, anytime)* (ubiquity), and *convenience and handiness* (availability), which shows at least some support for the Braudel Rule. The most used mobile service is SMS, which fulfills all three value propositions (mobility, availability, and ubiquity), and MMS follows the evolutionary path started by the SMS.

In this way we may yet be on the road to the Durlacher vision of a booming m-commerce market by 2005.

APPENDIX 11.1. THE SURVEY INSTRUMENT: QUESTION PHRASING

To you personally, major *benefits* of using mobile (wireless) services today or in the future are:

____My only connection to the Internet is through my mobile device (I do not own a computer, nor do I use one at work)
____I lack proficiency with computers, and therefore I prefer to use a mobile device over a computer
____Flexibility with respect to my location ("anywhere") and the time of the day ("anytime")
____The convenience and handiness of small, wireless mobile devices (in comparison to desktop computers)
____The possibility to get reminder and information services (for instance hot news) in real time, as the mobile device is always connected to the network, and always with me
____Entertaining features; mobile services are nice time killers/fillers
____Being trendy/ahead of my time
____Accentuation of my social status
____The possibility to get personalized information (e.g., personal horoscope) and personal service (e.g., health service reminders such as "remember to take your medicine")
____Enhanced communication features: Using short messages (text/audio/pictures/video) I can reach persons even when I cannot talk on the phone, or when the person I try to reach does not answer the phone
____The new dimensions of communication (picture/audio/video messages, streaming video; the possibility to have visual contact with the person you are talking to)
____The more effective use of time (I can, for instance, send e-mails, order groceries, check my bank account or pay bills while sitting in the dentist's waiting room)
____Uniqueness (the possibility to use services that are intended only for/available only through mobile devices—for instance pinpointing/routing services, making small payments such as parking fees, purchases at vending machines, etc.)
____Lower prices (some special offers are available only through mobile devices)

To you personally, major *impediments* to using mobile (wireless) services today or in the future are:

____High initial costs (costs of acquiring a mobile device)
____High operating costs (costs of subscriber connection and mobile services)
____Limited capacity/computing power of mobile devices in comparison to desktop computers
____Slow connection and/or data transfer (connecting to the service provider and/or downloading files takes too long)
____Complexity involved in operating mobile devices
____Complexity involved in using mobile services (time consuming, lack of graphical support, etc.)

____Small screen size of mobile devices
____Lack of new mobile devices on the markets
____Uselessness of services (purposeful and appealing mobile services are not available)
____Poor coverage of networks (faulting connections, or connection missing entirely in some areas)
____Security risks (concerns for the safety of personal information and/or the security of financial transactions)
____The fear of privacy invasion (for instance, as a result of numerous e-advertisements being sent to your mobile device)

NOTES

1. The abbreviations 2G (GSM), 2.5G (GPRS), 3G (UMTS), and so forth, refer to generations of network technology.

2. Broadly defined as the results or benefits customers receive in relation to total costs (McDougall and Levesque 2000), that is, a customer's overall assessment of the utility of a product (or service) based on perceptions of what is received and what is given (Zeithaml 1988).

3. In contrast, value is a relative concept that embodies an implicit assumption about a comparison between two or more alternatives.

4. Consumers in older age groups were excluded from the study, since previous surveys recently conducted in Finland (Anckar and D'Incau 2002) had indicated that consumers ages 65+ constitute an insignificant target group for most mobile services.

5. Enhanced communication features, flexibility, new dimensions of communication, and more effective use of time.

REFERENCES

Anckar, B. Rationales for consumer adoption or rejection of e-commerce: Exploring the impact of product characteristics. In *Proceedings of the SSGRR 2002s Conference.* L'Aquila, Italy (July 29–August 4), 2002a, p. 144 on CD.

———. Motivators for adoption of mobile commerce: Findings from a national consumer survey. In *Proceedings of the International Conference on Decision Making and Decision Support in the Internet Age (DSIage 2002).* Cork, Ireland (July 4–7), 2002b, 749–762.

Anckar, B., and D'Incau, D. Value creation in mobile commerce: Findings from a consumer survey. *Journal of Information Technology Theory and Application,* 4, 1 (2002), 43–64.

Booz Allen Hamilton. The wireless internet revolution. *Insights: The Communications, Media &Technology Group,* 6, 2 (2000), 1–8 (available at www.bah.de/content/downloads/6_1100_wi_rev.pdf.

Buellingen, F., and Woerter, M. Development perspectives, firm strategies and applications in mobile commerce. *Journal of Business Research,* 57, 12 (2002), 1402–1408.

Carlsson, C. The mobile process edge: An outline of a new research area. In *Proceedings of the International Conference on Decision Making and Decision Support in the Internet Age (DSIage 2002).* Cork, Ireland (July 4–7), 2002, pp. 775–784.

Carlsson, C., and Walden, P. The mobile commerce quest for value-added products and services. In *Proceedings of the SSGRRs 2001.* L'Aquila, Italy, 2001, p. 204 on CD.

———. Further quests for value-added products and services in mobile commerce. In *ECIS 2002 Proceedings.* Gdansk, Poland, 2002a, pp. 715–724.

———. Extended quests for value-added products and services in mobile commerce. In *DSIAge 2002 Proceedings.* Cork, Ireland, 2002b, pp. 763–774.

———. Mobile commerce: A summary of quests for value-added products and services. In *15th Bled International Conference on E-Commerce.* Bled, Slovenia, 2002c, 463–476.

———. Mobile commerce: Some extensions of core concepts and key issues. In *Proceedings of the SSGRR 2002s Conference.* L'Aquila, Italy (July 29–August 4), 2002d, p. 122 on CD.

Davis, F.D. perceived usefulness, perceived ease of use, and user acceptance of information technology. *MIS Quarterly,* 13, 3 (1989), 319–340.

Durlacher Research Institute. *UMTS Report.* Durlacher Research Report (March 2001) (available at www.durlacher.com).

Eggert, A., and Ulaga, W. Customer perceived value: A substitute for satisfaction in business markets? *Journal of Business and Industrial Marketing,* 17, 2 (2002), 107–118.

Eikebrokk, T.R., and Sørebø, Ø. Technology acceptance in situations with alternative technologies. In *Norsk konferanse for organisasjoners bruk av informasjonsteknologi.* Oslo, Norway (July 17–19), 1998, pp. 89–97.

Furnell, S.M., and Karweni, T. Security implications of electronic commerce: A survey of consumers and businesses. *Internet Research: Electronic Networking Applications and Policy,* 9, 5 (1999), 372–382.

Gillick, K., and Vanderhoof, R. Mobile e-commerce: Marketplace enablers and inhibitors. Paper presented at the *Smart Card Forum Annual Meeting* (September 25–28), 2000 (available at www.datacard.com/downloads/pdf/white_paper_ecommerce.pdf). Accessed July 2005.

Green, R. The internet unplugged. *eAI Journal* (October 2000), 82–86.

Guerley, W. Making sense of the wireless web. *Fortune* (August 15, 2000) (available at www.fortune.com).

Hampe, J.F.; Swatman P.M.C.; and Swatman, P.A. Mobile electronic commerce: Reintermediation in the payment system. In *Proceedings of the 13th Bled International Electronic Commerce Conference.* Bled, Slovenia (June 19–21), 2000, pp. 693–706.

Han, J., and Han, D. A framework for analyzing customer value of Internet business. *Journal of Information Technology Theory and Application,* 3, 5 (2001), 25–38.

Herman, J., and Neff, T. Managing through the m-commerce storm. *World Market Series Business Briefings: Wireless Technology 2002.* World Markets Research Centre, 2002, pp. 78–82.

Kalakota, R., and Robinson, M. *M-Business: The Race to Mobility.* New York: McGraw-Hill, 2001.

Keen, P., and Mackintosh, R. *The Freedom Economy: Gaining the M-commerce Edge in the Era of the Wireless Internet.* Berkeley, CA: Osborne/McGraw-Hill, 2001.

Langendoerfer, P. M-commerce: Why it does not fly (yet?). In *Proceedings of the SSGRRs 2002 Conference.* L'Aquila, Italy (July 29–August 4), 2002, p. 117 on CD.

Lee, D.; Park, J.; and Ahn, J. On the explanation of factors affecting e-commerce adoption. In *Proceedings of the 22nd International Conference on Information Systems.* New Orleans, Louisiana (December 16–19), 2001, pp. 109–120.

Lee, W.J.; Kim, T.U.; and Chung, J-Y. User acceptance of the mobile Internet. In *Proceedings of the First International Conference on Mobile Business.* Athens, Greece (July 8–9), 2002.

Li, V.K. Global m-commerce—business opportunities for wireless data services. *World Market Series Business Briefings: Wireless Technology 2002.* World Markets Research Centre, 2002, pp. 123–126.

Luckett, M.; Ganesh, J.; and Gillett, P. Quantitative tools in tourism research: An application of perceptual maps. In A. Pizam and Y. Mansfeld (eds.), *Consumer Behavior in Travel and Tourism.* Binghamton, NY: The Haworth Hospitality Press, 1999, pp. 307–333.

Malhotra, Y., and Galletta, D.F. Extending the technology acceptance model to account for social influence: Theoretical bases and empirical validation. In *Proceedings of the 32nd Hawaii International Conference on System Sciences.* Maui, Hawaii (January 5–8, 1999). Los Alamitos, CA: IEEE Computer Society Press, 1999.

Mathieson, K.; Peacock, E.; Chin, W.W. Extending the technology acceptance model: The influence of perceived user resources. *The Data Base for Advances in Information Systems,* 32, 3 (Summer 2001), 86–112.

May, P. *Mobile Commerce: Opportunities, Applications, and Technologies of Wireless Business.* Cambridge: Cambridge University Press, 2001.

McDougall, G.H.G., and Levesque, T. Customer satisfaction with services: Putting perceived value into the equation. *Journal of Services Marketing,* 14, 5 (2000), 392–419.

MobileInfo. *Europeans Willing to Pay Extra for 3G Services.* News Issue #2003–06 (February 2003) (available at www.mobileinfo.com).

Müller-Versee, F. *Mobile Commerce Report.* London: Durlacher Research Ltd., 1999.

Nokia 3G Market Research Centre. M-commerce: An end user perspective. Key learnings from global research. *Nokia 3G Market Research Report, Nokia Networks* (May 25, 2001) (available at www.nokia.com/3G). Accessed July 2005.

O'Cass, A., and Fenech, T.O. Web retailing adoption: Exploring the nature of Internet users web retailing behaviour. *Journal of Retailing and Consumer Services,* 10, 2 (2003), 81–94.

Paavilainen J. *Mobile Business Strategies.* Reading, MA: Wireless Press, Addison-Wesley, 2002.

Parasuraman, A. Reflections on gaining competitive advantage through customer value. *Journal of the Academy of Marketing Science,* 25, 2 (1997), 154–161.

Pavlou, P.A. What drives electronic commerce? A theory of planned behavior perspective. In *Proceedings of the Academy of Management Conference.* Denver, Colorado (August 9–14), 2002.

———. Consumer acceptance of electronic commerce—Integrating trust and risk with the technology acceptance model. *International Journal of Electronic Commerce,* 7, 3 (2003), 101–134.

Pedersen, P.E.; Methlie, L.B.; and Thorbjørnsen, H. Understanding mobile commerce end-user adoption: A triangulation perspective and suggestions for an exploratory service evaluation framework. In *Proceedings of the 35th Hawaii International Conference on System Sciences*, Hawaii (January 7–10, 2002). Los Alamitos, CA: IEEE Computer Society Press, 2002.

Ropers, S. New business models for the mobile revolution. *eAI Journal* (February 2001), 53–57.

Senn, J.A. The emergence of m-commerce. *Computer,* 33, 12 (December 2000), 148–150.

Shuster, T. Pocket Internet and m-commerce—(how) will it fly? (February 1, 2001) (available at www.gwu.edu/~emkt/Ecommerce/file/Mcommerce.pdf). Accessed November 2003.

Strong, C., and Old, J. How can mobile developments deliver customer end-value? *White Paper on Mobile Internet Applications.* London: NOP Research Group (November 2000). Accessed November 2003.

Sweeney, J.C., and Soutar, G.N. Consumer perceived value: The development of a multiple item scale. *Journal of Retailing,* 77 (2001), 203–220.

Teo, T.S.H.; Lim, V.K.G.; Lai. R.Y.C. Intrinsic and extrinsic motivation in Internet usage. *Omega—The International Journal of Management Science,* 27 (1999), 25–37.

Urbaczewski, A.; Wells, J.; Sarker, S.; and Koivisto, M. Exploring cultural differences as a means for understanding the global mobile Internet: A theoretical basis and program of research. In *Proceedings of the 35th Hawaii International Conference on System Sciences*, Hawaii (January 7–10, 2002). Los Alamitos, CA: IEEE Computer Society Press, 2002.

Varshney, U., and Vetter, R. A framework for the emerging mobile commerce applications. In *Proceedings of the 34th Annual Hawaii International Conference on System Sciences (HICSS-34)* (January 3–6, 2001) Maui, Hawaii. Los Alamitos, CA: IEEE Computer Society, 2001.

Varshney, U.; Vetter, R.J.; and Kalakota, R. Mobile commerce: A new frontier. *Computer,* 33, 10 (October 2000), 32–38.

Venkatesh, V., and Brown, S.A. A longitudinal investigation of personal computers in homes: Adoption determinants and emerging challenges. *MIS Quarterly,* 25, 1 (2001), 71–102.

Vittet-Philippe, P., and Navarro, J.M. Mobile e-business (m-commerce): State of play and implications for European enterprise policy. *European Commission Enterprise Directorate—General E-Business Report,* No. 3 (December 6, 2000) (available at www.ncits.org/tc_home/v3htm/v301008.pdf).

Vrechopoulos, A.P.; Constantiou, I.D.; Mylonopoulos, N.; and Sideris, I. Critical success factors for accelerating mobile commerce diffusion in Europe. In *Proceedings of the 15th Bled Electronic Commerce Conference.* Bled, Slovenia (June 17–19), 2002, pp. 477–492.

Yankee Group. Understanding the needs of European mobile phone users: Consumer survey results. *Wireless/Mobile Europe Report,* 4, 18 (November 2000). Boston: The Yankee Group.

Zeithaml, V.A. Consumer perceptions of price, quality and value: A means-end model and synthesis of evidence. *Journal of Marketing,* 52 (July 1988), 2–22.

CHAPTER 12

EXPLAINING THE SUCCESS OF NTT DOCOMO'S I-MODE

THE CONCEPT OF VALUE SCOPE MANAGEMENT

DETLEF SCHODER, NILS MADEJA, AND CHRISTIAN VOLLMANN

Abstract: *Mobile business, that is, conducting business activities as well as delivering content and services over the wireless Internet, is regarded as one of the key emerging areas in electronic business. Whereas adoption and usage of mobile business in several markets has remained far behind initial expectations, the case of NTT DoCoMo's i-mode in Japan is a famous example for success in mobile business, with many players at different steps in the mobile value chain thriving at the same time. In our analysis, we assume a perspective different from the existing approaches for explaining i-mode's success. Analyzing the economics of the i-mode system, we argue that NTT DoCoMo has been able to install its business model and secure its own position by employing a novel strategic management concept, which we term "value scope management."*

Keywords: *i-Mode, Information Management, Mobile Business, NTT DoCoMo, Standards, Value Scope Management*

INTRODUCTION

NTT DoCoMo's i-mode service is seen as one of the most successful examples of mobile business. Various attempts to explain i-mode's success have been undertaken, stressing the cultural peculiarities of Japanese society; technological contingencies in Japan; and economic factors, including the business model behind i-mode or market-related and consumer-group-specific aspects. In this paper, we challenge the existing attempts to explain i-mode's success. Although we admit that they provide good motivation for the success of a comprehensive mobile Internet service in general, we argue that they mostly fail to explain why i-mode in particular has become so successful. We contend that this is because they do not take into account NTT DoCoMo's unique and inimitable resources and its strategic moves to acquire them, which we regard as central and critical factors for explaining NTT DoCoMo's specific success.

We propose an analytical framework composed of the entire value chain for delivering the i-mode service, covering value-creating activities, players, and the underlying technologies and standards. We show that NTT DoCoMo employed a novel strategic management approach, which we term "value scope management," in order to gain significant control over this value chain and its players. Value scope management consists of advanced practices of information management directed toward suppliers and customers that employ such measures as branding, standards management, and management of information spheres. Specifically, we discuss how, in several

Figure 12.1 **Components of the I-Mode Value Network**

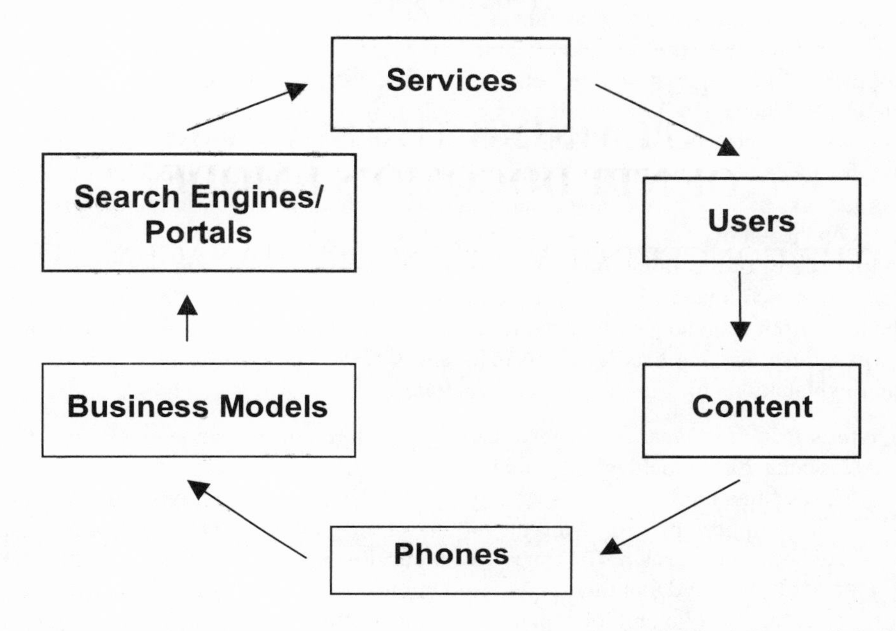

instances, through successful value scope management, NTT DoCoMo has managed to impropriate external resources and standards that were originally open and turn them into proprietary, inimitable, and, thus, unique resources and standards. We argue that these unique resources and standards are the key to explaining the astonishing success of i-mode.

The remainder of this paper is organized as follows. The second section describes parts of the business model of i-mode and sketches various attempts to explain i-mode's success, indicating that a more comprehensive approach should also recognize value scope management as one of the major success factors. For a better understanding of value scope management in mobile business, the necessary technical background on mobile communication systems and interfaces is briefly introduced in the third section, together with the proposed analytical framework. We will also link the proposed analysis to existing economic and management theory. Based on the i-mode case, the subsequent discussion will analyze the mobile business value chain and, more specifically, describe to what extent the single steps of value creation are dominated by NTT DoCoMo. The final section briefly summarizes the major findings and conclusions of the paper.

NTT DOCOMO'S I-MODE

NTT DoCoMo's service platform for mobile data communications, i-mode, enables NTT DoCoMo's subscribers to access mobile Internet content and services through specially equipped handsets. I-mode was launched in February 1999 and has become very popular in Japan: by April 2002, it had attracted more than 32 million subscribers (TCA 2002). I-mode is now seen as one of the most successful examples of mobile business, not only in terms of market penetration, but also in terms of financial returns. While the provision of information via mobile devices is at the core of the i-mode business model, the latter became viable only through the integration of users, content, handsets, portals, search engines, and additional services (as depicted in Figure 12.1).

The components of the model are closely interrelated. The size of the installed user base influences the amount and richness of available content, and vice versa. The size and growth rate of the user base determines the demand for, and thereby, indirectly, the supply of new handsets. The development of new, attractive handsets reinforces the demand for the service, since users are attracted by the latest and best mobile phones. An increase in the value of one component of the model spills over into other areas. Funk (2001) shows that NTT DoCoMo managed to ignite early positive feedback between the individual components of the business model, and, as the major success factors, he lists convenience and usability of the service, an attractive pricing model, emphasis on "reach over richness" (i.e., the fact that NTT DoCoMo designed the i-mode service with a low degree of media richness in order to keep handsets and use of the service simple and inexpensive so as to reach a broad customer base (Evans and Wurster, 1997)), initial focus on a young target group, and an attractive content lineup from the start. For more information on NTT DoCoMo and i-mode, see Bradley and Sandoval (2002).

Other explanations for i-mode's success include:

- Cultural factors in Japanese society, leading to different usage behavior (Baldi and Thaung 2002, Scuka 2000, Stiehler and Wichmann 2000). These include:
  - The fact that the Japanese, especially, spend a long time commuting on trains, providing an ideal opportunity for using the mobile service, although NTT DoCoMo's usage figures show that "peak traffic times for i-mode do not seem to correspond with peak traffic on the trains" and that there is a considerable contribution from "data traffic of customers in the Tohoku area of Japan, where most of the inhabitants tend to drive to work" (Macdonald 2002, 130)
  - A different attitude of Japanese users toward the mobile phone and services delivered via the mobile phone
- Technological contingencies in Japan: the low penetration of fixed Internet access when i-mode was introduced
- The business model involving multiple types of alliances leading to "win-win-relationships" between NTT DoCoMo and its partners (Natsuno 2002, 69–100). These alliances include:
  - Technology alliances with hardware and software manufacturers for the development of mobile handsets
  - Portal alliances with content and service providers for filling the i-mode portal with attractive contents and services
  - Platform alliances with companies from different industries, such as convenience stores, video rentals, arcade manufacturers, and so forth, in order to increase the usability of i-mode phones in users' daily lives

On its Web site,[1] NTT DoCoMo explains its own role within its business model as "coordinating [or: synchronizing] all stages of the mobile services value chain" for the purpose of "maximizing value for everyone," citing these activities as the main reason for the success of its i-mode service.

Although we do not deny the contribution of the above factors to i-mode's success, it is clear that they do not sufficiently explain why NTT DoCoMo's i-mode service, and not a competitor's service, became so successful. NTT DoCoMo's competitors faced the same market environment and could have implemented a quite similar business model, if it were for the above factors alone. The reasons why only i-mode succeeded and how NTT DoCoMo set itself apart from its competitors become clear when, in the following sections, we take a closer look at its effective value scope management and at the resources that NTT DoCoMo alone managed to accumulate as a result.

VALUE SCOPE MANAGEMENT

Definition and Theoretical Background

Value scope management not only takes advantage of the well-known economies of scope, but also consists of elements and instruments from well-established economic theory, especially industrial organization, management literature known under the terms of monopolization of the value chain, vertical integration, raising rivals' costs (Salop and Scheffman 1983), vertical foreclosure (Church and Ware 2000, 633), and the resource-based view of sustained competitive advantage (Barney 1991, 1996).

One of the strategic instruments applied for value scope management is *raising rivals' costs*. It represents a strategy for driving competitors out of the market, without starting a price war, through exclusionary practices. For example, by lobbying government bodies, companies can influence the regulation of (product) standards and thereby raise rivals' compliance costs. We will show below how NTT DoCoMo employed this strategy during the standardization process of the Japanese 2G mobile telephony protocol PDC (Personal Digital Cellular).

An extreme case of raising rivals' costs is known as *upstream vertical foreclosure*, which describes how, by vertically integrating a supplier, a firm can exclude rivals from products and services provided by that supplier. If these are of strategic importance, as was the case with the mobile phones produced by four big Japanese handset manufacturers, this strategy will put rivals at a distinct competitive disadvantage. Although NTT DoCoMo did not vertically integrate the four major suppliers of mobile phones, it found other ways of blocking rivals from the supply of that much-needed input for mobile telephony.

From the perspective of the resource-based approach, companies' internal resources are the sources of sustainable rents. In order to create sustainable rents, a firm strives to obtain sustained competitive advantages over its competitors (Bamberger and Wrona 1996). Those sustained competitive advantages result from valuable, rare, imperfectly imitable resources that have no substitutes (Barney 1991). Below we provide an analytical framework, and the subsequent sections will reveal sources of sustained competitive advantages that NTT DoCoMo has gained from imperfectly imitable and unique resources.

Analytical Framework

All mobile business value chains are based on technical standards. A need for technological standards exists where complementary systems have to communicate with one another. In order to facilitate communication across system boundaries, standardized interfaces have to be defined. Our proposed framework highlights those systems and interfaces underlying the main value-creating activities in mobile business (Durlacher 2000, 15, Sadeh 2002, 34). Thereby, we focus on systems and interfaces that are at the forefront in the battle between open and proprietary standards (Shapiro and Varian 1999, 261–296).

In the case of mobile telephony, at least five interdependent systems exist (Figure 12.2):

1. Content (source of information)
2. Network
3. Handset
4. Browser/Applications
5. End User (information sink)

Figure 12.2 **Systems and Interfaces in the Mobile Business Value Chain**

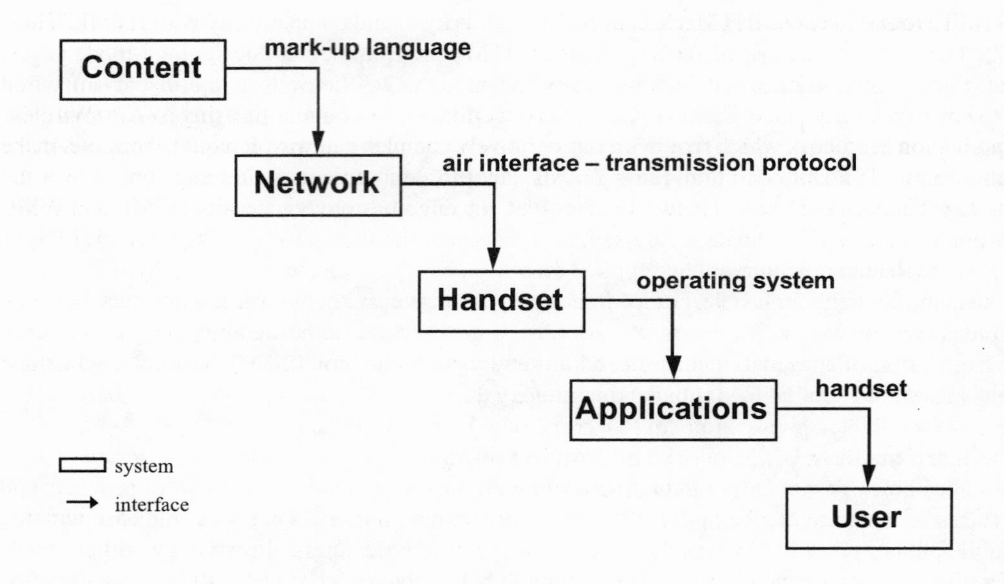

On its way through the network, data passes four interfaces:

1. Between content source and network (mark-up language)
2. Between network and handset (air interface, transmission protocol)
3. Between handset and application (operating system)
4. Between application and end user (handset)

In this model, the handset fulfills a double role. It is seen as an independent system, in communicating with the network, and as an interface in the link between user and application.

In the following paragraphs, the relevant technological standards for each of the four interfaces in the i-mode world are identified, and their degree of openness is determined. We will discuss how standards and resources, which were originally open, took on a proprietary character in the i-mode example.

In addition, we will explain how, through the establishment of information spheres, NTT DoCoMo has maintained a high degree of control over the content offered on the i-mode service, while encouraging organic network growth at the same time. We will therefore show how NTT DoCoMo has achieved control not only over the technical infrastructure, but also over the i-mode service itself, running on top of that technical infrastructure.

The Interface Between Content and the Network

Content for mobile devices has to be encoded in a predefined way so as to be well presented on displays, usually with limited resolution and size. For this purpose, NTT DoCoMo uses the iHTML mark-up language, which is based on compact HTML (cHTML). cHTML is an official World Wide Web Consortium (W3C) recommendation for use in mobile communications (W3C, 1998).

iHTML differs only marginally from cHTML. NTT DoCoMo used the term for branding reasons and the specification was available for free on its Web site.

NTT DoCoMo chose iHTML because of its similarity to and compatibility with HTML. Thus, NTT DoCoMo could draw on the large base of HTML programmers for designing i-mode pages, and, the conversion of wired Internet pages to i-mode pages (as well as the display of wired Internet pages on i-mode phones) was greatly facilitated, in contrast to using WAP (Wireless Application Protocol), which requires a comparatively complex gateway. It would, therefore, make no sense for NTT DoCoMo to develop iHTML any further in order to gain more control over the interface between content and network. Moreover, the ongoing convergence of cHTML and WML toward a single XHTML dialect, for example, will render the strategic choice between cHTML or WML obsolete in the future.

In summary, although NTT DoCoMo has only little actual control over the interface between content and network, with only very minor technical changes and mainly through intelligent branding, it has managed to impropriate an originally open standard. IHTML has become a unique resource of NTT DoCoMo's i-mode service.

The Interface Between Network and Handset

A different situation can be observed in the case of the Japanese 2G network protocol personal digital cellular (PDC). In 1990, the R&D department at NTT DoCoMo started working on the protocol specifications. In order to build a digital network based on PDC, the PDC protocol had to be ratified by the Japanese Association for Radio Industry Businesses (ARIB). The Japanese government authority for telecommunications insisted on the publication of the protocol in exchange for ratification. NTT DoCoMo accepted this requirement and published the specifications for PDC. Based on these openly available specifications, other mobile carriers also started to build their own 2G networks.[3]

However, Funk (2002a) argues that PDC is not as open a standard as one might suppose, listing the following arguments:

- The close ties between the mainly state-owned NTT and the Japanese Ministry of Posts and Telecommunications[4] enabled NTT's subsidiary company NTT DoCoMo to heavily influence the ratification of PDC. As a result, the protocol never went through the regular procedure for establishing a standard and ARIB basically ratified it without demanding any changes.
- NTT DoCoMo published the protocol specifications only after substantial delay. At the time of publication, NTT DoCoMo had already implemented the protocol in most of its own network and secured itself a head start over other carriers. In addition, NTT DoCoMo had already developed the protocol beyond the published specifications without sharing these enhancements with other carriers, thus securing for itself important technological advantages.
- The documentation of the protocol was weak compared to other standards (for example, GSM) and did not fulfill the requirements of typical standard-setting procedures. Parts of the air interface specifications were missing completely, while others were insufficiently detailed.

NTT DoCoMo used their advanced knowledge of the PDC standard to develop superior handsets in cooperation with four closely associated manufacturers: Matsushita, Mitsubishi, NEC, and Fujitsu. These four suppliers received preferential information about the PDC standard from NTT DoCoMo. NTT DoCoMo and its phone suppliers did not release any details of updates of the standard until they had been officially accepted by ARIB. As a result, these four manufacturers supplied almost 100 percent of the phones for use in NTT DoCoMo's networks (Funk 2002a, 85–186). In return for the exchange of preferential information about PDC, the four manufacturers agreed to sell their latest handsets to other carriers only after a six-month delay. It must be noted that the four manufacturers included in this cooperation are the major players in the Japanese market for telecom and consumer electronics devices. Since there are, if any, only a few other players left who have the necessary technological competence, production environment, and market power to supply several million units of cellular telephones a year (for example, SONY), it would be very difficult for competing network operators to make handsets available that are equal to the current generation of i-mode handsets. Consequently, competing network operators would also have a hard time trying to offer mobile Internet services equal to the last generation of i-mode services. In this context, it is also important to note that the current product life cycle for mobile phones in Japan has shrunk to just about six months.

In summary, we can conclude that NTT DoCoMo, by leveraging its initial control over the PDC standard, has ensured that its i-mode service maintains a head start of one product generation of handsets and, possibly, one generation of services, compared to competing network operators. These network operators have, therefore, been put at a distinct competitive disadvantage since the i-mode service was introduced. NTT DoCoMo's competitive position has not been weakened, although its degree of control over the PDC standard has been steadily declining as the knowledge of PDC continues to diffuse throughout the market (Funk 2002a, 191) and as PDC, de facto, becomes an open standard. Since NTT DoCoMo has managed to shift its power from initially controlling the transmission standard to largely controlling the degree of advancement of mobile phones in the Japanese market, the actual standard of the transmission network is no longer a critical issue.

In addition, during the definition phase of the W-CDMA standard employed in third-generation mobile telecommunication systems and, especially, in NTT DoCoMo's Freedom of Multimedia Access (FOMA) network, NTT DoCoMo has followed a pattern similar to that used during the definition phase of the PDC standard. First, it was heavily involved in the standardization process with the International Telecommunications Union (ITU) and made contributions on the basis of its in-house research. During that time, NTT DoCoMo acquired practical competence and developed technology needed for implementing mobile networks according to its W-CDMA standard proposal, for which it obtained protection through a list of several patents. Then, after the W-CDMA had become a part of the specification of the comprehensive IMT-2000 air interface, NTT DoCoMo began licensing its patented technology to other network operators and system vendors.[5] Therefore, although the W-CDMA specification is well documented and fully open, NTT DoCoMo has again managed to secure itself a competitive advantage (this time even on the international level) by leveraging its early R&D activities to influence the standardization process.

Interface Between Handset and Applications

The interface between handset and applications is managed by the operating system. Most i-mode-capable handsets run on proprietary operating systems developed by the manufacturers. One can argue that with mobile phones, the operating system is not as important as with PDAs, since the end user does not take much notice of it. Mobile phones rarely run more applications than a pre-installed browser. Java applications, which end users download to their phones, constitute one exception. However, in theory, these applications run completely independently of the underlying respective operating system on all Java-enabled phones. Nevertheless, in reality, different Java platforms hinder the interchangeability of Java applications between phones of different manufacturers. The specific Java platform used in the phone is, therefore, important. By employing the same Java platform on different phones, network effects become feasible, as applications can be interchanged between users. NTT DoCoMo uses Java 2.0 Micro Edition for its "i-appli" Java phones. Java is developed by SUN Microsystems and managed as an open software platform. Therefore, NTT DoCoMo's ability to influence this interface between handset and applications should be very limited. Nevertheless, NTT DoCoMo used its head start of six months, as discussed above, to establish a brand name ("i-appli") for its Java platform and application service as a sub-brand of i-mode. Therefore, even though a Java-enabled generation of devices has became available in the market, offering essentially the same functionality for competitors' networks, the already established sub-brand "i-appli" remains a feature that differentiates the i-mode service from other services, constituting another unique resource. Thus, as in the interface between content and network, NTT DoCoMo has seized control of the interface between handset and applications by appropriating an originally open standard.

Interface Between Applications and User

This interface determines the way in which users communicate with the application software on the phone, mainly using the browser for accessing information services. Methods for displaying data output, sound reproduction, input, and keyboard and voice control are defined through handset specifications. Due to its intensive R&D efforts and high degree of vertical integration, NTT DoCoMo develops many specifications for its i-mode phones itself and dictates them to manufacturers. Examples include display sizes, keyboard layouts, and i-mode's four-button operation. One of the four navigation buttons of every i-mode handset is the so-called "i-menu" button, featuring the i-mode logo.

On the one hand, this practice can be interpreted as "locking" the manufacturers into cooperation with NTT DoCoMo, since the manufacturers save their own R&D efforts when producing for NTT DoCoMo. They would have considerable switching costs if they decided to produce primarily for other network operators. On the other hand, NTT DoCoMo manages to establish and conserve a specific "look-and-feel" for its i-mode service through this practice, thereby generating a customer lock-in. In summary, NTT DoCoMo has managed to achieve control over the interface between applications and user and appropriate a resource that was equally open to its competitors in the beginning (namely, cellular phones made by Japan's largest manufacturers and their production capacity).

As far as the browser is concerned, NTT DoCoMo's influence is much more limited. Efforts to develop their own browsers have led most manufacturers to conclude that it is more complicated than anticipated and therefore not worth allocating the resources. As a result, the vast majority of manufacturers today use the microbrowser Compact NetFront developed by Access, giving it a monopoly-like market position (Ando et al. 2001, 3) and leaving NTT DoCoMo little choice about the browser. However, this situation doesn't put NTT DoCoMo at a competitive disadvantage, because its competitors equally depend on the Compact NetFront browser. Nor does it result in a lack of control over the interface between applications and the user, because the microbrowser remains transparent, and, thus, unnoticed by the mobile user, in contrast to browsers for the wired Internet.

Information Spheres and Control of Information Access

Finally, a central aspect of NTT DoCoMo's value scope management is the architecture of information spheres it has established for the i-mode service and the control it exercises over some of the featured contents and applications. The i-mode realm can be depicted as consisting of a closed inner information sphere, which is fully contained in an open outer information sphere. The inner information sphere is made up of the i-mode portal, which is directly accessible via the "i-menu" in subscribers' handsets. As discussed below, NTT DoCoMo maintains strict control over the contents and applications inside the i-mode portal, termed "official i-mode sites," and keeps it strictly closed. First, it is accessible only for i-mode subscribers, and not for subscribers to competing services. Second, there are no links between the inner and the outer information spheres. The outer information sphere consists of "unofficial i-mode sites," that is, all other sites complying with the iHTML standard, or even conventional Internet sites, which anyone is free to program. The outer information sphere is completely unregulated, and the sites can be accessed from any i-mode phone as long as they meet certain technical requirements, given mainly by device limitations of the handsets (for example, memory footprint, graphics format and size, and so forth), with which the "official i-mode sites" must also comply. This approach of a closed inner information sphere, which is fully contained in an open outer information sphere, has been described as a "semi-walled garden approach" (Funk 2001, 122) or as "open-out but closed-in" (Funk 2002b, 10). Clark (2000) compares NTT DoCoMo's domain in the wireless world to that of AOL in the fixed-line Internet.

The coexistence of these two information spheres, the fully controlled inner sphere, and the wholly unregulated outer one, fulfills two directly opposed purposes for NTT DoCoMo at the same time. The inner sphere, on the one hand, provides a safe and reliable basis for commercial content and services, thus resulting in a continuous revenue stream from providing the portal infrastructure. The openness of the outer sphere, on the other hand, encourages organic network growth. As the i-mode service is a network good, its attractiveness grows if more and more content and applications become available within its information realm. Yet the fact that an information sphere is unregulated and easy-to-access is a key motivator for individuals and organizations to launch content and applications in that sphere. Growth of the i-mode network, finally, will result in additional traffic.

NTT DoCoMo exercises its control over the i-menu portal mainly through the selection of content and content providers for the i-menu. NTT DoCoMo has developed a series of criteria that have to be met by content providers if they are to be considered for inclusion.[6] They include, *inter alia*, ethical guidelines prohibiting gambling and pornographic content. Advertisement on official i-menu sites can be sold only through D2C, a company in which NTT DoCoMo holds a 51 percent share. Official content providers are obliged to offer twenty-four-hour telephone support (Funk, 2001, 44). The harshest restriction is the ban on links from official to unofficial sites (Funk, 2001, 79, 122). In addition, NTT DoCoMo not only controls *what* can be offered within the i-menu, but also *who* can offer it. Only companies with the legal status of a Kabushiki Kaisha (K.K.), that is, corporations, are considered. Furthermore, NTT DoCoMo reserves the right to reject any application for inclusion based on its own business judgment, even if it fulfills all of the criteria. This gives NTT DoCoMo full control over who can become an official content provider.

Funk (2001, 123) points out that a thorough selection of high-quality content is very important for the functionality of the i-menu. Indeed, a prior selection of content is of great benefit to users of the mobile Internet, who, in comparison to fixed Internet users, pay (more) for content, have less time to assimilate it, and smaller displays on which to view it. Consequently, NTT DoCoMo's intensive content selection and aggregation generate additional value for users and are part of the success of the official i-menu.

Despite all the restrictions and arbitrariness in the selection process, there are several critical benefits from being listed in the "i-menu," making it very attractive to become an official content provider. The first is increased visibility to i-mode users and increased traffic from them. Second, official content providers benefit from NTT DoCoMo's positive brand image, which helps them gain a positive reputation and consumer trust. Third, and most importantly, official content and service providers are integrated into NTT DoCoMo's billing infrastructure. Via the subscribers' monthly cellular phone bills, NTT DoCoMo collects the revenues for the official content and service providers and keeps a share of 9 percent as a fee. Thereby, the official content and service providers do not need to operate their own billing infrastructure. In addition, the ease of use of their services for the subscribers to i-mode increases greatly, because it is very convenient for them to be billed via their monthly cellular phone bill and not to have a separate billing relationship.

Because of these clear advantages of becoming an official content provider, NTT DoCoMo has been overwhelmed with applications. In 2000, there was already a processing time of twelve months for new applications (Funk 2001, 28). These long waiting times and strict criteria for content selection have led to an explosive growth in unofficial content. In early 2002, the ratio of unofficial to official sites was eighteen to one. At the same time, unofficial sites contributed more to total i-mode traffic than official sites. There have also been improved conditions for providers of unofficial content. Portals outside the i-menu organize content offerings through their own selection processes and have thereby managed to build reputations. In addition, alternative payment solutions for unofficial content emerged, including credit cards, prepaid cards, bank account deductions, and monthly telephone bills (Funk 2001, 85–92).

When mobile Internet services first started in Japan, the information spheres that users of specific carriers could access with their mobile phones were clearly separated. NTT DoCoMo's i-mode was encoded in cHTML, KDDI's EZWeb in WML, and J-Phone's J-Sky in MML. These mark-up languages are not compatible without the use of gateways. As a result, users of a specific service were unable to access the contents of alternative services (Funk, 2002b, p. 10). Due to the growing lead of i-mode in terms of content, J-Phone and KDDI soon strove to develop gateways that would allow customers access to i-mode-based content. By so doing, they aimed to make their own services more attractive (Funk 2001, 184). KDDI managed to install a powerful gateway, allowing EZWeb users to access text and graphics of unofficial i-mode sites, while J-Sky users can access only the textual part of these sites. Official i-menu sites, however, remain within the i-mode information sphere and cannot be accessed from outside networks (Funk 2001, 42). Moreover, users of alternative services cannot use the full functionality of unofficial i-mode sites, since Java specifications and handset tracking mechanisms for use in location-based services differ between the networks (Funk 2002b, 10).

NTT DoCoMo holds a market share of 61.9 percent in the Japanese mobile Internet market (TCA 2002). The Japanese government has followed the development of NTT DoCoMo's market power with growing concern. Funk (2001, 195) comments: "NTT Docomo has probably become the most powerful firm in Japan, and its ability single-handedly to determine the i-mode official sites makes it potentially more powerful than any government regulator." Due to growing pressure from the government, NTT DoCoMo finally announced that it would open up the i-mode platform to other service providers (NTT DoCoMo 2002b). Starting in 2003, competing carriers and service providers were to be able to market their own services to the installed base of i-mode users. Since NTT DoCoMo would forgo a substantial amount of control over i-mode with the opening of its platform, and, since the i-mode service would lose some of its attractiveness along with its exclusiveness, it was anticipated that NTT

DoCoMo would try to make the conditions for interconnection as demanding as possible and raise entry barriers by, for example, introducing new technologies and specifications in the future (Fasol 2002). Thereby, NTT DoCoMo might be able to maintain some of the exclusiveness of the i-mode information sphere, even when the different mobile mark-up languages converge into XHTML.

CONCLUSIONS

In this chapter, we listed and evaluated the common approaches for explaining the groundbreaking success of NTT DoCoMo's i-mode service. We found that, although these approaches provide good reasons for the success of a comprehensive mobile Internet service in general, they generally fail to explain why it was specifically the i-mode service that became so successful. We have shown that a central reason for i-mode's success was that NTT DoCoMo managed to internalize and proprietarize external, originally open resources. Further, we have presented evidence that these achievements are due to NTT DoCoMo's successful value scope management. Value scope management is a new, comprehensive, and integrated strategic management approach, which aims at gaining control over the value chain and strongly relies on advanced information management practices.

As the result of our analysis, we argue that the issue of unique internal(ized) resources, as well as the applicability and sustainability of the value scope management approach, should be the main focus when discussing, for example, whether NTT DoCoMo will be able to maintain its leading position in Japan in the future, or whether NTT DoCoMo will be able to repeat the success story of i-mode in another country.

Further, our analysis also raises implications for regulation. Successful value scope management may severely inhibit competition, as in the i-mode example, especially in oligopolistic markets. Regulators might see the need to intervene if a single market player exhibits practices similar to NTT DoCoMo's.

Next, our analysis yields one more indication that the often-cited search for a single "killer application" (or a single class of applications) as the alleged key to success in mobile commerce may be severely misguided. In fact, the i-mode example strongly suggests that focusing on the applications alone may not be enough to make mobile commerce take off.

Finally, the lesson for managers from our analysis is that on top of favorable market conditions and a solid business model, value scope management may be the method that will strengthen and secure their company's competitive position. The question of how this method can be transferred to, and applied in, other industries remains an open issue to be investigated by further research.

NOTES

1. www.nttdocomo.com/corebiz/services/imode/what/bstrategy.html (Accessed August 3, 2005.)
2. For a comparison of cHTML (i-mode) and WML (WAP), see Pringle 2000.
3. au (the mobile phone subsidiary of KDDI) later switched its network from PDC to CDMAone.
4. Until 1985, NTT had been a government-controled monopoly for thirty-three years. In 1999 it was broken up into a holding company and one long-distance and two regional carriers (Choy 1999).
5. See www.nttdocomo/corebiz/network/3g/license.html (Accessed August 3, 2005.)
6. See www.nttdocomo.co.jp/english/p_s/i/tag/criteria.html (Accessed April 29, 2003.)

REFERENCES

Ando, Y.; Arisawa, K.; Takahashi, T.; and Tosa C. *Telecom Monthly.* (December 2001). Tokyo: Goldman Sachs Global Equity Research.

Baldi, S., and Thaung, H.P.P. The entertaining way to m-commerce: Japan's approach to the mobile Internet—a model for Europe? *Electronic Markets,* 12, 1 (2002), 6–13.

Bamberger, I., and Wrona, T. Der Ressourcenansatz und seine Bedeutung für die strategische Unternehmensführung. *Zeitschrift für betriebswirtschaftliche Forschung,* 48, 2 (1996), 130–153.

Barney, J.B. Firm resources and sustained competitive advantage. *Journal of Management,* 17, 1 (1991), 99–120.

———. *Gaining and Sustaining Competitive Advantage.* New York: Addison-Wesley, 1996.

Bradley, S.P., and Sandoval, M. NTT DoCoMo: The future of the wireless Internet? *Journal of Interactive Marketing,* 16, 2 (Spring 2002), 80–96.

Choy, J. NTT reorganization sparks telecommunications shuffle. *JEI Report* (1999). n.p.

Church, J., and Ware, R. *Industrial Organization: A Strategic Approach.* Boston: Irwin/McGraw-Hill, 2000.

Clark, R. *The NTT DoCoMo Success Story. America's Network,* 104, 4 (2000), 46–49.

Durlacher Research Ltd. *Mobile Commerce Report.* London, 2000.

Evans, P.B., and Wurster, T.S. Strategy and the new economics of information. *Harvard Business Review,* 75, 5 (September/October 1997), 71–83.

Fasol, G. *Re: opening of i-mode.* Keitai-l list archive, 2002 (available at www.appelsiini.net/keitai-l/archives/2002–01/0161.html/, accessed on April 16, 2002).

Funk, J.L. *The Mobile Internet: How Japan Dialed Up and the West Disconnected.* ISI Publications, Bermuda, 2001.

———. *Global Competition Between and Within Standards: The Case of Mobile Phones.* New York: Palgrave, 2002a.

———. Network effects, openness, gateway technologies and the expansion of a standard's "application depth" and "geographical breadth": The case of the mobile Internet. Kobe, Japan: Research Institute for Economics and Business Administration, Kobe University, 2002b (available at www.rieb.kobe-u.ac.jp/~funk/, accessed on March 16, 2002).

Macdonald, D. Exporting the i-mode concept. *WRMC Business Briefing Wireless Technology 2003.* London (2002), 129–131.

Natsuno, T. *I-Mode Strategy.* Chichester: John Wiley & Sons Ltd., 2002.

NTT DoCoMo. (English home page of NTT DoCoMo Japan). June 2, 2002a (available at www.nttdocomo.com/, accessed on June 6, 2002).

———. NTT DoCoMo to release conditions for accessing i-mode packet network, 2002b. (available at www.nttdocomo.com/presscenter/pressreleases/press/pressrelease.html?param[no]=100, accessed on August 3, 2005).

Pringle, D. Wireless war: WAP vs. i-mode. *Wall Street Journal* (June 6, 2000).

Sadeh, N. *M-Commerce—Technologies, Services, and Business Models.* New York: John Wiley & Sons, 2002.

Salop, S.C., and Scheffman, D.T. Rising rivals' costs. *American Economic Review,* 73, 2 (1983), 267–271.

Scuka, D. Unwired—Japan has the future in its pocket. J@pan Inc., June 2000 (available at www.japaninc.net/mag/comp/2000/06/jun00_unwired.html, accessed on April 24, 2003).

Shapiro, C., and Varian, H.R. *Information Rules: A Strategic Guide to the Network Economy.* Boston: Harvard Business School Press, 1999.

Stiehler, A., and Wichmann, T. Mobile Internet in Japan—Lessons for Europe? *ePSO Newsletter,* 1, 2 (2000), 13–15.

World Wide Web Consortium (W3C). *Compact HTML for Small Information Appliances,* 1998 (available at www.w3c.org/TR/1998/NOTE-compactHTML-19980209/#www1, accessed on March 8, 2002).

PART IV

TRUST, SECURITY, AND LEGAL ISSUES

CHAPTER 13

TRUST IN ONLINE CONSUMER EXCHANGES

EMERGING CONCEPTUAL AND THEORETICAL TRENDS

SIRKKA L. JARVENPAA AND V. SRINIVASAN RAO

Abstract: *Popular literature touts trust as the hallmark of online consumer commerce. But academic research has concentrated on examining the factors that engender trust without critically questioning the nature, processes, and roles of trust in online consumer commerce. Such neglect may have introduced biases into the trust literature and resulted in overly simplistic recommendations to managers and Internet practitioners on the importance of trust and how to generate it. There exists a need to expand and clarify our understanding of online consumer trust. This article identifies conceptual and theoretical trends on trust that, if addressed in future studies, may help in the overall quest for a deeper appreciation of the nature, processes, and role of trust in electronic commerce.*

Keywords: *e-Commerce, Online Consumer Commerce, Theoretical Foundations of Trust, Trust*

INTRODUCTION

Electronic commerce (e-commerce) is a telecommunication-based service, and, as such, must grapple with the conflict between access and control (Keen and McDonald, 2000). While e-commerce gives consumers access to many products, transactions, and relationships, at the same time they must surrender control and the ability to guard against the risk of uncertainties with those products, transactions, and relationships.

Trust is commonly defined as "a psychological state comprising the intention to accept vulnerability based upon positive expectations of the intentions or behavior of another" (Rousseau et al. 1998, 395). Without some threshold of trust in the seller and the Internet environment, a consumer is unlikely to engage in online commerce. Trust allows consumers to engage in transactions when they are at risk of harm or other negative consequences from doing so.

Internet-based consumer exchanges often involve many transacting parties (seller, financial institutions, shipping companies, and other intermediaries), and, as the complexity of relationships increases, so does the potential for opportunism (Grabner-Kraeuter 2002). Unethical and hurtful behaviors are known to increase in contexts without physical contact (Kelman and Hamilton 1989); for instance, Internet auctions have escalating levels of fraud (Boyd 2002, Kauffman and Wood 2000).

Consequently, consumers face three distinct facets of risk in e-commerce. First, consumers face *privacy* risks, in the sense that the customer's personal and financial information may be stolen, altered, or otherwise compromised by unauthorized third parties who are not part of the retailer–customer relationship. This can occur because an online customer's activities generate much more information than what is required to execute a particular sales transaction. Second, consumers face *technology* risks, where the retailer's online system for information search, order fulfillment, payment, and other business processes may falter. Because no party has total control over the systems and networks upon which the Internet-based transactions depend (Tan and Thoen 2000), the technology-mediated interfaces present barriers. Finally, consumers face risks of *retailer opportunism*—intentional misbehavior by the seller at the expense of the customer (Jarvenpaa and Tiller 2001). The retailer may falsely advertise product quality, intentionally defect from sales agreements, and misuse personal customer information by tracking customers for marketing purposes or selling customer data for profit. Virtual stores are more limited than brick-and-mortar ones in visual and auditory stimulation and communication synchrony (Tractinsky and Rao 2001) and can lead to a reduced sense of realism, or "presence" (Lombard and Ditton 1997). Consumers have to resort to indirect means, such as statements of store policies and practices as well as claims from other parties, rather than their own eyes and ears to make inferences on an online store's behavior (Kim 2003, Tan and Thoen 2000).

Moreover, the perception of risk may sometimes be even greater than the actual risk. Popular media continue to report countless instances of harmful and deceitful behavior on the Internet. Once alert to the possibility of harmful or deceitful behavior, potential victims can suspect deception even when none exists (Naguin and Paulson 2003).

Hence, it is of little surprise that trust is positioned as the single most powerful construct that retailers must manage both initially and in long-term business-to-consumer (B2C) relationships (Cheskin Research 1999, Keen and McDonald 2000, Urban et al. 2000). Indeed, a large body of research has accumulated on online trust across several disciplines, much of it focused on studies that are antecedents to trust in an online environment. Studies ask questions such as "What factors produce trust?" or "How can Web sites build trust?"

Although examining the antecedents of online trust helps conceptual advancement and provides pragmatically useful information, such research tells only part of the story. The studies unquestionably assume that trust is intrinsically beneficial to online sales, and dismiss the possibility that trust may have limited direct ability to sway a consumer to purchase from a site. To develop a more complete picture, researchers must begin to build a richer nomological model of trust in online consumer commerce. Future research needs to go beyond studying antecedents of trust to understanding the nature, role, and consequences of trust.

The interest in trust research is expected to continue in both the short and the medium term, especially with the advent of new technologies such as peer-to-peer computing and mobile computing (Balasubramanian et al. 2002). What's more, technological and legal developments are likely to affect the nature, processes, and role of trust in e-commerce. Issues of trust no doubt affect the nature of giving, and consequently the reciprocal nature of distributed computing and file-sharing arrangements.

To enable future research to focus on issues that will help develop deeper understanding, we identify gaps or areas that are underresearched or unresearched (to the best of our knowledge) in the broader nomological net of trust. We present these areas as emerging trends in the hope that more researchers will contribute to making them primary themes of exploration and theorizing. We identify seven trends, but by no means do these represent an exhaustive list, nor does the order in which trends are discussed reflect their importance. We first establish a vocabulary to discuss trust in consumer–seller relationships.

ELEMENTS OF TRUST IN CONSUMER–SELLER RELATIONSHIPS

The key elements in consumer–seller relationships are the consumer (truster), object of trust (trustee), trust-initiating factors, trustworthiness (beliefs of trust), and forms of trust (trusting intentions). We selected these elements because they are common building blocks of trust models (see, for example, Doney and Cannon 1997, McKnight et al. 1998). Our vocabulary regarding the elements of trustworthiness and forms of trust builds on the beliefs–intentions notions of trust (Fishbein and Ajzen 1975).

The *truster* may be an individual or a collection of consumers, vulnerable to the opportunistic behavior of others. The *object of the trust* (also referred to as the target of trust) can be an individual Internet store, the Internet as a whole, or one of the other components in the Internet commerce system. Internet stores fall into two categories: a new Internet store or the Internet version of an existing physical or catalog store. Salespeople are rarely an object of trust online, as the essence of Internet shopping is the absence of a salesperson.

Trust initiating factors refer to the antecedents (for example, store reputation, store size) that trigger the evaluations of trustworthiness of the object. These factors may also help sustain trust over time. The factors can be classified into four categories:

- *Seller factors* refer to features of the seller observed by a consumer. For instance, the general reputation of a store or the layout of an online store can trigger customer trust.
- *Referential factors* are individuals or organizations willing to recommend that the object of trust can be trusted. These are usually other customers or third-party guarantee agencies such as BBBOnline, Verisign, TrustE, and so on.
- *Guarantee factors* are agencies that have enforcement powers in terms of overseeing transactions and being able to correct the effects of any opportunistic behavior. Such agencies include governmental regulatory agencies, which have legal clout. They may also include trade associations, which impose a code of conduct on their members.
- *Self-initiated factors* are generated by the customer. The customer can *self-initiate* trust through his or her traits and propensities, such as a highly trusting disposition (Rotter 1980) and/or a propensity to take risks.

While *trustworthiness* captures the expectations and beliefs regarding the seller, it is the trust-initiating factors that signal trustworthiness. Trustworthiness can take on different dimensions (Sirdeshmukh et al. 2002):

- *Competence:* Signals the ability of the seller to execute the transactions and provide the service.
- *Benevolence:* Reflects restraint from self-serving opportunism.
- *Problem-solving responsiveness:* Refers to the responsiveness to customer problems during and after the online interaction.

Forms of trust are trusting intentions and refer to the consumer's willingness to accept vulnerability and proceed with the interaction. Dimensions of trustworthiness and forms of trust are closely related, the former refers to beliefs and the latter to intentions. Like categories of trustworthiness, there are many classifications of the forms of trust (see, for example, McAllister 1995). We use the classification that identifies three forms of trust: calculus-based, knowledge-based, and identification-based.

• *Calculus-based* trust (also called deterrence-based) conceptualizes trust as a willingness to be vulnerable, based on a rational calculative judgment of the awareness of a retailer's motivations and goals, and the ability to rely on deterrence and control mechanisms to prevent opportunism of a retailer. These factors affect the customer estimation of gain or loss in undertaking a transaction. Consumers trust the merchant as long as they believe that retailers have more to gain from cooperative rather than from opportunistic behavior. In other words, the costs of possible punishment decrease the gain from opportunistic behavior. Such punishment or deterrence may include the loss of future opportunities, one's reputation, valued relationships, and other investments (Lewicki and Bunker,1996).

• A *knowledge-based* view of trust is rooted in social exchange theory (Blau 1964) and argues that people will continue to cooperate voluntarily as long as they believe other parties will do the same.[1] Knowledge-based trust emerges from information about others' past voluntary behavior rather than from deterrence. In other words, trust is grounded on information about the seller that allows the buyer to understand and predict the seller's cooperative behavior. If the seller has been dependable and reliable in the past, the buyer can develop a generalized trust expectancy of the seller.

• *Identification-based* trust derives from social categorization and identity/identification theory (Hogg and Terry 2000), and suggests that people categorize themselves into "in-group" and "out-group" based on perceived similarities versus differences. Consumers trust sellers if there is a perceived similarity in values between the seller and the consumer. Identification-based trust engenders confidence that the retailer will protect the consumer's interests, and no surveillance or monitoring of a seller's actions is necessary. The manifestation of trust is limited to those with a common identity, whether or not they have any direct contact. For instance, a salesman who is an alumnus of one university may engender trust in other alumni on the basis of a common alma mater. Another example would be environmentally conscious consumers trusting organizations that espouse "green marketing." Common bases for identification may be culture, ethnic origins, language, professional or personal affiliation, and so forth.

The trust literature also acknowledges the existence of a fourth form of trust, that is, institutional trust. According to Luhmann (1979), institutional trust is based on the appearance of "everything . . . in proper order." Institutional trust is tied to institutional norms and beliefs, and so remains unexamined until the norms are violated (Zucker 1986). For example, institutional trust can facilitate entry into commercial contracts as long as the truster has faith in the country's legal system. Institutional trust is a form of calculus-based trust. Deterrence includes the social and cultural norms and legal regulations governing the transacting parties (the "institutional environment").

Figure 13.1 summarizes the basic elements of trust. Trust-initiating factors elicit beliefs of the trustworthiness of a trustee. The beliefs in turn will prompt different forms of trust in a truster. For example, trust will encourage the shopper to accept the vulnerability inherent in the potential exchange with an online store (trustee). The greater the risks, the higher the trust levels needed before the consumer is willing to explore an online site and possibly engage in a transaction. The trust elements have applicability in both an interpersonal context, where the trustee is a virtual salesperson, as well as in contexts where the trustee is a collective group, such as a Web site, department, or organization. We use below the basic trust elements to find relevant research and discern gaps in our understanding.

EMERGING TRENDS IN ONLINE CONSUMER RESEARCH

This paper aims to identify opportunities for future research that will fill some of the existing conceptual and theoretical gaps in the literature. We reviewed trust literature in both academic marketing and information systems (IS) journals as well as recent IS conference proceedings.

Figure 13.1 **Elements of Trust**

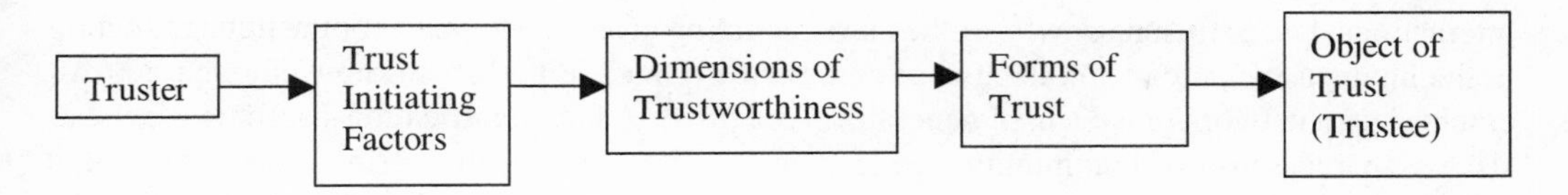

Note: Arrows do not denote causality

Many of the gaps on which trends are based on are not unique to e-commerce research on trust, but have counterparts in trust literatures in other areas.

From Unidimensional Views to Multidimensional Views of Trust

Trust is widely recognized as a multifaceted, multilevel, and dynamic concept (Butler 1991). Although e-commerce researchers do acknowledge the plethora of trust conceptualizations, individual studies in e-commerce treat trust theoretically and empirically as a unidimensional construct. The assessment of trust is seen predominantly as a calculative undertaking, reduced to a subjective probability of the other party behaving in a certain way because of deterrence. A consumer engages in an ongoing calculation of the costs of punishment and rewards of opportunistic behavior for the seller. As long as the rewards of opportunism do not exceed the costs of punishment for the seller, the consumer trusts the seller. In calculus-based trust, "opportunities are pursued and risks continually monitored" (Rousseau et al. 1998, 399). Sellers do what they say because of fear of punishment or deterrence.[2]

Much less researched in online consumer trust are psychological and sociological forms of trust that build on how people relate to each other either through reciprocity or social identification.[3] Some research is now emerging that enriches the calculus form with knowledge- and identification-based forms. For example, the knowledge-based view of trust has been studied in peer-to-peer auctions (e.g., eBay) that include feedback systems where buyers rate sellers and these ratings are available for future consumers (Ba and Pavlou 2002). Knowledge-based trust develops because consumers gain knowledge of the seller's behavior both through direct interactions and through *indirect* or secondary knowledge, that is, knowledge of the experiences of others with the seller.

The third form of trust, the identification-based view, is even less studied in online commerce (for an exception, see Cazier and Gill 2003). Identification-based trust exists when the truster believes that the trustee shares his or her goals, empathy, and common values. Lewicki and Bunker (1996) cite the arguments of Kramer (1993) and Kramer and Brewer (1986) "that a certain form of group-based trust is linked with group membership and develops as individuals identify with the goals espoused by particular groups and organizations" (Lewicki and Bunker 1996 122). In the early years of the commercialization of the Internet, online stores primarily sold high-tech goods, and those buying them were technically knowledgeable. Technology provided the common identity and generated identification-based trust. For instance, in 1996, "Amazon.com was appealing to a particularly sophisticated and computer-savvy audience: The top selling book on Amazon.com in 1996 was *Creating Killer Web Sites: The Art of Third-Generation Site Design* by David Siegel" (Spector 2000, 159).

The different forms of trust have important theoretical ramifications. The calculus-based trust advocates a focus on individuals, individual purposes, and mostly on individual outcomes of interactions. It sees trust narrowly, as the basis for acting in self-interest, not as the basis for acting in the interests of a broader collective or community. On the other hand, knowledge-based trust emphasizes a network or a chain of generalized reciprocity, and identification-based trust emphasizes a shared sense of community with a common fate. Hence, the various forms provide a different locus for research on trust.

The forms also imply different levels of initial trust. Many studies assume low levels of initial trust (Stewart 2003). Lewicki and Bunker (1996) offer a stage-wise evolution model in which trust begins with calculus-based trust (deterrence), maturing to knowledge-based trust, and eventually to identification-based trust. According to Lewicki and Bunker (1996), the "three forms are linked in a sequential interaction in which achievement of trust at one level enables the achievement of trust at the next level" (119). However, McKnight et al. (1998) propose a model where initial trust can be high. Similarly, Myerson et al. (1996) suggest a high level of initial trust. Consider, for example, an individual engaging in an initial transaction based on secondary knowledge, that is, knowledge acquired from another customer. In such a case, the first stage is knowledge-based trust. Alternately, consider a customer identifying with a "green marketer." Here the first stage is identification-based trust. Identification-based trust can develop rapidly (or even instantaneously) and reach high levels when a consumer identifies a commonality of values. Such commonality may be promoted through the use of virtual communities or discussion groups. For example, two individuals, though strangers to each other, may belong to the same group or club, and membership in the group reflects a set of common values. So, even before there is any significant interaction or mutual discovery of goals and values, there can be a high level of initial trust. Thus, identification-based trust does not necessarily need a period of time to develop. Instead, it can be spontaneous and immediate.

We encourage research with greater recognition of trust as a multidimensional construct. A multidimensional perspective of trust will provide richer theoretical bases for the study of consumer trust. Multidimensionality will also help trust research to break out from distinct disciplinary boundaries and allow greater possibilities to study inherent features of the phenomenon without disciplinary constraints (Kramer 1999).

From Factors to Processes of Trust

Much of the existing research regarding online trust has been factor research. Studies have examined factors that initiate trust or shift it above the threshold necessary to stimulate buying behavior (see Jarvenpaa et al. 2000, Yoon 2002). A large number of factors has been identified, leading some researchers to create integrative models of how these factors affect trust (see, for example, Appan and Mellarkod 2003, Kim et al. 2003). But all in all, the search for factors has encouraged empiricism over theoretical advances. Empiricism has ruled particularly because studies have not theorized about the mechanisms that produce the effects on trust.

To counter this trend, some researchers have begun to shift away from factors to processes. The research focuses on factors that trigger certain processes to establish the initial level of trustworthiness and trust, and then examines how other processes come into play, either increasing or decreasing the level of trust as time goes by. A process focus tames empiricism and stimulates theoretical advances on the mechanisms underlying trust.

In the context of traditional industrial buying, Doney and Cannon (1997) identified five trust processes: calculative, predictive, capability, intentionality, and transference. They compiled these processes by spanning literature across a variety of fields, including psychology, sociology, economics, organization science, and marketing. These five processes appear to be fundamental in the sense that they explain trusting behavior across a wide range of situations. The processes also map to different theories of economic and social exchange. The emerging trend is to build on these processes with good prospects for new insights.

In the *calculative* process, the truster predicts the trustee's trustworthiness based on an assessment of the costs of betrayal versus the benefits of nonbetrayal. Many factors can evoke the calculative process. The amount of resources committed to a relationship by the seller—perhaps via personalization and customization—affects the costs of being caught engaging in opportunistic behavior, as does the value of the seller's reputation. The calculative process affects the competence dimension of trustworthiness. A truster infers trustworthiness from the types of investments and self-controls instituted by the seller to signal the ability to consummate transactions. The calculative process engenders a calculus-based form of trust, whereby the truster engages in ongoing calculations of the costs and benefits of the other party cheating versus cooperating in a relationship. A seller's forbearance from opportunistic behavior forms the basis of a truster's trusting behavior. Both transaction cost theory (Williamson 1985) and agency theory provide the tenets to understand the calculative process (Bergen et al. 1992).

In the *predictive* process, the truster assesses the likelihood that the trustee will behave opportunistically based on first- or secondhand knowledge of past opportunistic behavior. Repeated interactions increase the amount and variety of experiences as well as the ability to make accurate predictions of another's behavior. The accumulated experience is important for strengthening the competence appraisals of the store as well as for building the knowledge-based form of trust. This knowledge can, in turn, raise the cost of switching to another site. Hence, trust can be best explained through social interactions entailing repeated exchanges. Social exchange theory, with its variants (Blau 1964), can shed light on the underlying processes.

In the *capability* process, the truster predicts whether the trustee can be trusted to overcome external uncertainties, once again based on prior knowledge, first- or secondhand. This relates to the seller's ability to anticipate and satisfactorily resolve problems as they arise. The manner in which the seller has dealt with problems in the past will determine the problem-solving orientation of trustworthiness, which in turn will affect the consumer's level of knowledge-based trust. Consumers use the evidence of problem-solving orientation to gauge the amount of risk they are willing to take. Here again, the theoretical approaches that address both social and economic interactions can shed light on underlying processes (for example, social exchange theory and generalized social exchange theory).

In the *intentionality* process, consumers base their prediction of trustworthiness on the knowledge of the seller's commonality of views and values. This process requires a disclosure or signaling of a seller's goals and intentions and a consumer's ability to interpret these intentions. The intentionality process is related to both the benevolence process of trustworthiness and identification-based trust. In identification-based trust, a truster allows a trustee to act as an agent for the other without the presence of monitoring. Strub and Priest (1976) found that in the intentionality process there initially tends to be a search for selective behavior cues, then the sharing of information, and then validation of shared goals and values. The factors that evoke the intentionality process may be explicit words or statements in the form of management policies, or behavior in the form of store practices. The process of discovering the intentions may be gradual or abrupt. The more a trustee resembles a truster in interests, backgrounds, and memberships, the faster the process of discovering shared intention. Social identification theories (for example, Hogg and Terry 2000) shed light on the underlying processes.

In the *transference* process, a consumer accepts someone else's evaluation of trust in an unknown object of trust (trustee). If a trusted third party appraises an unknown trustee to be trustworthy, then the truster assumes that this unknown trustee is also trustworthy. Trust in the third party is transferred to the unknown party. Transference can be formal or informal. Formal transference occurs when the first agent introduces the trustee to the second agent and explicitly vouches for the second agent's trustworthiness. An example of informal transference is when the trustworthy behavior of an online store leads to trust in other online stores. The factors that evoke the transference process are the perceived strength of the relationship between the trusted third party and the unknown party (similarity in appearance, image, and setting between the two) and the reputation of the trusted party. Social network theories (see, for example, Granovetter 1973) provide insight into the transference process, particularly in their treatment of structural balance and mutual reciprocity.

An example of a study that focuses on process is Stewart's (2003) work on the transference of trust from a known retailer to an unknown online retailer. Stewart studied the conditions of transference as well as its underlying mechanisms. Transference was found to occur to the extent that two sites are considered to be related or form a group, in other words, are enabled by "entitativity," or the grouping of elements based on their relative similarity, promixity, or common fate. Besides identifying the conditions for transference, Stewart suggested that the nature of the trust transference process is bidirectional (Stewart and Zhang 2003). This is in contrast to Doney and Cannon's (1997) original articulation of a unidirectional nature of trust. Stewart's work advances theoretical understanding, as it goes deeper into the conditions and mechanisms underlying transference than previously reported.

Table 13.1 maps trust processes to trust-initiating factors, dimensions of trustworthiness, and forms of trust. The processes of trust are closely linked with dimensions of trustworthiness and forms of trust. New insight on processes may be more likely with research that breaks away from calculus-based trust and economic theories and considers the social dynamics underlying the relationship between a consumer and a seller.

From Contextless Views to Situated Models of Trust

The existing studies on Internet stores do not sufficiently acknowledge the broader context: that the store and the consumer are a part of the overall Internet commerce system that is composed of other online stores, physical stores, customers, the underlying Internet architecture, financial institutions, regulatory agencies, various third-party guarantors, and so on.

Figure 13.2 provides a conceptual view of the Internet commerce system. The collection of online stores constitutes the online business environment built on the Internet infrastructure. The customer's relationship with the stores is moderated by enabling agents, such as credit card processors, or malicious agents, such as hackers. Regulating agencies play an oversight role, and third-party guarantors play the role of facilitating intermediaries. We include physical stores as part of the Internet commerce system because a single organization may own both physical and online stores and may provide cross-services. Customers' relationships with the physical stores are moderated by enabling agencies and overseen by regulating agencies.

Thus, if trust in an individual store is affected, it reflects on the overall system. Or, if trust in the Internet system is affected, it will reflect on the trust in the individual stores. In discussing trust in international business, Brenkert (1998) says, " . . . a complicated pattern of interaction among individuals, firms, industries, international organizations, and governmental structures will be required to overcome the obstacles [to trust]" (p. 289). Analogously, an understanding of

Table 13.1

Trust-Initiating Factors, Trustworthiness, Forms of Trust, and Trust Processes in Online Stores

Trust process	Trust-initiating factors	Trustworthiness	Trust forms	Possible theoretical foundations
Calculative	Amount of invested resources (e.g., customization, personalization)	Competence	Calculus-based (deterrence-based trust)	Agency theory
	Penalties of nonperformance			Transaction cost theory
	Reputation			
Prediction	Length of relationship	Competence	Knowledge-based trust	Social exchange theory
	Ratings by past customers			
Capability	Disclosure of past problem-solving history	Problem-solving orientation	Knowledge-based trust	Social exchange theory
	Expertise of store staff			
Intentionality	Explicit words and behavior illustrating motives and values	Benevolence	Identification-based trust	Social identification theory
	Similarity in perceived backgrounds			
Transference	Similarity or "entitativity" between the trusted third party and the unknown "trustee"	Benevolence and competence through attribution	Identification-based trust/ calculus-based trust	Social network theory

Figure 13.2 **The Internet Commerce System**

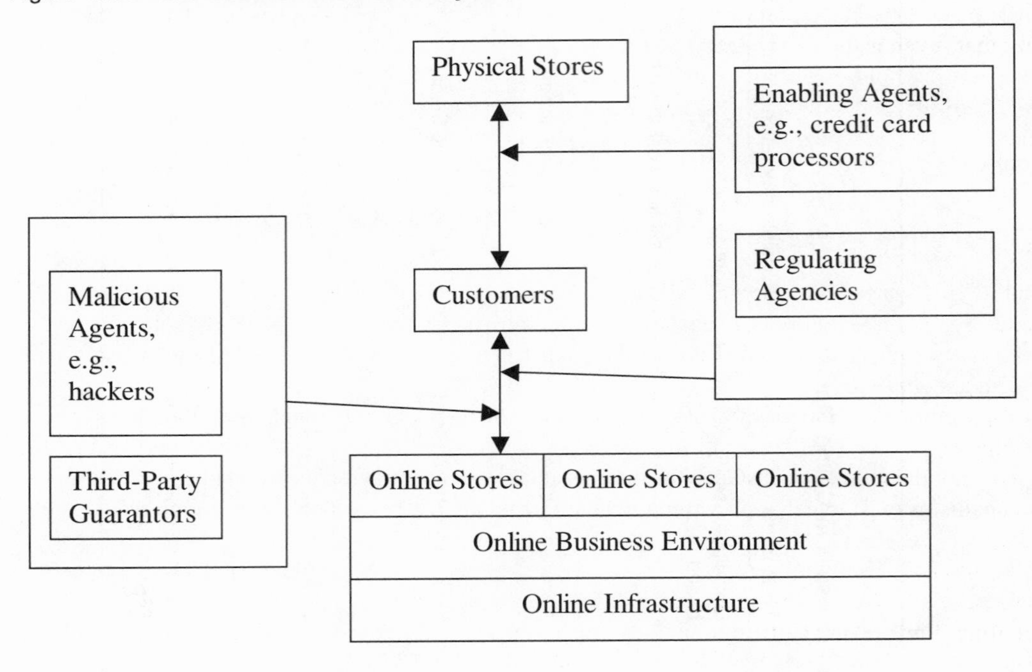

trust in B2C e-commerce requires an understanding of the consequences of trust in the overall sociotechnical environment.

Existing studies' lack of focus on context is a bit perplexing, especially since practitioners have been calling for contextual marketing (Kenny and Marshall 2000) and experience economy (Gilmore and Pine 1999), stressing the importance of context in e-commerce. Rarely have e-commerce researchers even considered the theoretical implications of product or service characteristics on trust (for an exception, see Lee et al. 2000, examining low-involvement versus high-involvement products), let alone the cultural setting or the industry segment (Huang 2001; Jarvenpaa and Tractinsky 1999, Lee and Rao 2003).

This disregard to context may arise from the focus on calculative trust that sees trust as the basis for acting in self-interest. The other views of trust more readily recognize the social embeddedness of individuals and how this embeddedness may affect trust. Buchan et al. (2002) reported both theoretically and empirically how reciprocity (underlying knowledge-based trust) appears to develop at different speeds in different cultures because of the differences in social networks. Consumers are known to reduce opportunism in high-uncertainty situations by relying on within-network exchanges and partners with whom they are socially connected (DiMaggio and Louch 1998). The importance of context likely increases rather than decreases when shopping moves to the Internet. Context introduces distinctive characteristics that need to be considered explicitly. The unique context should also caution researchers to be careful about directly translating the findings from other contexts to the online consumer–seller exchanges.

Some research is emerging that takes a broader sociotechnological focus. Rosenbaum et al. (2003) single out situational trust and strive to develop a grounded view of trust that emphasizes the roles of buyers in social and organizational contexts and various designer values in the design, implementation, and use of the Web site. Trust is viewed as an outcome of the social interactions among these various participants, with intended and unintended consequences. They also emphasize that "even in the same context, the scope of the trust may vary, depending on the relationship's history, stage of development, and cues in the immediate setting" (398). We encourage an increasing focus on context and situated change perspectives. In situated change, the context surrounding the actors plays a crucial role in influencing cognitive and behavioral changes (Orlikowski 1996).

From Unidirectional to Bidirectional and Asymmetric Views of Trust

Online trust research has largely viewed trust as unidirectional, that is, the trust is placed in the seller by the buyer, without regard to the seller's trust in a buyer. This goes against some of the seminal writings on trust that contend, "each trusts on the assumption that the others trust" (Luhmann 1979, 69).

Opportunistic behavior by customers may take the form of nonpayment for goods and services and improper returns of goods. Most established retailers have control mechanisms in place against risk of nonpayment. For instance, in Internet retailing, most payments are made by credit cards. Mechanisms exist to get approval immediately from the credit card company and to receive payment while the amount is debited to the customer's credit card account. Thus, the need to trust a customer may seem minimal. However, there are reports that the ratio of fraudulent to authentic credit card transactions by customers is significantly higher in Internet retailing than in traditional retailing. Further, in an effort to manage the losses from this source, credit card companies have transferred the risks associated with fraudulent credit card use to the merchant. For example, if an Internet merchant ships goods based on a stolen credit card, the credit card company will not pay the merchant, even if it has approved the charge, in contrast to earlier practices in which the credit card company bore the loss.

Improper returns of goods refers to the practice of ordering items, such as books or clothes, using them briefly, and returning them for credit within the money-back guarantee period. A similar practice related to software is the downloading of trial versions of software, which are needed only for a short period, and then discontinuing their use when payment is required. The extreme version of this is the downloading of the trial software a second time, when the first trial term is over. While these examples do not transgress the law, the practices are a violation of seller trust if the customer had no intention of buying the product in the first place. The extent of such violations of trust is not known. Businesses consider such trust violations by customers a cost of doing business. In the case of books and clothes, the merchant can track the history of returns and discontinue shipments to customers who appear to be taking advantage of seller trust. In the case of software, identifying the untrustworthy customer is more difficult. Even if the customer repeatedly downloads the same trial software, it is easy to hide behind different false identities.

Thus, e-commerce presents risks not just to buyers, but also to sellers (Grazioli and Jarvenpaa 2003). Deception, whether by the buyer or the seller, exploits the complexities of the system and the weaknesses of the human cognitive system. With the growth in auction sites such as E-bay, the problem of seller trust in the buyer is as important as buyer trust in the seller. Both are susceptible to misuse. In fact, 46 percent of the complaints received by the Internet Fraud Complaint Center (IFCC) in 2002 related to auction fraud (IFCC 2003). Complaints included both nondelivery of merchandise and nonpayment, but no breakdown was provided. Individual sellers have no mechanism to ascertain the trustworthiness of the buyer, and so often demand cashier's checks[4] as payment, particularly for large-ticket items. This not only slows the speed of the transaction, but also puts the buyer at greater risk, with little (or a complicated process of) recourse if the goods are not shipped or are of bad quality. On the other hand, sellers on auction sites have also been known to act in bad faith. They may refuse to ship goods that did not fetch a reasonable price, even though they are obligated. Thus, in a growing number of fraud cases, deception is perpetrated by individuals against other individuals. The fraudulent schemes are simple, such as buyers promising to pay with no intention of doing so. As commerce takes place more in peer-to-peer and mobile platforms, the seller's risk increases along with that of the buyer. Hence, there is a need to understand the seller's trust in a consumer in addition to a consumer's trust in a seller. The bidrectional focus will help to instill an element of dynamicity in trust studies.

From One-Night Stands to Trust Marriages

There has been a preponderance of studies on initial encounters with new Internet stores, but there has been little focus on repeat visits. Little is known about how trust affects learning and practice, which have been found to serve as powerful lock-ins for repeat visits and online purchasing (Johnson et al. 2003). For example, on an initial visit, a consumer learns how to use a Web site to accomplish his or her goals. After learning to use the site, the customer should find it more efficient to use than another unfamiliar site, since browsing and buying can be executed at a faster rate at the familiar site. Gefen (2000) showed that familiarity with an Internet vendor, familiarity with process, and trust in the Internet vendor all influenced intentions to purchase. In a separate study, Gefen (2002) showed that customer loyalty increased with trust. Collectively, these findings argue that initial trust is an important first step in initiating familiarity and loyalty. Having established this, researchers need to move on to an examination of ways to maintain trust over time.

Some scholars believe that trust is fragile, that is, that it is easier to destroy than create (Kramer 1999), and argue that once initial trust has been engendered, the merchant has to be vigilant in ensuring that it is maintained over the longer term. Despite high levels of vigilance, there is no way to guarantee that every transaction will be perfect. Fallibility is to be expected of individuals and the organizations to which they belong. Whether the consequences of the fallibility are marginal or serious may depend on the amount of familiarity and loyalty the merchant has accumulated over time. Familiarity increases the cost of switching, the cost associated with abandoning one merchant, learning about another, and establishing a new relationship. Loyalty provides a psychological bond that makes customer defection less likely. Individually and collectively, familiarity and loyalty ensure that minor lapses on the part of the merchant do not produce disproportionate responses from the customer. It is possible that they may even help a merchant survive egregious errors.

Thus, it is easy to see the need to move from one-time studies to longitudinal studies. The various antecedents examined to date in cross-sectional studies may have different effects on initial trust and trust development in the long run.

From Positive Trust to Negative Trust

Trust is good for e-business. This has become a truism even in academic research on online trust, as studies have a strong normative bias toward the inherent value of trust. Retailers, both online and offline, are assumed to have intentions that are in the interest of the consumer; and if the consumer trusts the seller, both merchant and consumer welfare increase. For example, consumer trust in the seller has been found to increase the consumer's willingness to disclose personal information (Culnan and Armstrong 1999). Disclosure of personal information in turn helps the seller customize the offerings to the needs of the consumer, and thereby increase consumer satisfaction and welfare.

Research showing a positive bias toward trust has dwarfed research on the dual role of antecedents. The same antecedents that engender trust might also promote distrust. The classic ploy of a criminal is to gain a victim's trust by donning the trappings of trustworthiness. False store fronts are a common ruse, and can be set up with ease on the Internet. For example, Netware International Bank (Radcliff 1999) was a fraudulent façade with no real bank behind it. Its Web site displayed seals claiming deposit insurance in an effort to engender trust. Such ruses may cause customers to be suspicious of the very signals, such as seals of approval, that are indicative of trustworthiness. Positively framed antecedents and consequences of trust may tell only half of the story. A trustworthy history engenders trust, but that can be misleading too. IFCC Report cites a case in which an individual sold computers for two years, and then held a mock auction, but failed to deliver goods for orders worth more than $400,000 (IFCC 2003). Kramer et al. (1996, 380) observe that "the very properties of identity-based trust that contribute to its resilience might sometimes render individuals more vulnerable to misplaced trust." Moreover, betrayal of higher levels of trust can have more negative consequences than betrayal of lower levels of trust (Robinson 1996). For the most part, studies about online consumer trust have failed to explore the negative effects of antecedents. Grazioli and Jarvenpaa (2000) found that even sophisticated, technologically competent Internet shoppers have difficulty detecting fraud in a Web site that includes trust-inducing features.

Finer-grained insights about trust require examination of the positive–negative duality of trust. How do various antecedents build consumer trust but at the same time increase the likelihood of seller opportunism and lead to the mistrust of those same antecedents? Also, research must consider that behaviors in one context might render trust, whereas in others they might build distrust or produce no effect. For sure, the likely existence of the positive–negative duality should be a caution against simple prescriptions of any particular factors building trust unidirectionally and affecting consumers positively.

From Direct to Moderator Effects of Trust

Assuming that the seller's intentions are honest, there is still little systematic evidence of a direct positive impact of trust on actual shopping behavior. Much online consumer research has examined the consequences of perceived trust on outcomes such as shopping intention (Gefen 2000, Jarvenpaa et al. 2000), not actual purchase choice. Although some researchers claim direct effects of trust in the seller on the economic behavior of buyers, for example, higher price premiums (Ba and Pavlou 2002), others found only indirect effects (Li 2003, Pavlou 2003). In situations where trust has an indirect effect, increases or decreases in trust may have little impact on economic outcomes (Li 2003, Naguin and Paulson 2003). Finally, in some situations, increases in trust may enhance the potential for deceptive and/or opportunistic behavior (Grazioli and Jarvenpaa 2000).

The concern about overly enthusiastic claims of trust affecting actual behavior has attracted interest in both marketing and organizational literatures (Atuahene-Gima and Haiyang 2002; Dirks and Ferrin 2001, Sirdeshmukh et al. 2002). In the brick-and-mortar marketing context, trust has been found to affect the choice set and intentions to engage in interaction in the future, but not the purchase choice (Doney and Cannon 1997). Only if trust affected the consumer's perception of the value of the good or service did trust have an effect on loyalty (Sirdeshmukh et al. 2002). In the organizational literature, Dirks and Ferrin (2001) reviewed a large amount of organizational science literature and found that only in limited situations does trust directly influence behavior. Although trust likely matters in e-business, its effects may be somewhat different than conventional knowledge suggests. Trust helps a store convince the consumer to browse, but does not necessarily close the sale unless trust directly increases the value of the exchange. Other aspects of the marketing mix are relevant in the final choice.

Hence, the effect of trust is more conditional than might be portrayed in the existing literature. This calls for examination of the direct versus moderator effects of trust. In the organizational trust setting, Dirks and Ferrin (2001) advanced models to explain the role of trust in behavioral and attitudinal outcomes depending on the "situational strength" present. The first model applies to "weak situations," where individuals face novelty and time pressure and lack clear and consistent signals that allow them to interpret the situation consistently. In these weak situations, trust has a main effect on outcomes because the situation lacks other, more powerful factors to influence behaviors or judgments. But, in such situations, trust arises from the people themselves, either in the form of propensities or prior standings (self-initiating factors). For instance, the pioneers of Internet buying faced a novel situation, and presumably their propensity to trust was important in the decision to use the online channel. Also, people's prior beliefs and attitudes, manifested in trust, dictate their behaviors and judgments. Hence, if trust has a direct effect, it is likely to arise from a person's prior experiences of shopping online and on the same or similar Web sites.

According to the arguments of Dirks and Ferrin (2001), in the "moderately strong situations" where there are some signals that allow an assessment of the behavior of the seller, trust has a moderator effect. In these situations, other cues, such as the reliability of delivery, are available to directly affect outcomes, and hence trust has a *moderating* influence on the relationship between these cues and attitudinal and performance outcomes: trust either facilitates or hinders these other determinants or outcomes. Dirks and Ferrin (2001) identify two underlying processes to explain the moderator effect based on cognitive consistency: (1) "trust affects how one *assesses the future behavior* of another party with whom one is interdependent (or who may take action that affects oneself)" and (2) "trust also affects how one *interprets the past (or present) actions* of the other party, and the motives underlying the actions" (p. 456, italics original). This can be seen when a customer engages in a unsatisfactory transaction with a trading partner of long standing. For instance, a customer may have been buying clothes from the same boutique for many years, and finds that her latest purchase is of poor quality. The decision to continue purchasing at the same boutique is determined by the buyer's assessment of future behavior and also the buyer's rationalization of the poor quality goods. Most of the reasons for the long-standing relationship are still valid, but now trust moderates the intention to continue shopping at the same location.

In the "strong" situation, the Dirks and Ferrin (2001) theory expects no effect of trust on behavior. The situation is structured and highly controlled, rendering the outcomes "overdetermined." In such situations, there is low uncertainty, and trust is not likely to have an effect. This is typical of low-risk products bought in face-to-face environments, such as books in local bookstores. The transaction is highly structured, where money is exchanged for the immediate acquisition of a product. Any damage in the product is readily identifiable; no long-term support is needed. Thus, there is little or no need for trust in the seller.

In their extensive review of trust and its consequences in organizational sciences, Dirks and Ferrin (2001) found that less than 10 percent of empirical studies had examined the moderator effect of trust. We are unaware of any such studies in online consumer research. An understanding of the role of trust in online consumer commerce is sorely needed.

Table 13.2

Emerging Trends for Future Research

No.	From
1	Unidimensional views to multidimensional views of trust
2	Factors to processes of trust
3	Contextless views to situated models of trust
4	Unidirectional to bidirectional views of trust
5	One-night stands to trust marriages
6	Positive trust to negative trust
7	Direct to moderator effects of trust

CONCLUSIONS

Both practitioner and academic literatures tout the importance of trust in online retailing. Research in online trust has exploded over the last few years, with both marketing and IS scholars bringing their respective expertise to bear on the area. Yet, there is insufficient understanding of how and why trust is important in purchasing decisions and how the Internet context affects the processes of trust. Much refinement as well as extensions of current research are needed.

What we do know is that a wide variety of factors can help establish initial trust in a new online store. The empirical evidence suggests that trust affects a buyer's anticipated future interaction with the site. This is consistent with what Doney and Cannon (1997) found in industrial buying decisions: trust affects whether the customer is likely to include the retailer as part of the consideration set. Undoubtedly, it is important for the retailer to be part of the consideration set.

However, we do not know how trust affects the value of a particular exchange and buyer choice. Although we know how various antecedents affect consumer trust, we do not understand the effect on the seller and subsequent seller behavior. Bidirectionality of trust needs to be considered along with the dual effects of antecedents. Otherwise, results can be very misleading. Whether factors have negative or positive effects and whether these effects are linear or asymmetric is likely to be contingent on the context (Sirdeshmukh et al. 2002). We also have little knowledge of the effects of trust in the broader sociotechnical context of the Internet commerce system. Given the major gaps in our understanding, researchers should avoid simple blanket statements proclaiming the singular importance of trust in online consumer commerce such as, "Customers make Internet buying decisions on the basis of trust." . . . or . . . "Consumers must make online research and purchasing decisions almost *solely* [our italics] on the basis of trust" (Urban et al. 2000, 39).

The primary purpose of this article is to outline gaps in our current understanding and to propose trends for future research (see Table 13.2). Many of the trends are a function of research maturity rather than any deep insight on our part, and more are likely to emerge as new and innovative technologies and business models of e-commerce are conceptualized and implemented.

The community of researchers in online trust continues to grow, but their voluminous research to date has left us with limited understanding. With interest in trust remaining unabated, the prospect of research in the area maturing and contributing to a richer understanding remains promising.

NOTES

1. A knowledge-based view is centered on interpersonal relationships that are not purely economic, but based on social exchanges.

2. Trust does not necessarily have to be the result of calculations, but can be the result of historical calculations of like environments that have been incorporated as habit and norms into the human utility function, through the process of human evolution (Fukuyama 2001).

3. The literature offers many categorizations of trust. For example, McAllister (1995) distinguished between cognitive and affective trust. We are using the classification developed by Shapiro, Sheppard, and Cheraski (1992).

4. The term demand drafts is used in some countries.

REFERENCES

Appan, R., and Mellarkod, V. The impact of website design effectiveness on customer's trusting beliefs about a pure Internet retailer: A conceptual study. In *Proceedings of Ninth Americas Conference on Information Systems.* Tampa, Florida, 2003, pp. 257–268.

Atuahene-Gima, K., and Haiyang, L. When does trust matter? Antecedents and contingent effects of supervisee trust on performance in selling new products in China and the United States. *Journal of Marketing,* 66 (July 2002), 61–81.

Ba, S., and Pavlou, P.A. Evidence of the effect of trust building technology in electronic markets: Price premiums and buyer behavior. *MIS Quarterly,* 26, 3 (September 2002), 243–268.

Balasubramanian, S.; Peterson, R.A.; and Jarvenpaa, S.L. Exploring the implications of m-commerce for markets and marketing. *Journal of the Academy of Marketing Science,* vol. 30, issue 4 (Fall 2002), 348–361.

Bergen, M.; Dutta, S.; and Walker, O. Agency relationships in marketing: A review of the implications and applications of agency and related theories. *Journal of Marketing,* 56 (July 1992), 1–24.

Blau, P.M. *Exchange and Power in Social Life.* New York: Wiley, 1964.

Boyd, J. In community we trust: Online security communication at eBay. *Journal of Computer Mediated Communication,* 7, 3 (2002) n.p. (available at jcmc.indiana.edu/vol7/issue3/boyd.html).

Brenkert, G. Trust, morality and international business. In C. Lane and R. Bachman (eds.), *Trust Within and Between Organizations: Conceptual Issues and Empirical Applications.* New York: Oxford University Press, 1998, pp. 273–297.

Buchan, N.R.; Croson, R.T.A.; and Dawes, R.M. Swift neighbors and persistent strangers: A cross-cultural investigation of trust and reciprocity in social exchanges. *American Journal of Sociology,* 108, 1 (June 2002), 168–206.

Butler, J.K., Jr. Toward understanding and measuring conditions of trust: Evolution of a conditions of trust inventory. *Journal of Management,* 17 (1991), 643–663.

Cazier, J., and Gill, M.A. Values in e-business: Testing value compatibility and trust production in e-commerce. In *Proceedings of the Ninth American Conference on Information Systems.* Tampa, Florida, 2003, pp. 1723–1730.

Cheskin Research. eCommerce trust study, 1999 (available at www.cheskin.com, click "expertise").

Culnan, M.J., and Armstrong, P.K. Information privacy concerns, procedural fairness and impersonal trust: An empirical investigation. *Organization Science,* 10,1 (1999), 104–115.

DiMaggio, P., and Louch, H. Socially embedded consumer transactions: For what kinds of purchases do people most often use networks. *American Sociological Review,* 63, 5 (1998), 619–637.

Dirks, K.T., and Ferrin, D.L. The role of trust in organizational settings. *Organization Science,* 12, 4 (July–August 2001), 450–467.

Doney, P.M., and Cannon, J.P. An examination of the nature of trust in buyer-seller relationships. *Journal of Marketing,* 61 (1997), 35–51.

Fishbein, M., and Ajzen, I. *Belief, Attitude, Intention and Behavior: An Introduction to Theory and Research.* Reading, MA: Addison-Wesley, 1975.

Fukuyama, F. Social capital, civil society and development. *Third World Quarterly,* 22, 1 (2001), 7.

Gefen, D. E-commerce: The role of familiarity and trust. *Omega: The International Journal of Management Science,* 28, 6 (2000), 725–737.

———. Customer loyalty in e-commerce. *Journal of the Association of Information Systems,* 3 (2002), 27–52.

Gilmore, J.H., and Pine, B.J. *The Experience Economy.* Boston: Harvard Business School Press, 1999.

Grabner-Kraeuter, S. The role of consumer's trust in online shopping. *Journal of Business Ethics,* 39 (2002), 43–50.

Granovetter, M.S. The strength of weak ties. *American Journal of Sociology,* 78 (1973), 1360–1380.

Grazioli, S., and Jarvenpaa, S. Perils of Internet fraud. *IEEE Transaction on Systems, Man, and Cybernetics,* 30, 4 (2000), 395–410.

———. Consumer and business deception over the Internet: Content analysis of documentary evidence. *International Journal of Electronic Commerce,* 7, 4 (Summer 2003), 93–118.

Hogg, M.A., and Terry, D.J. Social identity and self-categorization processes in organizational contexts. *Academy of Management Review,* 25 (2000), 121–140.

Huang, J-H. Consumer evaluations of unethical behaviors of web sites: A cross cultural comparison. *Journal of International Consumer Marketing,* 13, 4 (2001), 51–71.

IFCC (The Internet Fraud Complaint Center). *IFCC 2002 Internet Fraud Report* 2003 (available at www1.ifccfbi.gov/strategy/2002_IFCCReport.pdf, accessed August 17, 2003).

Jarvenpaa, S.L., and Tiller, E.H. Consumer trust in virtual environments: A managerial perspective. *Boston University Law Review,* 81, 3 (June 2001), 665–686.

Jarvenpaa, S.L., and Tractinsky, N. Consumer trust in an Internet store: A cross-cultural validation. *Journal of Computer Mediated Communication,* 5, 2 (1999), 1–35.

Jarvenpaa, S.L.; Tractinsky, N.; and Vitale, M. Consumer trust in an Internet store. *Information Technology and Management Special Issue on Electronic Commerce,* 1, 1–2 (2000), 45–72.

Johnson, E.J.; Bellman, S.; and Lohse, G.L. Cognitive lock-in and the power law of practice. *Journal of Marketing,* 67 (April 2003), 62–73.

Kauffman, R., and Wood, C. Running up the bid: Modeling seller opportunism in Internet auctions. In *The Proceedings of the 2000 Americas Conference on Information Systems.* Long Beach, CA, August 10–13, 2000, n.p.

Keen, P., and McDonald, M. *The eProcess Edge: Creating Customer Value and Business in the Internet Era.* New York: McGraw-Hill, 2000.

Kelman, H.C., and Hamilton, V.L. *Crimes of Obedience.* New Haven, CT: Yale University Press, 1989.

Kenny, D., and Marshall, J.F. Contextual marketing: The real business of the Internet. *Harvard Business Review,* 78, 6 (2000), 119.

Kim, D. The effects of trust-assuring arguments on consumer trust in Internet stores. In *Proceedings of the Ninth Americas Conference on Information Systems.* Tampa, Florida, 2003, pp. 3332–3337.

Kim, D.J.; Ferrin, D.L.; and Rao, H.R. Antecedents of consumer trust in B-to-C electronic commerce. In *Proceedings of the Ninth Americas Conference on Information Systems.* Tampa, Florida, 2003, pp. 157–167.

Kramer, R.M. Cooperation and organizational identification. In K. Murnighan (ed.), *Social Psychology in Organizations: Advances in Theory and Research.* Englewood Cliffs, NJ: Prentice Hall, 1993, pp. 244–268.

———. Trust and distrust in organizations: Emerging perspectives, enduring questions. *Annual Review of Psychology,* 50 (1999), 569–598.

Kramer, R.M., and Brewer, M.A. Social identity and emergence of cooperation in resource conservation dilemmas. In H. Wilke, C. Rutter, and D.M. Messick (eds.), *Experimental Studies of Social Dilemmas.* Frankfurt, Germany: Peter Lang, 1986, pp. 205–234.

Kramer, R.M.; Brewer, M.B.; and Hanna, B.A. Collective trust and collective action: The decision to trust as a social decision. In R.M. Kramer and T.R. Tyler (eds.), *Trust in Organizations: Frontiers of Theory and Research.* Thousand Oaks, CA: Sage Publications, 1996, pp. 357–389.

Lee, J.K., and Rao, H.R. A study of customers' trusting beliefs in government-to-customer online services. In *Proceedings of the Ninth Americas Conference on Information Systems.* Tampa, Florida, 2003, pp. 821–826.

Lee, J.; Kim, J.; and Moon, J.Y. What makes Internet users visit cyber stores again? Key design factors for customer loyalty. In *Proceedings of CHI 2000.* New York, April 2000, pp. 305–312.

Lewicki, R.J., and Bunker, B.B. Developing and maintaining trust in work relationships. In R.M. Kramer and T.R. Tyler (eds.), *Trust in Organizations: Frontiers of Theory and Research.* Thousand Oaks, CA: Sage Publications, 1996, pp. 114–139.

Li, Y. Is trust the whole story? Rethinking online auction via network exchange theory. In *Proceedings of the Ninth Americas Conference on Information Systems.* Tampa, Florida, 2003, pp. 2919–2924.

Lombard, M., and Ditton, T. At the heart of it all: The concept of presence. *Journal of Computer-Mediated Communication,* 3, 2 (1997) (available at jcmc.indiana.edu/jcmc/o13/issue2/lombard.html). jcmc.indiana.edu/vol3/issue2/lombard.html.

Luhmann, N. *Trust and Power.* Chichester, UK: Wiley, 1979.

McAllister, D.J. Affect and cognition-based trust as foundations for interpersonal cooperation in organizations. *Academy of Management Journal,* 13 (1995), 363–380.

McKnight, D.H.; Cummings, L.L.; and Chervany, N.L. Initial trust formation in new organizational relationships. *Academy of Management Review,* 23, 3 (1998), 473–490.

Myerson, D.; Weick, K.E.; and Kramer, R.M. Swift trust and temporary groups. In R.M. Kramer and T.R. Tyler (eds.), *Trust in Organizations: Frontiers of Theory and Research.* Thousand Oaks, CA: Sage Publications, 1996. pp. 166–195.

Naguin, C.E., and Paulson, G.D. Online bargaining and interpersonal trust. *Journal of Applied Psychology,* 88, 1 (2003), 113–120.

Orlikowski, W. Improvising organizational transformation over time: A situated change perspective. *Information Systems Research,* 7, 1 (1996), 63–92.

Pavlou, P.A. Consumer acceptance of electronic commerce: Integrating trust and risk with the technology acceptance model. *International Journal of Electronic Commerce,* 7, 3 (Spring 2003), 101–134.

Radcliff, D. Trusting the Internet. *Computerworld,* 33, 18 (1999), 46–47.

Robinson, S.L. Trust and the breach of the psychological contract. *Administrative Science Quarterly,* 41, 4 (1996), 574–599.

Rosenbaum, H.; Davenport, E.; and Swan, M. Situational trust in digital markets: A socio-technical exploration. In *Proceedings of the Ninth Americas Conference on Information Systems.* Tampa, Florida, 2003, pp. 1761–1765.

Rotter, J. Inter-personal trust, trustworthiness and gullibility. *American Psychologist,* 35 (1980), 1–7.

Rousseau, D.; Sitkin, S.; Burt, R.; and Camerer, C. Not so different after all: A cross-discipline view of trust. *Academy of Management Review,* 23, 3 (1998), 393–404.

Shapiro, D.L.; Sheppard, B.H.; and Cheraski, L. Business on a handshake. *Negotiation Journal,* 3 (1992), 365–377.

Sirdeshmukh, D.; Singh, J.; and Sabol, B. Consumer trust, value, and loyalty in relational exchanges. *Journal of Marketing,* 66 (January 2002), 15–37.

Spector, R. *Amazon.com: Get Big Fast.* New York: HarperCollins Publishers, 2000.

Stewart, K.J. Trust transfer on the world wide web. *Organization Science,* 14, 1 (2003), 5–18.

Stewart, K.J., and Zhang, Y. Effects of the nature and direction of hypertext links on trust transfer. A paper presented at the *Academy of Management Conference,* Seattle, Washington, August 4, 2003, n.p.

Strub, P.J., and Priest, T.B. Two patterns of establishing trust: The marijuana user. *Sociological Focus,* 9, 4 (1976), 399–411.

Tan, Y-H, and Thoen, W. Formal aspects of a generic model of trust for electronic commerce. In *Proceedings of the 33rd Hawaii International Conference on Systems Sciences.* Los Alamitos, CA: IEEE Computer Society Press, 2000, pp. 1–8.

Tractinsky, N., and Rao, V.S. Social dimensions of Internet shopping: Theory-based arguments for web-store design. *Human Systems Management,* 20, 2 (2001), 105–122.

Urban, G.L.; Sultan, F.; and Qualls, W.J. Placing trust at the center of your Internet strategy. *Sloan Management Review,* 42, 1 (Fall 2000), 39–49.

Williamson, O.E. *The Economic Institutions of Capitalism: Firms, Markets, and Relational Contracting.* New York: The Free Press, 1985.

Yoon, S-J. The antecedents and consequences of trust in online-purchase decisions. *Journal of Interactive Marketing,* 16, 2 (Spring 2002), 47–63.

Zucker, LG. Production of trust: Institutional sources of economic structure 1840–1920. *Research in Organizational Behavior,* 8 (1986), 53–111.

CHAPTER 14

SPOTTING LEMONS IN THE PKI MARKET

ENGENDERING TRUST BY SIGNALING QUALITY

JAMES BACKHOUSE, CAROL HSU, JOHN BAPTISTA, AND JIMMY C. TSENG

Abstract: *Public key infrastructure (PKI) has emerged as a critical technology for identity management in e-commerce and e-government and over a hundred certification authorities (CAs) across the globe offer certification services. Despite the passing of legislation in many countries to give equal legal weight to electronic and handwritten signatures, the overall market for digital certificates has not expanded as much as it was originally expected to. The literature indicates a range of possible issues that are holding back wide-scale adoption of PKI, ranging from technical to policy, legal, and regulatory hindrances. In this paper, we focus on the question of quality uncertainty, and hence on trust, and use an economic theory, the lemons principle, to examine the market context for digital certificates. A review follows of three ways—brand names, guarantees, and licensing—to signal the quality of certificates and so engender some of the trust that is required for the relying party to accept and use certificates when they are offered.*

Keywords: *Asymmetry of Information, Economics of Information Systems, Information Security, Interoperability, Public Key Infrastructure*

INTRODUCTION

The value of economic theories in the study of information systems (IS) has been demonstrated both by IS researchers and economists. In the IS field, for example, such work includes Malone, Yates, and Benjamin (1987) on the use of the market and hierarchy model, Ciborra (1993) on the use of transaction cost theory, and Wigand (1997) on the summary of economic approaches to study electronic commerce (e-commerce). In the economics field, Shapiro and Varian (2002) have used economic theory to analyze information goods and their dynamics in markets. More recently, researchers in the IS security area have begun to use economic theory to better understand the economic phenomena underpinning security threats and the properties of the markets for security services (Anderson 2003). In 2002, well-known scholars and practitioners in the IS and economics fields, such as Ross Anderson, Lawrence Gordon, Bruce Schneier, and Hal Varian, set up an annual workshop, "Economics and Information Security," illustrating the growth in interest in this interdisciplinary approach.[1] In keeping with this shift in thinking, this chapter examines the current disappointing market situation of public key infrastructure (PKI) through the lens of economic theory.

In recent years, PKI has been developed as a key security technology to provide trust in online transactions and communications. However, some argue that technical difficulties (Ellison and

Schneier 2000, Lloyd 2001), legal and regulatory obstacles (Froomkin 1996), and privacy concerns (Greenleaf and Clarke 1997) have prevented PKI from reaching the expected level of success and use. In this chapter, we take a market approach to examine the underlying economic dynamics surrounding PKI. We argue that some of the hesitancy in adopting PKI arises from the existence of quality uncertainty in the PKI market. To demonstrate our argument, we apply Akerlof's lemons principle and illustrate the problem of asymmetric information in the PKI market. The implications of information asymmetry for e-commerce (Bakos 2001) and electronic marketplaces (Kauffman and Wood 2000) have not gone unnoticed, and the concept is used increasingly in the design of countermeasures (Lai et al. 1994, Millen and Wright 2000).

In the second section, below, we describe PKI and its current vicissitudes. Akerlof's economic theory, the lemons principle, is used in the third section to explain the problem of quality uncertainty resulting from asymmetry of information between buyers and sellers in markets. In the same section, we also briefly discuss the three countermeasures proposed by Akerlof. In the fourth section, we identify the existence of a "lemons problem" in the PKI market and examine how countermeasures might be adopted to reduce this quality uncertainty.

PKI AS A TRUST MECHANISM IN E-COMMERCE

Trust in e-commerce can be understood in terms of security principles such as authentication, confidentiality, authorization, and nonrepudiation (Wilson 1999). In the world of written contracts, these principles can be realized through face-to-face encounters, contracts supported by handwritten signatures, and by the established legal framework. To foster the growth of e-commerce, both consumers and businesses need to have confidence in the enforceability and confidentiality of any electronic contract or message exchanged. Accordingly, PKI has been developed with the intention of realizing these security principles in an electronic environment.

Adams and Lloyd (1999) define PKI as "a pervasive security infrastructure whose services are implemented and delivered using public-key concepts and techniques" (33). Indeed, the concept of PKI is nothing new. The use of public key cryptography, also known as asymmetric key cryptography, began in the late 1970s (Clarke 2001). In order to resolve the problem of key distribution in symmetric key cryptography, Diffie and Hellman in 1976 proposed the concept of public key cryptography: the use of different keys to encrypt and decrypt a message. After years of development and evolution, this technique in conjunction with PKI provides the basis for digital signatures and other secure networking protocols.

Public key algorithms provide the mechanisms of digital signatures and message integrity that serve as forensic evidence in electronic transactions (Ford and Baum 1997). The reliability of the forensic evidence depends on the ability of the certification authority (CA) to bind identities to their public keys in a digital certificate. A public key infrastructure therefore consists of digital certificates issued by CAs and registration authorities to subscribers and relied upon by relying parties. Each PKI domain is based on a certificate policy that "indicates the applicability of a certificate to a particular community and/or class of application with common security requirements" (Chokhani and Ford 1999). Each CA within a PKI domain may also publish a Certificate Practice Statement (CPS) detailing the practices it employs when issuing certificates. It is through these important documents that CAs "reduce risk in transacting, establish trust among e-trading parties, thus providing the much-needed security for electronic commerce" (Tseng and Backhouse 2000).

Thus, in the PKI model, CAs bear the greatest responsibility for establishing trust in the electronic world between two mutually unfamiliar identities. CAs are responsible for verifying an applicant's identity, issuing the digital identity certificate, and managing the certificate life cycle. If a CA makes a mistake at any stage of the certificate life cycle, it increases the opportunity for fraud or other malpractice occasioned by the reliance on a certificate. For example, an incident in January 2001 resulted in VeriSign issuing two code-signing digital certificates to someone posing as a Microsoft employee (Liew 2001). VeriSign was found at fault in its identification procedures. If this mistake had not been discovered in time, the consequences could have been damaging.

With the expansion of e-commerce, many companies have been setting up as CAs offering the service of certificate issuance to the public. Our research shows that around the world there are currently at least 100 public-facing CAs. However, we maintain that the considerable growth of PKI services within such a short time scale has led to quality uncertainty in the market. In a typical electronic transaction, trading parties use digital identity certificates as their means of identification and authentication. In the situation of open e-commerce, a digital identity certificate offered as a credential by a subscriber may come from any CA within or outside the same PKI domain. In the marketplace there exist many different PKI policy domains, each with its own practices for binding an identity to a certificate. As a result of these variances in certificate policy and security procedures, relying parties cannot be completely certain that certificates emanating from an unknown CA can be trusted and, hence, whether to rely on them.

The role of quality uncertainty and asymmetric information and its impact on markets has been a core subject of study within the economics field. From an economics perspective, the situation we describe above, the existence of quality uncertainty in the PKI market, is a classic example of a "lemons problem" originating in asymmetry of information. The next section explains this concept and some possible countermeasures for addressing it.

THE LEMONS PRINCIPLE

The 2001 Nobel Prize for Economics was awarded jointly to George Akerlof, Michael Spence, and Joseph Stiglitz for their analyses of markets with asymmetric information. This recognition confirms the timeless significance of research on how buyers and sellers come together to form markets. Understanding the dynamics of markets is fundamental not only for traditional markets, but also for new ones, such as the markets for trust and security services.

In his seminal paper, "The market for 'lemons': quality uncertainty and the market mechanism," Akerlof (1970) studied markets with informational gaps between buyers and sellers, and developed the "lemons principle" as a theoretical framework for understanding the dynamics of markets with this characteristic. He argues that in markets where the quality of the goods is not assessed in the same way by buyers and sellers, the bad-quality goods and services tend to drive out the good-quality ones, and as a consequence lead to market extinction. Akerlof uses the used-car market as an example. The buyer fears getting stuck with a lemon, and the seller of a good-quality car fears not being able to get a fair price for it.

Akerlof explains that, although each individual seller knows the real quality of the good, the buyer does not have access to the same information and is not able to distinguish between good- and bad-quality wares. Therefore, the buyer measures the quality of the goods from the market as a whole and is led to assume that all goods in the market have the same average quality. Owing to this asymmetry of information, the seller has an incentive to market lower-quality goods for the same average price. At the same time, the better-quality goods will not be traded in the market because their true value may not be captured. Consequently, the average quality of goods tends to fall, as well as the size of the market. In extreme circumstances, no market will exist at all.

To illustrate this phenomenon, Akerlof uses the example of the used-car market in the United

States. In this market, there are used cars of good and bad quality available. However, the sellers have more information about the true quality of the cars than the buyers, which creates asymmetry of information. Because of the imperfect information in the market (buyers are not able to assess the true quality of the cars offered by the sellers and are led to assume a market average quality), the price of a given used car will be the same, regardless of its quality. Akerlof (1970) further points out that the market price will always be the bad car price. As a result, the good-quality car owners will not sell their cars in this market because they cannot realize the true value of their cars. The bad cars gradually drive the good cars out of the market and only bad cars will be traded.

The lemons model may also be used to analyze the cost of dishonesty. In a market where goods are sold both honestly and dishonestly, quality may be represented fairly or misrepresented. The buyer's problem is to identify quality. As in the "lemons" car case, the existence in the market of people willing to offer inferior goods tends to drive the market out of existence. Thus, dishonest dealings have a tendency to force honest dealings out of the market, to the extent that no market is possible. To strengthen his argument as to the negative impact of information asymmetry on markets, Akerlof (1970) also analyzes the situation of symmetry of information, where all parties share good-quality information and there is information transparency. In this case, a market is possible and all parties are better off for being able to distinguish the good from the bad cars.

There are two possible consequences of asymmetric information in markets: adverse selection and moral hazard. Adverse selection is illustrated by the example of the insurance market, where, as the premiums rise, the more likely it is that only people that need the insurance (those in the worst health conditions) will buy it. Still, in the insurance example, moral hazard is illustrated by the fact that the insured will not be as careful in taking risks as they would without the insurance. The work of Akerlof has been widely used in the study of markets and adopted by several authors as a generic model of market failure caused by quality uncertainty (Bond 1982; Heinkel 1981; Leland 1979).

More recently, the June 2002 edition of the *American Economic Review* contains the papers of Akerlof, Spence, and Stiglitz, based on their public lectures upon being awarded the 2002 Nobel Prize in Economics. In these papers they challenge neoclassical economic models and advocate the use of the more robust behavioral economics. Akerlof (2002) revisits his lemons principle and argues for the need to incorporate asymmetry of information in economic models. Spence and Stiglitz both reexamine their proposed countermeasures for the lemons problem. The former describes *signaling* devices that enable the well-informed part to signal their true quality to the less informed part, while the latter examines *screening* devices, where the less informed are able to distinguish the quality from the better informed by inscribing an auto-selection process in their decisions. The next section elaborates on the concept of signaling in combating lemons problems.

Concept of Signaling

Many researchers have suggested ways in which the market problems of quality uncertainty and information asymmetry may be reduced. One possible solution is through the concept of *signaling* (Spence 1973). Advocates argue that sellers of the product or service should be allowed to issue costly signals of the quality being offered. In a rational equilibrium, prospective buyers could use these signals to discriminate accurately between products of differing quality (Bhattacharya 1979, 1980, Ross 1977, Spence 1973, 1974, 1977). Campbell and Kracaw (1980) propose another solution: that sellers make side payments to information producers to acquire the necessary information at a cost, and convey it to the market. Following this line of thinking, Thakor (1982) proposes the idea of the third party. He identifies three parties in the market structure: a group of sellers, each aware of the quality of its own product; a set of buyers who satisfy the rational-expectations assumption that they are aware of the average quality of the products in the market, but are unable to distinguish one seller from the other on the basis of product quality; and "third-party" information producers who expend resources to produce information about the quality of each product offered for sale. Thakor argues that market failure as explained by the lemons principle can be prevented if imperfectly informed buyers of a given product can somehow revise their initial, *a priori,* conditional estimates of product quality.

At a specific level, Akerlof (1970) suggests that market players can implement three types of countermeasures to mitigate the effects of asymmetry of information: guarantees, brand names, and licensing. Guarantees exist to assure the buyer of normal expected quality. Brand names not only serve to indicate quality but also offer a better chance of consumer retaliation should quality not match expectation. Umbrella branding (where new products are associated with older brands) is often used for quality perception extension. Licensing, certification, and even education can also reduce quality uncertainty. For example, skilled labor often requires certain licenses and certificates to work and employers also use educational qualifications, such as degrees, to reduce uncertainty about an employee's quality.

This part of the chapter has briefly identified some countermeasures for overcoming the lemons problem. The next section applies the lemons principle to the PKI context. From this analysis it is possible to recognize the existence of quality uncertainty in the PKI market. We also examine how the market is currently institutionalizing the three countermeasures proposed by Akerlof to combat this problem.

APPLYING THE LEMONS PRINCIPLE TO THE PKI MARKET

As discussed in the preceding section, Akerlof (1970) considers a general class of situations in which quality uncertainty about a product combines with "unravelling effects" on individual behavior to influence the average quality of the products traded and sometimes the actual existence of the market for the good. We now apply the lemons principle to the PKI environment and have chosen the used-car market as an analogy for information asymmetry in the PKI market.

In the used-car market there are two main parties involved: the seller and the buyer. In the PKI market, there is, on the one hand, the party that accepts (or not) the digital certificate, that is, the relying party, and there is, on the other hand, the issuer of the certificate, that is, the CA. Trust is required when the relying party has to make a transaction decision based on the credibility of the information provided by the digital certificate.

In Akerlof's example, used cars could be of various grades of quality between good and bad. Likewise, in the PKI market there are certificates with various qualities. As discussed above, the spread of CAs throughout the world, with their different procedures, technologies, and legal frameworks, has contributed to the existence in the market of certificates with variable quality. In addition, we argue that consumers' unfamiliarity with the use of digital certificates for electronic authentication and transactions has further exacerbated the problem of imperfect information. Many certificate users have no technical or legal understanding of how digital certificates really work and what the associated risks are. This creates the incentive for opportunistic behavior by CAs to underinvest in technology and operational procedures for the creation of digital certificates, which in turn compromises the quality of the certificate. Following the logic of the "lemons principle," we maintain that this market exhibits an asymmetry of information between the CA and the relying party. As a consequence, relying parties are unable to distinguish the quality of a digital certificate and hence assume that all certificates are of average quality. Therefore, good-quality certificates will be seen and accepted as if they are of average quality. This could lead, after several feedback loops, to only low-quality certificates remaining in the market, the bad-quality certificate driving out the good.

However, as suggested by Akerlof (1970), the problem of information asymmetry can be circumvented or mitigated. Three different signaling mechanisms can provide credible information about the quality of the digital certificate to the relying party, and, as a result, the relying party is able to assess the real quality of the digital certificate and the level of risk associated with its acceptance. Incorporating this new information into a risk-management strategy, a relying party can then make an informed decision as to whether to accept a particular certificate or not. Without the signaling devices, it can be a difficult task to distinguish the quality of the incoming certificate, and the "lemons" effect may sink the PKI market entirely.

Signaling of Certificate Quality in the PKI Market

As indicated above, Akerlof (1970) suggests three mechanisms for reducing quality uncertainty in the market: guarantees, brand names, and licensing. For this research, we utilized primarily secondary data sources, for example, government reports, industry reports, and online search results. We conducted data analysis in accordance with the criteria of guarantees, brand names, and licensing and discuss below how these mechanisms were implemented and what issues remain for further consideration.

On the implementation of guarantees, Akerlof (1970) makes a point that the provision of a guarantee by the seller can offer a degree of assurance about the product or service to the buyer. In the PKI market, the disclosure of certification practices is intended to establish confidence in the CA. However, the mechanism used to signal quality is curtailed by statements limiting liability in a CPS. The industry CPS standard RFC2527 recommends that the CA should declare its liability clearly under the section "Limitation and Warranty." However, our research shows that in reality there is no standard practice regarding the extent of liability of a CA in the event of a security breach or for any other damages caused by the use or reliance on a digital certificate. Furthermore, most CAs set a limit for liability associated with different types of certificates. These are crafted to limit the CA's liability. To complicate the problem further, each CA often has its own classification scheme defining the types of certificates and its associated limitations.

There are other concerns regarding this countermeasure. In general, before accepting a digital certificate, a relying party needs to understand the limitations or conditions of liability. Thus, for each unknown certificate, relying parties need to go through the exercise of locating the CPS as well as understanding its content. There are several problems in this process. First, our research shows that not all CPSs are available online. Since the CPS may contain detailed information on its security procedures, some CAs maintain that publishing a CPS increases risk unacceptably. Second, there is no guarantee that the language in which the CPS is written is intelligible to the relying party. In the case that the CPS is inscrutable, the relying party has no way of knowing what protection is available from the CA under the terms of the guarantees in the CPS. Finally, with no case law yet to establish precedent, it is unclear which laws might apply to digital certificates and how the courts might apply them. Hence, until there are precedents, it may be difficult to use liability as a sole device for eliminating poor-quality certificates in the market.

The second countermeasure, in Akerlof's view, is the use of brand names. Market research literature has shown that, when purchasing a product, a brand name is an important element in a consumer's decision-making process (Chu and Chu 1994, Jacoby 1977). Thus, in promoting a new product or service, manufacturers can use brand names as a signal for product quality. In the PKI market, we also detect the adoption of branding as a marketing strategy for attracting potential certificate subscribers and assuring quality to the relying party. Our research indicates that many CAs in the market have been established by either telecommunication companies or postal service companies. Such companies already have experience in providing trust services, such as passport registration or telephone directories. It would be natural for them to extend their existing services to the trust services market. Instead of setting up a new company, these organizations are using their existing brand names to advertise their new services. This fits well with what Wernerfelt (1988) described as "umbrella branding." The practice of umbrella branding is to use the established brand name for promoting new experience goods. Wernerfelt refers to experience goods as products "whose quality cannot be determined by inspection, so that consumers need to buy the product to learn its quality" (1988, 458). Further, he asserts that only firms with two good-quality products would use this branding strategy, otherwise, an old product with bad quality would consequently lead to the loss of both products. In the context of the PKI market, many consumers have already relied on the same telecommunication or postal services for many years, and generally have good faith in their quality. Therefore, when these companies launch a new service, such as certification, consumers may tend to assume that the service quality offered by these companies will be better than that of others in the market.

Chain stores can have the same level of impact in the market as brand names. One good example is the dominant position of McDonald's as compared with a local hamburger joint. In the PKI market, we found that the chain store strategy is also alive and prospering for such companies as VeriSign or GlobalSign. To penetrate the market, as well as to capture a large market share, these companies have seized the first-mover advantage by entering the market early and have expanded by establishing a network of CAs in different parts of the world. The "chain store" network is constructed either by strategic alliances or by setting up local companies. For instance, our research shows that, at present, GlobalSign and VeriSign have established networks of global alliance or partnerships. From the perspective of the chain store strategy, when consumers face the choice of different CAs, they often choose the one with a global reputation: companies such as VeriSign and GlobalSign will stand out from other CAs. As well as utilizing multinational branding, the chain store strategy can also be implemented through the game of being "one of the club," such as VeriSign Network and Identrus. VeriSign demonstrated the success of this strategy by reporting an increase in earnings in 2001 (see VeriSign Financial Report 2001). However, we recommend that more research is required before a judgment can be made on the effectiveness of the brand name and the chain store strategy as signals for certificate service quality.

The third mechanism for signaling product quality is the method of licensing. In the economics field, the notion of imposing minimum quality standards has been applied both to professions and to products. Leland (1979) offers the example of licensing doctors or accountants as well as drugs. Swann and Temple (1996) investigate the effect of standards on trade performance. In their work, they analyzed the impact of British standards on exports and imports performance in the UK context. The findings suggest that "UK standards appears to increase UK exports and UK imports, though the effect on exports is stronger than on imports" (1311). In the IS security field, licensing and minimum quality standards have also been around for a long time. Examples include the Orange Book on security product evaluation, BS7799 on IS security management, and Certified Information Systems Auditor (CISA) on IS security professionals. In the context of the PKI market, we discern two broad types of licensing methods: compulsory licensing and voluntary accreditation. The former refers to the situation in which a CA needs to meet certain legal requirements in order to operate in a

Table 14.1

Signaling Strategy in the PKI Market

Examples of CAs in the PKI market	Guarantee	Brand name	Licensing
VeriSign	CPS	VeriSign Network	WebTrust, Gatekeeper[1]
Baltimore	CPS	Global subsidiaries and alliance	WebTrust, Gatekeeper
GlobalSign	CPS	GlobalSign strategic license program	WebTrust
Entrust	CPS	Global subsidiaries and alliance	WebTrust
OnSite, BT Ignite	CPS	Extension of the telecommunication service	tScheme
Australia Key Post	CPS	Extension of the postal service	Gatekeeper
Hong Kong Post	CPS	Extension of the postal service	Compliance with the Electronic Transactions Ordinance

[1]VeriSign Australia is operated under the name of eSign.

country or a particular community. The latter refers to the situation in which a CA voluntarily takes up an accreditation scheme. Compulsory schemes are practiced in some countries, such as those embodied in the Digital Signature Act in Malaysia and the Digital Document Regulations in Italy. In these countries, governments can assure consumers that all CAs meet the minimum quality standard. In legal terms, this is also known as the technology-specific approach (Kuner et al. 2000, Wilson 2001).

Voluntary accreditation can also be offered by government agents or commercial entities. Examples of these schemes include Gatekeeper in Australia, WebTrust in North America, and tScheme in the UK. This type of scheme is most likely to be implemented in countries that subscribe to a technology-neutral or two-tier legal approach. In these countries, there are no mandatory requirements governing the operation of CAs. We consider two reasons why a CA might pursue a particular voluntary accreditation scheme. First, a CA might take up a scheme because of business requirements. In the case of Gatekeeper, the government only accepts certificates issued by a Gatekeeper-certified CA. In the case of WebTrust, Microsoft now requires that, for Root CAs to be included in Microsoft Explorer, they must have succeeded in the WebTrust audit (KPMG 2002). Thus, in order to attract certificate subscribers who wish to do business, say, with the Australian government or through Microsoft Explorer, a CA must invest in acquiring voluntary accreditation. Second, a CA might decide to use an accreditation scheme as a device to increase the level of consumer trust in general. For instance, with the seal of approval from tScheme accreditation in the UK, CAs such as Certificate Factory and OnSite can demonstrate their quality service to the public. Nevertheless, there are variances in the evaluation criteria that apply to the existing CA accreditation schemes. In our view, more government and industry effort is still needed to ensure the quality standard across different accreditation schemes.

Table 14.1 shows an example of CAs that undertake different signaling mechanisms in the PKI markets. VeriSign, Baltimore, GlobalSign, and Entrust are global market leaders, while OnSite, Australia Key Post, and Hong Kong Post are examples of CAs operating in specific geopolitical areas.

CONCLUSIONS

In this chapter we have demonstrated the nature of information asymmetry in the PKI market by using the "lemons principle." We then examined both the problems of, and possible countermeasures for, quality uncertainty in the current PKI market. Besides applying the model to analyze the PKI market, we further discussed the current value of three countermeasures for addressing quality uncertainty in the market. In this discussion, we examined how each method is currently implemented in the PKI market and what further problems need to be addressed in order to increase the effectiveness of any such signal. As a result of this discussion, we hope to increase understanding of the barriers holding back adoption of PKI and to offer an economic perspective on a resolution. While we acknowledge the technical difficulties and the legal and policy obstacles addressed within the information security literature, we contend that the problem of information asymmetry is a contributory factor in the slow take-up of digital certificates in the PKI market. Embracing an economic perspective brings additional insight into the mechanisms for enhancing the level of trust and confidence in third-party trusted services and consequently for e-commerce in general.

ACKNOWLEDGMENTS

Funding support from grant number L142251004, the ESRC/DTI Management of Information LINK program, is gratefully received. An earlier version of this paper was presented at the 11th European Conference on Information Systems.

NOTE

1. The workshop information is available at www.sims.berkeley.edu/resources/affiliates/workshops/econsecurity/.

REFERENCES

Adams, C., and Lloyd, S. *Understanding Public Key Infrastructure: Concepts, Standards and Deployment Consideration.* Indianapolis, IN: Macmillan Technical Publishing, 1999.

Akerlof, G. The market for 'lemons': Quality uncertainty and the market mechanism. *Quarterly Journal of Economics,* 89 (1970), 488–500.

Akerlof, G. Behavioral macroeconomics and macroeconomics behavior. *American Economic Review,* 92, 3 (2002), 411–423.

Anderson, R. Economics and security resource page (available at www.cl.cam.ac.uk/~rja14/econsec.html, accessed on 23 April 2003).

Bakos, Y. The emerging landscape for retail e-commerce. *Journal of Economic Perspectives* (January 2001), 69–80.

Bhattacharya, S. Imperfect information, dividend policy, and the "bird in the hand fallacy." *The Bell Journal of Economics,* 10 (1979), 259–270.

———. Nondissipative signaling structures and dividend policy. *Quarterly Journal of Economics,* 95 (1980), 1–24.

Bond, E.A. Direct test of the lemons model: The market for used pick-up trucks. *The American Economic Review,* 72 (1982), 836–840.

Campbell, T., and Kracaw, W. Information production, market signaling and the theory of financial intermediation. *Journal of Finance,* 35 (1980), 863–882.

Chokhani, S., and Ford, W. Internet X.509 public key infrastructure—Certificate policy and certification practices framework. *IETF RFC 2527,* 1999 (available at www.ietf.org/rfc/rfc2527.txt;accwssed on September 30, 2005).

Chu, W., and Chu, W. Signaling quality by selling through a reputable retailer: An example of renting the reputation of another agent. *Marketing Science,* 13, 2 (1994), 177–189.

Ciborra, C. *Teams, Markets and Systems: Business Innovation and Information Technology.* Cambridge, UK: Cambridge University Press, 1993.

Clarke, R. The fundamental inadequacies of conventional public key infrastructure. In *Global Co-Operation in the New Millennium.* Bled, Slovenia, June 27–29, 2001, pp. 148–159.

Ellison, C., and Schneier, B. Ten risks of PKI: What you are not being told about public key infrastructure. *Computer Security Journal,* XVI (2000), 1–8.

Ford, W., and Baum, M. *Secure Electronic Commerce: Building the Infrastructure for Digital Signatures and Encryption.* Upper Saddle River, NJ: Prentice Hall, 1997.

Froomkin, M.A. The essential role of trusted third parties in electronic commerce. *Oregon Law Review,* 75 (1996), 49.

Greenleaf, G., and Clarke, R. Privacy implications of digital signatures. *IBC Conference on Digital Signatures,* Sydney, 1997.

Heinkel, R. Uncertainty product quality: The market for lemons with an imperfect testing technology. *The Bell Journal of Economics,*12 (1981), 625–636.

Jacoby, J.; Szybillo, G.; and Busato-Schach, J. Information acquisition behavior in brand choice situations. *Journal of Consumer Research* 3, 4 (1977), 209–216.

Kauffman, R.J., and Wood, C. Analyzing competition and collusion strategies in electronic marketplaces with information asymmetry. *University of Minnesota Management Information Systems Research Center Working Paper* No. 00–19, 2000.

KPMG. *Digital Certificates, Authentication and Trust on the Internet* (available at www.kpmg.nl/irm, accessed on August 2002).

Kuner, C., Barcelo, R.; Baker, S. and Greenwald, E. An analysis of international electronic and digital signature implementation initiatives. *The Internet Law and Policy Forum,* September 2000 (available at www.ilpf.org/groups/analysis_IEDSII.htm, accessed September 30, 2005).

Lai, C.; Medvinsky, G.; and Neuman, C. Endorsements, licensing, and insurance for distributed system services. In *Proceedings of the 2nd ACM Conference on Computer and Communication Security.* November 1994, pp. 170–175.

Leland, H. Quacks, lemons and licensing: A theory of minimum quality standards. *Journal of Political Economy,* 87 (1979), 1328–1346.

Liew, M. Digital certificate fraud. *Computerworld* 7, 21 (April 2001), 6–12.

Lloyd, S.; Fillingham, D.; Lampard, R.; and Orlowski, S. CA-CA interoperability. White paper, PKI Forums Technology Working Group (March 2001) (available at www.pk.forum.org/pdfs/ca-ca_interop.pdf, accessed September 30, 2005).

Malone, T.; Yates, J.; and Benjamin, R. Electronic markets and electronic hierarchies. *Communications of the ACM* 30, 6 (1987), 484–497.

Millen, K., and Wright, R. Reasoning about trust and insurance in a public key infrastructure. In *Proceedings of The 13th Computer Security Foundations Workshop.* July 3–5, 2000, Cambridge, England.

Ross, S. The determination of financial structure: The incentive signaling approach. *The Bell Journal of Economics,* 8 (1977), 23–40.

Shapiro, C., and Varian, H. *Information Rules: A Strategic Guide to the Network Economy.* Boston: Harvard Business School Press, 2002.

Spence, M. Job market signaling. *Quarterly Journal of Economics,* 87 (1973), 355–374.

———. Competitive and optimal responses to signals: Analysis of efficiency and distribution. *Journal of Economic Theory,* 7 (1974), 296–332.

———. Consumer misperceptions, product failure and producer liability. *Review of Economic Studies,*3 (1977), 561–572.

Swann, P., and Temple, P. Standards and trade performance: The UK experience. *The Economic Journal* 106, 438 (1996), 1297–1313.

Thakor, A. An exploration of competitive signaling equilibria with "third party" information production: The case of debt insurance. *Journal of Finance,* 37 (1982), 717–739.

Tseng, J., and Backhouse, J. Searching for meaning—Performatives and obligations in public key infrastructure. In *Proceedings of The Fifth International Workshop on the Language-Action Perspective on Communication Modeling.* LAP2000: Aachen, Germany, 2000, n.p.

VeriSign Financial Report. 2001 (available at www.verisign.com/static/000745.pdf).

Wernerfelt, B. Umbrella branding as a signal of new product quality: An example of signaling by posting a bond. *Rand Journal of Economics,* 190 (1988), 458–466.
Wigand R. Electronic commerce: Definition theory and context. *The Information Society,* 13 (1997), 1–16.
Wilson, S. Digital signatures and the future of documentation. *Information Management & Computer Security,* 7, 2 (1999), 83–87.
———. A comparison of authentication technologies in e-business. *The Asia Business Law Review* (July 2001), 49–56.

CHAPTER 15

PRIVATE LAW ON THE INTERNET

THE PERFORMANCE OF THE ICANN/UDRP SYSTEM

JAY P. KESAN AND ANDRES A. GALLO

Abstract: *This chapter presents an empirical study of the performance of Uniform Domain-Name Dispute Resolution Policy (UDRP) providers. In contrast to most empirical studies of the UDRP, which analyze the resulting verdicts in each case, we concentrate on the general performance of the different private providers, taking into account efficiency considerations. We use duration econometric analysis of the cases handled by these providers as the main variable to measure the general efficiency of each provider. From our empirical analysis, we conclude that there are important differences in performance among the UDRP providers. We found that the providers have different processes and technologies for resolving cases, giving rise to opportunities for forum shopping. This result supports claims of forum shopping in the UDRP regime, even though, in this case, the forum shopping is based on important institutional differences among the providers, instead of simple bias toward the complainants.*

Keywords: *Domain Names, ICANN, Internet Law, Internet Regulation, Law and Economics, Self-Regulation, Uniform Domain-Name Dispute Resolution Policy (UDRP)*

INTRODUCTION

The impressive growth of the Internet in the 1990s and the boom of the e-economy generated competition for domain names in the most coveted, top-level domains, that is, the .com space (Miller 1981). Nonetheless, the other original generic top-level domains (gTLDs) open to commercial use—.org, and .net—were also in high demand from businesses (Froomkin 2002b, Nguyen 2001). Other types of top-level domain names, especially the country code TLDs (ccTLDs), were of little commercial value, and registration was not as important as in the case of gTLDs (Froomkin 2002b). As a result, the artificial scarcity of TLDs created by the managers of the Domain Name System (DNS) sharply increased the value of the registered and most popular domain names. Just recently, a new set of gTLDs were introduced in the root system (Solomon 2001).

Since 1998, the management of names and addresses on the main root server has been in the hands of the Internet Corporation for Assigned Names and Numbers (ICANN). One of the main problems for ICANN was the need to create a system to handle the growing number of problems among users because of the—sometimes indiscriminate—registration of domain names that collided with already established trademarks in real-life markets (Froomkin 2002b). In 1999, after a series of consultations with many interest groups, ICANN created the Uniform Domain-Name Dispute Resolution Policy (UDRP) (Solomon 2001). This system was thought of as a decentralized regime for dispute resolution in which ICANN created the general rules and a series of competing private providers were authorized to manage and resolve disputes. Theoretically, the system seemed to work perfectly. Nonetheless, a few years after its creation, the regime has been subject to hard criticism from scholars and commentators. The debate about the performance of the system has been strong, with both favorable and unfavorable comments.[1]

Most of the empirical studies of the UDRP have been based on the analysis of cases handled by the providers, and the results from various panel decisions. The most common criticisms are that the providers have an incentive to favor the complainants and that the rules have been designed to favor proprietary interests on the Internet (Froomkin 2002b). Some of these facts follow from the political structure of ICANN, which we have analyzed elsewhere (Kesan and Gallo 2005). In this chapter, we present a thorough empirical study of the performance of the UDRP providers. Based on our previous research, we identify the duration of the dispute resolution procedure employed to decide these cases as one of the main variables that determines the efficiency of the system (Kesan and Gallo 2003). We have applied regression models based on the analysis of this duration to identify different factors that determine the performance of the system. Among our main findings, we claim that the UDRP providers have different duration functions, implying a different technology in treating the cases before them, which then implies the existence of forum shopping. The existence of forum shopping based on the performance of the providers is different from the forum shopping mentioned in the literature of UDRP, which notes that there is a bias among the dispute resolution services providers toward the complainant (Froomkin 2002b). These results are emphasized by the finding that the two most important providers are located at the extremes of the possible technological structures for dispute resolution within the UDRP. Second, the providers have an unambiguous bias toward specific countries. This finding is very important, because most of the literature discusses the bias between individuals. Nonetheless, the bias toward countries of origin of the providers could be an important element that must be taken into account in the design of a general dispute system, such as the UDRP. Furthermore, the evidence of such a bias delivers a hard blow to ICANN's claim that the system is intended to handle the most diverse claims on the Internet, regardless of the origin of the parties (Segal 2001).

ICANN UDRP CHARACTERISTICS

ICANN is a nonprofit organization supported by many governments, but mainly the United States government, through the Department of Commerce, which promoted its creation in 1998.[2] Among its various activities, the management of the domain name system has proved to be a delicate area in which property and trademark rights from the real world collide with the unregulated nature of the Internet (Kesan and Gallo 2004). New domain names assigned on the Internet could have been protected by trademark and property rights laws in different countries. However, because of various problems, local courts cannot adequately handle Internet-based disputes (Lee 2002). As a result, conflicts in the rights over domain names on the Internet have generated a need for an arbitration mechanism to resolve these disputes (Hejny 2001). Many private actors, with interests in the creation of such a system and with influence over ICANN, together with other organizations, like the World Intellectual Property Organization (WIPO), promoted the creation of a dispute resolution mechanism for domain names.[3] WIPO's report was the blueprint for the new regime created by ICANN afterward (Froomkin 2002b). Consequently, in 1999, ICANN enacted the Uniform Domain Name Dispute Resolution Policy (UDRP) (Helfer and Dinwoodie 2001). Under this policy, ICANN authorized a number of private third-party institutions (providers) to evaluate disputes among Internet users regarding rights over domain names.[4] ICANN designed a series of general rules to regulate the dispute resolution procedures, leaving the private providers to add their own complementary rules to the system.[5] The UDRP has been harshly criticized by some scholars and commentators, and at the same time it has received support from others. The capacity of ICANN in enforcing and applying the UDRP regime to the registered domain names is based on the contractual relationship each user enters with ICANN at the moment of registering a new domain name (Goldstein 2002). In this section, we describe the main characteristics of the UDRP system, identifying the weaknesses and strengths of this regime, as well as delineating the questions to be tested with our regression model.

Procedure and Enforcement

The general procedure for considering complaints is competitive and one in which different organizations can offer dispute resolution services to users.[6] This is different from the usual alternative dispute resolution providers that handle privacy rights on the Internet, in which one of the parties is subject to the private provider imposed by the Web site visited and, in addition, there are multiple rules created by a number of providers (Kesan and Gallo 2004). In the UDRP system, Internet users can choose the provider knowing that the underlying set of rules is uniform and consistent among providers. However, by letting the complainant choose the provider, ICANN has created an incentive for providers to favor complainants in their decisions (Froomkin 2002b; Geist 2002). ICANN provides a set of rules that delimits the issues to be regulated, the cases that providers should evaluate, the minimum requirements for the composition of the panel, and the penalties to be applied.[7] However, it permits providers freedom to implement further rules and to charge the corresponding fees. As a result, we have a system where users face a common set of rules, but complainants can choose the provider they prefer. This framework has created good incentives for competition among providers of domain name dispute resolution services offered at a reasonably low cost. However, it has also generated problems of bias in favor of complainants, who are the entities choosing the provider (Geist 2002). Therefore, in the current system, complainants have an incentive to choose the provider who is friendlier to complainants, and the providers' optimal strategy is to favor complainants in order to ensure that they continue to be chosen in the future.[8]

The complaints that are evaluated under this system are only those related to domain name disputes.[9] Figure 15.1 shows the different stages the claim goes through during the procedure. The procedure depicted in Figure 15.1 can vary marginally because of the different supplemental rules of the providers.

The complainant can file a complaint with any of the approved providers that ICANN has authorized. The selection of the provider resting in the hands of the complainant has been one of the most critical issues in the analysis of bias in the UDRP procedure (Froomkin 2002b). Once the provider receives the complaint, it has to evaluate its validity. If the complaint is not valid, then the provider could either ask for further information or discard the complaint. In case the complaint is found to be valid, we then have a case that has to be resolved by the provider. The provider asks the respondent to submit a defense responding to the complaint. Once the respondent has submitted an answer, or the legal time period for a response has expired, that is, the respondent is declared in default, the provider forms a panel. This panel can be either a one- or a three-member panel, as requested by the parties.[10] However, in contrast to other alternative

Figure 15.1 **UDRP General Procedure**

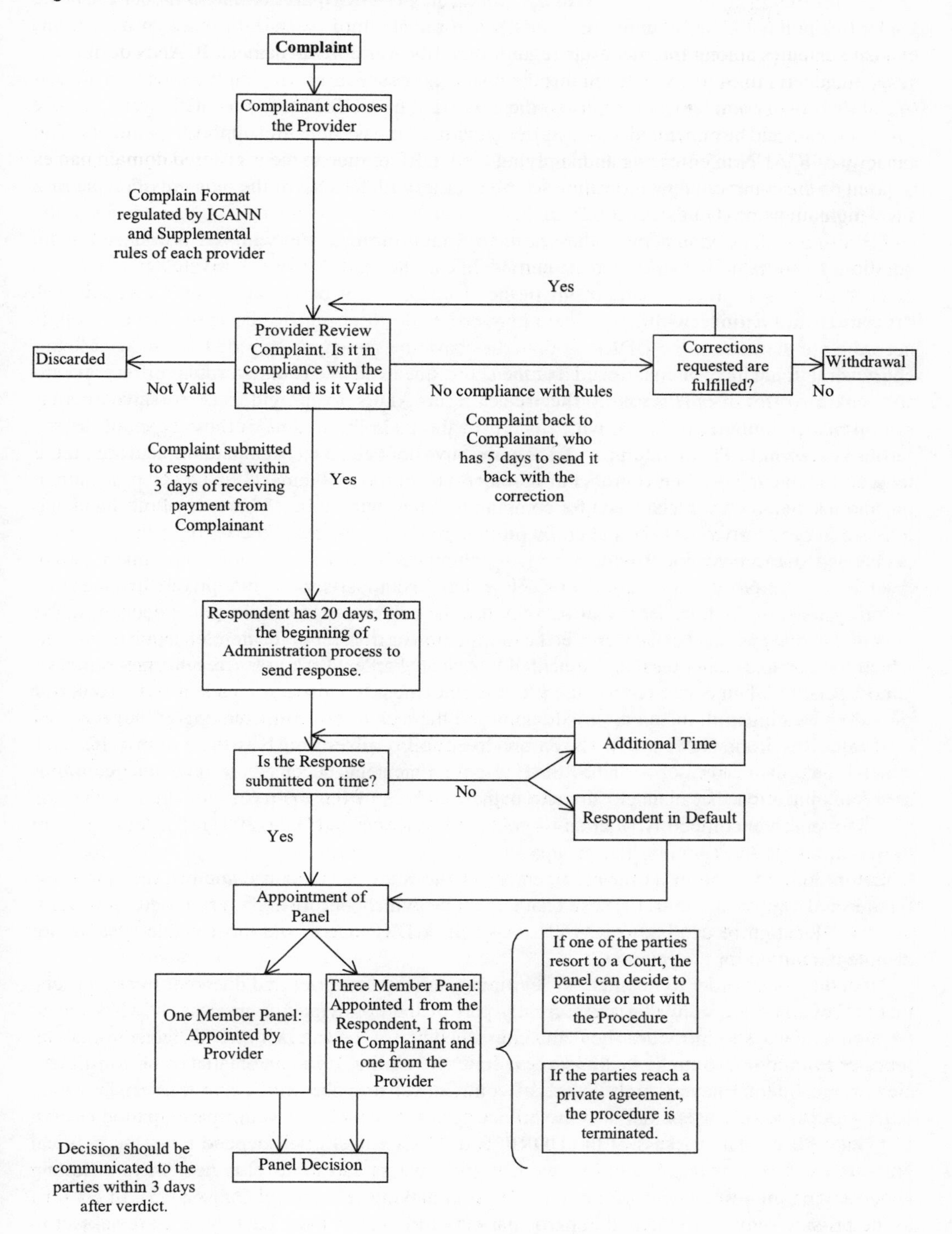

dispute resolution forums (ADRs) that operate in the privacy rights area, here the panelists are elected from a list elaborated by the provider and in agreement with the parties, at least in the three-member panel case. As a result, even though the complainant can elect the provider, the respondent has the choice of determining the panel composition, making the panel more transparent than in the case of privacy rights forums, where the panelists are appointed directly by the provider, without the parties' intervention. Nonetheless, the participation of the respondents takes place just in the case of three-member panels. Otherwise, the provider is the one in charge of appointing the panelist. This procedure has been criticized because of the bias providers have in favoring complainants (Thornburg 2002).

Once the panel is constituted, they have to decide on the case, with the power to ask for additional information from any of the parties. In case the parties reach a private agreement, the panel terminates its process, without any further decision. If any of the parties initiate a court trial, the panel can continue with its deliberations or decide to terminate the case.[11] Even though, according to the rules of the UDRP, both parties have the same grace period to take the case to a court, some scholars have mentioned that the short time available is unfavorable for respondents (Froomkin 2002b). As in the case of the privacy rights ADRs, the providers do not have jurisdiction in matters initiated in court, which is one of the main limitations of these types of dispute resolution regimes. That said, most UDRP cases have not been contested in court, and the parties have accepted the panel decisions.[12] Furthermore, one of the problems of the UDRP procedure is the absence of a review mechanism for complaints (Thornburg 2002). This type of mechanism is in place in other private ADRs and could provide for better review and control of the panelists' decisions (Kesan and Gallo 2004).

One of the main advantages of the UDRP regime in comparison to other private dispute resolution systems in the Internet is that ICANN has the power to enforce the panel decisions. The only action that the panel can enforce is the termination or transfer of the domain name in dispute, which is, of course, under the management of ICANN (Mueller 2002a). As a result, enforcement is almost perfect, when compared to the lack of enforcement that privacy rights dispute resolution providers, dealing with different jurisdictions and the lack of government support, have to contend with (Kesan and Gallo 2003). The enforcement ability arises from both the design of ICANN, which is an organization supported by the U.S. government and accepted by some other countries as the organization that manages domain names, and also from the design of the root system, which favors an uncompetitive market for root names (Kesan and Gallo 2003). The legitimacy of its functions, at least among the groups that have direct influence on the ICANN Board of Directors, provides the basis for enforcement of the rules on domain name dispute resolution (Helfer and Dinwoodie 2001). These characteristics, which, surprisingly, are based on governmental delegation of powers to ICANN, make the UDRP one of the most viable systems for dispute resolution on the Internet.

Nonetheless, in order to maintain its legitimacy among countries and different Internet users, that is, beyond the groups that are currently part of the policymaking process, ICANN has to develop new ways to introduce the many constituencies of the Internet into its decision-making process (Froomkin 2002b). If we look at how ICANN is formed, we can see that some constituencies on the Internet have a high degree of control over its policymaking process, meanwhile, other groups, mainly users, but also the private sector, have a low level of participation (Kesan and Gallo 2005). The success of the UDRP, and ICANN itself, will depend upon the political pressure exerted over ICANN to involve new participants and to develop new ways of letting wide-ranging interest groups influence its decision making (Kesan and Gallo 2005). In contrast to the privacy rights providers, this particular structure makes the UDRP both more subject to criticism but also more susceptible to change, while at the same time creating an opportunity to maintain the consensus around the common set of rules of the system.

Number of Participants

Under the UDRP system, every person or entity that registers a new domain name is subject to the policies created by ICANN, since the companies that manage domain name assignments on the Internet are subject to ICANN authorization.[13] As a result, most of the domain name owners are subject to the regulations of the UDRP (Mueller 2002a). This provides the system with wide coverage and uniform regulation throughout most of the Internet. This feature is another important difference with respect to other attempts to create private dispute resolution systems in which the adoption of their regulatory regime is voluntary (Kesan and Gallo 2004). The specific design of ICANN as the only institution that manages domain names, and the support from different governments, generates a quasi-automatic jurisdiction for those who request a new domain name in any of the gTLDs.

International Cooperation

In the UDRP, since ICANN controls the registry of domain names (at least for gTDLs), enforcement of the rules is better than in other cases, like e-commerce. (Thornburg 2002). However, international cooperation is needed to sustain the policy that is put in place throughout the Internet. Since ICANN has relied on the support of the U.S. government, other developed countries have followed suit and now support the jurisdiction of ICANN to resolve domain name disputes.[14] Nonetheless, most ccTLDs are still out of the jurisdiction of ICANN with respect to UDRP policy.[15] However, the technical dependency of ccTLDs on ICANN, and in the end, on the U.S. government, hinders the sovereignty of country code managers (Ware 2002). Reforms in ICANN's political structure in 2002, which gave more participation to ccTLDs, could be considered a political maneuver to reach a wider international consensus about ICANN policies (Kesan and Gallo 2003).

There are some characteristics of the ICANN structure that help explain this success in reaching international consensus. First, the management structure of ICANN has become more open to participation and, especially the 2002 reforms, the international community has more say on ICANN policymaking (Kesan and Gallo 2003). Different constituencies from all around the globe can participate in the decision-making and shaping of ICANN policies.[16] Given the interest of ICANN in becoming an international body with jurisdiction over the Internet, it is not surprising that there have been major changes in the way board members are elected and also regarding the participation of country code registries (ccTLDs).[17] These changes will permit more cooperation at the international level, which will allow for better enforcement of dispute resolution policies.[18] Nonetheless, the inclusion of international actors will also increase the need for reform in the UDRP in order to accommodate different international perspectives. For example, the growth of the Internet in Asia and the interest of ICANN in continuing to be the main source of control and regulation over domain names have prompted the creation of two new offices, one in Hong Kong and the other in Beijing, to resolve disputes in the Asian region.[19] As a result, the UDRP can accommodate different views and be open to changes, even though groups with more power inside ICANN can resist such reforms. Second, the constituencies that form the board of ICANN were created to permit people from different countries to be part of it and have a voice in the political process.[20] Nonetheless, the governance of ICANN has been relegated to groups and constituencies that were introduced as initial parts of the organization. As ICANN tries to move to a more international environment, these constituencies should accommodate other interests mainly from other countries—the private sector, Internet users, and governments. In this sense, we can say that ICANN is an institution in its formative stage, in which different constituencies and groups try to establish positions in the management of the institution, but without an already established procedure or representation.[21] However, the forces that shape the political characteristics of ICANN will also shape the rules of its dispute resolution policy. In the end, if ICANN succeeds in promoting and enforcing a set of dispute resolution rules for domain names throughout the Internet, it will be due to the capacity of its constituencies to accommodate different demands and to the political process inside the corporation that enables such a process to occur.

User Participation

In the case of the UDRP, user participation is much higher than in the previous case study of the privacy rights (Kesan and Gallo 2004) of Third Party Institutions (TPIs).[22] First, every user that registers a domain name on the ICANN-managed root server is automatically under the jurisdiction of the providers and is subject to the rules of the UDRP.[23] Second, ICANN has provided, in theory, numerous ways by which users can contact the organization and propose reforms to the dispute resolution system.[24] Furthermore, in ICANN, users have direct participation on the board of directors through the election of representatives in the at-large group, and in the Generic Name Supporting Organization (GNSO) group, under the constituency of noncommercial users.[25] However, user participation in ICANN policymaking has been scarce and the commercial private sector is the main power that is in control of ICANN. As a result, although ICANN fares better than the privacy rights TPIs, as seen from our previous analysis (Kesan and Gallo 2004), it is still biased toward private firms' interests regarding domain name policies.

There are many critics pointing to the lack of democratic participation in the decision making of ICANN.[26] For example, ICANN has strictly controlled the number of top-level domain names, which has created an artificial scarcity in the market (Mueller 2002a). Furthermore, this scarcity has favored specific private firms with interests in controlling this resource (Mueller 2002a). By letting private firms compete with each other to provide options in the top-level domain name arena, ICANN could improve users' welfare by providing more alternatives than what currently exists (Mueller 2002a). However, competition at this level will decrease the value of the top domain names that already exist today, hurting the profits of the firms that control them. As these firms have significant influence over ICANN's decisions, it is to be expected that they will exert pressure to avoid such competition. Nonetheless, if ICANN wants to promote cooperation and continue to advance in its governance of the domain name system, it should accommodate users' demands. For example, one of the most common criticisms of the UDRP is that the domain name rules enforced by providers are designed to protect trademark holders' interests on the Internet, at the expense of free speech interests (Blackman 2001). For example, if somebody registers a domain name called FIFAWorldCup.com, which is devoted to criticizing the way the Fédèration Internationale de Football Association (FIFA) has designed the classification groups for the 2006 World Cup in Germany, FIFA could claim that this domain name infringes on its own trademark rights and seek to cancel this registration by initiating a complaint with a UDRP provider. These kinds of problems have arisen because of the small number of top-level domain names and the broad definitions applied for the type of content that is admissible under each top-level domain name. For example, if ICANN creates a new top-level domain name for free speech, such as .fsp, in which all domain name registrants have to be individuals or noncommercial entities and in which all names, including trademarks, can be used, together with a prohibition against undertaking commercial activities in this space, many of the free speech concerns can be accommodated.

ICANN can then have a commercial set of top-level domain set of names in which trademarks are the rule for name assignment, and also a free speech section in which users can express themselves without fear of their domain names and free speech rights being suppressed. Nonetheless, under the current interests that dominate ICANN, such a simple technical change cannot be expected (Kesan and Gallo 2005).

More Internet users employ UDRP dispute procedures rather than privacy rights forums (Kesan and Gallo 2004). The reasons are that, first, both parties have the opportunity to take part in the formation of the panel, guaranteeing a higher degree of impartiality and independence than in the case of panels constituted directly by the private providers with interests dominated by private businesses.[27] Nonetheless, it is clear that the ICANN system is far from being independent, given its bias toward private firms, although this bias is less than in the case of the totally private privacy rights forums. Second, given that the general governing rules employed by the UDRP providers are supplied by ICANN, and users do have the opportunity—although limited—to place representatives on ICANN's Board of Directors, these rules could be subject to review in order to insure a more fair treatment of noncommercial parties (Kesan and Gallo 2003). Third, international users have more say in the rules and management of ICANN compared to privacy rights providers, given the attempts to construct a more international organization (Mueller 2002a). As a result, more cooperation can be expected on the international sphere, and a broader consensus may be achieved around the UDRP (Thornburg 2002). Finally, as governments participate in the process, it is more probable that consumers and other users can exert more influence over ICANN's decisions when compared to the totally private system that regulates privacy in e-commerce (Kesan and Gallo 2004).

UDRP PROVIDERS

ICANN has authorized private providers to manage the complaints presented by Internet users.[28] These providers are supposed to follow the policy guidelines designed by ICANN, but they can complement these rules with their own.[29] Initially, ICANN authorized two providers, the World Intellectual Property Organization (WIPO) and the National Arbitration Forum (NAF), on December 1 and 23, 1999, respectively. Afterward, in 2000, ICANN added two more providers, eResolution (eRes) in January and CPR Institute for Dispute Resolution (CPR), approved in May. Of these providers, eRes ceased to operate in November 2001. In February 2002, a new provider was approved, Asian Domain Name Dispute Resolution Centre, with two offices in Beijing and Hong Kong.[30] In this work we will analyze the cases of the initial four providers of the UDRP.

WIPO is an agency of the United Nations system of organizations.[31] It was created in 1994 with the aim of providing mediation services between private parties in specific areas. Its headquarters are located in Geneva, Switzerland. WIPO has been one of the main actors that influenced the creation of the UDRP regime by ICANN. In April 1999 WIPO produced a final report on the creation of a domain name resolution system, which was the blueprint for ICANN's own UDRP.[32] The National Arbitration Forum (NAF) was created in 1986 in order to provide alternative dispute resolution services to different parties. The NAF is composed of judges and lawyers around the world, who aim solely to provide mediation and arbitration services.[33] It is located in the United States, and most of the UDRP cases evaluated by NAF are from the North American region. The Center for Public Resources (CPR) was formed in 1979 by major corporations in order to provide alternative dispute resolution forums for private business.[34] This is a nonprofit organization with more than 500 private corporations as members. Finally, eResolution (eRes) suspended its activities in 2001. This provider was located in Quebec, Canada.

In 2002 ICANN approved the addition of an Asian dispute resolution provider, Asian Domain Name Dispute Resolution Centre (ADNDRC), with offices in Hong Kong and Beijing. This new provider is composed of the China International Economic and Trade Arbitration Commission (CIETAC) and the Hong Kong International Arbitration Centre (HKIAC).[35] CIETAC is the only dispute resolution provider for the top domain name .cn. Meanwhile, HKIAC was created in 1985 as an alternative dispute resolution system, and in 2001 it was appointed as the sole dispute resolution provider for the top domain name .hk.[36]

Characteristics of the Providers

As explained before, ICANN provides the rules for the administration of the UDRP. Accordingly, the authorized providers have to follow these rules in resolving the cases. Nonetheless, there are some differences between the providers, because ICANN has left some room for the providers to differ. In this section we analyze the differences between these providers in terms of supplemental rules, fees, and relative representation in their panels of arbitrators.

Supplemental Rules

Besides the UDRP rules provided by ICANN, the private providers can add their own rules, if they do not contradict ICANN policy.[37] Most of these additional rules are about general procedures for the cases evaluated by the provider, and how participants should present information and proofs in terms of characteristics and time schedule. Table 15.1 presents the main characteristics of the supplemental rules for each provider. As we can see, even though the differences in the supplementary rules are minimal, and most of them concern the format and timing of the submissions of information and proofs to the panel, the effects of such differences in procedure could have important consequences on the efficiency and results of the procedure. Some of the providers, such as WIPO, have a more complex system of procedures than others, such as NAF and CPR (King 2000). For example, in the case of CPR, the rules are minimal and most of the decisions are left to the panel. It is worth mentioning that NAF is the only provider that offers incentives to keep the amount of information to be submitted and the time spent at a minimum. This is done by introducing extra fees if there are supplemental submissions or if time extensions are requested. However, these fees could be a problem for parties attempting to propose new proofs or information regarding the case (Froomkin 2002b). Nonetheless, the general fee of NAF is lower than the other providers, and the extra fees are much smaller. Beyond these small differences, most of the rules are similar for all of the providers (see Table 15.1).

Fees

Another of the main issues that can differentiate providers is the fees they charge for different types of cases. Differences among the fees the providers charge can induce complainants to switch from one provider to another, given that the set of rules applied is the same. Table 15.2 shows the schedule of fees charged by each provider. From this table, there are two main characteristics worth mentioning. First, the cost of the procedure across providers is not prohibitive and it is much lower than the expected costs of resorting to court action to solve the conflict (Thornburg 2002). Second, the differences in prices among providers are not big enough to promote a high substitution among providers. For example, the most popular provider is WIPO, which charges a higher fee than NAF, which is second in popularity. The fees of WIPO are 16 percent higher on

Table 15.1

Supplemental Rules of UDRP Authorized Providers

	WIPO	NAF	CPR	eRes
Submission requirements	Coversheet and copies to registrar(s) and respondent	Coversheet plus three copies (single panel) or five copies (three-member panel)	Five copies	Three parts: Complaint proper, annexes, and cover sheet
Compliance review	Center has five days to review		Left to the panel without specific requirement	Clerk has ten days to review and complainant has five days to correct any deficiency.
Official administrating the case	Center appoints case administrator			Clerk's office
Panel appointment	Three-member panel: Parties should provide list of three candidates, ordered by preference. The third panelist appointed is the president. Parties can agree on naming the president.	Single-member panel: appointed by the forum Three-member panel: Chair elected by the provider and no part of the parties list of candidates.	Not mentioned	Single-member panel: appointed by the clerk's office Three-member panel: appointed by provider: one panelist from the lists of each party and the third appointed by the provider (president).
Recusation of panelists	Not mentioned	Not mentioned	Not mentioned	Decided by the clerk's office
Respondent default	Panel should be appointed by the center.	Panel appointed by the center. Option to change to a one-member panel should be provided.	Not mentioned	Panel appointed by provider

Table 15.1 *(continued)*

	WIPO	NAF	CPR	eRes
Limits to submission	Word limit: Paragraph 3(b)(ix) 5,000 words; 5(b)(i) 5,000 words; 15(e) no word limits.	Complaint and response no longer than ten pages total	Complaint and response not to exceed ten pages plus annexes and exhibits	Not mentioned
Extension for response	Not mentioned	Extension can be given subject to: parties agreement, communicated to the forum, state exceptional circumstances, state extension (no more than twenty days) and pay extension fee $100. Forum will decide on the extension.	Not mentioned	Could be extended by the panel
Additional submissions	Not mentioned	Within five days of submission of the response and it should be accompanied by a fee of $250.	Not mentioned	Not mentioned

Source: Authors' elaboration, based on www.udrpinfo.com/eres/supprules.htm, arbiter.wipo.int/domains/background/index.html, www.arbforum.com/domains/UDRP/rules.asp, and www.cpradr.org.

(continued)

Table 15.2

Fees Charged by Providers (in U.S. dollars)

Number of domain names	Single-panel	Three-member panel
NAF		
1	1,150	2,500
2	1,300	2,600
3–5	1,400	2,800
6–10	1,750	3,500
11–15	2,000	4,000
16 or more	*	*
WIPO		
1–5	1,500	4,000
6–10	2,000	5,000
More than 10	*	*
CPR		
1–2	2,000	4,500
3–5	2,500	6,000
More than 6	*	*

Sources: arbiter.wipo.int/domains/, www.arbforum.com/domains/, www.cpradr.org/ICANN _Menu.htm. http//www.cpradr.org/ICANN_Menu.asp?M=1.6.6.
*To be determined.

average than NAF's for those cases in which the number of domain names involved is between one and five. For the cases involving between six and ten domain names, the difference is just 14 percent between these two providers. In the case of CPR, the difference in price with respect to NAF is 24 percent higher for the cases involving one to five domain names. Accordingly, we can conclude that the system is providing affordable dispute resolution services without producing a high level of competition among providers.

Geographical Representation of Arbitrators

The third main variable among providers is the kind of panelists they offer to complainants and respondents. In most of the cases, those panelists are former judges or lawyers from different countries.[38] The different backgrounds of these panelists could have an influence over their final verdicts. This is a very important issue on the Internet, where people from different parts of the world are getting in contact with each other and doing business. As a result, a common set of rules for the Internet for every user around the world should correlate with the diversity of the panelists offered by each provider. Of course, those countries with higher levels of connectivity to the Internet will be represented by a number of panelists in proportion to their relative importance. Table 15.3 shows the distributions of panelists for each provider across countries. In this case there are important differences between providers. WIPO is the organization that has the most diverse group of panelists from both developed and less-developed countries, even though countries from the OECD represent 87 percent of all panelists and account for 75 percent of Internet users in the world. The most-favored countries in WIPO are Australia, Canada, France, Spain, Switzerland, and the UK, which account for 33.4 percent of the panelists and just 13.95 percent of

Internet users. The less-represented countries, among OECD members, are Japan, Germany, and Korea, which account for 8 percent of the panelists and 22.5 percent of Internet users. In the case of the United States, its representation in the group of panelists is almost equal to its share of world Internet users. WIPO may be the most diversified of the UDRP providers because of its relationship with the United Nations and its need to have worldwide representation. On the other hand, in both CPR and NAF, the United States is heavily represented, providing most of the panelists in the list of both providers. In the next section we will explore the effects panelists and specific country cases have on the performance of the providers.

One of the regions that is treated unfavorably, compared with the number of Internet users located in this region, is Asia, especially East Asia. This region accounts for 26 percent of total Internet users, but their representation is just 10 percent of panelists for WIPO, 8 percent of panelists for NAF, and 2.4 percent of panelists for CPR. This bias could explain the creation of new providers for the East Asian region in 2002.

EMPIRICAL EVIDENCE

The development of the UDRP system has drawn the attention of many researchers since the beginning of the regime in 1999. The creation of a global dispute resolution system that covered the entire gTLDs domain names, and as a consequence most of the Internet, was an ambitious task for an environment that was mostly unregulated, except for regulations through code (Mueller 2000, 2002a, b). Most of the studies about ICANN's UDRP are devoted to the theoretical debate of the virtues and failures of the system in providing effective regulation of domain name complaints. However, there are few works designed to evaluate performance of the UDRP with exhaustive empirical analysis.

One of the first empirical attempts to understand UDRP was done by Milton Mueller at Syracuse University (Mueller 2002a). Mueller constructed a database with most of the data concerning the cases evaluated at ICANN's UDRP regime.[39] The first empirical work from Mueller was an attempt to describe the performance of the system and explain the differences in market share that the providers had (Mueller 2000). This work provided useful empirical information on the characteristics of the providers and the performance of both the system as a whole and individual private providers. From the empirical analysis the author concluded that there is a bias in the system, since those providers that favored complainants are also the ones that received the higher market share. As it is noted in this work, WIPO and NAF received 61 percent and 31 percent of the cases, respectively, having a winning rate for complainants of 67.5 percent and 71.5 percent, respectively. On the other hand, eRes, which was more lenient with respondents, had a market share of just 7 percent, with a winning rate percentage for complainants of just 44.2 percent. However, as Mueller noted, the main difference in the winning rates was in those cases in which the respondent was in default. When the respondent contested the complaint, the winning percentage for the complainant was 43 percent with eRes, 50 percent with NAF, and 54 percent with WIPO. This work also presented an econometric analysis of the cases, concluding that the share of the market that NAF and WIPO received depended on their influence over the United States and the rest of the world, respectively, while for eRes, the market share was determined by the high complainant loss rate. The main conclusions of this work were that the system is biased toward the complainants and that the eRes low market share was due to the fact that respondents were favored by this provider.

The author also proposed some changes in the system in order to avoid forum shopping. Nonetheless, the results of this research effort have been strongly criticized by an INTA report (Branthover

Table 15.3

Panelists

	WIPO	NAF	CPR	Internet users (% world total)	Panelists (% of total) WIPO	NAF	CPR
Argentina	4	2		0.66	1.2	1.4	
Australia	19	1	1	1.44	5.8	0.7	2.7
Austria	2	1		0.52	0.6	0.7	
Belgium	5	1		0.64	1.5	0.7	
Brazil	8	3		1.60	2.4	2.2	
Canada	21	7	1	2.69	6.4	5.0	2.7
Chile	5			0.62	1.5		
China	2	2	1	6.72	0.6	1.4	2.7
Colombia	2	3		0.23	0.6	2.2	
Croatia	1			0.05	0.3		
Cyprus	1			0.03	0.3		
Czech Republic	3			0.28	0.9		
Denmark	2	1		0.58	0.6	0.7	
Ecuador	1	1		0.07	0.3	0.7	
Egypt	3			0.12	0.9		
Finland	1			0.45	0.3		
France	17	2		3.12	5.2	1.4	
Germany	9			6.14	2.8		
Ghana	1			0.01	0.3		
Greece	2			0.28	0.6		
Hungary	2	1		0.30	0.6	0.7	
India	6	2		1.40	1.8	1.4	
Ireland	2	2		0.18	0.6	1.4	
Israel	5	2		0.36	1.5	1.4	
Italy	10	2	1	3.27	3.1	1.4	2.7
Jamaica	2			0.02	0.6		
Japan	8	1		11.15	2.4	0.7	
Liechtenstein		1		0.00		0.7	
Malaysia	2	1		1.30	0.6	0.7	
Mexico	6	2		0.72	1.8	1.4	
Netherlands	6			1.58	1.8		
New Zealand	6	1		0.22	1.8	0.7	
Nigeria	1			0.02	0.3		
Norway	4			0.54	1.2		
Pakistan	1			0.10	0.3		
Paraguay		1		0.01		0.7	
Puerto Rico		1		0.12		0.7	
Portugal	3			0.50	0.9		
Republic of Korea	9	5		4.86	2.8	3.6	
Romania	1			0.20	0.3		
Singapore	6			0.30	1.8		
South Africa	2	1		0.61	0.6	0.7	
Spain	10	3	3	1.47	3.1	2.2	8.1
Sweden	6	2		0.92	1.8	1.4	
Switzerland	14	2		0.44	4.3	1.4	
Uganda	1	1		0.01	0.3	0.7	
UK	28	2		4.79	8.6	1.4	
United States	93	85	30	28.48	28.4	61.2	81.1
Vietnam		1		0.20		0.7	
Zimbabwe	1			0.02	0.3		
Total	327	139	37				

Sources: arbiter.wipo.int/domains/; www.arbforum.com/domains/; www.cpradr.org/ and World Bank Country Indicators, at www.worldbank.org/

2002). This report notes major flaws in Mueller's analysis, such as misunderstandings in the functioning of UDRP, inappropriate statistical evidence to support the claims of bias, inadequate review of UDRP cases, and a lack of analysis and data showing the rate of challenges to UDRP decisions. According to this report, Professor Mueller's analysis "distorts facts and misuses statistics to achieve a predetermined end—to show that the UDRP is somehow biased in favor of trademark owners and does harm the domain name system" (10).

Professor Michael Geist provides another major piece of empirical evidence on the ICANN UDRP system (Geist 2002). His work is based on the analysis of general data from UDRP cases. His conclusions are similar to Mueller's, finding evidence of bias and forum shopping among providers. Furthermore, the author finds that panel performance is quite different if separated into one-member and three-member panels. This work shows that, in the case of panel composition, three-member panels offer a lower winning rate for complainants: 62 percent (WIPO), 4 percent (NAF), and 50 percent (eRes) versus 83 percent (WIPO), 86 percent (NAF), and 64 percent (eRes) for single-member panels. Accordingly, the main proposal derived from this work is that by simply changing to a mandatory three-member panel regime, the system bias will be reduced. However, this work has been strongly criticized by INTA (2002). The critical review claimed that Geist's work is based on simple statistical analysis of the cases without offering adequate measuring for fairness. Besides, it does not consider the default cases in the calculation of the winning percentage for complainants; it does not analyze other causes that could justify a high winning percentage ratio; nor does it consider that forum selection can be the result of other factors, such as quality and reputation, costs, and so forth, rather than bias. Both of INTA's reports (Branthover 2002; INTA 2002) criticize the assumptions of Geist and Muller that a 50 percent winning rate for complainants and respondents should be the norm. They assert that the UDRP was created to solve the problem of abusive registration and that a higher winning rate for complainants than for respondents should be the expected norm.

Finally, the last major piece of empirical work on ICANN is the exhaustive work of Anne Kur at the Max-Plank-Institute (Kur 2002). This paper shows an excellent empirical description of the performance of the UDRP system, taking into account the most disparate variables and characteristics of the panels' decisions. The main conclusion of the work is that:

> [G]enerally speaking, the survey shows that fears concerning the risk that the policy might be misused by large companies in order to freeze competition and free speech are largely unfounded. In the vast majority of the cases considered, the domain name at stake was identical with, or incorporated, or otherwise clearly resembled the trademark belonging to someone else, and whenever the respondent could make out a plausible case of bona fide business interests or fair use, chances were good that the complaint would be rejected. Only a rather small amount of cases could be identified where issues such as reverse hijacking or critical comments on the right owner's product or business conduct, etc. were involved. On the other hand, a more detailed analysis of the cases or groups of cases reveals that several issues still need further clarification. In other words: although UDRP is functioning well as a matter of principle, there are certain points where the picture becomes somewhat unclear. (57–58)

This empirical work presents the latest addition to the analysis of ICANN's UDRP. Most of the current theoretical debate is based on the assumption that the main variable that matters in explaining users and provider behavior in this regime is the provider bias toward complainants. As we will show in the next sections, even though bias is important, the performance of each provider can be more important in determining the users' choice of provider. In this respect, our work in this matter offers a richer empirical analysis, looking at the different factors that explain the performance of the UDRP (Kesan and Gallo 2003). Furthermore, as we demonstrate, there are other variables, like efficiency of the providers, which help to explain the process of selection better than the argued bias toward complainants. As a consequence, the aim of our work is to reevaluate the claims of the main empirical works and to provide a more accurate explanation of the performance of the UDRP.

Econometric Analysis

To analyze the UDRP system, we used duration models to test the performance of each provider and the system as a whole. Duration models have been widely used in medicine and labor economics to measure the expected length, in time, of an event. For example, in labor economics, researchers have been interested in measuring the probability of duration for a strike. As the strike goes on, there is a probability that it will end the very next day, or it will continue for an extra day. These models measure the probability that the strike will be maintained an extra day. Accordingly, we use this model in the case of the UDRP. Once a trial begins, there is a probability that it will be terminated the next day, or else it will continue to be analyzed by the designated provider.

Data

We use a database for the cases of the four providers—WIPO, NAF, eRes, and CPR—for the period January 2000 to November 2002. This database was obtained from the UDRP Web site and it consists of 7,148 cases. The cases are separated by provider and by the duration, in days, of each case.

Duration Models

Let's introduce the duration model and its relationship to our case of the UDRP. In our case, let's define the random variable T, which is the failure time for the cases of the UDRP. That is, T represents how many days it takes each case to be decided by a given provider. The distribution function of T is defined as $F(t)$ and density $f(t)$.[40] Accordingly, we define the survival function of T as,

$$S(t) = F(t) = \Pr(T > t) \tag{1}$$

Equation (1) tells us that $S(t)$ is the probability of t being greater than t, that is, the probability that the final decision of the case (failure) will occur after time t.[41] Now, lets define the conditional density of failure at time t, which is the conditional instantaneous measure of failure at time t, given survival to time t. This measure is called the hazard rate, and is denoted $\lambda(t)$. The hazard rate considers the following question: given that the case has lasted under a provider revision until time t, what is the probability that it will end in the next short interval of time D? Then,

$$\lambda(t) = \lim_{\Delta \to 0} \frac{\Pr ob(t \leq T \leq t + \Delta \mid T \geq t)}{\Delta} = \lim_{\Delta \to 0} \frac{\Pr ob(t + \Delta) - F(t)}{\Delta S(t)} = \frac{f(t)}{S(t)} \tag{2}$$

Finally, the integrated hazard function (cumulative hazard function) is given by

$$\Lambda(t) = \int_0^t \lambda(t)dt = -\ln S(t) \qquad \text{then} \qquad S(t) = e^{-\Lambda(t)} \tag{3}$$

From this theoretical background there are several definitions for the distribution of the variable *T*, like the constant, exponential, Weibull, lognormal, and log-logistic distributions. These are called parametric models of survival analysis. One of the most important drawbacks of these models is the imposed structure on the data, which could distort the estimated hazard rates. Instead, we will use nonparametric and semiparametric models, which are less restrictive over the characteristics of the data. First we use the Kaplan-Meier product limit estimator, which is a strictly empirical approach to survival and hazard-function estimation.[42]

Results

The UDRP was created in 1999 and immediately attracted the attention of Internet users, especially business. This was the first attempt at creating a dispute system with the global reach to comprehend most of the Internet. As a consequence, providers have been busy evaluating the most diverse complaints. The evolution of the total number of cases presented in each month is depicted in Figure 15.2. As we can see, there was a sharp increase in the number of complaints presented during the initial months of 2000, which could be a consequence of the implementation of the UDRP regime itself (Mueller 2000). From August 2000, the number of cases steadily decreased throughout 2001. In 2002, there was a short jump in the number of cases from March to June, but afterward the number of cases continued to decline. This declining tendency in the number of cases can be the consequence of two main factors: first, as most of the disputes associated with earlier domain names were already settled during 2000 and part of 2001, the incoming number of disputes was much lower. Furthermore, the existence of the UDRP system could have acted as a deterrence mechanism for users engaged in mass registration of names or looking for fast profits from registering already proprietary names and brands. Second, the economic downturn of technology-related economic activities, especially e-commerce, could have had an impact on the number of complaints and disputes about domain names. Nonetheless, it is expected that the number of disputes will increase in the future, as the Internet is becoming a more international environment and is becoming more popular in other countries besides the United States and the European Union.

During the period of time between January 2000 and June 2003, the UDRP evaluated 8,549 cases, and most of them were divided among two main providers, NAF and WIPO (Figure 15.3). As Figure 15.3 shows, WIPO and NAF decided 95.5 percent of the cases. The closest follower, with just 3.3 percent, eRes, is no longer a provider for the UDRP regime.

If we look at the evolution of the number of cases received by each provider through time, we can see how the system evolved around two main providers (Figure 15.4). During the first year we can appreciate the dominance of WIPO, which was an active participant in the process of delineating the UDRP. Accordingly, the number of cases received by WIPO (60 percent of the total) strongly surpassed those of NAF (32 percent), eRes (7.6 percent), and CPR (0.7 percent). In the second year, this tendency was maintained, with WIPO receiving 60 percent of the cases, but NAF increased its participation to 37 percent, thanks to a reduction in the number of cases of eRes to 3.4 percent. Meanwhile, CPR stood at 0.6 percent. In 2002, the tendency changed, as we

Figure 15.2 **UDRP Number of Cases per Month**

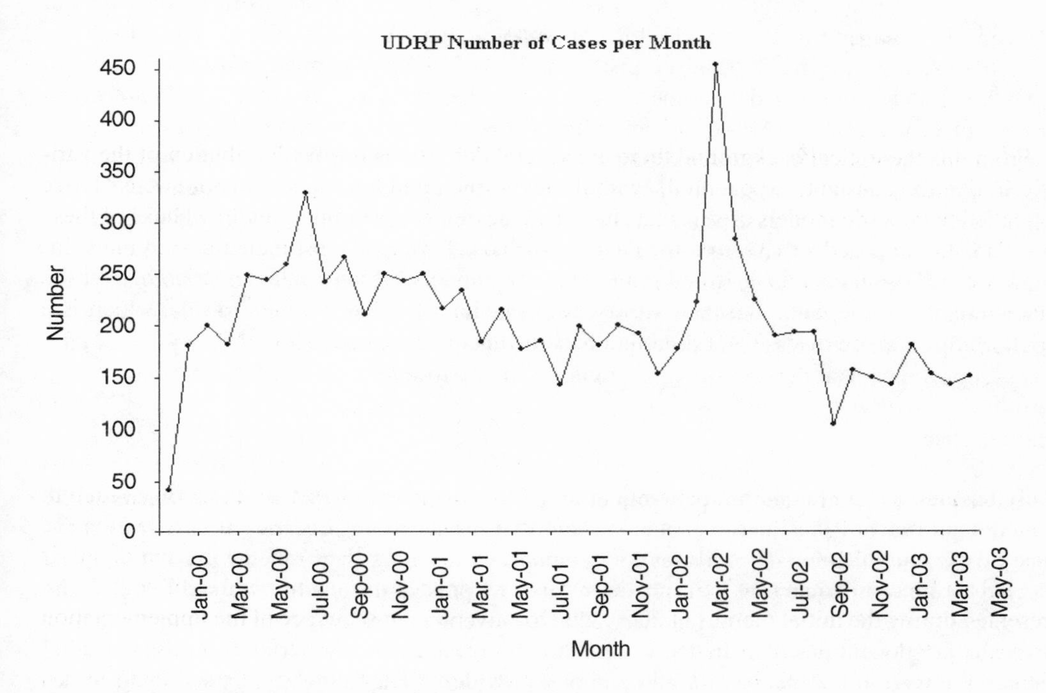

Figure 15.3 **Total Number of Cases by Provider**

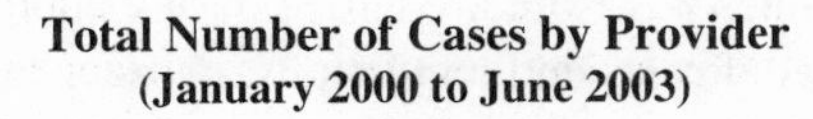

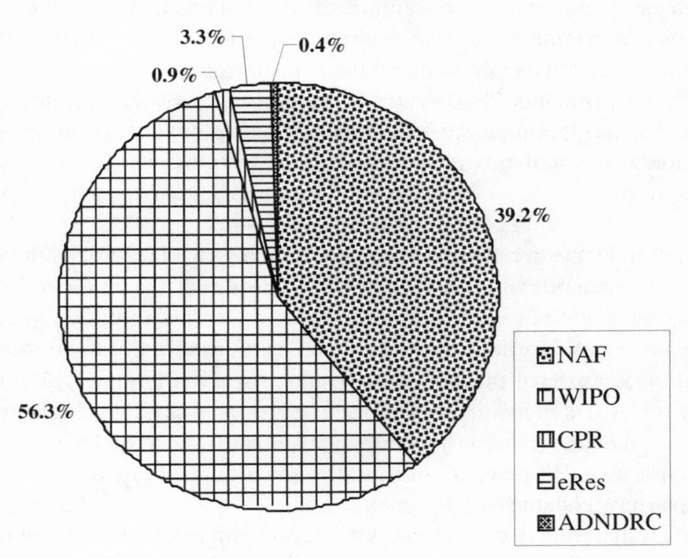

observe a convergence in the number of cases between NAF and WIPO. NAF increased its participation to 46 percent and WIPO decreased its own to 52 percent. At the same time, eRes went out of business at the end of 2001 and CPR continued to have an insignificant share. In 2002, ADNDRC was created, but it managed just 0.8 percent of the total number of cases. Finally, in 2003, this tendency continued, with the two main providers polarizing the cases. WIPO received 50 percent of the cases, NAF 46 percent, CPR 1.6 percent, and ADNDRC 2 percent. In this situation, the system seems to have reached equilibrium, with two main providers receiving an almost similar quantity of cases. In the future, it is expected that the new provider, ADNDRC, will increase its number of cases, as it has been granted an exclusive geographic region of operations. If we look at the actual duration of cases from month to month, we can see that there were almost no differences in the duration of the cases (Figure 15.5). There were some outliers at the initial stages of the system, but then, most of the months show, on average, similar values for duration. Building on this general description of the data and the evolution of the system, in the next section we present the econometric results on the performance of the UDRP system.

Econometric Results

In this section we study the duration of a case, that is, what the factors are that determine the expected number of days a case is under review. The answer to this question is very important, since this is one of the main variables for providers in reaching their objectives, that is, to be selected by the complainants as their provider. First, we present the results obtained based on the database covering the months from January 2000 to November 2002. With this sample we answer two main questions: first, what are the general duration characteristics of the system as a whole? Second, are there differences in duration among providers? The first question will help to describe the procedure and determine the expected duration times of the system as a whole. In evaluating the second question, we are looking at a more interesting issue, which is forum shopping. One of the main objectives of ICANN has been to establish a system with many private providers, but a common set of rules and regulations, in order to ensure all the parties a similar treatment with any provider. Since the complainant is the one that picks the provider, differences among them can determine a bias that could be exploited by the complainants. Accordingly, if the duration time, which depends on many factors and characteristics of each provider, proves to be different for each provider, then we are in the presence of structural differences among them and, as a result, forum shopping opportunities can be exploited. Nonetheless, if we find that the duration functions are statistically the same among providers, then the system designed by ICANN has proved to be successful in providing a homogeneous system for dispute resolution on the Internet.

In order to analyze the performance of the system, Figure 15.6 shows the Kaplan-Meyer survival function. The horizontal axis measures the duration of the cases in days, and the vertical axis shows the probability of surviving one extra day. Accordingly, the expected mean duration for the whole system is fifty-four days (Table 15.4). Furthermore, if we look at different probabilities of survival we have the following results: for a duration of up to thirty-one days, the probability of survival is higher than 90 percent; up to forty days, it is higher than 70 percent; for forty-seven days, the probability is higher than 50 percent; above fifty-six days, the probability of survival is higher than 30 percent; and finally, for a duration of up to eighty-three days, the probability of survival is at least 10 percent.

From these results, we can see that the system is providing a relatively fast procedure for evaluating complaints, since the median duration is just forty-seven days for the system as a whole.

Figure 15.4 **UDRP Number of Cases by Provider**

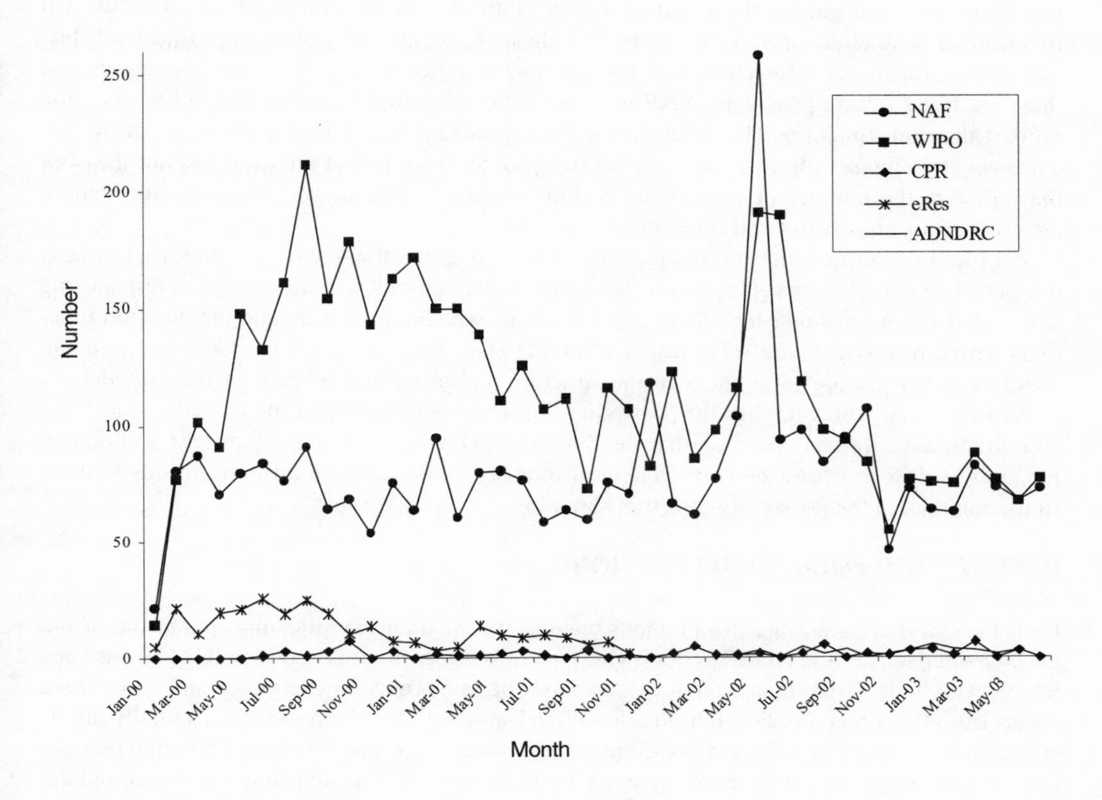

Figure 15.5 **Duration of Cases per Month**

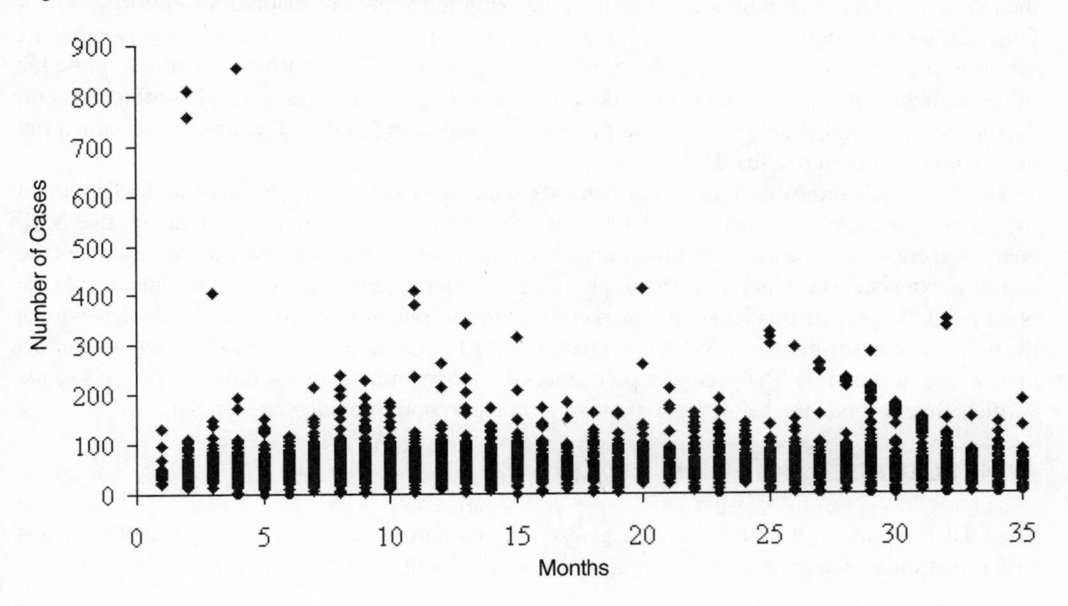

To answer our second question, we will now analyze the differences in duration among providers, and determine if these differences are important or not. First, let's draw a survival function for each of the providers. Figure 15.7 shows the results we obtain by drawing a different survival function for each provider. From a simple inspection of Figure 15.7 we can see that there are two extreme providers, NAF with the lowest duration function, and WIPO with the highest duration function. The other providers are located somewhere in between these two extremes. It is interesting to notice that the two providers located at the extremes are the ones that polarize the number of complaints within the whole system. We will evaluate if these differences are significant and important.

In order to determine the statistical differences among duration curves, we use a set of tests designed to compare survival functions. The tests are the log-rank test, the Wilcoxon test, and the Cox test. Table 15.5 shows the values for these tests, which corroborate that the duration functions between providers are statistically different. This result is very important, since we can conclude that there are differences in the structure and procedure of each of the providers in evaluating cases, which implies the possibility of forum shopping under the UDRP system.

Furthermore, we can conclude that the duration function, and consequently the technology function, is different for each court. These differences could result in different results in decisions, and then in the possibility of forum shopping.

RESULTS AND POLICY IMPLICATIONS

From the empirical analysis in the previous sections we can draw the following conclusions about the characteristics of the UDRP system. The system is not as homogeneous as ICANN has been telling everybody. Even though the providers have the same rules for every case and they cannot depart from this general policy, our duration model shows that each provider has a totally different technology function that induces different performance in terms of expected duration for each case. Accordingly, these differences give rise to the possibility of forum shopping for complainants. This possibility is reinforced by the fact that the two most popular providers are located at the extremes of the technological diversity, polarizing the supply of dispute resolution services. Other minor providers, who get some marginal cases, are located somewhere in between. The different performance is also reinforced by the different factors and variables that determine the different behavior between these providers. As a result, given the variables that affect general performance, complainants will choose the provider according to their idiosyncratic characteristics, which can influence the decision.

Eliminating extreme differences between providers can be effected by further standardization of the general procedures for handling and deciding the claims. For example, the extra fees that NAF charges to create an incentive for shorter response time and to reduce the total duration of each case could be extended as a general rule to all providers in order to generate the right incentives. On the other hand, if the system is let be, the market demand for low duration for cases could drive down the number of cases that go to WIPO compared to NAF, and induce WIPO to improve its performance. Furthermore, WIPO's lengthy procedures do not generate many differences in terms of the verdicts they receive: the results of the cases presented to both providers are similar.

CONCLUSIONS

The UDRP regime of ICANN has been analyzed by numerous scholars and commentators. Most of these studies concentrate on the general empirical results of the system. From different per-

Figure 15.6 **Kaplan-Meyer Survival Estimate**

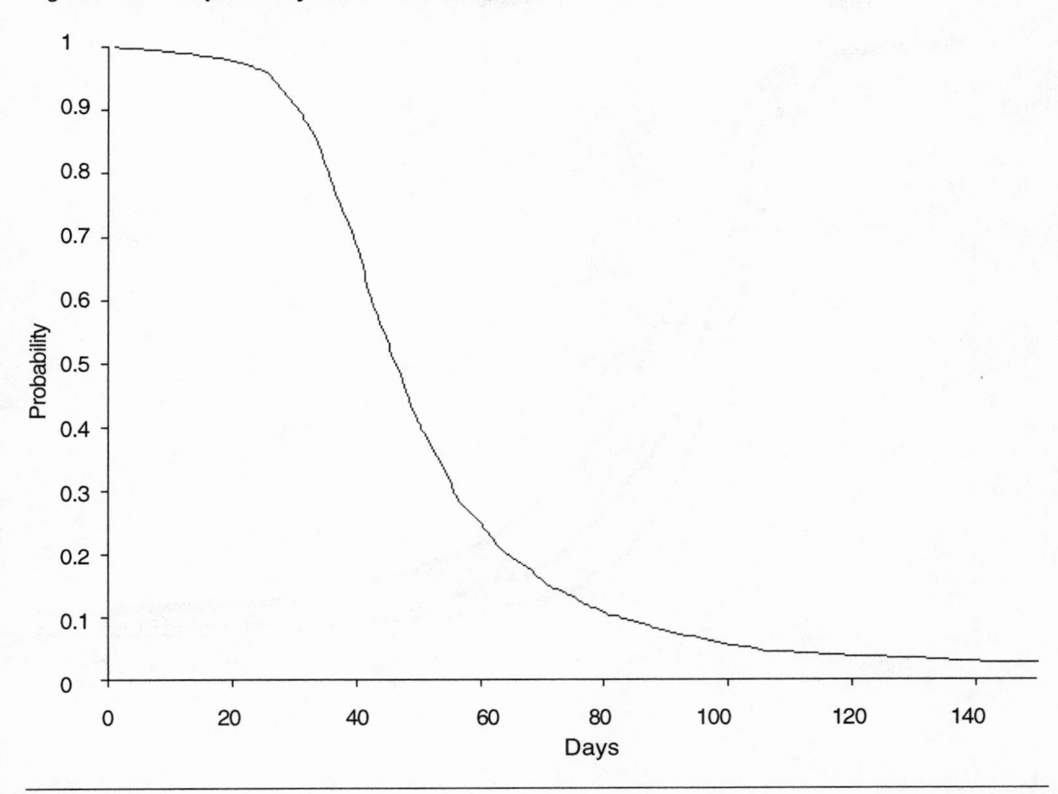

Table 15.4

Duration Characteristics

Category	Total	Mean	Min	Median	Max
No. of subjects	7,330				
No. of records	7,330	1	1	1	1
(first) Entry time	0	0	0	0	
(final) Exit time	54.368	1	47	856	
Subjects with gap	0				
Time on gap if gap	0				
Time at risk	398,521	54.368	1	47	856
Failures	7,148	0.975	0	1	1

spectives, these studies generally criticize the UDRP providers for being biased toward complainants and leaving the respondents without a fair defense of their rights. In this chapter, we claim that there are other variables that are important in a firm's decision to choose the most suitable dispute resolution provider. Complainants seem to regard the performance of the providers as the main variable that is taken into account at the moment of deciding on a provider. Accordingly, the

Figure 15.7 **Kaplan-Meyer Survival Estimate by Provider**

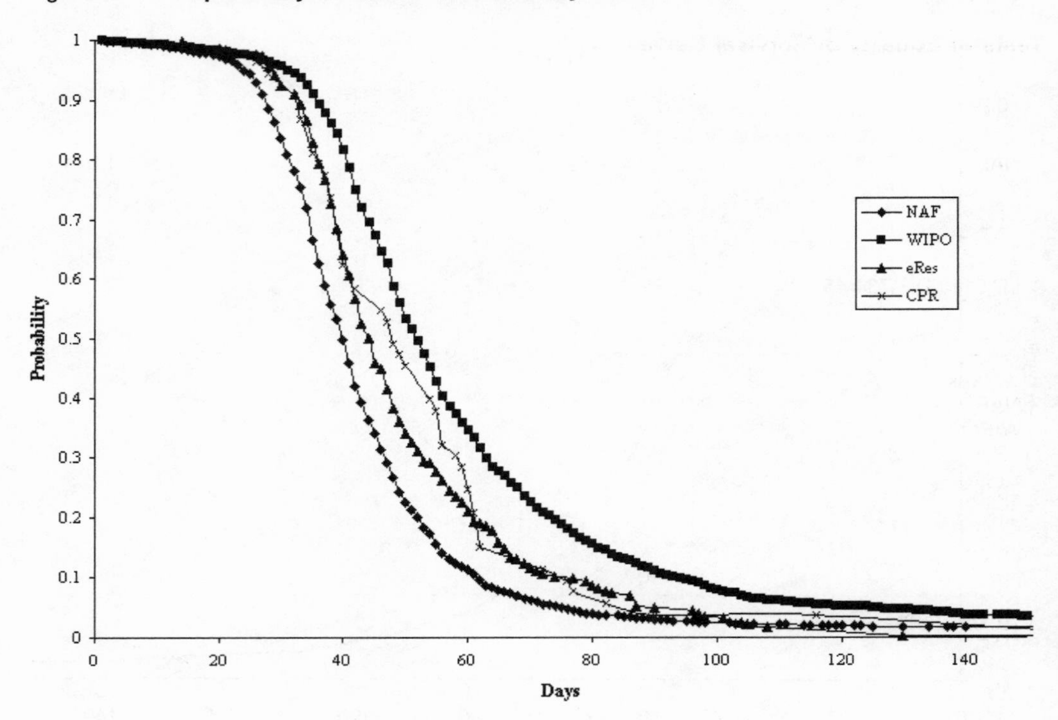

procedural rules of dispute resolution should be analyzed not just in terms of bias and fairness, which is a bit overdone in the recent literature, but in terms of the incentives they generate for the rapid and efficient solution of the claims presented under the UDRP. The UDRP can be better understood by paying more attention to efficiency and the performance indicators from providers and panelists.

Based on our findings about the importance of the performance of the UDRP, we analyzed the procedural structure for each provider. We identified the duration of the procedure as one of the main indicators of efficiency. Accordingly, we used duration models to identify the different factors that have an influence in determining the performance of each provider. We tested whether the duration functions for each provider were homogeneous. This characteristic is very important, given that ICANN created the UDRP as a homogeneous regime for the entire Internet. Accordingly, the selection of providers should not matter in terms of the result or efficiency of the system. However, we find that the providers have different technologies for solving cases, giving rise to opportunities for forum shopping. Despite the attempts by ICANN to provide uniform rules and policies, the providers still have differences among them that can be exploited. In general, we found that NAF is the most efficient provider, while WIPO is the least efficient provider, with the other providers ranking somewhere between these two extremes. This result supports claims of forum shopping within the UDRP regime, even though, in this case, the forum shopping is based on institutional differences among providers, instead of a simple bias toward the complainant.

Table 15.5

Tests of Equality of Survival Curves

Court	Observed	Expected	Hazard
Cox Regression-Based Test			
NAF	2731	1740.85	1.674
WIPO	4079	5110.42	0.830
ERes	286	246.24	1.223
CPR	52	50.48	1.081
Total	7148	7148	1.000
LR Chi²(4) = 734.45		Prob. Chi² = 0.000	

Court	Observed	Expected
Log-Rank Test		
NAF	2,731	1,740.85
WIPO	4,079	5,110.43
eRes	286	246.24
CPR	52	50.48
Total	7,148	7148
Chi²(3) = 834.61		Prob. Chi² = 0.0000

Court	Observed	Expected	Sum of Ranks
Wilcoxon Test			
NAF	2,731	1,740.85	5,440,025
WIPO	4,079	5,110.43	–5,562,113
eRes	286	246.24	126492
CPR	52	50.48	–4404
Total	7,148	7,148	0
Chi²(3) = 1,131.40		Prob. Chi² = 0.0000	

NOTES

1. There is a wide range of criticism and some support of the UDRP established by ICANN. The following is an incomplete list of some papers that deal with the problems and challenges of the system: Baratta and Hanaman (2000); Batavia (2002); Bernstein (2002); Blackman (2001); Blasbalg (2000); Brooks (2001); Brunet (2002); Falzone (2001); Froomkin (2000; 2002a,b); Fuller (2001); Geist (2002); Goldstein (2002); Hadfield (2002); Hejny (2001); Helfer and Dinwoodie (2001); Hestermeyer (2002); Kelley (2002); King (2000); Litman (2000); Look (2002); Mueller (2002a, b); Post (2000); Rains (2000); Segal (2001); Sharrock (2001); Sims and Bauerly (2002a, b); Sorkin (2001); Speidel (2002); Thornburg (2002); Ware (2002); Weinberg (2001).

2. See www.icann.org/general.

3. See www.icann.org/udrp/udrp-schedule.htm (describes the timetable of creation of the UDRP, with links to WIPO initiative).

4. See www.icann.org/dndr/udrp/approved-providers.htm.

5. See www.icann.org/udrp/. For supplemental rules, see www.icann.org/dndr/udrp/approved-providers.htm.

6. See www.icann.org/udrp/.

7. See www.icann.org/dndr/udrp/policy.htm

8. It is interesting to notice that the only provider that declared bankruptcy was e-resolution, which was the one with more cases won by respondents.

9. See www.icann.org/dndr/udrp/policy.htm.

10. See www.icann.org/dndr/udrp/policy.htm (for the rules about panel formation).

11. See UDRP part 4.k, at www.icann.org/dndr/udrp/policy.htm.

12. According with UDRPLaw.net until July 2002, just sixty-five UDRP cases were taken to court. This is a small number compared with the more than 6,000 cases UDRP providers had considered since 1999. See www.udrplaw.net/.

13. (1) Purpose. This Uniform Domain Name Dispute Resolution Policy (the "Policy") has been adopted by the Internet Corporation for Assigned Names and Numbers ("ICANN"), is incorporated by reference into your Registration Agreement, and sets forth the terms and conditions in connection with a dispute between you and any party other than us (the registrar) over the registration and use of an Internet domain name registered by you. Proceedings under Paragraph 4 of this Policy will be conducted according to the Rules for Uniform Domain Name Dispute Resolution Policy (the "Rules of Procedure"), which are available at www.icann.org/udrp/udrp-rules-24oct99.htm, and the selected administrative-dispute-resolution service provider's supplemental rules. (UDRP part 1, at www.icann.org/dndr/udrp/policy.htm).

14. See www.iana.org/cctld/cctld-whois.htm (lists all of the countries that participate in ICANN).

15. Up to now only a handful of ccTLDs have signed Sponsorship Agreements with ICANN. See www.icann.org/cctlds/ (lists the number of ccTLDs agreeing to follow UDRP).

16. See www.icann.org/general/archive-bylaws/bylaws-15dec02.htm (lists the new bylaws of ICANN with important changes in the influence of different groups on the policy process).

17. Until December 15, 2002, the Board of Directors of the ICANN was composed of nineteen members. Five of them came from the original Board of Directors established in 1998 and the other fourteen came from the following organizations listed. Five came from at-large membership. Each of these directors was to represent a different geographic unit: Africa, Asia/Australia/Pacific, Europe, Latin America and the Caribbean, and North America. Three board members came from the Domain Name Supporting Organization (DNSO). The DNSO was composed of different constituency groups: business, noncommercial, ccTLD registries, gTLD registries, ISPs, registrars, and intellectual property. Three board members came from the Address Supporting Organization (ASO). This group was composed of the Asian Pacific Network Information Center (APNIC), American Registry for Internet Numbers (ARIN), Latin American and Caribbean Internet Address Registry (LACNIC), and Réseaux IP Européens Network Coordination Centre (RIPENCC). Finally, three board members came from the Protocol Supporting Organization (PSO). The PSO was composed of the Internet Engineering Task Force (IETF), the World Wide Web Consortium (W3C), International Communication Union (ITU-T), and the European Telecommunications Standard Institute (ETSI).By the new bylaws of the ICANN, beginning December 15, 2002, the Board of Directors was to be composed of fifteen members elected as follows: eight directors from the nominating committee, two from ASO, two from the Country Code Name Supporting Organization (ccNSO), two from the Generic Name Supporting Organization (GNSO), and one who is the president of ICANN. The nominating committee is composed as follows: five from at-large representation, two from the business constituency of GNSO, one from the gTLD Registry, one from the gTLD registrars, one from the Council Country Code NSO, one from the ISP constituency GNSO, one from the intellectual property constituency GNSO, one from ASO, one designated by the ICANN Board to represent academic and other similar institutions, one from consumer and civil society groups from the noncommercial constituency of GNSO, one from IETF, and one from the ICANN Technical Liaison Group. See www.icann.org/general/archive-bylaws/bylaws-15dec02.htm#VI for a complete version of the new bylaws of ICANN.

18. See www.icann.org/cctlds/ (describes the objectives and activities of ccTLDs in ICANN).

19. See www.adndrc.org/so (describes the characteristics of the Asian providers).

20. See www.icann.org/general/support-orgs.htm (describes the different constituencies that support ICANN).

21. The reform process initiated in 2002 and the debate about the role of ICANN and the division of power among different constituencies is one indication that ICANN is an organization in a formative stage.

22. As evidenced by the many critics mentioned in footnote 1, user participation in ICANN is far from ideal. However, we found more user participation than in the case of purely private regulation systems.

23. The uniform domain-name dispute resolution policy (UDRP) has been adopted by ICANN-accredited registrars in all GTLDS (.aero, .biz, .com, .coop, .info, .museum, .name, .net, .org, .pro). (www.icann.org/udrp/#udrp).

24. See www.icann.org/ (describes multiple instruments users have to reach ICANN and participate).

25. See www.icann.org/committees/alac/ (describes the tasks and composition of the at-large group) and gnso.icann.org/ (describes and informs about the different constituencies that are part of the GNSO).

26. See P. Kasan and Andres Gallo, Pondering the Politics of Private Procedures. Working paper posted at www. ssrm.com.

27. See www.icann.org/dndr/udrp/uniform-rules.htm (describes the rules for appointing the panel).

28. See www.icann.org.

29. See www.icann.org/dndr/udrp/uniform-rules.htm.

30. See www.adndrc.org/adndrc/index.html (the Web site of the Asian provider) and www.icann.org/announcements/announcement-03dec01.htm (the announcement of ICANN creating the new Asian provider for the UDRP regime).

31. See www.wipo.int/about-wipo/en/overview.html.

32. See Final Report of the First WIPO Internet Domain Name Process, at wipo2.wipo.int/process1/report/index.html.

33. See www.arbforum.com.

34. See www.cpradr.org/ICANN_Menu.asp?M=1.6.6.

35. See www.adndrc.org/adndrc/index.html.

36. Ibid.

37. See www.icann.org/dndr/udrp/uniform-rules.htm.

38. See www.udrpinfo.com/panl.php (provides information and profiles of the panelists of the UDRP system).

39. To access the database, see dcc.syr.edu/markle/mhome.htm.

40. This section is based on the literature of duration models: Greene (1997), London (1997), Miller (1981), and STATA (1999).

41. Observe that $F(t)=\Pr(T<t)$ and thus,

$$f(t) = \frac{d}{dt}F(t) = -\frac{d}{dt}S(t), \qquad t \geq 0$$

then,

$$F(t) = \int_0^t f(t)dt \quad \text{and} \quad F(t) = \int_t^\infty f(t)dt$$

42. The survival function can be estimated as,

$$\hat{S}(t_k) = \prod_{j=1}^{k} \hat{p}_j$$

the hazard function is defined as,

$$\hat{\lambda}(t_k) = \sum_{j|t_j \leq t} \frac{d_j}{n_j}$$

REFERENCES

Baratta, O., and Hanaman, D. A global update on the domain name system and the law: Alternative dispute resolution for increasing Internet competition. Oh, the times they are a-changin'! *Tulane Journal of International & Comparative Law,* 8 (Spring 2000), 325–390.

Batavia, N. That which we call a domain by any other name would smell as sweet: The overboard protection of trademark law as it applies to domain names on the Internet. *South Carolina Law Review*, 53, 2 (2002), 461–486.

Bernstein, D.H. The alphabet soup of domain name dispute resolution: The UDRP and ACPA. 716 PLI/Pat (2002), 251–305.

Blackman, K. The uniform domain name dispute resolution policy: A cheaper way to hijack domain names and suppress critics. *Harvard Journal of Law & Technology*, 15, 1 (2001), 211–256.

Blasbalg, G. Masters of their domains: Trademark holders now have new ways to control their marks in cyberspace. *Roger Williams University Law Review*, 5, 2 (2000), 563–600.

Branthover, N. UDRP—a success story: A rebuttal to the analysis and conclusions of professor Milton Mueller in "Rough Justice." *International Trademark Association (INTA) Internet Committee* (available at www.inta.org/downloads/tap_udrp_1paper2000.pdf), (May 2002), 1–11.

Brooks, W. Wrestling over the World Wide Web: ICANN's uniform dispute resolution policy for domain name disputes. *Hamline Journal of Public Law & Policy*, 22, 2 (2001), 297–333.

Brunet, E. Defending commerce's contract delegation of power to ICANN. *Journal of Small & Emerging Business Law*, 6, 1 (2002), 1–42.

Falzone, L.P. Playing the Hollywood name game in cybercourt: The battle over domain names in the age of celebrity-squatting. *Loyola Los Angeles Entertainment Law Review*, 21, 1 (2001), 289–325.

Froomkin, M. Wrong turn in cyberspace: Using ICANN to route around the APA and the Constitution. *Duke Law Journal*, 50, 1 (2000), 17–186.

———. Form and substance in cyberspace. *Journal of Small & Emerging Business Law*, 6, 1 (2002a), 93–124.

———. ICANN's uniform dispute resolution policy—Causes and (partial) cures. *Brooklyn Law Review*, 67, 3 (2002b), 605–718.

Fuller, K. ICANN: The debate over governing the Internet. *2001 Duke Law & Technology Review* (February 2001), 2–41.

Geist, M. Fair.com? An examination of the allegations of systemic unfairness in the ICANN UDRP. *Brooklyn Journal of International Law*, 27, 3 (2002), 903–938.

Goldstein, A. ICANNSUCKS.BIZ (and why you can't say that): How fair use of trademarks in domain names is being restrained. *Fordham Intellectual Property Media & Entertainment Law Journal*, 12, 4 (2002), 1151–1186.

Greene, W. *Econometric Analysis*, 3rd ed. Saddle River, NJ: Prentice Hall, 1997.

Hadfield, G. Privatizing commercial law: Lessons from ICANN. *Journal of Small & Emerging Business Law*, 6, 2 (2002), 257–288.

Hejny, S. Opening the door to controversy: How recent ICANN decisions have muddied the waters of domain name dispute resolution. *Houston Law Review*, 38, 3 (2001), 1037–1064.

Helfer, L.R., and Dinwoodie, G.B. Designing non-national systems: The case of the uniform domain name dispute resolution policy. *William & Mary Law Review*, 43, 1 (2001), 141–273.

Heller, K. The young cybersquatter's handbook: A comparative analysis of the ICANN dispute. *Cardozo Online Journal Conflict Resolution*, 2, 2 (2001), 2–28.

Hestermeyer, H.P. The invalidity of ICANN's UDRP under national law. *Minnesota Intellectual Property Review*, 3, 1 (2002), 1–57.

INTA. The UDRP by all accounts works effectively: Rebuttal to analysis and conclusions of professor Michael Geist in Fair.com? and Fundamentally fair.com? International Trademark Association, INTA Internet Committee (available at www.org/downloads/tap_udrp_1paper2000.pdf), May 2002.

Kelley, P.D. Emerging patterns in arbitration under the uniform domain-name dispute resolution policy. *Berkeley Technology Law Journal*, 17, 1 (2002), 181–204.

Kesan, J., and Gallo, A. ICANN/UDRP performance. *Michigan Telecommunications and Technology Law Review*, October (2003).

———. Optimizing regulation of electronic commerce. *University of Cincinnati Law Review*, 72, 4 (2004), 14.

———. Pondering the politics of private procedures: The case of ICANN. Manuscript, on file with authors. (2005).

King, S. The "law that it deems applicable": ICANN dispute resolution, and the problem of cybersquatting. *Hastings Communications & Entertainment Law Journal*, 22, 3/4 (2000), 453–507.

Kur, A. UDRP. A study by the Max Plack Institute for Foreign and International Patent, Copyright and Competition Law, Munich, in cooperation with the Institute for Intellectual Property Law and Market Law, University of Stockholm. Karlsruhe: Institute for Information Law, Technical University of Karlsruhe (2002).

Lee, E. Rules and standards for cyberspace. *Notre Dame Law Review*, 77, 5 (2002), 1275–1372.

Litman, J. The DNS wars: Trademarks and the Internet domain name system. *Journal of Small & Emerging Business Law*, 4, 1 (2000), 149–165.

Look, J.J. Law and order on the wild, wild west (www). *University of Arkansas Little Rock Law Review*, 24, 4 (2002), 817–854.

London, D. *Survival Models and Their Estimation*, 3rd ed. Winsted, CT: ACTEX Publications, 1997.

Miller, R.G. *Survival Analysis*. New York: John Wiley & Sons, 1981.

Mueller, M. Rough justice. An analysis of ICANN's Uniform Dispute Resolution Policy. Working paper V2.1, Syracuse University School of Information Studies (November 2000) (available at dcc.syr.edu/miscarticles/roughjustice.pdf).

———. A new profile of domain name trademark disputes under ICANN's UDRP. Syracuse University School of Information Studies Working Paper, June 2002a (on file with the authors).

———. *Ruling the Root. Internet Governance and the Taming of Cyberspace.* Cambridge: MIT Press, 2002b.

Nguyen, X-T.N. Cyberproperty and judicial dissonance: The trouble with domain name classification. *George Mason Law Review*, 10, 2 (2001), 183–214.

Post, D. Of black holes and decentralized law-making in cyberspace. *Vanderbilt Journal of Entertainment Law & Practice,* 2, 1 (Winter 2000), 70–75.

Rains, C. A domain by any other name: Forging international solutions for the governance of Internet domain names. *Emory International Law Review*, 14, 1 (Spring 2000), 355–403.

Segal, P. Attempts to solve the UDRP's trademark holder bias: A problem that remains unsolved despite the introduction of new top level domain names. *Cardozo Online Journal of Conflict Resolution*, 3, 1 (December 2001), 1–47.

Sharrock, L.M. The future of domain name dispute resolution: Crafting practical international legal solutions from within the UDRP framework. *Duke Law Journal*, 51, 2 (2001), 817–849.

Sims, J., and Bauerly, C.L. A reply to Professor Froomkin's form and substance in cyberspace. *Journal of Small & Emerging Business Law*, 6, 1 (2002a), 125–128.

———. A response to Professor Froomkin: Why ICANN does not violate the APA or the Constitution. *Journal of Small & Emerging Business Law*, 6, 1 (2002b), 65–92.

Solomon, B. Domain name disputes: New developments and open issues. *Trademark Reporter*, 91 (2001), 833–866.

Sorkin, D.E. Judicial review of ICANN domain name dispute decisions. *Santa Clara Computer & High Technology Law Journal*, 18, 1 (December 2001), 35–55.

Speidel, R.E. ICANN domain name dispute resolution, the revised uniform arbitration act, and the limitations of modern arbitration law. *Journal of Small & Emerging Business Law*, 6, 1 (2002), 167–190.

STATA. *STATA References Manual Release 6*, Vol. 3. College Station, TX: Stata Press, 1999.

Thornburg, E.G. Fast, cheap and out of control: Lessons from the ICANN dispute resolution process. *Journal of Small & Emerging Business Law*, 6, 1 (2002), 191–233.

Von Arx, K.G., and Hagen, G.R. Sovereign domains: A declaration of independence of ccTLDs from foreign control. *Richmond Journal of Law & Technology*, 9, 1 (2002), 1–84.

Ware, S.J. Domain name arbitration in the arbitration-law context: Consent to, and fairness in, the UDRP. *Journal of Small & Emerging Business Law*, 6, 1 (Spring 2002), 129–165.

Wienberg, J. ICANN and the problem of legitimacy. *Duke Law Journal*, 50, 1 (2001), 187–260.

ABOUT THE EDITOR AND CONTRIBUTORS

Bill Anckar is an associate research fellow at the Institute for Advanced Management Systems Research, Abo Akademi University, and the managing director of the hotel chain Omenahotellit, both in Finland. He earned his doctoral degree at the Department of Information Systems at Abo Akademi University, Turku, Finland. His current research focuses on e- and m-commerce in B2C markets, in particular applications in the travel and tourism industry. His work has been published in several international journals and conference proceedings.

James Backhouse is director of the IS Integrity Group at the London School of Economics, Department of Information Systems. He currently advises the UK Office of Science and Technology on policy matters in the Foresight CyberTrust and Crime Prevention Project and is an expert adviser to the Royal Society's Science in Society program. He is an activities coordinator for the EU FIDIS (Future of Identity in the Information Society) Network of Excellence.

John Baptista is a doctoral student in the Department of Information Systems at the London School of Economics. Additionally, he is teaching assistant in the same department and research assistant for the LSE's Information Systems Integrity Group. His current research analyzes the fostering of trust in a large e-government procurement environment. He studies the role of digital certification as a trust fostering device through the establishment of common norms among participants in the procurement system.

Daniel Beimborn graduated with a Ph.D degree in economics and business administration at Goethe University, Frankfurt, where he works as a research assistant at the Institute of Information Systems. He is member of the postgraduate program Enabling Technologies for Electronic Commerce of the German Science Foundation. His research interests include controlling and standardization of IS infrastructures and especially the impact of Web services technologies on their design.

Christer Carlsson is the director of the Institute for Advanced Management Systems Research, and has been a professor of management science at Abo Akademi University in Finland since 1985. He has lectured extensively at various universities in Europe, the United States, Asia, and Australia. His research covers multiple criteria, including optimization, knowledge-based systems, fuzzy real options valuation, and software agents. He is an editor of *Electronic Commerce Research and Applications* and on the editorial boards of eleven other journals. He has published more than 220 papers.

Kai Fischbach is a research associate at WHU, Otto Beisheim Graduate School of Management (chair of Electronic Business, Vallendar, Germany). His current research interests include the economics of ubiquitous and peer-to-peer computing and the impacts and development of Web services. He is a co-editor of a volume on P2P systems (Springer, 2002). He is also the co-chair of the Peer-to-Peer Paradigm minitrack at HICSS, 2004.

Dennis F. Galletta is an associate professor at Katz Graduate School of Business, University of Pittsburgh; is an AIS Fellow; and has published in *Management Science, ISR, JMIS, Decision Sciences, CACM, Data Base, AMIT*, and other outlets. He has served on several editorial boards, including those of *MIS Quarterly, ISEB*, and *Data Base*. He has served as AIS vice president of member services, ICIS treasurer, inaugural AMCIS conference chair, AIS council member, and AMCIS 2003 program co-chair.

Andres A. Gallo is an assistant professor at the Department of Economics, University of North Florida. He received his Ph.D. from the University of Illinois at Urbana-Champaign in 2003. Gallo writes in the areas of law and regulation of cyberspace, patent law, and economics. He has published several articles studying the impact of government and private regulation on the Internet. He has also written in the areas of economic development, institutional economics, and political economy issues, with an emphasis on Latin America. His latest research includes the effects of property rights on seed markets in developing countries.

Xianjun Geng is an assistant professor in the Department of Management Science, University of Washington School of Business. His research interests include the impact of emerging technologies information on the digital economy, economics of electronic markets, and digital marketing. He received a Ph.D. in information systems from the University of Texas at Austin.

Ram Gopal is an associate professor in the Department of Operations and Information Management, School of Business, University of Connecticut. His research interests include electronic markets, intellectual property rights, and database systems. Gopal received a Ph.D. in information systems from the State University of New York at Buffalo.

Carol Hsu is a tutorial fellow at the London School of Economics, Department of Information Systems, and also a researcher of the Information Systems Integrity Group. Her current research examines contextual and institutional aspects of standardization and information technology.

Sirkka L. Jarvenpaa is the James Bayless/Rauscher Pierce Refsnes Chair in Business Administration at the University of Texas at Austin, where she serves as a director of the Center for Business, Technology and Law and a track leader in the cross-functional Customer Insight Center. She is the editor of the *Journal of AIS* and co-editor-in-chief of the *Journal of Strategic Information Systems*. Her current research projects focus on electronic business and mobile business.

P.K. Kannan is Harvey Sanders Associate Professor of Marketing and associate director of the Center for Excellence in Service at the Robert H. Smith School of Business at the University of Maryland. His current research focuses on pricing information products and product lines, CRM and online loyalty, and new product development. He has received grants from NSF, Mellon Foundation, and SAIC, and has published papers in *Management Science, Marketing Science, Journal of the Academy of Marketing Science,* and *Communications of the ACM.*

Jay P. Kesan is a professor at the University of Illinois at Urbana-Champaign in the College of Law and the Department of Electrical & Computer Engineering, and he is the director of the Program on Intellectual Property and Technology Law at the College of Law. He teaches, writes, and consults in the areas of law and regulation of e-commerce, intellectual property, and patent law. He has a J.D., summa cum laude, from Georgetown University, and a Ph.D. in electrical and computer engineering from the University of Texas at Austin.

Stefan Klein is the John E. Sharkey Professor of Electronic Commerce at the MIS Department, University College Dublin, Ireland, and director of the Department of IS at the University of Muenster, Germany. He has held teaching or research positions at the universities of Linz, Austria; Koblenz-Landau, Germany; and St. Gallen, Switzerland; and at Harvard University, the German National Research Center for Computer Science (GMD), and the University of Cologne. His research interests include ICT impact on industry structures and interorganizational arrangements, electronic business strategies, and information management.

Frank Köhne is a Ph.D. student at the Department of Information Systems at Hohenheim University, Stuttgart, Germany. He studied information systems at the University of Muenster and has been involved in different research projects in Muenster and at RWTH Aachen. His research interests include human-computer interaction, electronic markets, and intelligent systems. He currently works on a research project on electronic negotiation support.

Nevena T. Koukova is a doctoral candidate at the R.H. Smith School of Business at the University of Maryland. Her research interests include pricing of digital products, bundling and unbundling of electronic content, and behavioral aspects of bundling. She has presented at many major conferences and published in their proceedings, including those of the Association for Consumer Research, AMA Marketing Educators, Marketing Science, and the Haring Symposium.

Hermann-Josef Lamberti is a member of the Board of Managing Directors of Deutsche Bank AG. As chief operating officer (COO), he is responsible for Deutsche Bank Group's cost and infrastructure management, information technology and operations, building and facilities management, and purchasing worldwide. Until January 2002, he was the board member responsible for the client and distribution group within the Private Clients and Asset Management (PCAM) Division. as chief information officer (CIO), he was in charge of Deutsche Bank's information technology.

Hau L. Lee is the Thoma Professor of Operations, Information and Technology at the Graduate School of Business, Stanford University. He is also a co-director of the Stanford Global Supply Chain Management Forum, an industry–academic consortium to advance the theory and practice of supply chain management. His research focuses on global supply chain management, e-business, and global logistics.

Fu-ren Lin is a professor at the Department of Information Management of National Sun Yat-sen University. His current research interests are B2B e-commerce, agent technologies for supply chain management and knowledge management, data mining, and knowledge discovery. He has published related articles in *Decision Support System; IEEE Intelligent Systems; IEEE Transactions on Systems, Man, and Cybernetics; International Journal of Flexible Manufacturing Systems;* and *Journal of Organizational Computing and Electronic Commerce.*

Nils Madeja is a research assistant, and doctoral candidate at the DaimlerChrysler Chair of Electronic Business at the Otto-Beisheim Graduate School of Management (WHU Koblenz). His research and teaching activities include success factors in electronic and mobile business and his research has been presented at several international conferences. He holds a graduate degree in electrical engineering from the University of Kiel, Germany, and has a broad background in high tech and telecommunications.

Matthew L. Nelson is an assistant professor in accounting and information systems at Illinois State University. His research interests include innovation diffusion, standards development organizations, interorganizational systems standards, and the value of information technology. Nelson was a senior analyst with Electronic Data Systems (EDS) and has participated in several conferences, including the Americas Conference on Information Systems, Informs, and the American Accounting Association conference. He holds an undergraduate degree in accounting from the University of Michigan and a Ph.D. in information systems from the University of Illinois.

Daniel E. O'Leary received his Ph.D. from Case Western Reserve University and his M.B.A. from the University of Michigan. O'Leary, now a professor, has been at the University of Southern California since 1985. He has been an active contributor to research on computer and information systems, including enterprise resource planning (ERP) systems and e-business. He is the author of *Enterprise Resource Planning Systems*, published by Cambridge University Press.

Barchi Peleg is the research director of the Stanford Global Supply Chain Management Forum, an industry–academic consortium to advance the theory and practice of supply chain management. She directs research in e-business, cross-enterprise collaboration, and supply chain management, and teaches global supply chain project coordination at Stanford.

R. Ramesh is a professor in the Department of Management Science and Systems, School of Management, State University of New York at Buffalo. His research interests include Web-caching architectures, electronic trading systems, and ontologies. Ramesh received a Ph.D. in industrial engineering from SUNY at Buffalo.

V. Srinivasan Rao is an associate professor in information systems at the University of Texas at San Antonio. He obtained his Ph.D. from the University of Texas at Austin. His areas of research interest include computer support of groups and e-commerce. He has published in leading academic journals, such as *MIS Quarterly, Management Science,* and *Group Decision and Negotiation.*

Brian T. Ratchford is professor of marketing and Pepsico Chair in Consumer Research at the Robert H. Smith School of Business at the University of Maryland. His research interests are in economics applied to the study of consumer behavior, information economics, and marketing productivity. He has published over thirty articles in the leading journals in marketing and related fields, including *Journal of Consumer Research, International Journal of Electronic Commerce, Marketing Science, Management Science,* and *Journal of Marketing Research.*

Detlef Schoder is full professor and chairs the Department of Information Systems and Information Management at the University of Cologne, Germany. He has conducted several of Europe's largest empirical studies of Web-based e-commerce. He has recently been appointed adviser to the German parliament (Bundestag) for issues related to e-commerce. Schoder lists more than 130 reviewed publications, including articles in leading international and German journals.

Mary Schoonmaker is vice president of industry development at RosettaNet, an independent, self-funded, nonprofit consortium dedicated to the development and deployment of standardized electronic interfaces to align the processes between supply chain partners in the high technology industry. Her experience in the technology industry spans more than twenty years.

Michael J. Shaw is Hoeft Endowed Chair in Information Technology Management and director of the Center for Information Technology and e-Business Management at the University of Illinois at Urbana-Champaign, where he has been on the faculty of the Department of Business Administration since 1984. He is also a faculty member of the Beckman Institute for Advanced Science and Technology.

Carsten Totz is a Ph.D. student at the Department of Information Systems, University of Muenster, Germany. His research interests include electronic business strategies, online-marketing, and strategic management.

Jimmy C. Tseng worked on the Fiducia project based at the London School of Economics and Political Science, and is currently assistant professor of electronic commerce at the Rotterdam School of Management, Erasmus University, Rottherdam, in the Netherlands.

Christian Vollmann is director of Business Development at Spirit Link, a German IT services company. Prior to this position he worked in South America for the online auction company DeRemate.com. In 1999, he was the first employee of the newly founded alando AG, which was soon after acquired by eBay Inc. and now operates the highly successful German platform of eBay. Vollmann graduated from the Otto-Beisheim Graduate School of Management (WHU Koblenz).

Pirkko Walden is a professor of marketing and information systems, a research director of the Institute for Advanced Management Systems Research, and the leader of the Mobile Commerce Laboratory at Abo Akademi University. Her research interests are focused on knowledge-based support systems, electronic, and m-commerce. Walden was in charge of the Valentine research program, which implemented e-commerce technology for SMEs in the Vakka-Suomi region. The research of the Mobile Commerce Laboratory is focusing on finding new, effective products and services.

Tim Weitzel received his Ph.D. from Goethe University, Frankfurt, where he works as an assistant professor at the Institute of Information Systems. His research interests include standardization, network analysis, e-finance, and IS support of the HR function. Since 1997, he has also been head of the institute's XML Competence Center. Weitzel has written over eighty scientific articles and books.

Andrew B. Whinston is the director of the Center for Research in Electronic Commerce at the University of Texas at Austin. His research interests focus on laying the theoretical and practical foundations of a digital economy. Whinston received a Ph.D. in management from Carnegie-Mellon University.

Charles A. Wood is an assistant professor at the University of Notre Dame who specializes in e-commerce research, investigating how technology changes buyer and seller behavior, especially in online auctions. He holds patents on specialized data collecting agents used to gather data from any Web page. He has authored five books on database system development, contributed to five other books, and published in several academic journals, including *Communications of the ACM, Information Technology and Management,* and others.

SERIES EDITOR

Vladimir Zwass is Distinguished Professor of Computer Science and Management Information Systems at Fairleigh Dickinson University. He holds a Ph.D. in computer science from Columbia University. Dr. Zwass is the founding editor-in-chief of the *Journal of Management Information Systems*; one of the three top-ranked journals in the field of information systems, the journal recently celebrated twenty years of publication. He is also the founding editor-in-chief of the *International Journal of Electronic Commerce,* ranked as the top journal in its field. Dr. Zwass is the author of six books and several book chapters, including entries in the *Encyclopaedia Britannica,* as well as a number of papers in various journals and conference proceedings. He has received several grants, consulted for a number of major corporations, and is a frequent speaker to national and international audiences. He is a former member of the professional staff of the International Atomic Energy Agency in Vienna, Austria.

INDEX

D

E

F

G

H

I

J

R

S

T

U

V

W–X